JUSTICE LEAGUE of AMERICA

THE RISE OF ECLIPSO

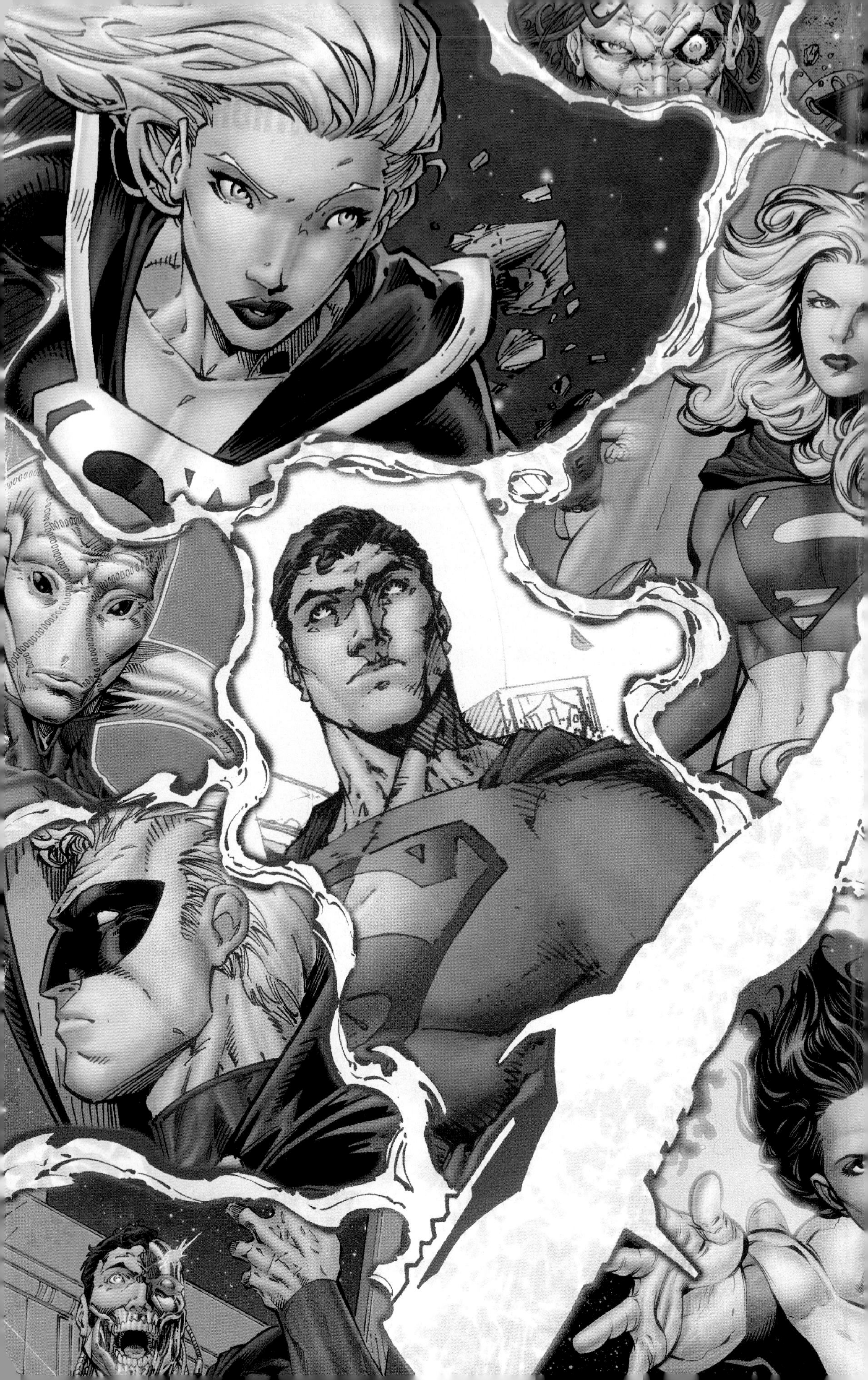

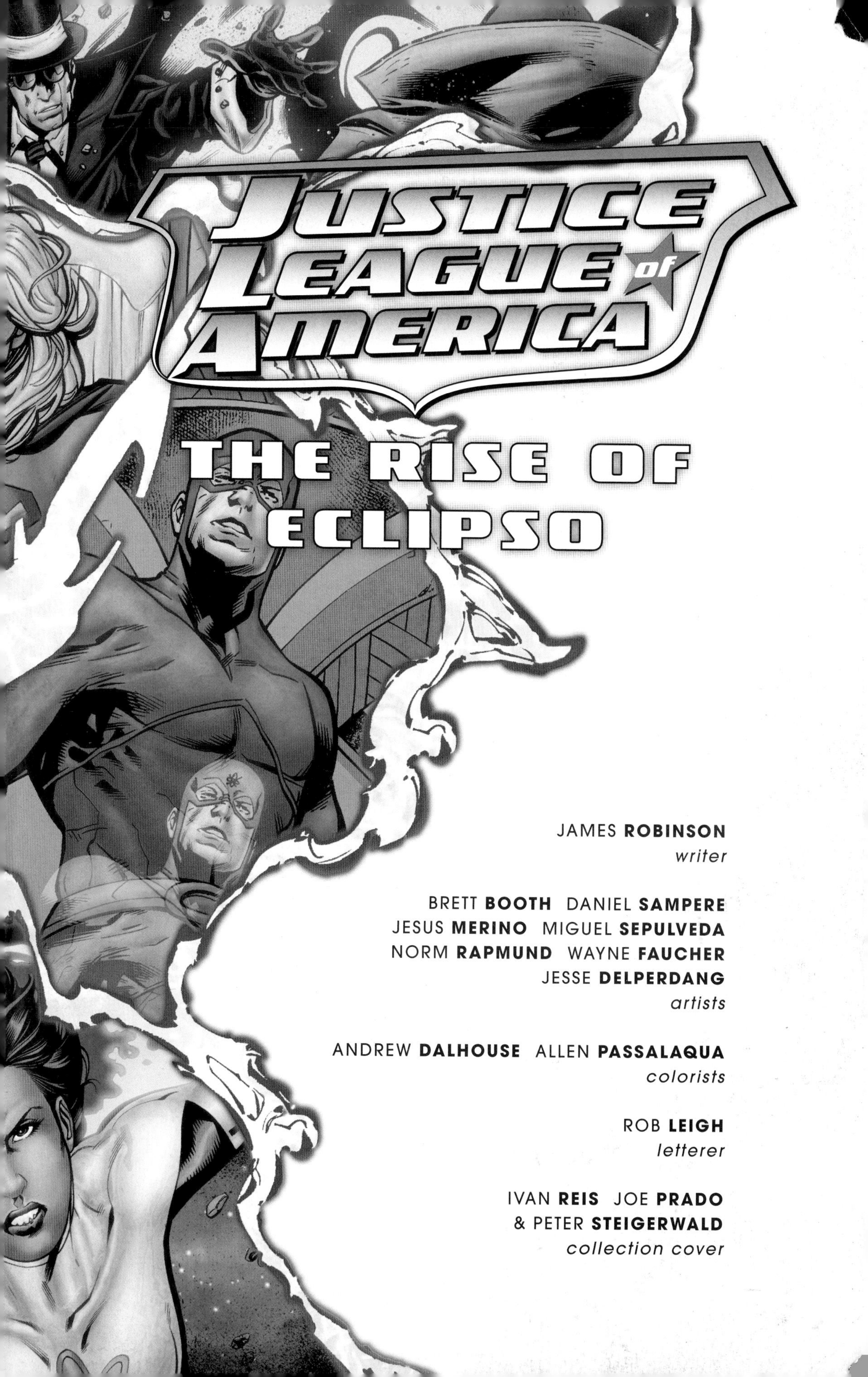

JUSTICE LEAGUE of AMERICA

THE RISE OF ECLIPSO

JAMES **ROBINSON**
writer

BRETT **BOOTH** DANIEL **SAMPERE**
JESUS **MERINO** MIGUEL **SEPULVEDA**
NORM **RAPMUND** WAYNE **FAUCHER**
JESSE **DELPERDANG**
artists

ANDREW **DALHOUSE** ALLEN **PASSALAQUA**
colorists

ROB **LEIGH**
letterer

IVAN **REIS** JOE **PRADO**
& PETER **STEIGERWALD**
collection cover

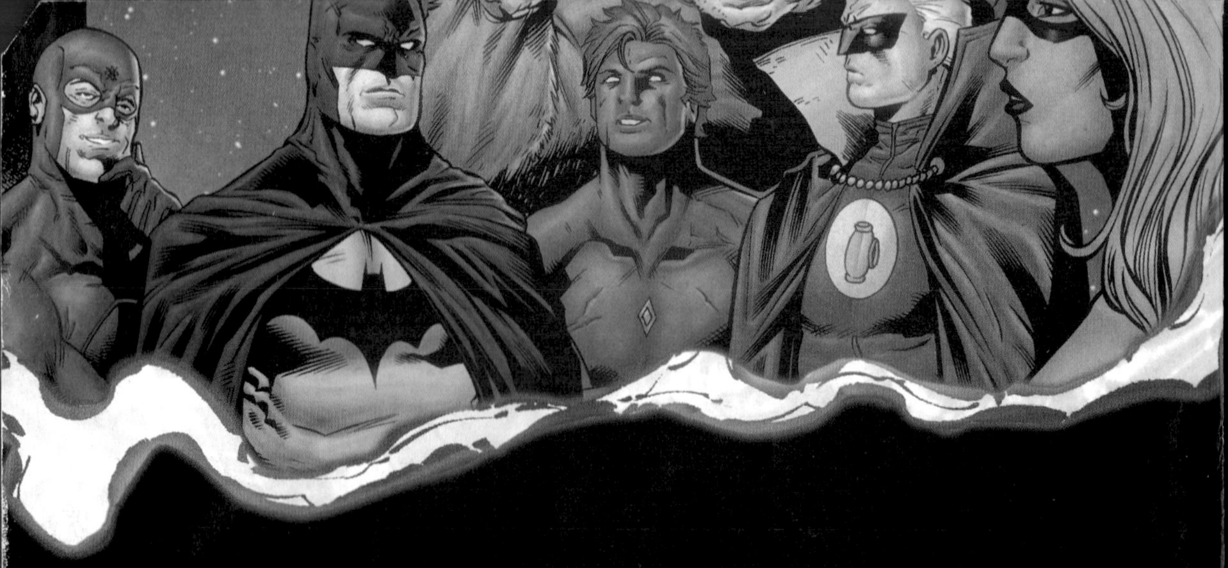

Eddie Berganza Rex Ogle Mike Carlin Editors - Original Series
Rachel Gluckstern Associate Editor - Original Series
Robbin Brosterman Design Director - Books
Robbie Biederman Publication Design

Bob Harras VP - Editor-in-Chief

Diane Nelson President
Dan DiDio and **Jim Lee** Co-Publishers
Geoff Johns Chief Creative Officer
John Rood Executive VP - Sales, Marketing and Business Development
Amy Genkins Senior VP - Business and Legal Affairs
Nairi Gardiner Senior VP - Finance
Jeff Boison VP - Publishing Operations
Mark Chiarello VP - Art Direction and Design
John Cunningham VP - Marketing
Terri Cunningham VP - Talent Relations and Services
Alison Gill Senior VP - Manufacturing and Operations
Hank Kanalz Senior VP - Digital
Jay Kogan VP - Business and Legal Affairs, Publishing
Jack Mahan VP - Business Affairs, Talent
Nick Napolitano VP - Manufacturing Administration
Sue Pohja VP - Book Sales
Courtney Simmons Senior VP - Publicity
Bob Wayne Senior VP - Sales

JUSTICE LEAGUE OF AMERICA: THE RISE OF ECLIPSO

DC Comics, 1700 Broadway, New York, NY 10019
A Warner Bros. Entertainment Company.
Printed by RR Donnelley, Salem, VA, USA. 8/31/12. First Printing.
ISBN: 978-1-4012-3413-3

SUSTAINABLE FORESTRY INITIATIVE
Certified Chain of Custody
At Least 25% Certified Forest Content
www.sfiprogram.org
SFI-01042
APPLIES TO TEXT STOCK ONLY

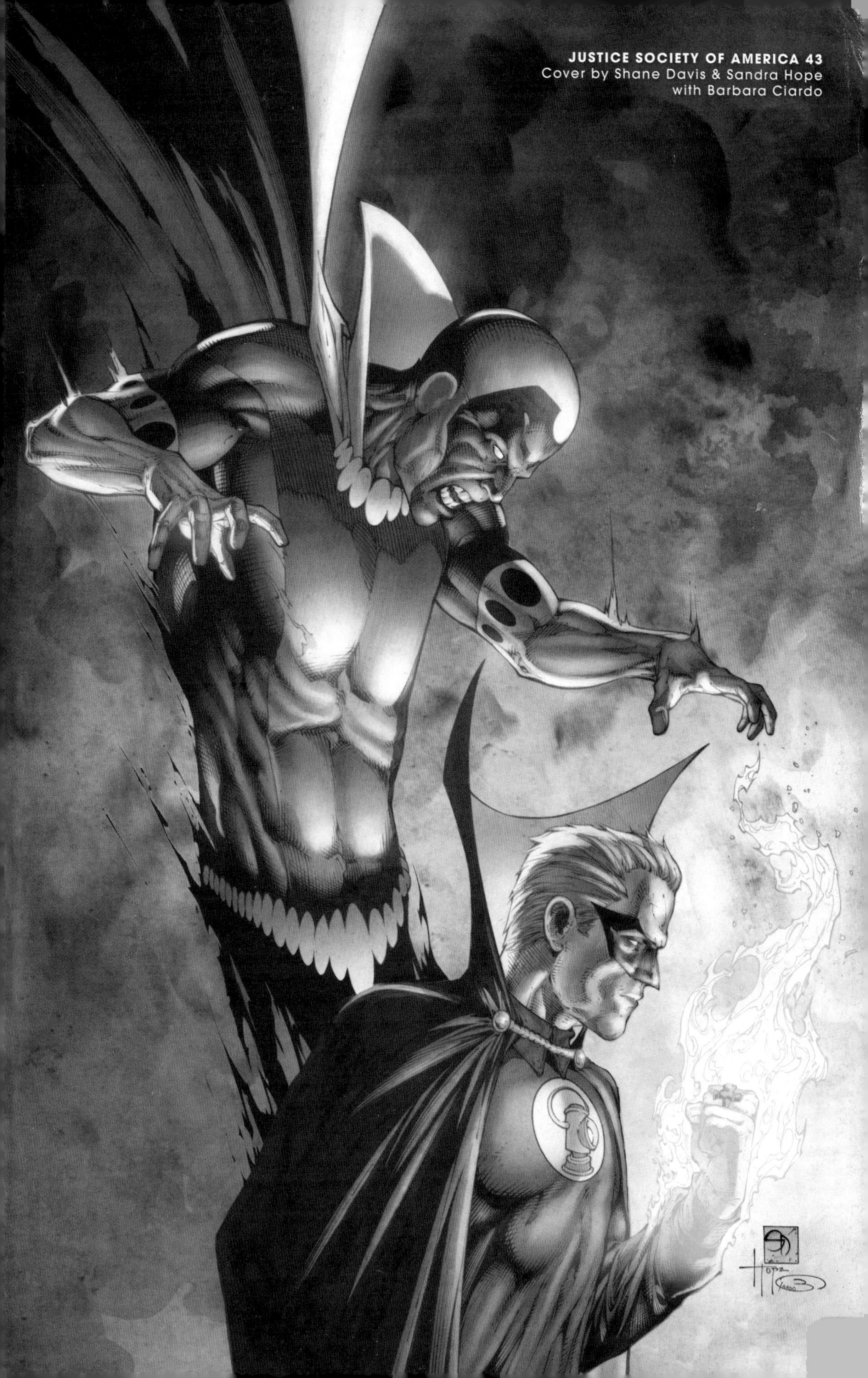

JUSTICE SOCIETY OF AMERICA 43
Cover by Shane Davis & Sandra Hope
with Barbara Ciardo

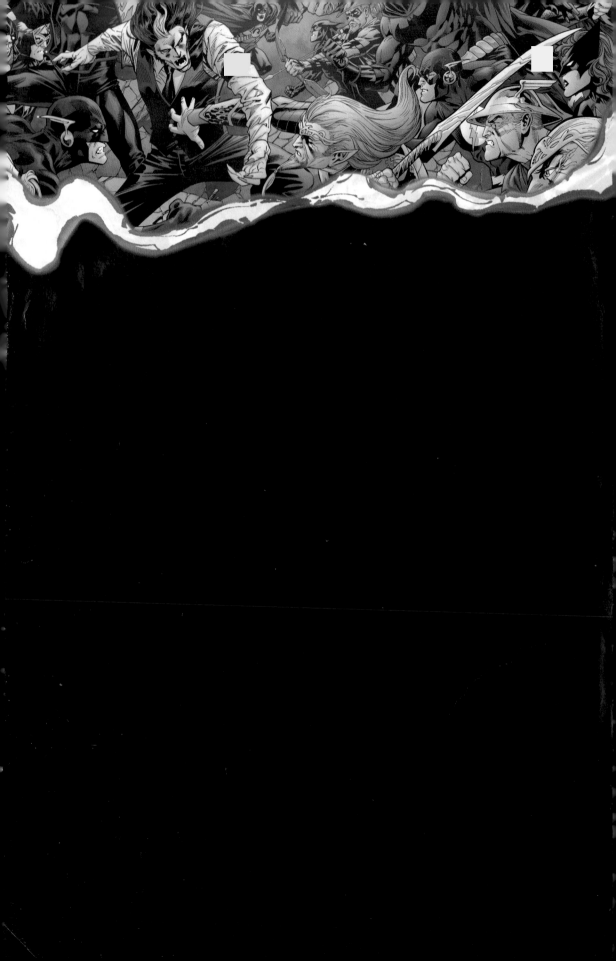

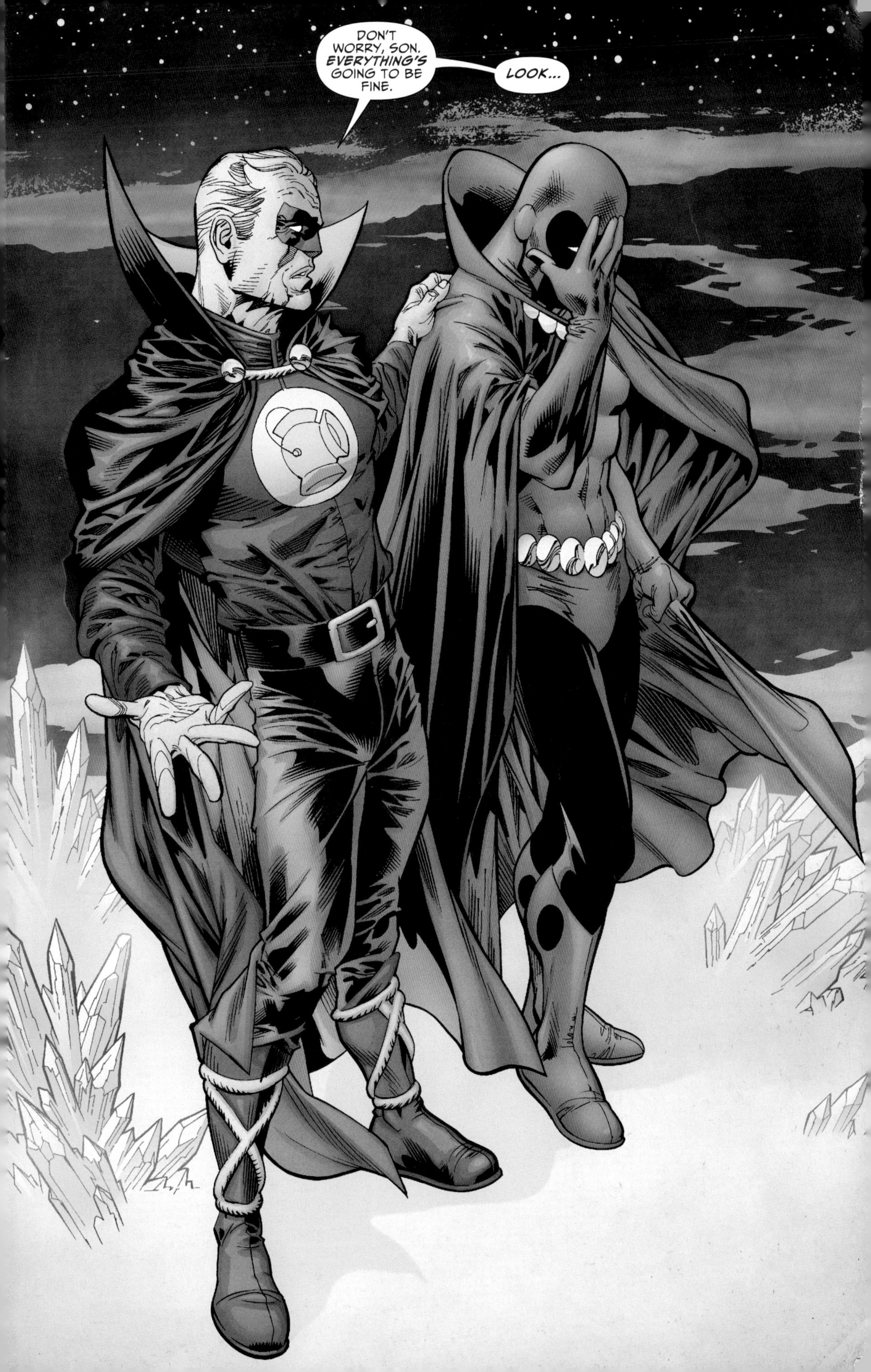
DON'T WORRY, SON. EVERYTHING'S GOING TO BE FINE.
LOOK...

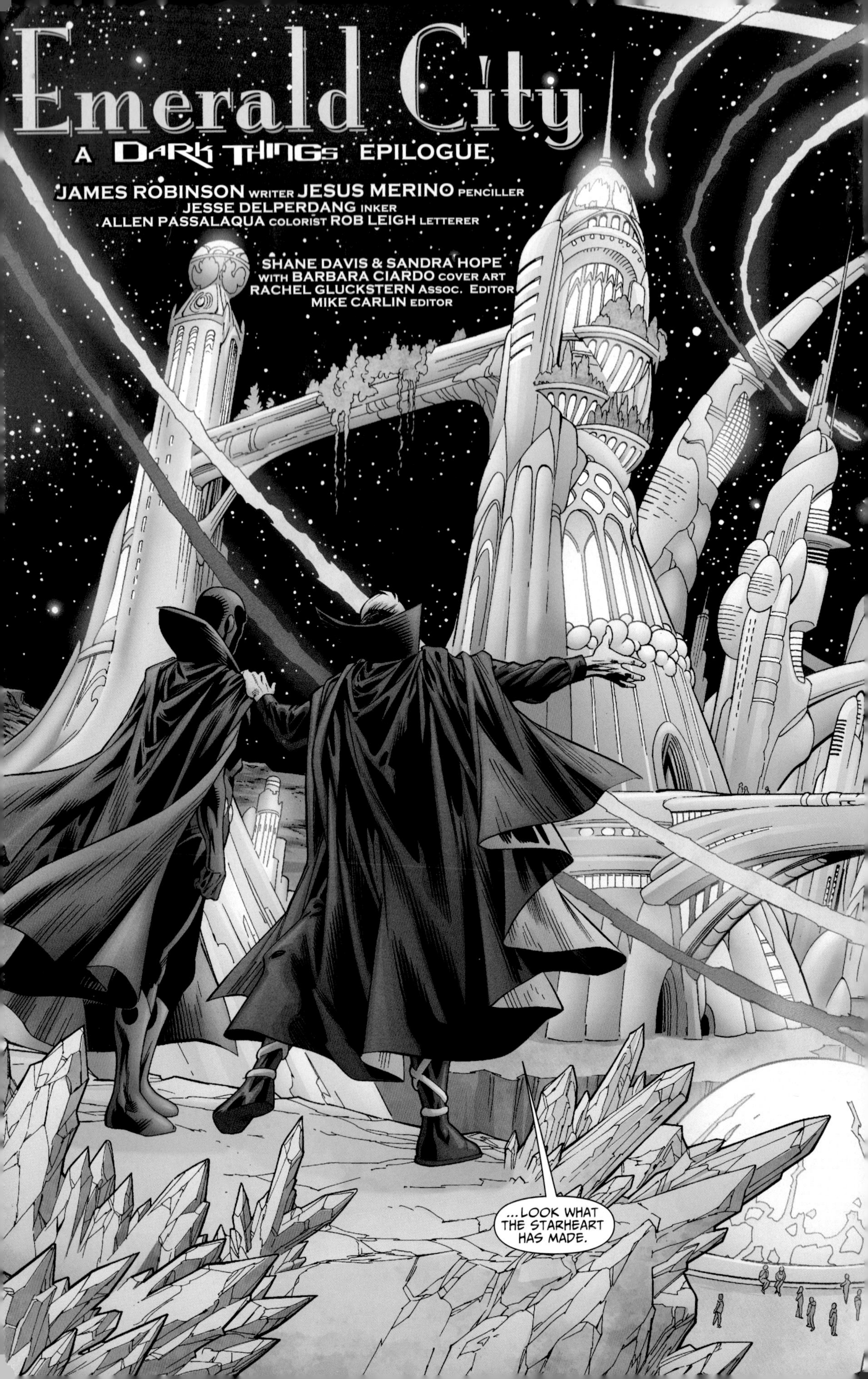
Emerald City
A DARK THINGS EPILOGUE
JAMES ROBINSON WRITER JESUS MERINO PENCILLER
JESSE DELPERDANG INKER
ALLEN PASSALAQUA COLORIST ROB LEIGH LETTERER
SHANE DAVIS & SANDRA HOPE
WITH BARBARA CIARDO COVER ART
RACHEL GLUCKSTERN ASSOC. EDITOR
MIKE CARLIN EDITOR
...LOOK WHAT THE STARHEART HAS MADE.

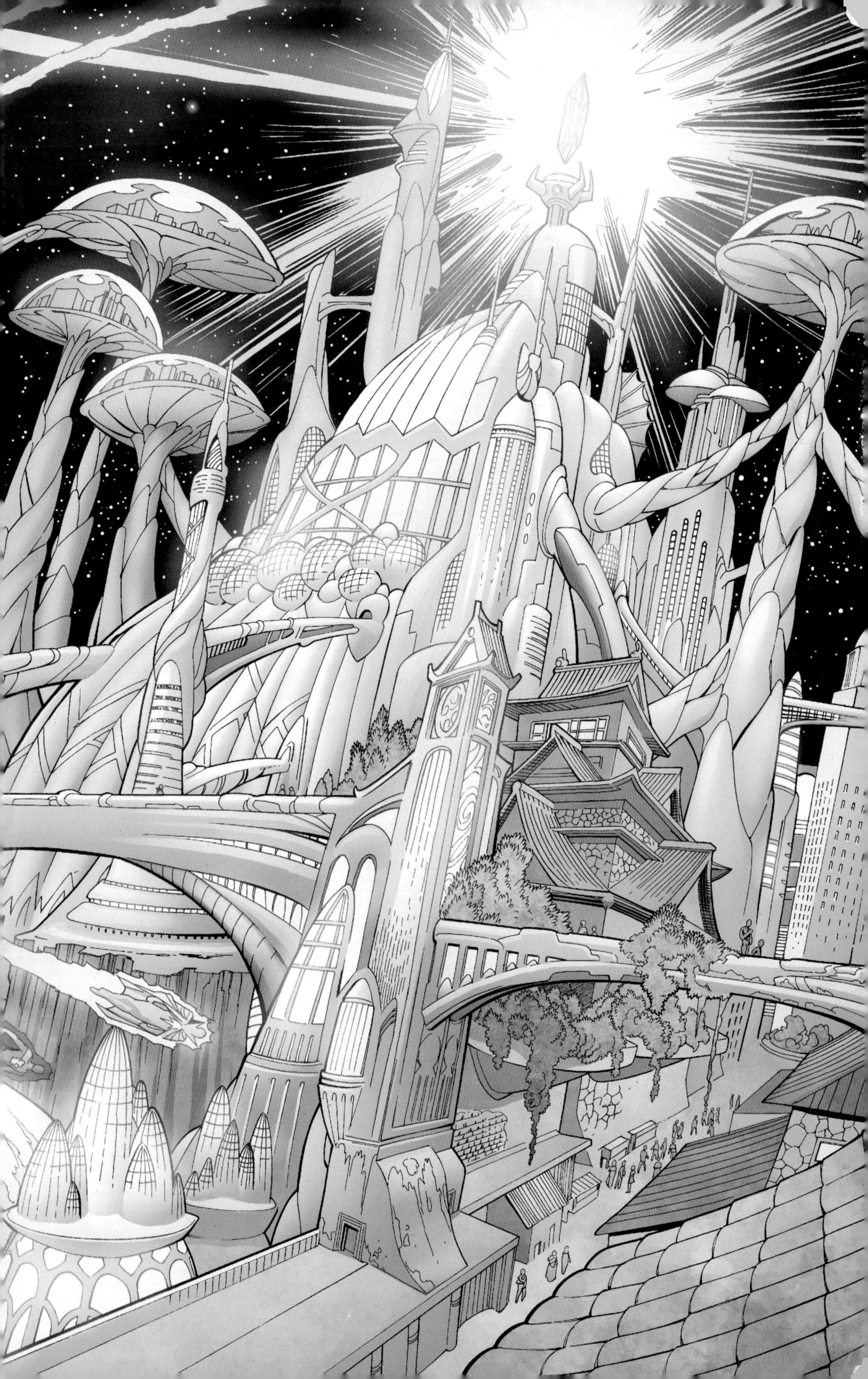

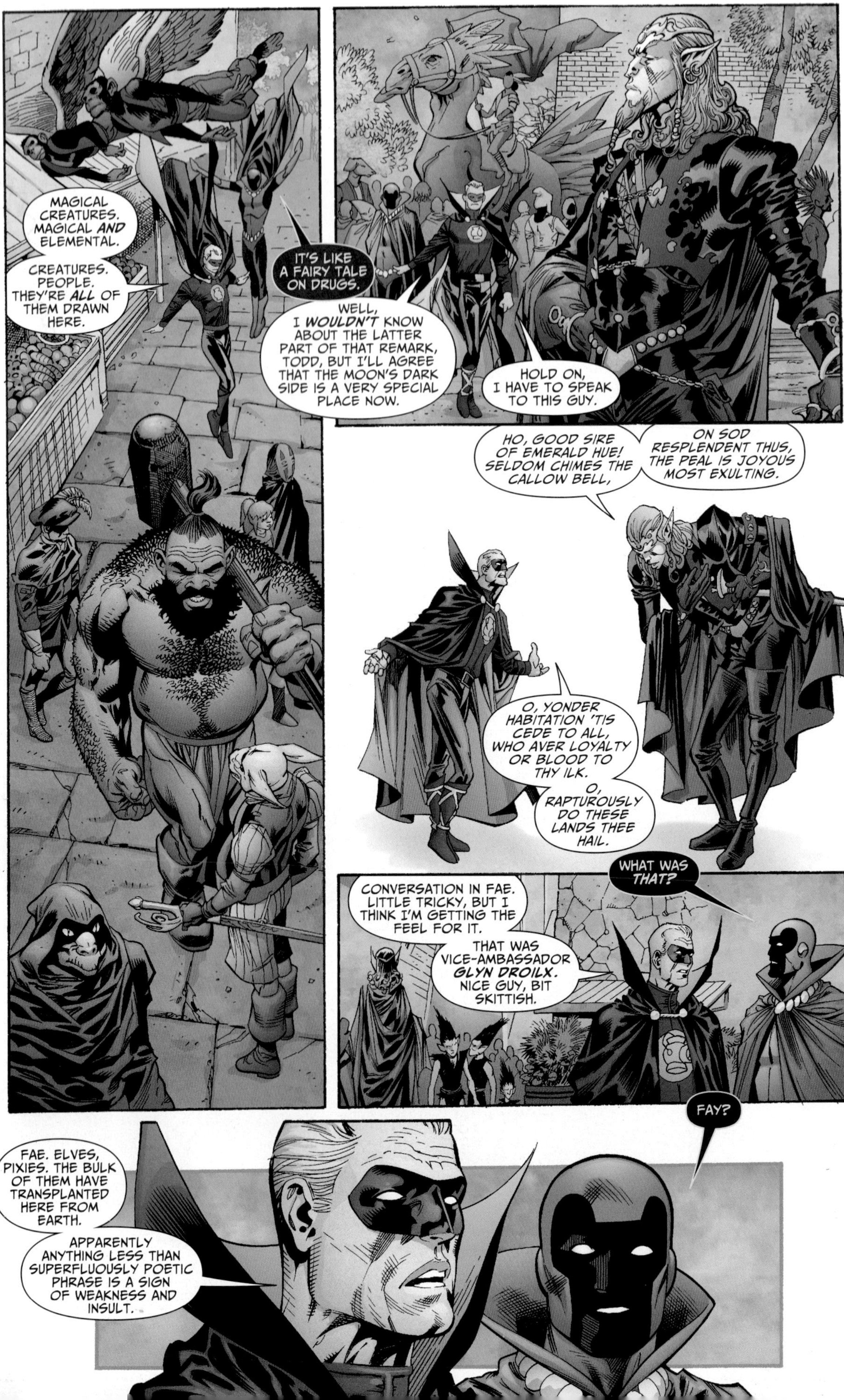
MAGICAL CREATURES. MAGICAL AND ELEMENTAL.
CREATURES. PEOPLE. THEY'RE ALL OF THEM DRAWN HERE.
IT'S LIKE A FAIRY TALE ON DRUGS.
WELL, I WOULDN'T KNOW ABOUT THE LATTER PART OF THAT REMARK, TODD, BUT I'LL AGREE THAT THE MOON'S DARK SIDE IS A VERY SPECIAL PLACE NOW.
HOLD ON, I HAVE TO SPEAK TO THIS GUY.
HO, GOOD SIRE OF EMERALD HUE! SELDOM CHIMES THE CALLOW BELL,
ON SOD RESPLENDENT THUS, THE PEAL IS JOYOUS MOST EXULTING.
O, YONDER HABITATION 'TIS CEDE TO ALL, WHO AVER LOYALTY OR BLOOD TO THY ILK.
O, RAPTUROUSLY DO THESE LANDS THEE HAIL.
CONVERSATION IN FAE. LITTLE TRICKY, BUT I THINK I'M GETTING THE FEEL FOR IT.
WHAT WAS THAT?
THAT WAS VICE-AMBASSADOR GLYN DROILX. NICE GUY, BIT SKITTISH.
FAY?
FAE. ELVES, PIXIES. THE BULK OF THEM HAVE TRANSPLANTED HERE FROM EARTH.
APPARENTLY ANYTHING LESS THAN SUPERFLUOUSLY POETIC PHRASE IS A SIGN OF WEAKNESS AND INSULT.

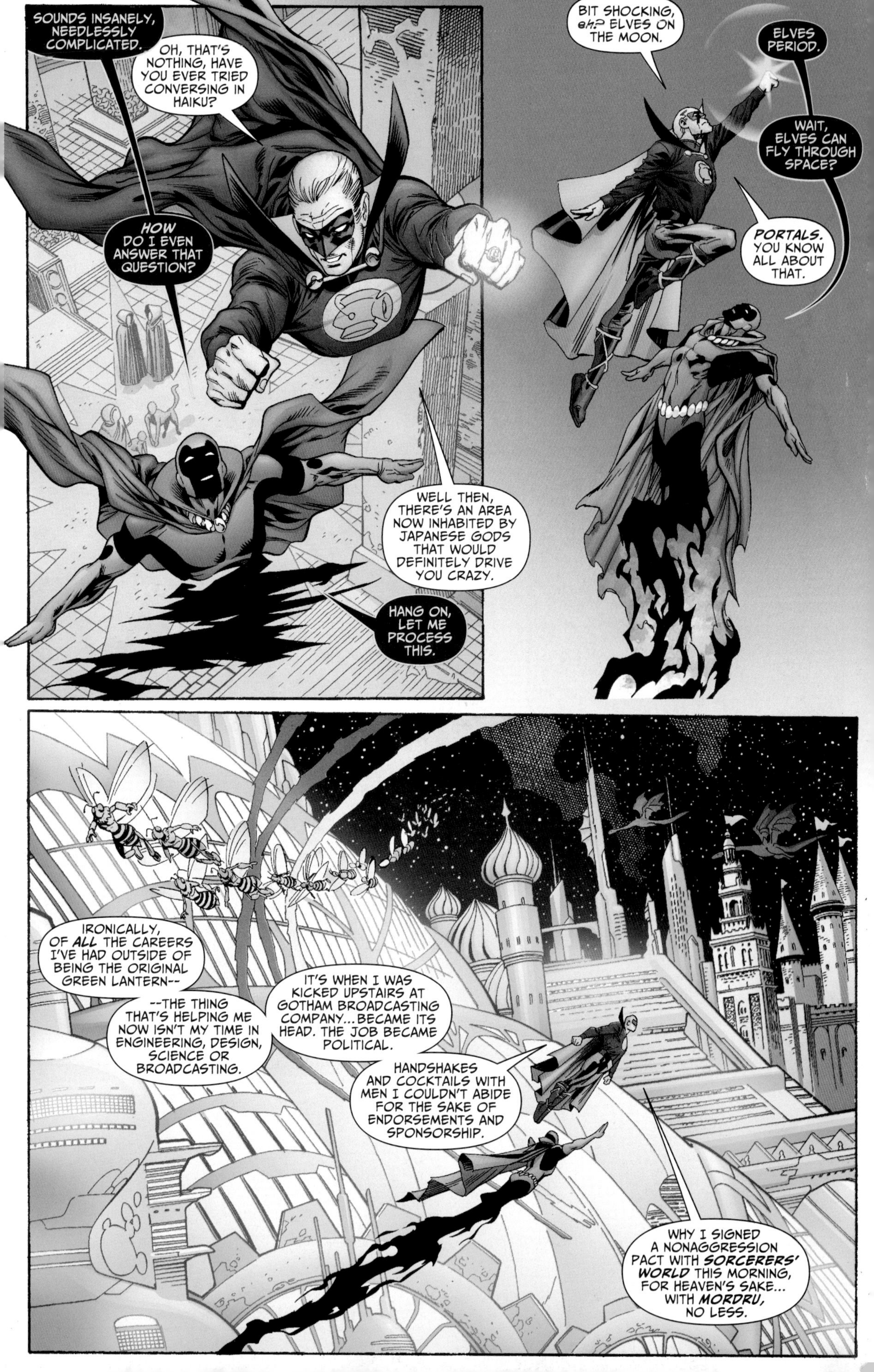

SOUNDS INSANELY, NEEDLESSLY COMPLICATED.
OH, THAT'S NOTHING, HAVE YOU EVER TRIED CONVERSING IN HAIKU?
HOW DO I EVEN ANSWER THAT QUESTION?
WELL THEN, THERE'S AN AREA NOW INHABITED BY JAPANESE GODS THAT WOULD DEFINITELY DRIVE YOU CRAZY.
HANG ON, LET ME PROCESS THIS.
BIT SHOCKING, eh? ELVES ON THE MOON.
ELVES PERIOD.
WAIT, ELVES CAN FLY THROUGH SPACE?
PORTALS. YOU KNOW ALL ABOUT THAT.
IRONICALLY, OF ALL THE CAREERS I'VE HAD OUTSIDE OF BEING THE ORIGINAL GREEN LANTERN--
--THE THING THAT'S HELPING ME NOW ISN'T MY TIME IN ENGINEERING, DESIGN, SCIENCE OR BROADCASTING.
IT'S WHEN I WAS KICKED UPSTAIRS AT GOTHAM BROADCASTING COMPANY...BECAME ITS HEAD. THE JOB BECAME POLITICAL.
HANDSHAKES AND COCKTAILS WITH MEN I COULDN'T ABIDE FOR THE SAKE OF ENDORSEMENTS AND SPONSORSHIP.
WHY I SIGNED A NONAGGRESSION PACT WITH SORCERERS' WORLD THIS MORNING, FOR HEAVEN'S SAKE... WITH MORDRU, NO LESS.

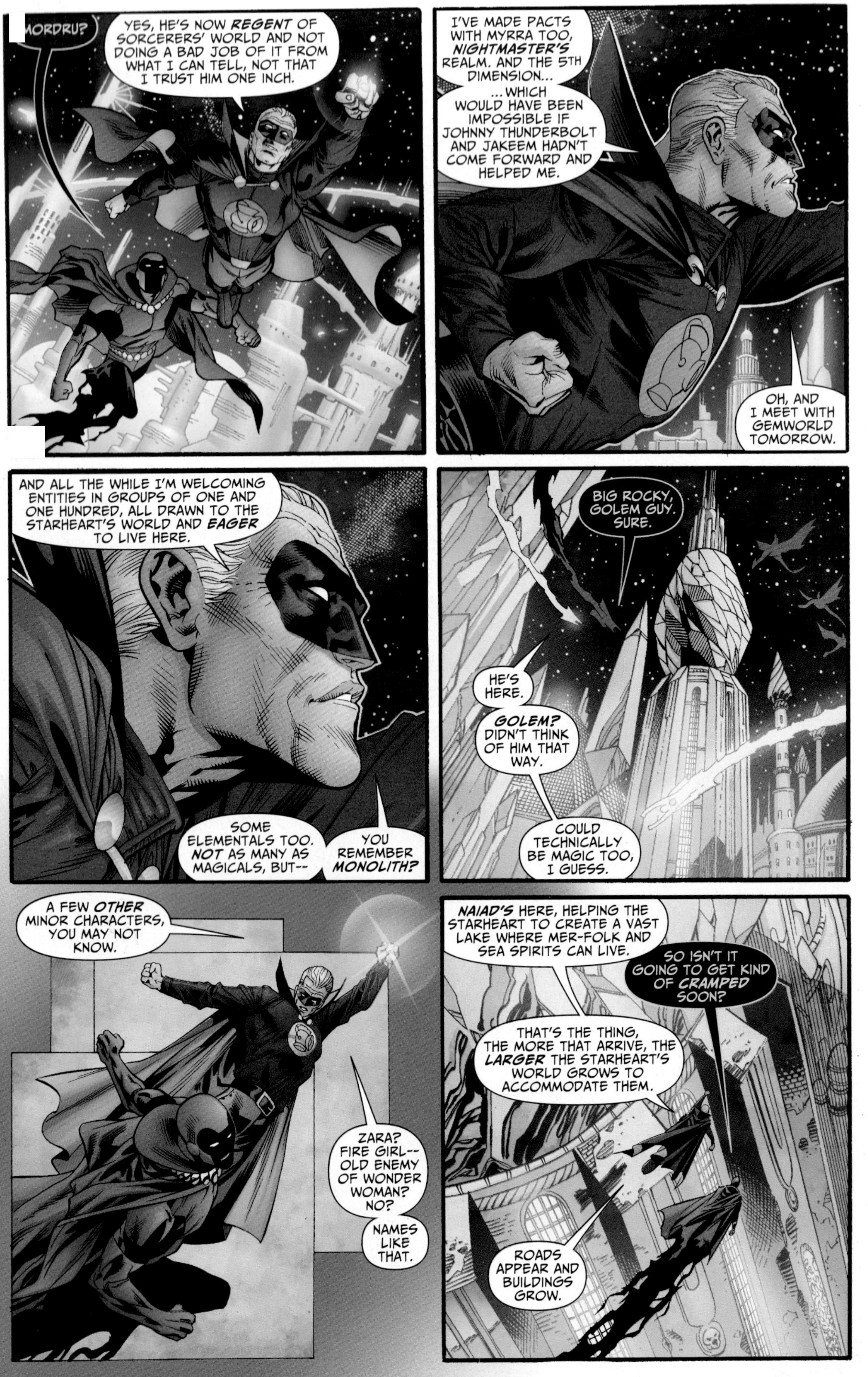
MORDRU?
YES, HE'S NOW REGENT OF SORCERERS' WORLD AND NOT DOING A BAD JOB OF IT FROM WHAT I CAN TELL, NOT THAT I TRUST HIM ONE INCH.
I'VE MADE PACTS WITH MYRRA TOO, NIGHTMASTER'S REALM. AND THE 5TH DIMENSION...
...WHICH WOULD HAVE BEEN IMPOSSIBLE IF JOHNNY THUNDERBOLT AND JAKEEM HADN'T COME FORWARD AND HELPED ME.
OH, AND I MEET WITH GEMWORLD TOMORROW.
AND ALL THE WHILE I'M WELCOMING ENTITIES IN GROUPS OF ONE AND ONE HUNDRED, ALL DRAWN TO THE STARHEART'S WORLD AND EAGER TO LIVE HERE.
SOME ELEMENTALS TOO. NOT AS MANY AS MAGICALS, BUT--
YOU REMEMBER MONOLITH?
BIG ROCKY, GOLEM GUY. SURE.
HE'S HERE.
GOLEM? DIDN'T THINK OF HIM THAT WAY.
COULD TECHNICALLY BE MAGIC TOO, I GUESS.
A FEW OTHER MINOR CHARACTERS, YOU MAY NOT KNOW.
ZARA? FIRE GIRL--OLD ENEMY OF WONDER WOMAN? NO?
NAMES LIKE THAT.
NAIAD'S HERE, HELPING THE STARHEART TO CREATE A VAST LAKE WHERE MER-FOLK AND SEA SPIRITS CAN LIVE.
SO ISN'T IT GOING TO GET KIND OF CRAMPED SOON?
THAT'S THE THING, THE MORE THAT ARRIVE, THE LARGER THE STARHEART'S WORLD GROWS TO ACCOMMODATE THEM.
ROADS APPEAR AND BUILDINGS GROW.

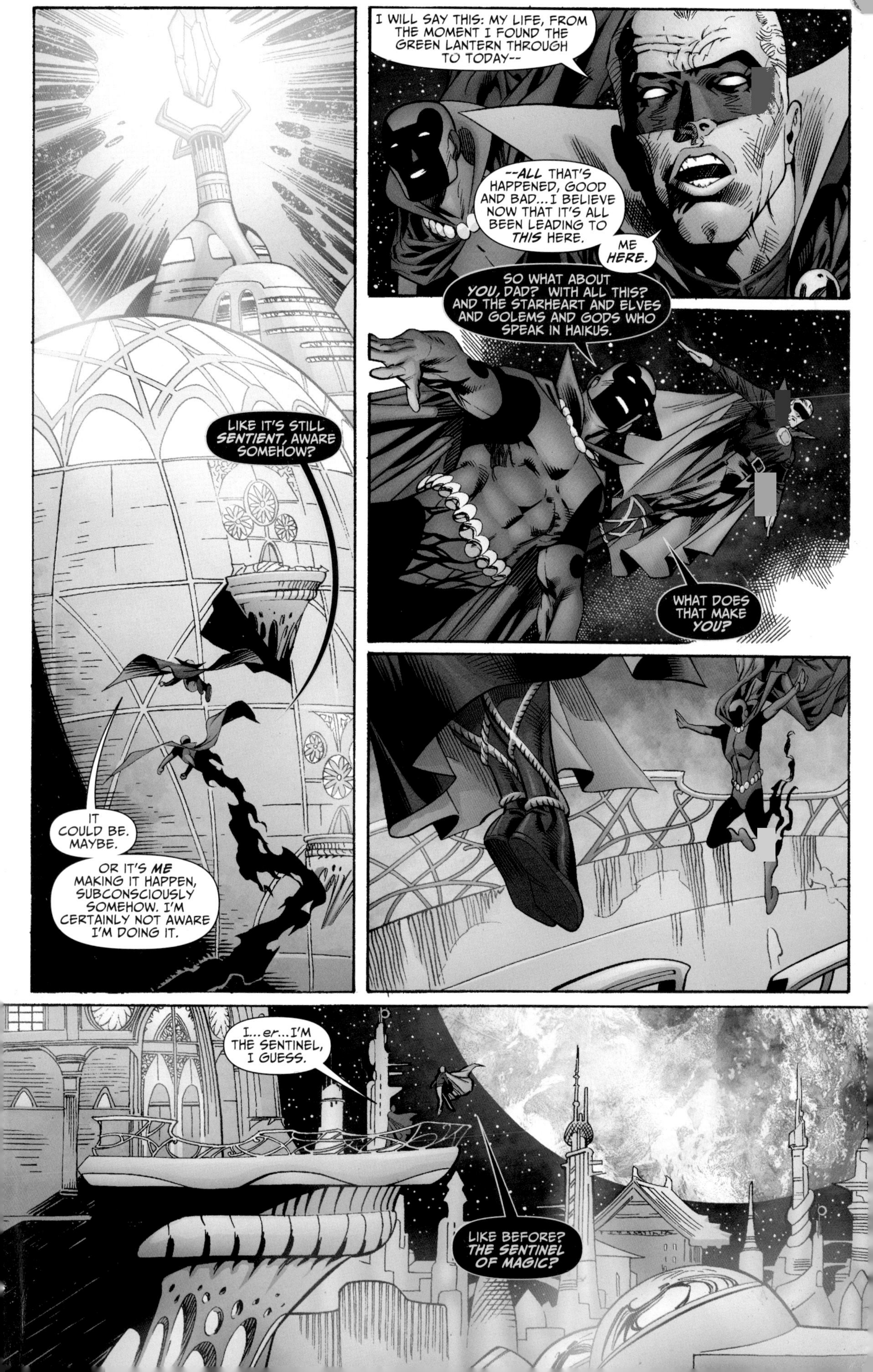
LIKE IT'S STILL SENTIENT, AWARE SOMEHOW?
IT COULD BE. MAYBE.
OR IT'S ME MAKING IT HAPPEN, SUBCONSCIOUSLY SOMEHOW. I'M CERTAINLY NOT AWARE I'M DOING IT.
I WILL SAY THIS: MY LIFE, FROM THE MOMENT I FOUND THE GREEN LANTERN THROUGH TO TODAY--
--ALL THAT'S HAPPENED, GOOD AND BAD...I BELIEVE NOW THAT IT'S ALL BEEN LEADING TO THIS HERE.
ME HERE.
SO WHAT ABOUT YOU, DAD? WITH ALL THIS? AND THE STARHEART AND ELVES AND GOLEMS AND GODS WHO SPEAK IN HAIKUS.
WHAT DOES THAT MAKE YOU?
I...er...I'M THE SENTINEL, I GUESS.
LIKE BEFORE? THE SENTINEL OF MAGIC?

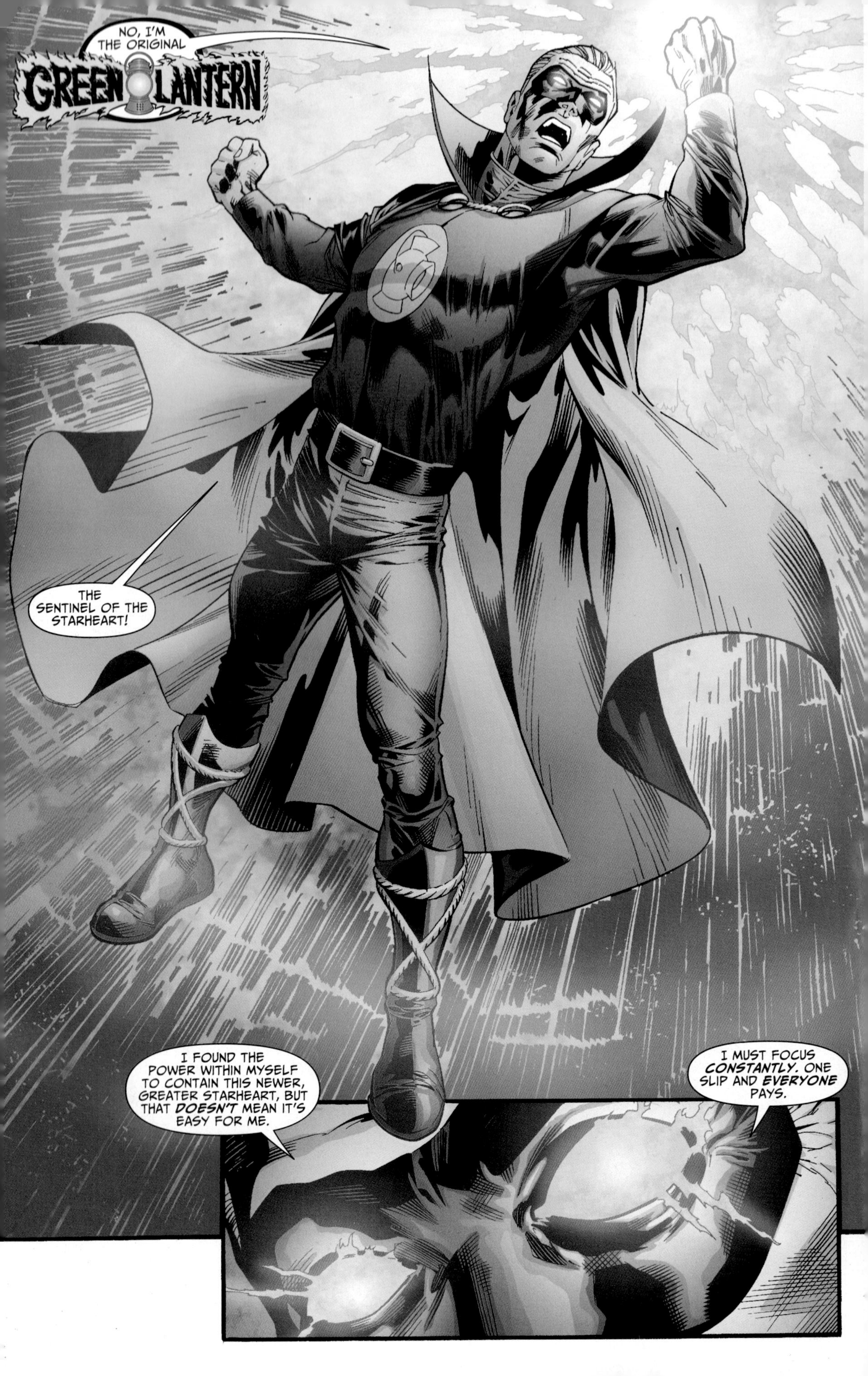
NO, I'M THE ORIGINAL
GREEN LANTERN
THE SENTINEL OF THE STARHEART!
I FOUND THE POWER WITHIN MYSELF TO CONTAIN THIS NEWER, GREATER STARHEART, BUT THAT DOESN'T MEAN IT'S EASY FOR ME.
I MUST FOCUS CONSTANTLY. ONE SLIP AND EVERYONE PAYS.

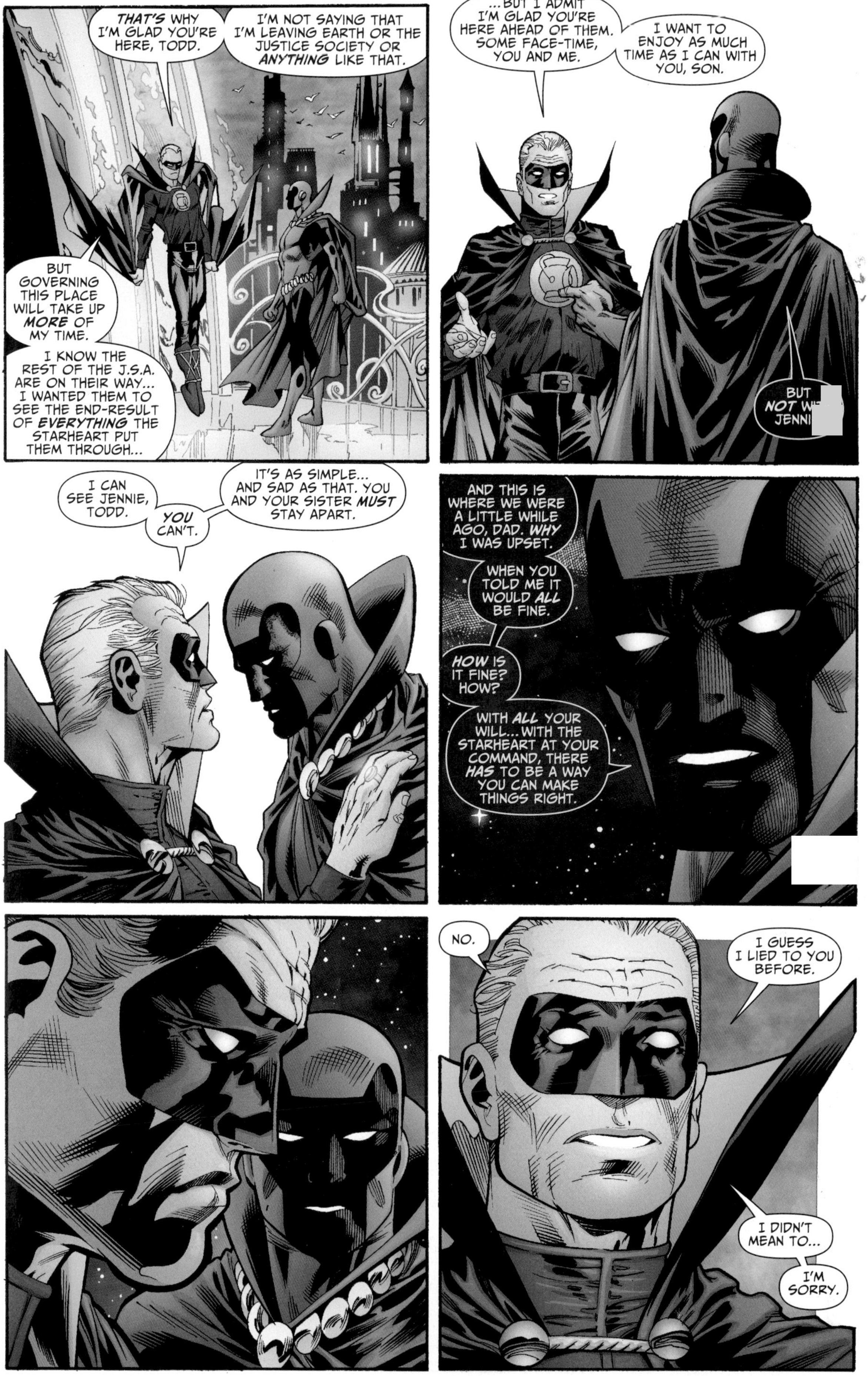

THAT'S WHY I'M GLAD YOU'RE HERE, TODD.
I'M NOT SAYING THAT I'M LEAVING EARTH OR THE JUSTICE SOCIETY OR ANYTHING LIKE THAT.
BUT GOVERNING THIS PLACE WILL TAKE UP MORE OF MY TIME.
I KNOW THE REST OF THE J.S.A. ARE ON THEIR WAY... I WANTED THEM TO SEE THE END-RESULT OF EVERYTHING THE STARHEART PUT THEM THROUGH...
...BUT I ADMIT I'M GLAD YOU'RE HERE AHEAD OF THEM. SOME FACE-TIME, YOU AND ME.
I WANT TO ENJOY AS MUCH TIME AS I CAN WITH YOU, SON.
BUT NOT W
JENNI
I CAN SEE JENNIE, TODD.
YOU CAN'T.
IT'S AS SIMPLE... AND SAD AS THAT. YOU AND YOUR SISTER MUST STAY APART.
AND THIS IS WHERE WE WERE A LITTLE WHILE AGO, DAD. WHY I WAS UPSET.
WHEN YOU TOLD ME IT WOULD ALL BE FINE.
HOW IS IT FINE? HOW?
WITH ALL YOUR WILL... WITH THE STARHEART AT YOUR COMMAND, THERE HAS TO BE A WAY YOU CAN MAKE THINGS RIGHT.
NO.
I GUESS I LIED TO YOU BEFORE.
I DIDN'T MEAN TO...
I'M SORRY.

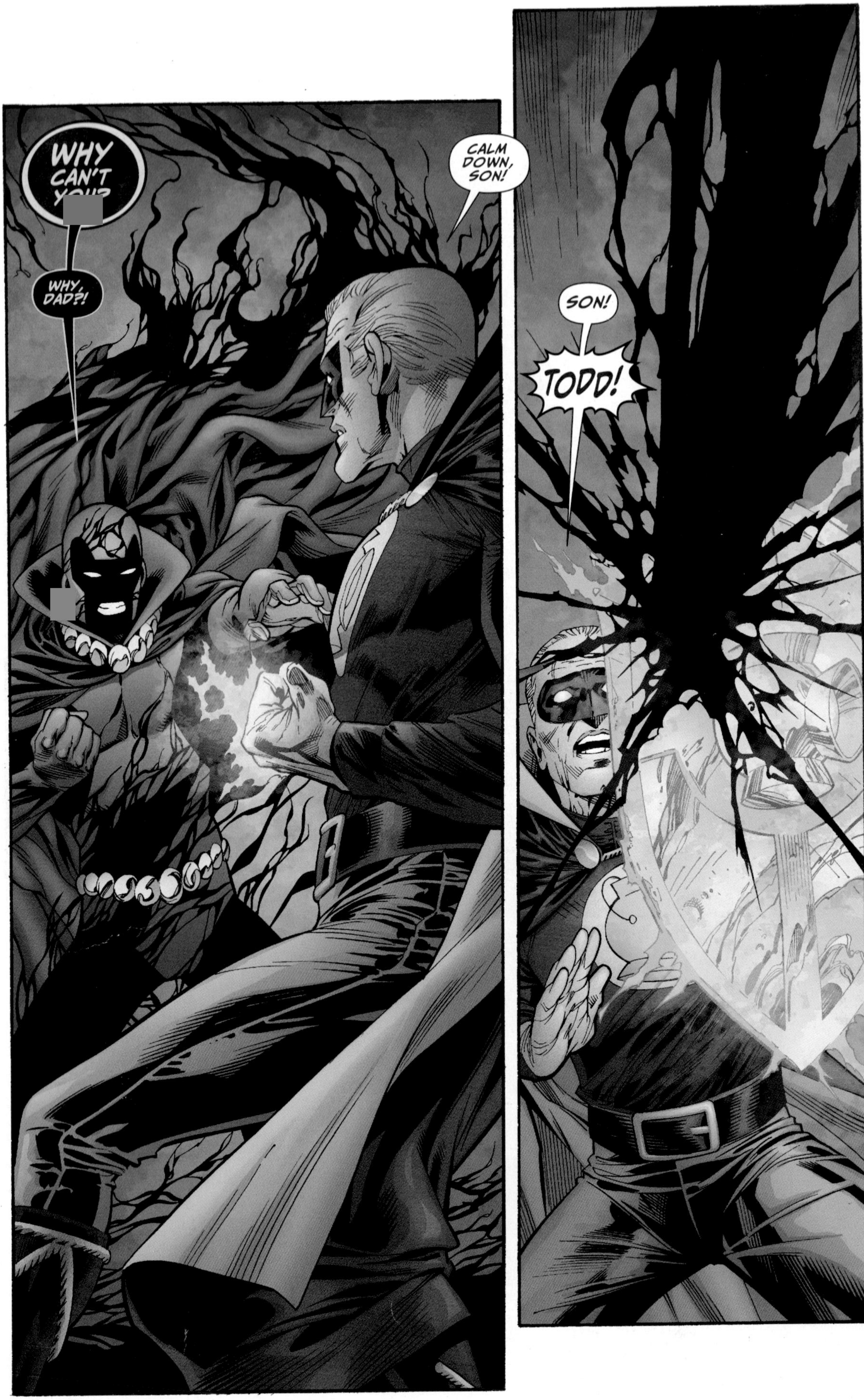
WHY CAN'T YOU?
WHY, DAD?!
CALM DOWN, SON!
SON!
TODD!

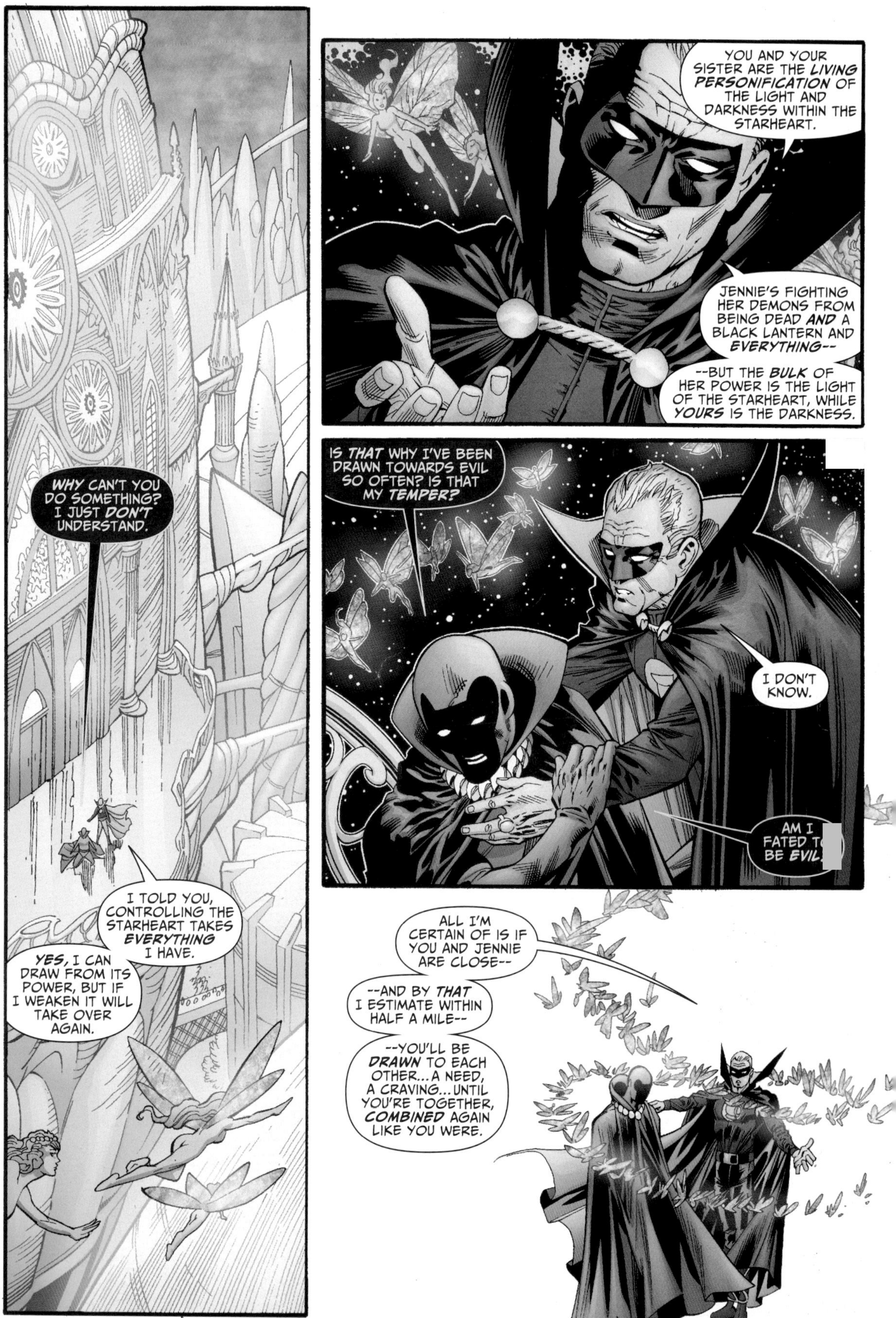

WHY CAN'T YOU DO SOMETHING? I JUST DON'T UNDERSTAND.
I TOLD YOU, CONTROLLING THE STARHEART TAKES EVERYTHING I HAVE.
YES, I CAN DRAW FROM ITS POWER, BUT IF I WEAKEN IT WILL TAKE OVER AGAIN.
YOU AND YOUR SISTER ARE THE LIVING PERSONIFICATION OF THE LIGHT AND DARKNESS WITHIN THE STARHEART.
JENNIE'S FIGHTING HER DEMONS FROM BEING DEAD AND A BLACK LANTERN AND EVERYTHING--
--BUT THE BULK OF HER POWER IS THE LIGHT OF THE STARHEART, WHILE YOURS IS THE DARKNESS.
IS THAT WHY I'VE BEEN DRAWN TOWARDS EVIL SO OFTEN? IS THAT MY TEMPER?
I DON'T KNOW.
AM I FATED T BE EVIL
ALL I'M CERTAIN OF IS IF YOU AND JENNIE ARE CLOSE--
--AND BY THAT I ESTIMATE WITHIN HALF A MILE--
--YOU'LL BE DRAWN TO EACH OTHER...A NEED, A CRAVING...UNTIL YOU'RE TOGETHER, COMBINED AGAIN LIKE YOU WERE.

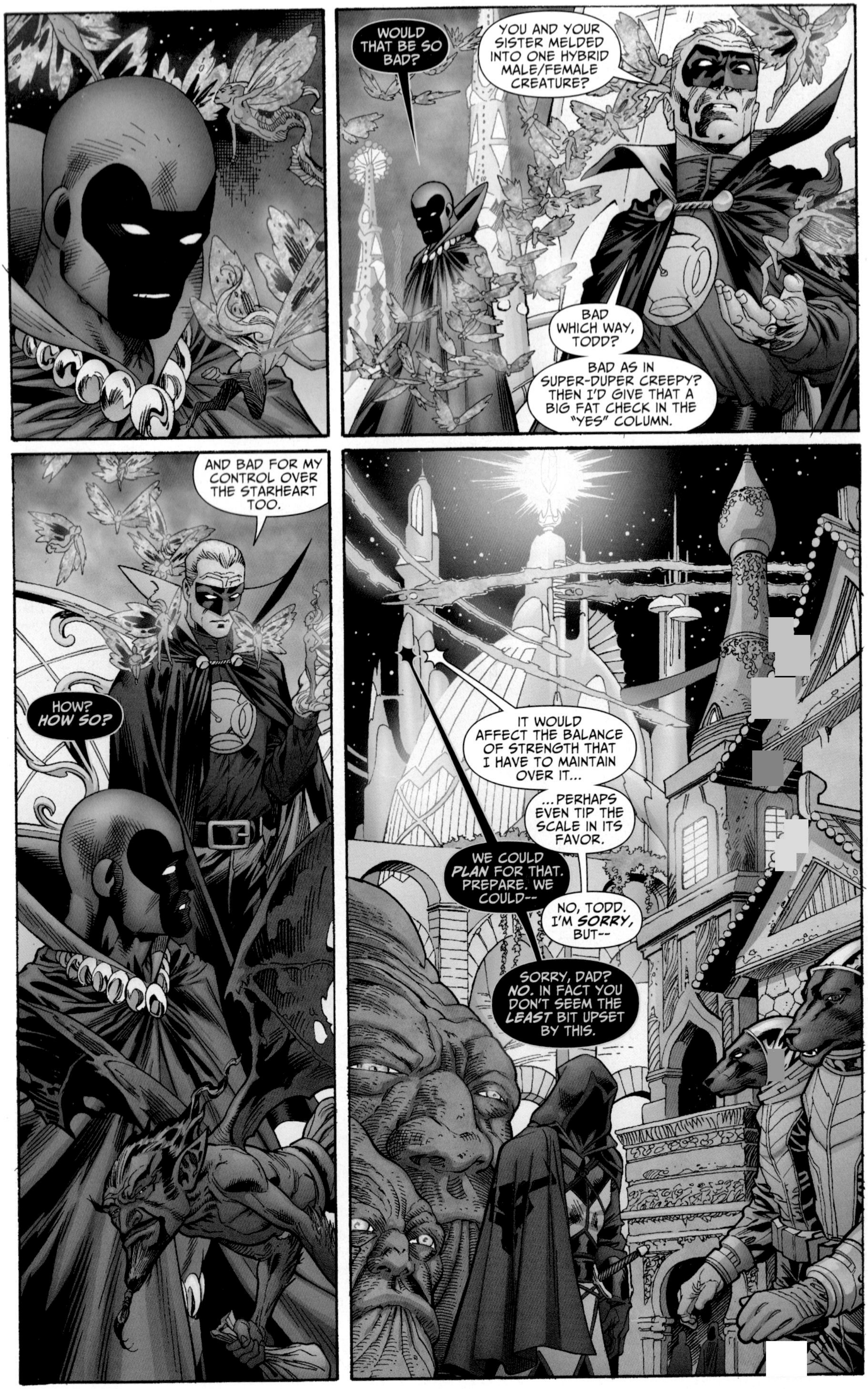
WOULD THAT BE SO BAD?
YOU AND YOUR SISTER MELDED INTO ONE HYBRID MALE/FEMALE CREATURE?
BAD WHICH WAY, TODD?
BAD AS IN SUPER-DUPER CREEPY? THEN I'D GIVE THAT A BIG FAT CHECK IN THE "YES" COLUMN.
AND BAD FOR MY CONTROL OVER THE STARHEART TOO.
HOW? HOW SO?
IT WOULD AFFECT THE BALANCE OF STRENGTH THAT I HAVE TO MAINTAIN OVER IT...
...PERHAPS EVEN TIP THE SCALE IN ITS FAVOR.
WE COULD PLAN FOR THAT. PREPARE. WE COULD--
NO, TODD. I'M SORRY, BUT--
SORRY, DAD? NO. IN FACT YOU DON'T SEEM THE LEAST BIT UPSET BY THIS.

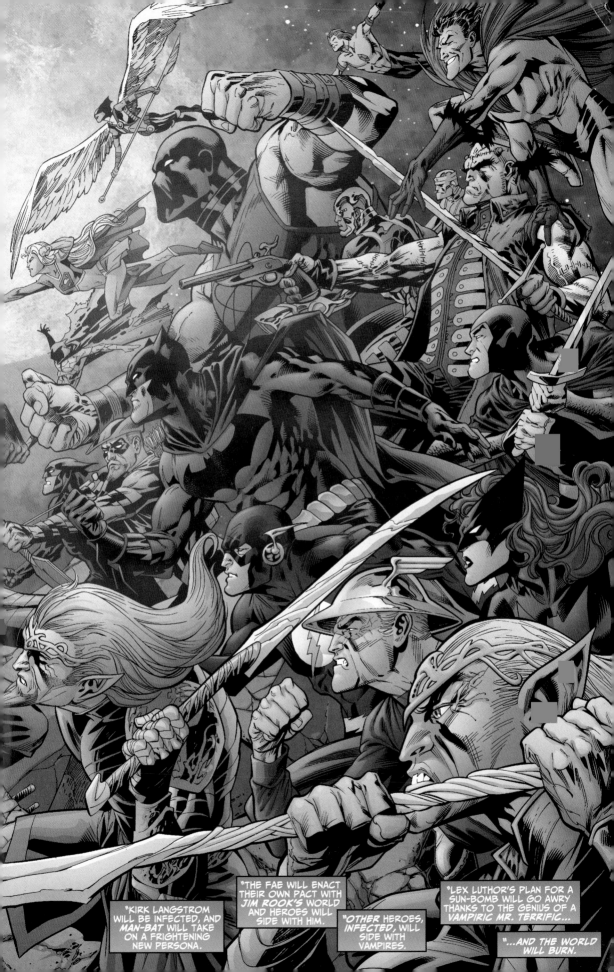

"KIRK LANGSTROM WILL BE INFECTED, AND MAN-BAT WILL TAKE ON A FRIGHTENING NEW PERSONA.

"THE FAE WILL ENACT THEIR OWN PACT WITH JIM ROOK'S WORLD AND HEROES WILL SIDE WITH HIM.

"OTHER HEROES, INFECTED, WILL SIDE WITH VAMPIRES.

"LEX LUTHOR'S PLAN FOR A SUN-BOMB WILL GO AWRY THANKS TO THE GENIUS OF A VAMPIRIC MR. TERRIFIC...

"...AND THE WORLD WILL BURN.

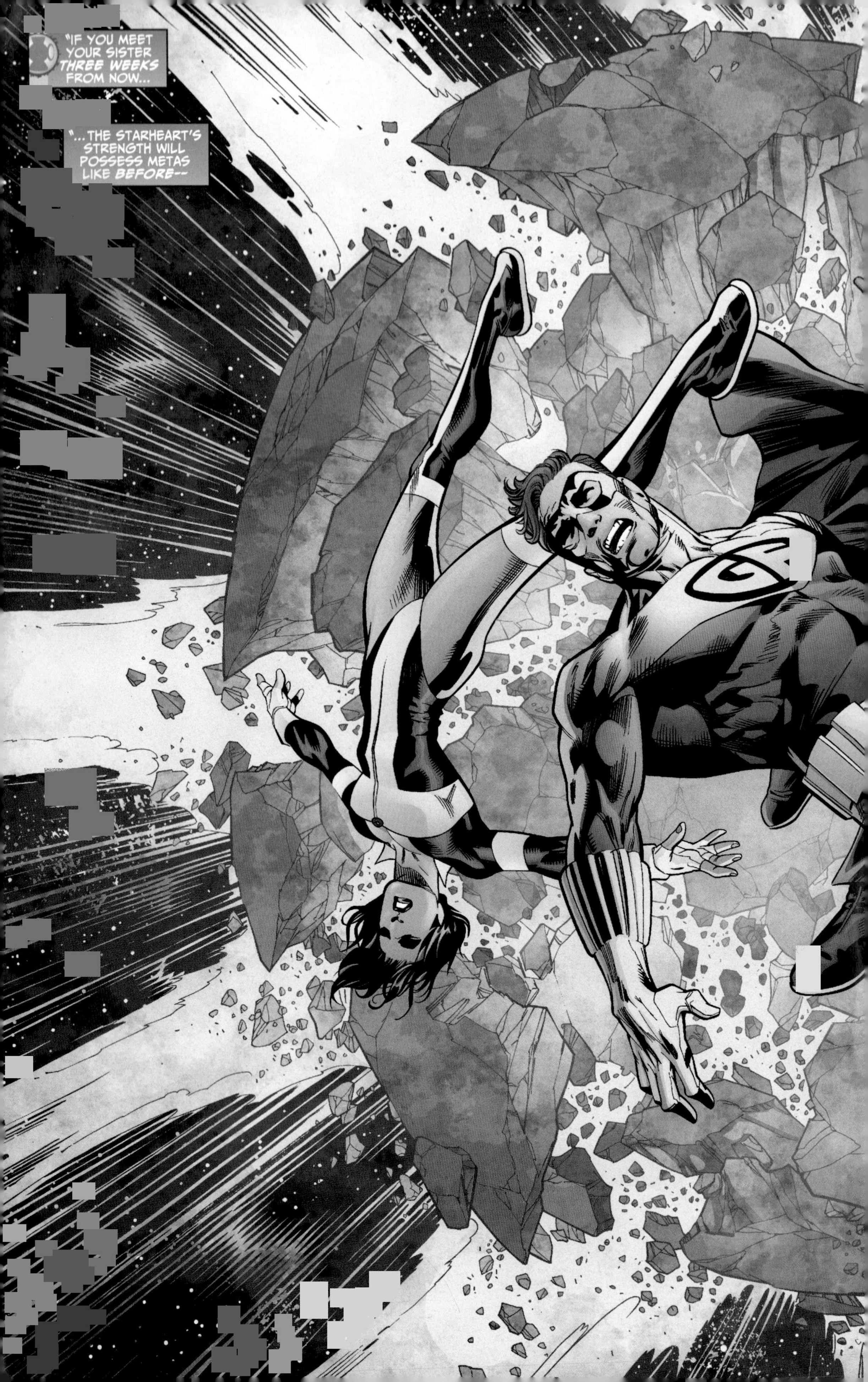
"IF YOU MEET YOUR SISTER THREE WEEKS FROM NOW...
"...THE STARHEART'S STRENGTH WILL POSSESS METAS LIKE BEFORE--

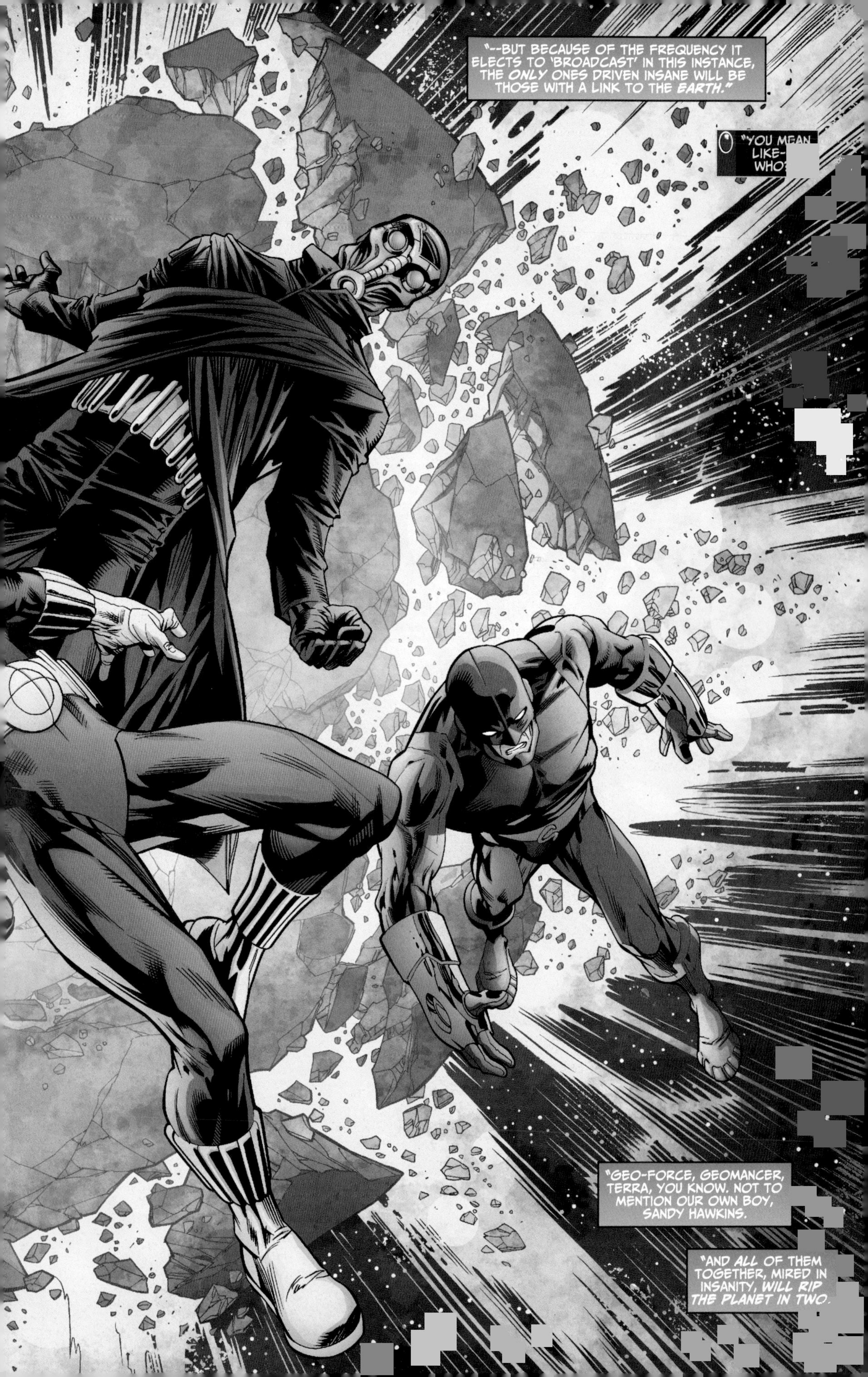
"--BUT BECAUSE OF THE FREQUENCY IT ELECTS TO 'BROADCAST' IN THIS INSTANCE, THE *ONLY* ONES DRIVEN INSANE WILL BE THOSE WITH A LINK TO THE *EARTH*."
"YOU MEAN LIKE- WHO
"GEO-FORCE, GEOMANCER, TERRA, YOU KNOW. NOT TO MENTION OUR OWN BOY, SANDY HAWKINS.
"AND *ALL* OF THEM TOGETHER, MIRED IN INSANITY, ***WILL RIP THE PLANET IN TWO.***

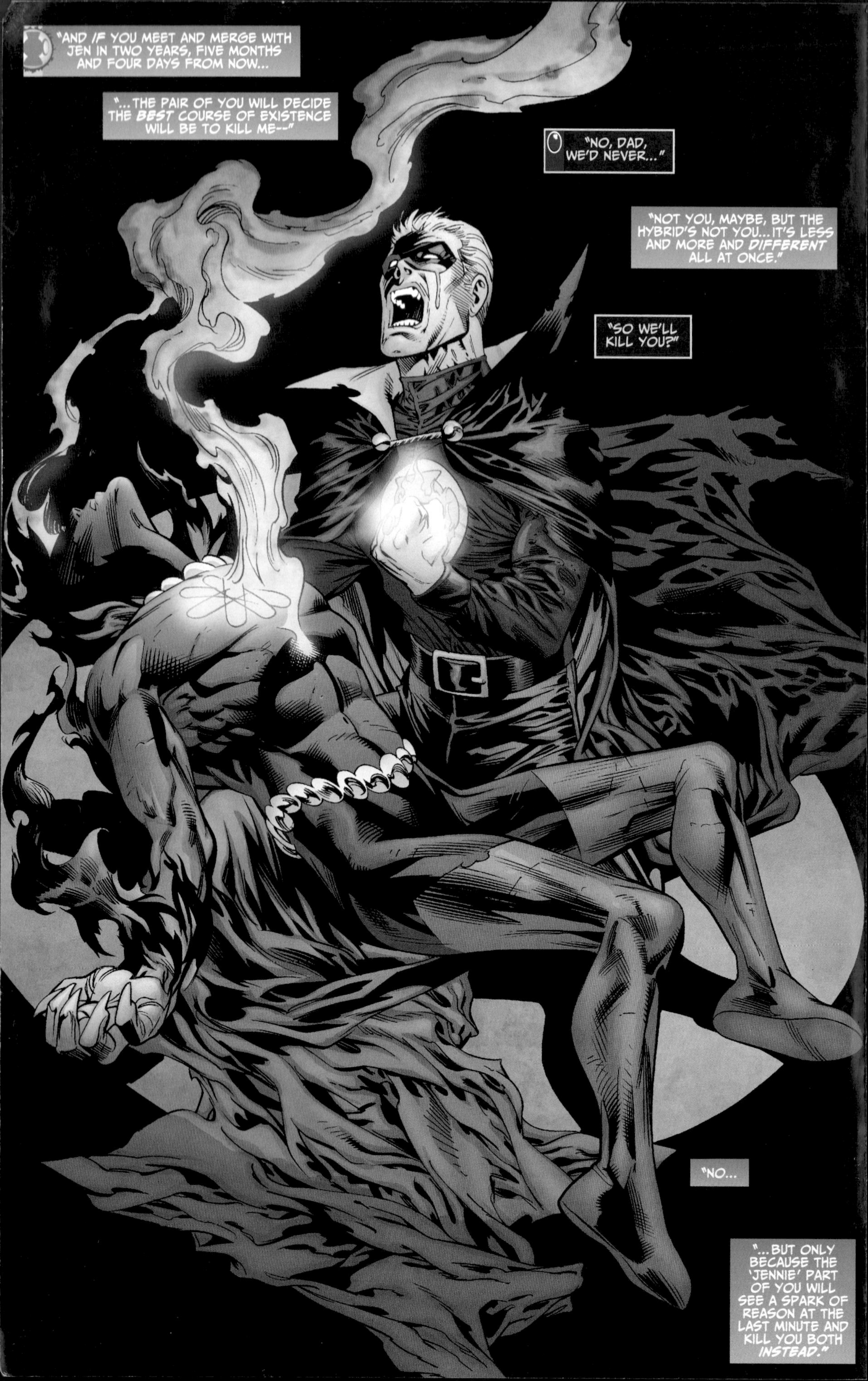
"AND IF YOU MEET AND MERGE WITH JEN IN TWO YEARS, FIVE MONTHS AND FOUR DAYS FROM NOW...
"...THE PAIR OF YOU WILL DECIDE THE BEST COURSE OF EXISTENCE WILL BE TO KILL ME--"
"NO, DAD, WE'D NEVER..."
"NOT YOU, MAYBE, BUT THE HYBRID'S NOT YOU...IT'S LESS AND MORE AND DIFFERENT ALL AT ONCE."
"SO WE'LL KILL YOU?"
"NO...
"...BUT ONLY BECAUSE THE 'JENNIE' PART OF YOU WILL SEE A SPARK OF REASON AT THE LAST MINUTE AND KILL YOU BOTH INSTEAD."

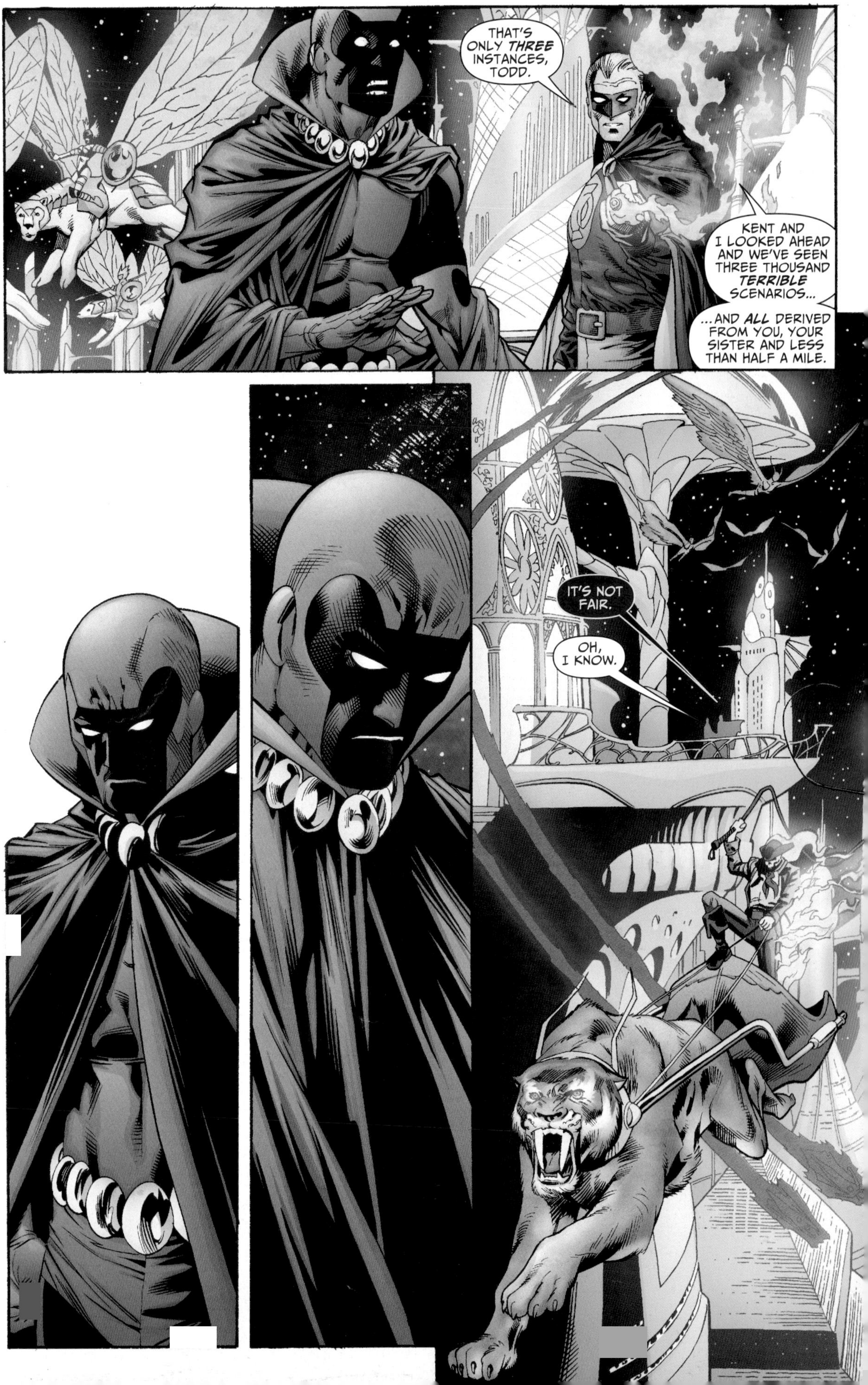
THAT'S ONLY *THREE* INSTANCES, TODD.
KENT AND I LOOKED AHEAD AND WE'VE SEEN THREE THOUSAND *TERRIBLE* SCENARIOS...
...AND *ALL* DERIVED FROM YOU, YOUR SISTER AND LESS THAN HALF A MILE.
IT'S NOT FAIR.
OH, I KNOW.

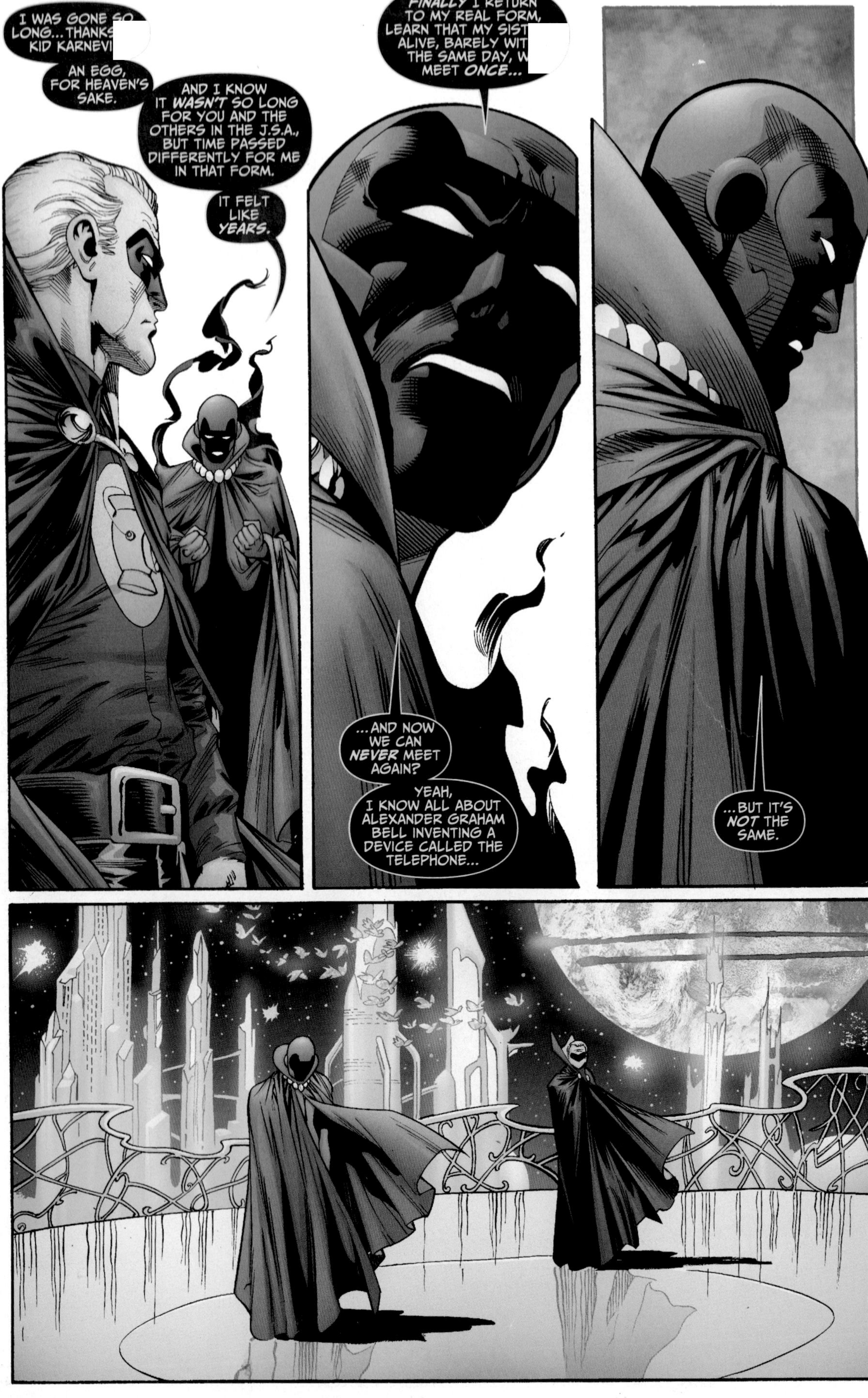

I WAS GONE SO LONG...THANKS KID KARNEVI
AN EGG, FOR HEAVEN'S SAKE.
AND I KNOW IT WASN'T SO LONG FOR YOU AND THE OTHERS IN THE J.S.A., BUT TIME PASSED DIFFERENTLY FOR ME IN THAT FORM.
IT FELT LIKE YEARS.
FINALLY I RETURN TO MY REAL FORM, LEARN THAT MY SIST ALIVE, BARELY WIT THE SAME DAY, W MEET ONCE...
...AND NOW WE CAN NEVER MEET AGAIN?
YEAH, I KNOW ALL ABOUT ALEXANDER GRAHAM BELL INVENTING A DEVICE CALLED THE TELEPHONE...
...BUT IT'S NOT THE SAME.

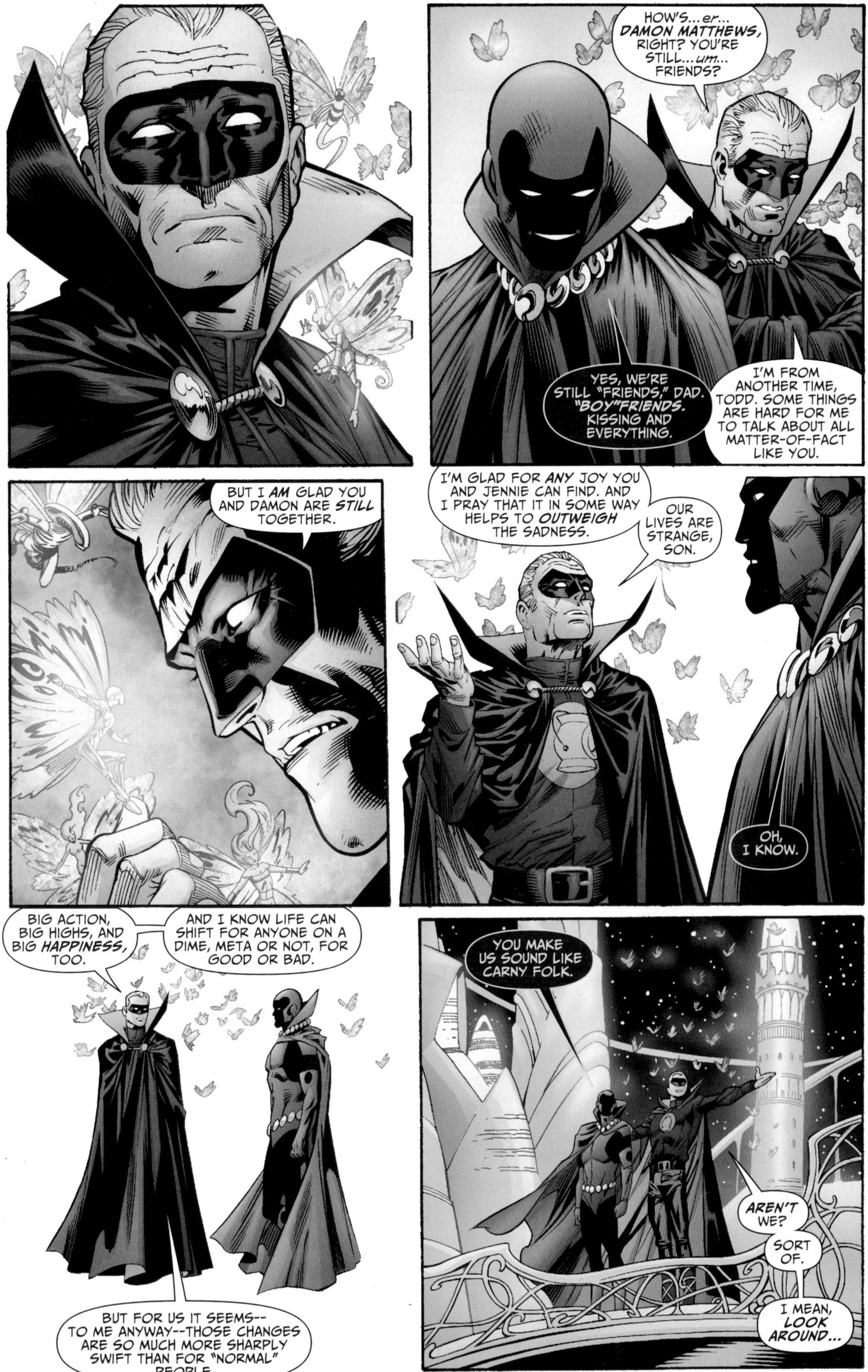
HOW'S...er...
DAMON MATTHEWS, RIGHT? YOU'RE STILL...um... FRIENDS?
YES, WE'RE STILL "FRIENDS," DAD. "BOY"FRIENDS. KISSING AND EVERYTHING.
I'M FROM ANOTHER TIME, TODD. SOME THINGS ARE HARD FOR ME TO TALK ABOUT ALL MATTER-OF-FACT LIKE YOU.
BUT I AM GLAD YOU AND DAMON ARE STILL TOGETHER.
I'M GLAD FOR ANY JOY YOU AND JENNIE CAN FIND. AND I PRAY THAT IT IN SOME WAY HELPS TO OUTWEIGH THE SADNESS.
OUR LIVES ARE STRANGE, SON.
OH, I KNOW.
BIG ACTION, BIG HIGHS, AND BIG HAPPINESS, TOO.
AND I KNOW LIFE CAN SHIFT FOR ANYONE ON A DIME, META OR NOT, FOR GOOD OR BAD.
BUT FOR US IT SEEMS-- TO ME ANYWAY--THOSE CHANGES ARE SO MUCH MORE SHARPLY SWIFT THAN FOR "NORMAL" PEOPLE.
YOU MAKE US SOUND LIKE CARNY FOLK.
AREN'T WE?
SORT OF.
I MEAN, LOOK AROUND...

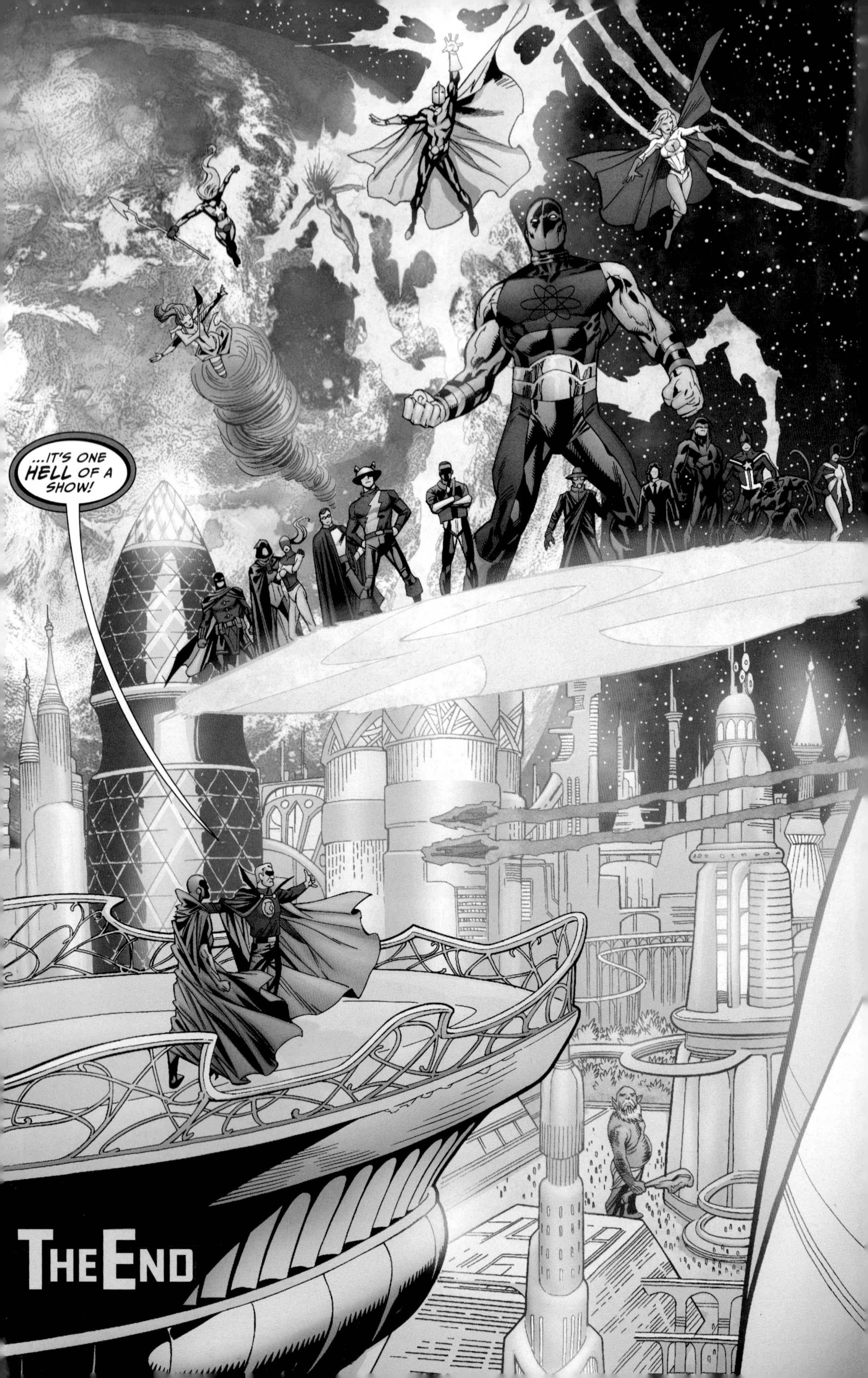
...IT'S ONE HELL OF A SHOW!
THE END

JUSTICE LEAGUE OF AMERICA 54
Cover by Brett Booth & Andrew Dalhouse

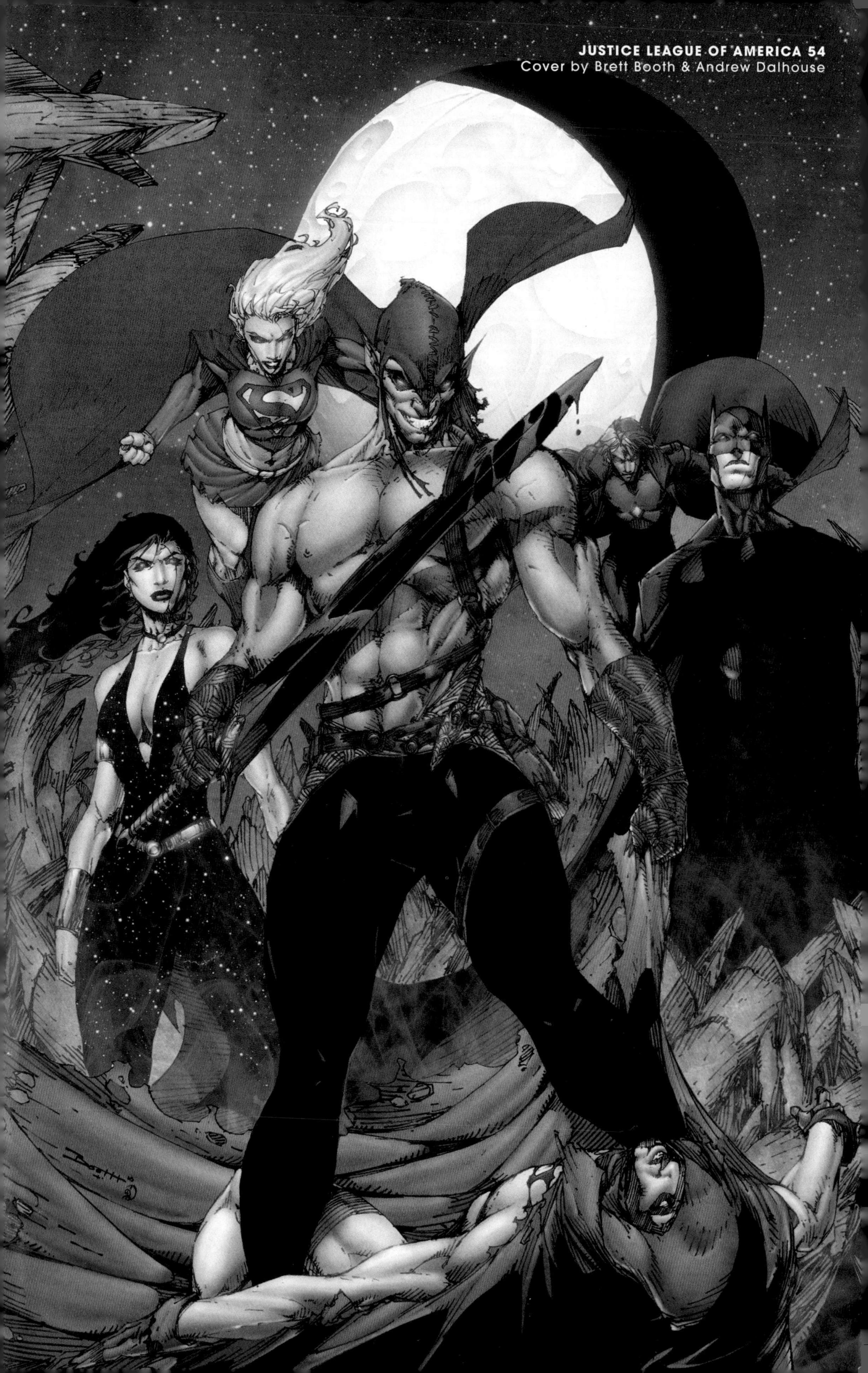

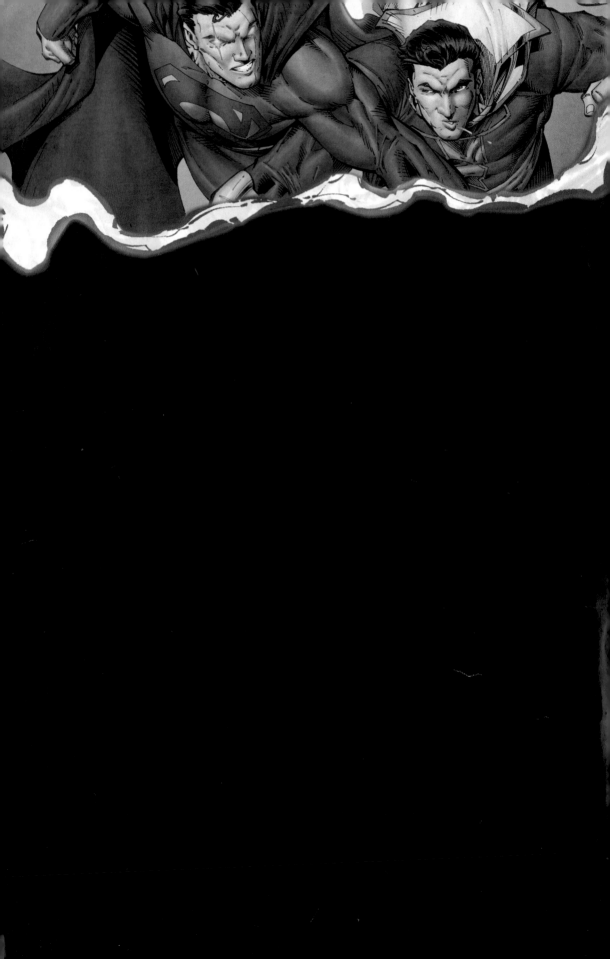

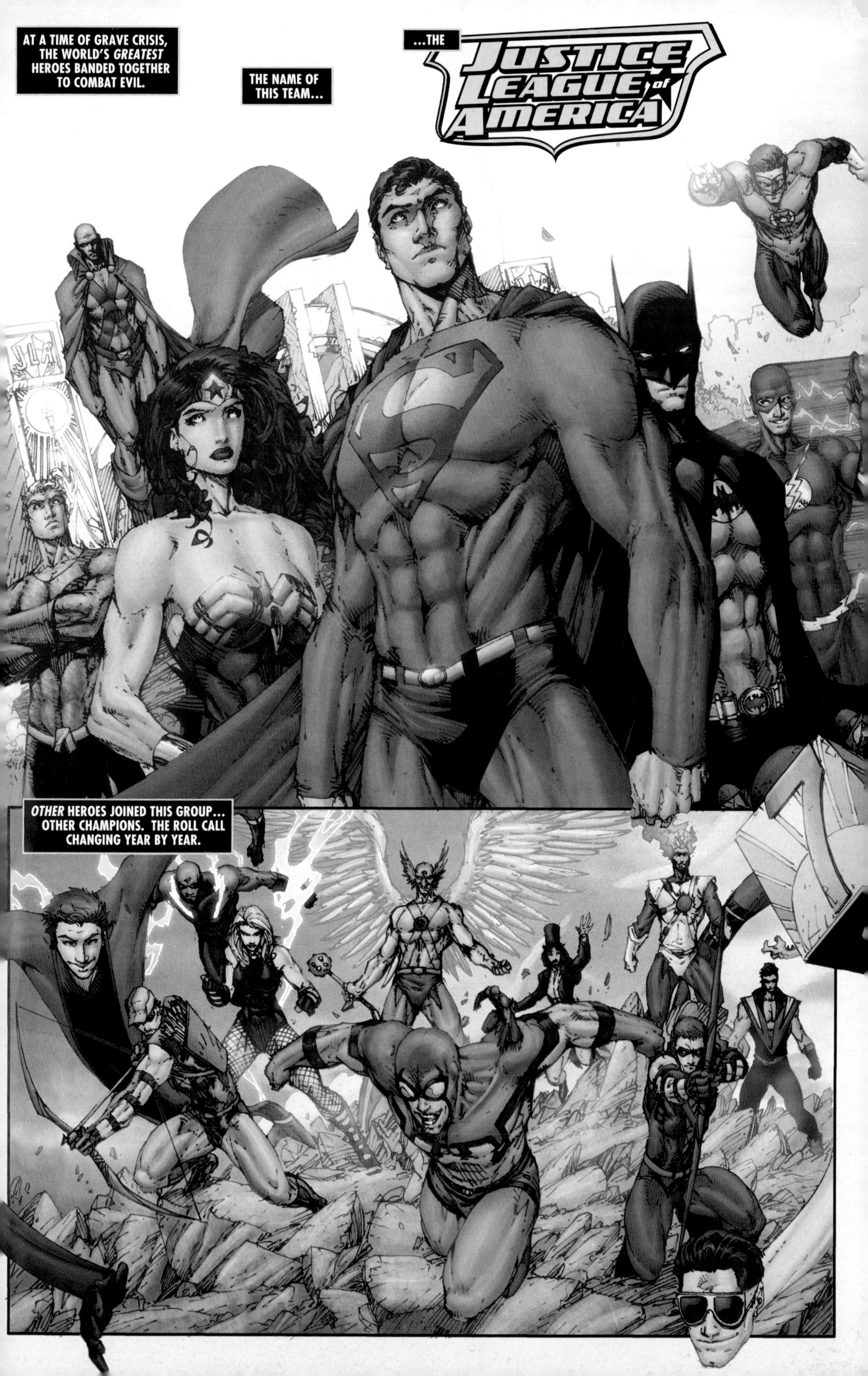
AT A TIME OF GRAVE CRISIS, THE WORLD'S *GREATEST* HEROES BANDED TOGETHER TO COMBAT EVIL.
THE NAME OF THIS TEAM...
...THE
JUSTICE LEAGUE of AMERICA
JLA
OTHER HEROES JOINED THIS GROUP... OTHER CHAMPIONS. THE ROLL CALL CHANGING YEAR BY YEAR.

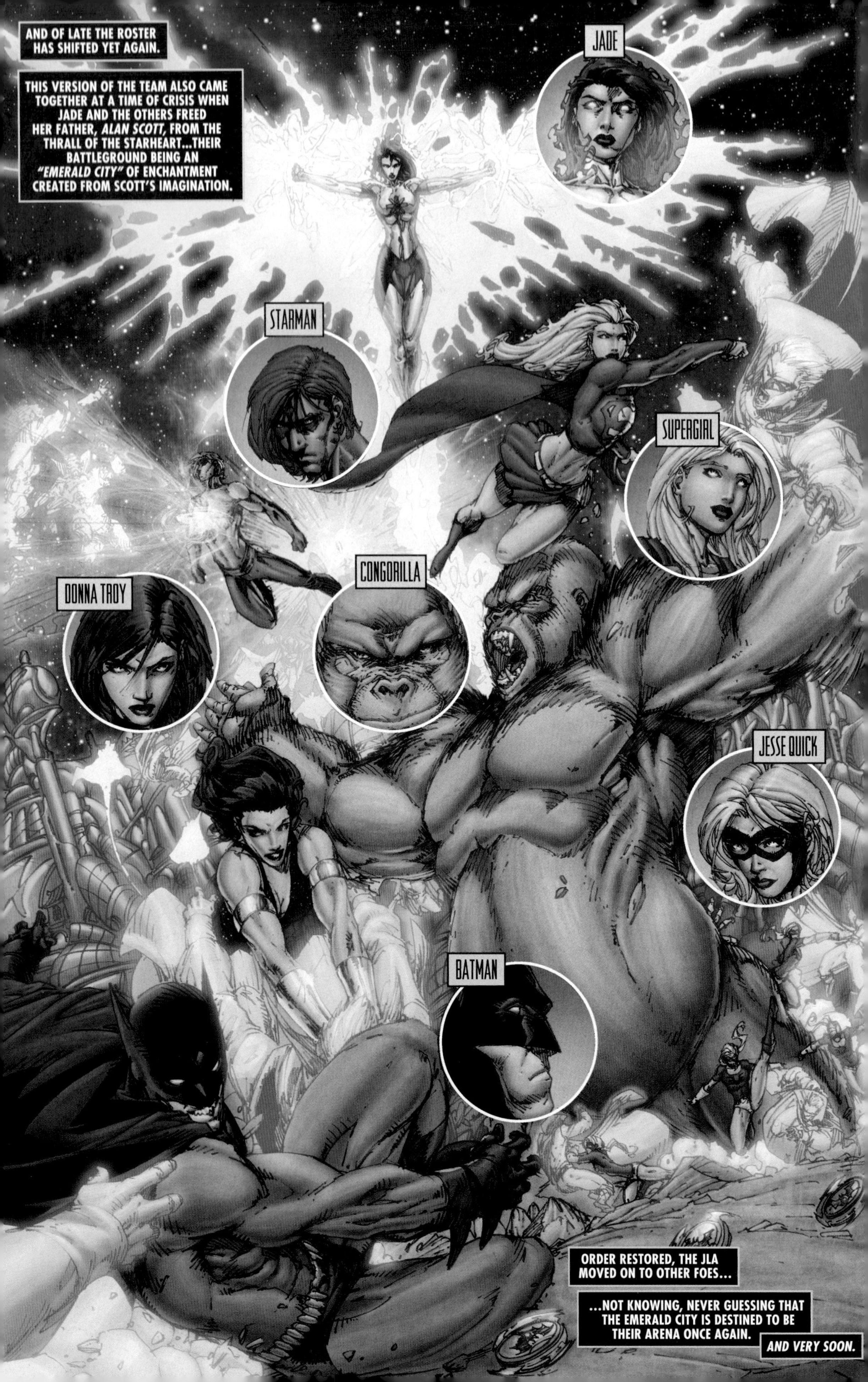
AND OF LATE THE ROSTER HAS SHIFTED YET AGAIN.
THIS VERSION OF THE TEAM ALSO CAME TOGETHER AT A TIME OF CRISIS WHEN JADE AND THE OTHERS FREED HER FATHER, *ALAN SCOTT*, FROM THE THRALL OF THE STARHEART...THEIR BATTLEGROUND BEING AN *"EMERALD CITY"* OF ENCHANTMENT CREATED FROM SCOTT'S IMAGINATION.
JADE
STARMAN
SUPERGIRL
CONGORILLA
DONNA TROY
JESSE QUICK
BATMAN
ORDER RESTORED, THE JLA MOVED ON TO OTHER FOES...
...NOT KNOWING, NEVER GUESSING THAT THE EMERALD CITY IS DESTINED TO BE THEIR ARENA ONCE AGAIN.
AND VERY SOON.

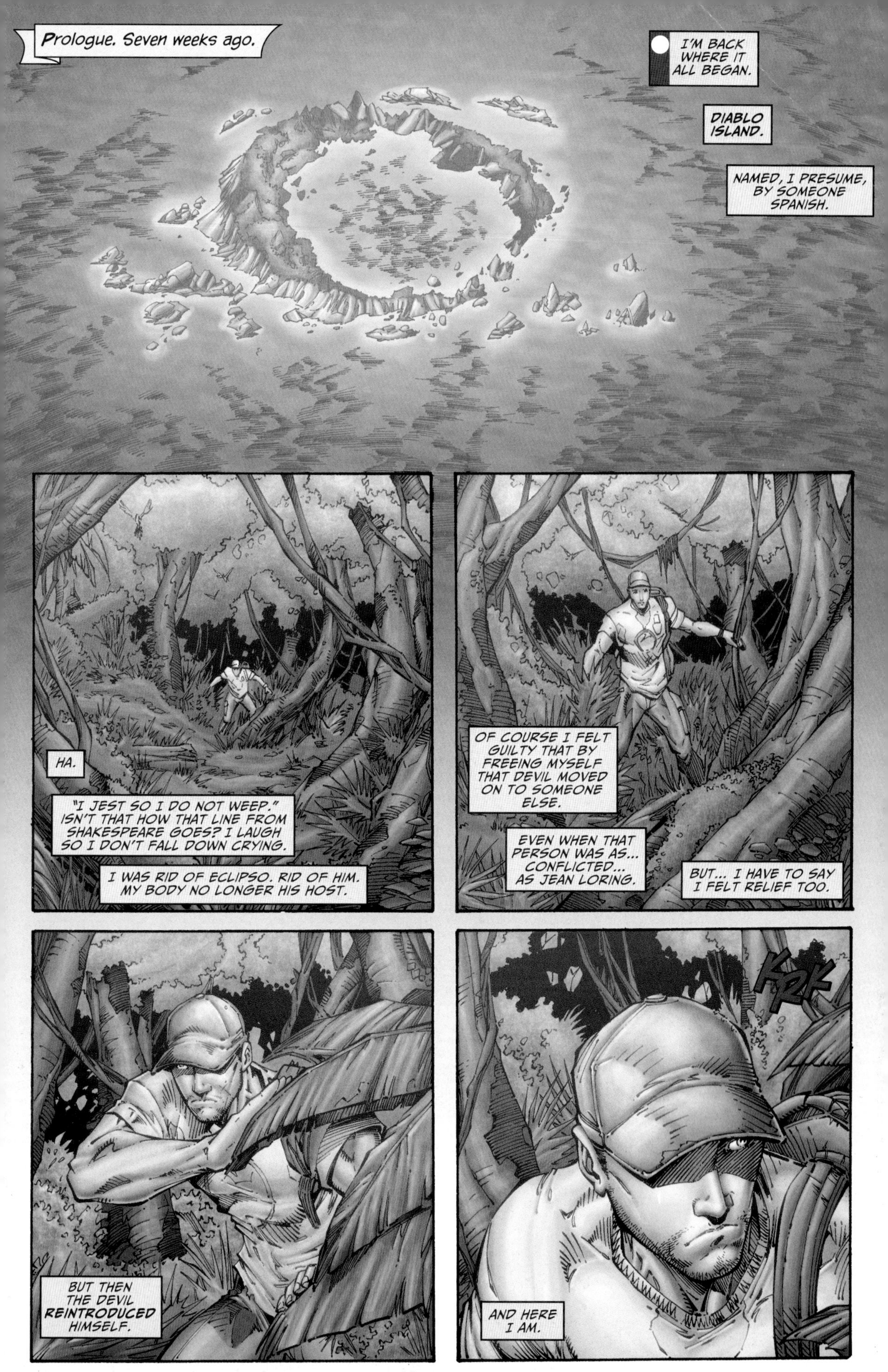
Prologue. Seven weeks ago.
I'M BACK WHERE IT ALL BEGAN.
DIABLO ISLAND.
NAMED, I PRESUME, BY SOMEONE SPANISH.
HA.
"I JEST SO I DO NOT WEEP." ISN'T THAT HOW THAT LINE FROM SHAKESPEARE GOES? I LAUGH SO I DON'T FALL DOWN CRYING.
I WAS RID OF ECLIPSO. RID OF HIM. MY BODY NO LONGER HIS HOST.
OF COURSE I FELT GUILTY THAT BY FREEING MYSELF THAT DEVIL MOVED ON TO SOMEONE ELSE.
EVEN WHEN THAT PERSON WAS AS... CONFLICTED... AS JEAN LORING.
BUT... I HAVE TO SAY I FELT RELIEF TOO.
BUT THEN THE DEVIL REINTRODUCED HIMSELF.
KRK
AND HERE I AM.

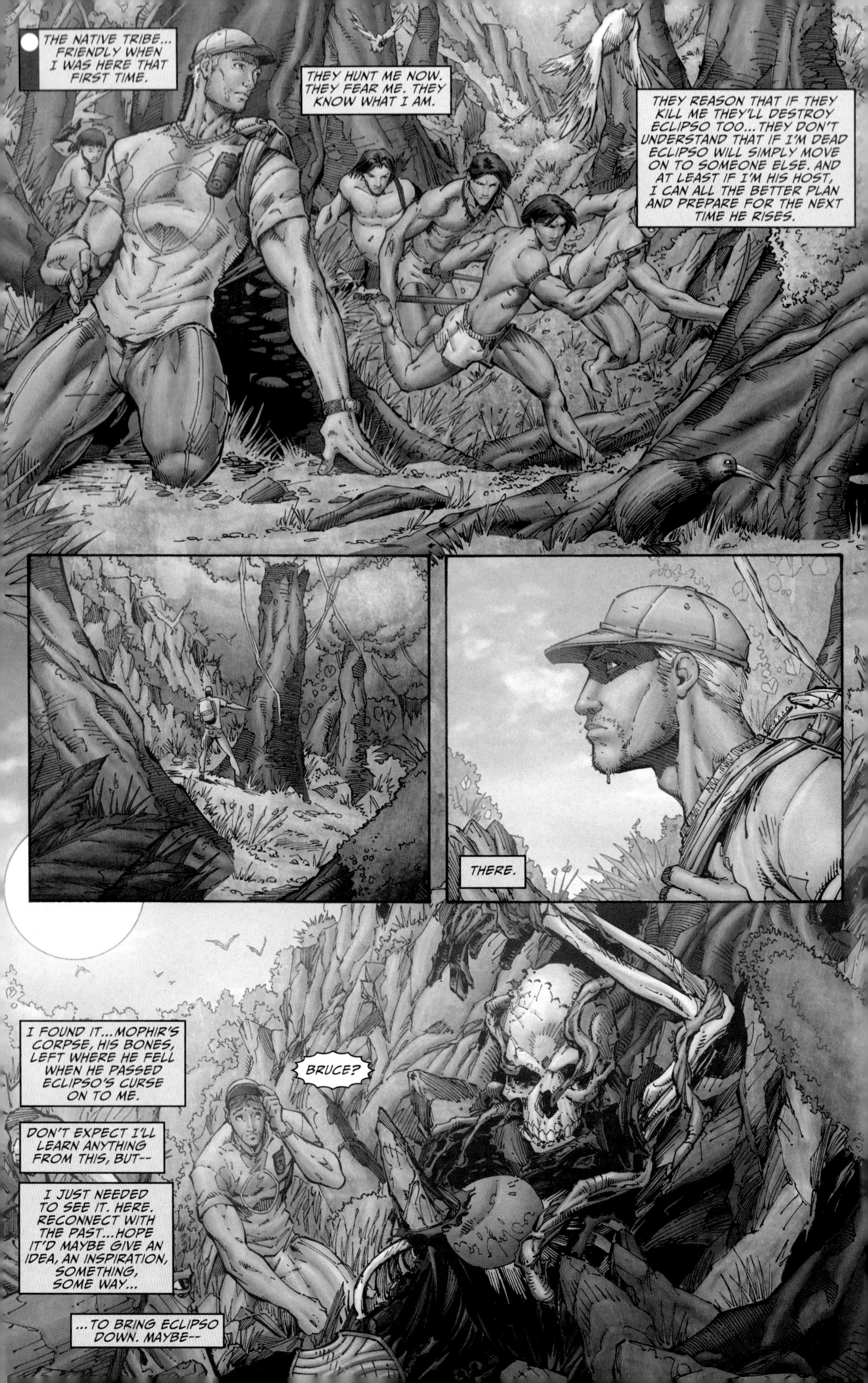
THE NATIVE TRIBE... FRIENDLY WHEN I WAS HERE THAT FIRST TIME.
THEY HUNT ME NOW. THEY FEAR ME. THEY KNOW WHAT I AM.
THEY REASON THAT IF THEY KILL ME THEY'LL DESTROY ECLIPSO TOO...THEY DON'T UNDERSTAND THAT IF I'M DEAD ECLIPSO WILL SIMPLY MOVE ON TO SOMEONE ELSE. AND AT LEAST IF I'M HIS HOST, I CAN ALL THE BETTER PLAN AND PREPARE FOR THE NEXT TIME HE RISES.
THERE.
I FOUND IT...MOPHIR'S CORPSE, HIS BONES, LEFT WHERE HE FELL WHEN HE PASSED ECLIPSO'S CURSE ON TO ME.
BRUCE?
DON'T EXPECT I'LL LEARN ANYTHING FROM THIS, BUT--
I JUST NEEDED TO SEE IT. HERE. RECONNECT WITH THE PAST...HOPE IT'D MAYBE GIVE AN IDEA, AN INSPIRATION, SOMETHING, SOME WAY...
...TO BRING ECLIPSO DOWN. MAYBE--

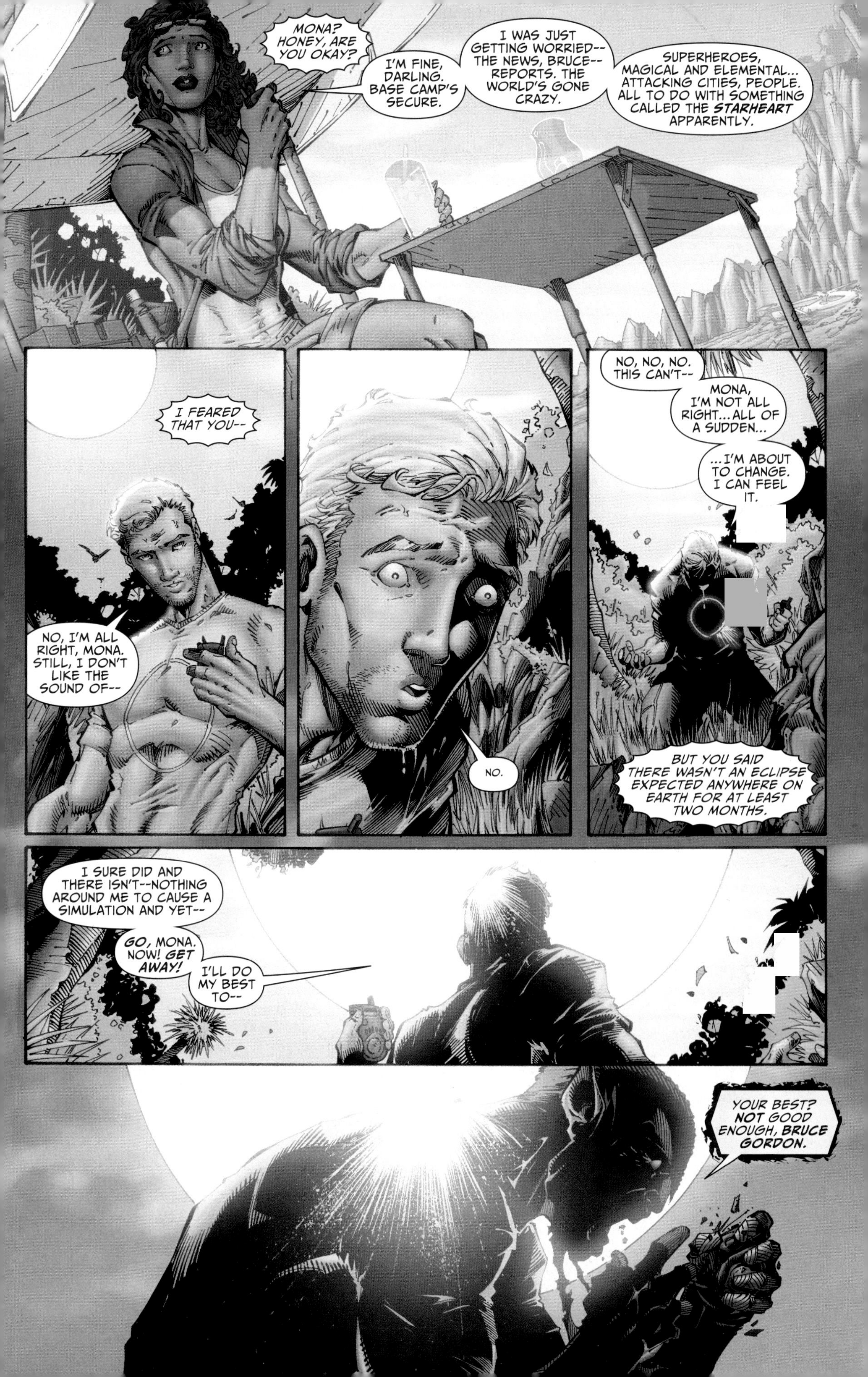
MONA? HONEY, ARE YOU OKAY?
I'M FINE, DARLING. BASE CAMP'S SECURE.
I WAS JUST GETTING WORRIED-- THE NEWS, BRUCE-- REPORTS. THE WORLD'S GONE CRAZY.
SUPERHEROES, MAGICAL AND ELEMENTAL... ATTACKING CITIES, PEOPLE. ALL TO DO WITH SOMETHING CALLED THE STARHEART APPARENTLY.
I FEARED THAT YOU--
NO, I'M ALL RIGHT, MONA. STILL, I DON'T LIKE THE SOUND OF--
NO.
NO, NO, NO. THIS CAN'T--
MONA, I'M NOT ALL RIGHT... ALL OF A SUDDEN...
...I'M ABOUT TO CHANGE. I CAN FEEL IT.
BUT YOU SAID THERE WASN'T AN ECLIPSE EXPECTED ANYWHERE ON EARTH FOR AT LEAST TWO MONTHS.
I SURE DID AND THERE ISN'T--NOTHING AROUND ME TO CAUSE A SIMULATION AND YET--
GO, MONA. NOW! GET AWAY!
I'LL DO MY BEST TO--
YOUR BEST? NOT GOOD ENOUGH, BRUCE GORDON.

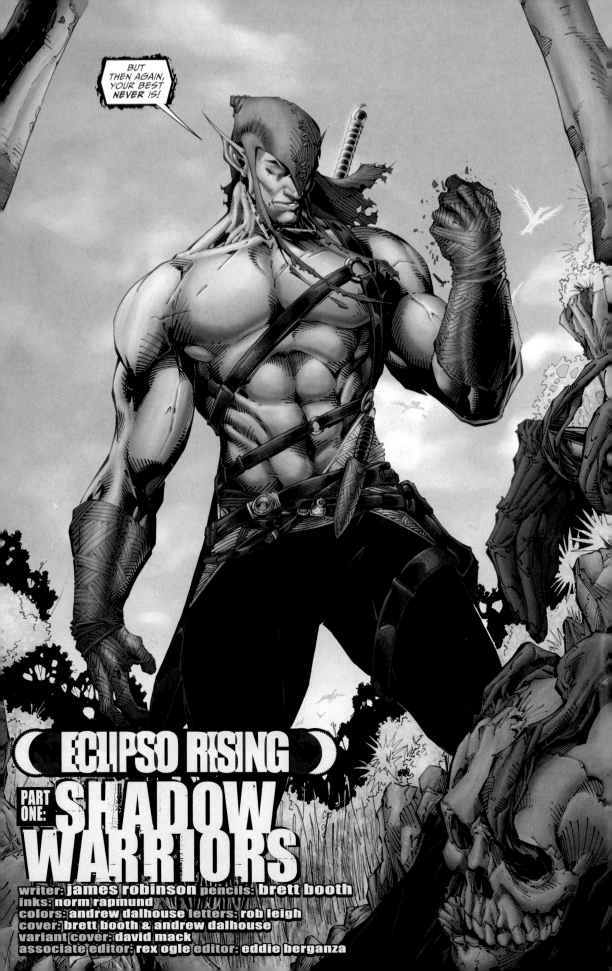

BUT THEN AGAIN, YOUR BEST NEVER IS!

ECLIPSO RISING
PART ONE: SHADOW WARRIORS

writer: james robinson pencils: brett booth
inks: norm rapmund
colors: andrew dalhouse letters: rob leigh
cover: brett booth & andrew dalhouse
variant cover: david mack
associate editor: rex ogle editor: eddie berganza

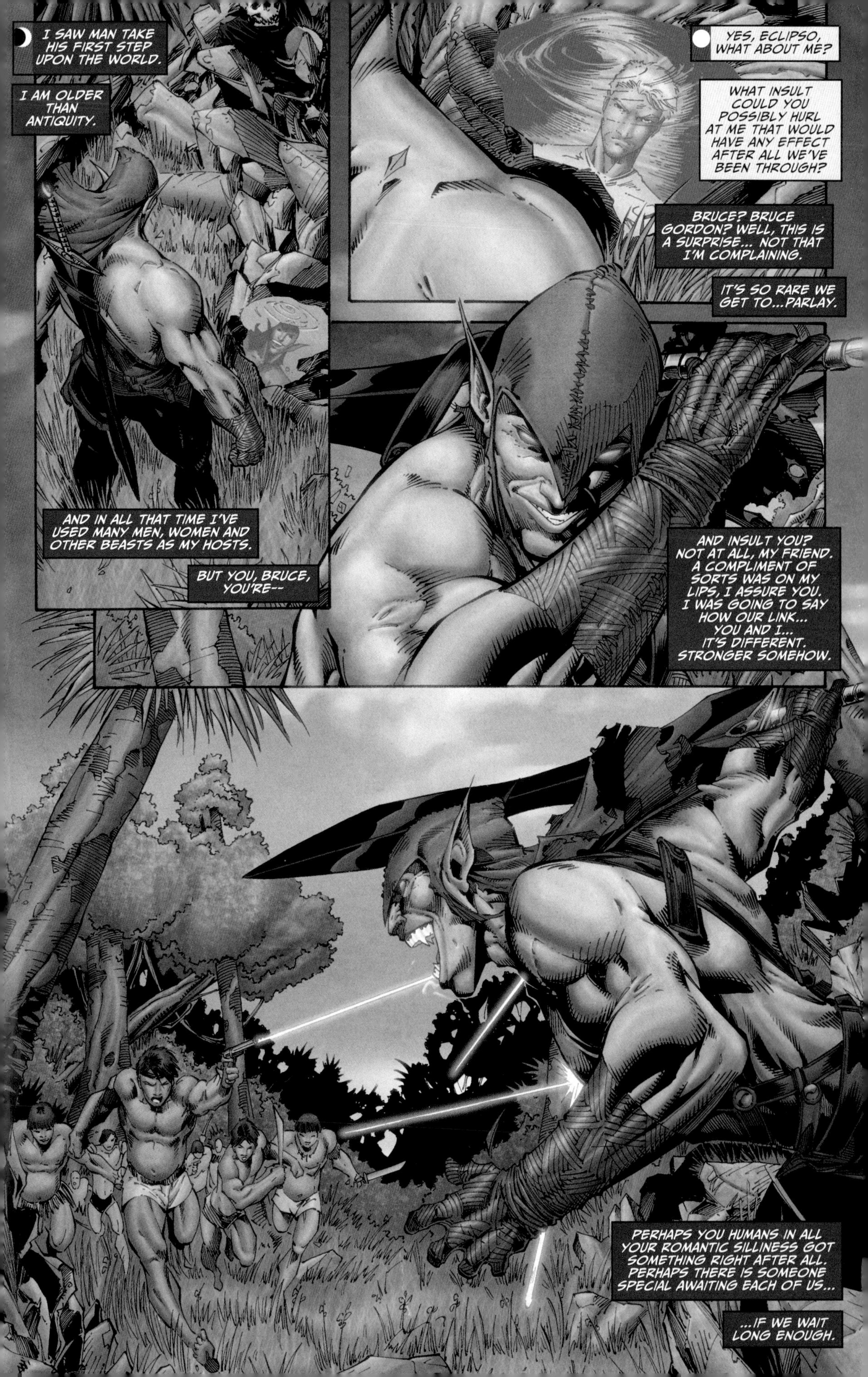
I SAW MAN TAKE HIS FIRST STEP UPON THE WORLD.
I AM OLDER THAN ANTIQUITY.
YES, ECLIPSO, WHAT ABOUT ME?
WHAT INSULT COULD YOU POSSIBLY HURL AT ME THAT WOULD HAVE ANY EFFECT AFTER ALL WE'VE BEEN THROUGH?
BRUCE? BRUCE GORDON? WELL, THIS IS A SURPRISE... NOT THAT I'M COMPLAINING.
IT'S SO RARE WE GET TO...PARLAY.
AND IN ALL THAT TIME I'VE USED MANY MEN, WOMEN AND OTHER BEASTS AS MY HOSTS.
BUT YOU, BRUCE, YOU'RE--
AND INSULT YOU? NOT AT ALL, MY FRIEND. A COMPLIMENT OF SORTS WAS ON MY LIPS, I ASSURE YOU. I WAS GOING TO SAY HOW OUR LINK... YOU AND I... IT'S DIFFERENT. STRONGER SOMEHOW.
PERHAPS YOU HUMANS IN ALL YOUR ROMANTIC SILLINESS GOT SOMETHING RIGHT AFTER ALL. PERHAPS THERE IS SOMEONE SPECIAL AWAITING EACH OF US...
...IF WE WAIT LONG ENOUGH.

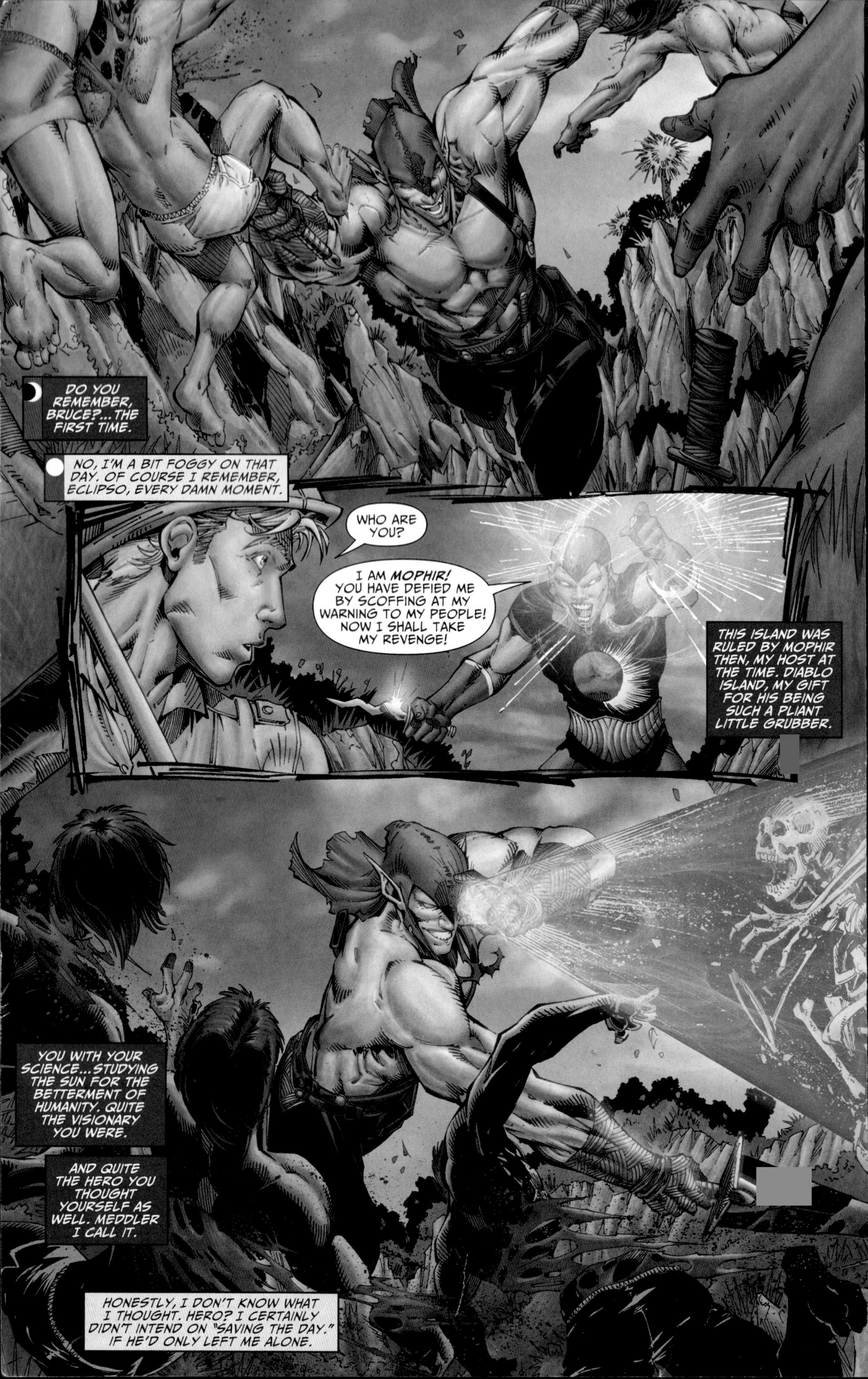
DO YOU REMEMBER, BRUCE?...THE FIRST TIME.
NO, I'M A BIT FOGGY ON THAT DAY. OF COURSE I REMEMBER, ECLIPSO, EVERY DAMN MOMENT.
WHO ARE YOU?
I AM MOPHIR! YOU HAVE DEFIED ME BY SCOFFING AT MY WARNING TO MY PEOPLE! NOW I SHALL TAKE MY REVENGE!
THIS ISLAND WAS RULED BY MOPHIR THEN, MY HOST AT THE TIME. DIABLO ISLAND, MY GIFT FOR HIS BEING SUCH A PLIANT LITTLE GRUBBER.
YOU WITH YOUR SCIENCE...STUDYING THE SUN FOR THE BETTERMENT OF HUMANITY. QUITE THE VISIONARY YOU WERE.
AND QUITE THE HERO YOU THOUGHT YOURSELF AS WELL. MEDDLER I CALL IT.
HONESTLY, I DON'T KNOW WHAT I THOUGHT. HERO? I CERTAINLY DIDN'T INTEND ON "SAVING THE DAY." IF HE'D ONLY LEFT ME ALONE.

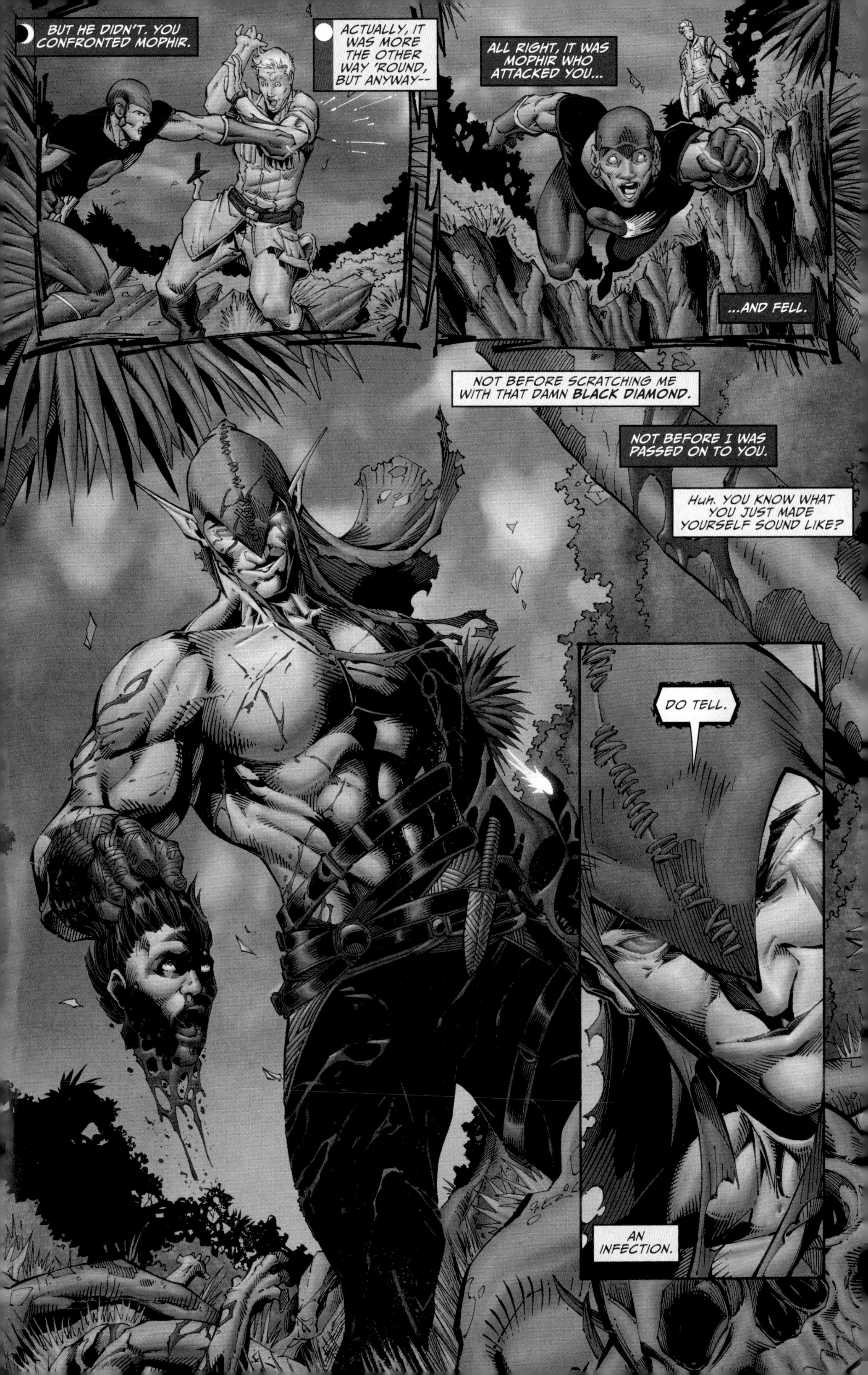
BUT HE DIDN'T. YOU CONFRONTED MOPHIR.
ACTUALLY, IT WAS MORE THE OTHER WAY 'ROUND, BUT ANYWAY--
ALL RIGHT, IT WAS MOPHIR WHO ATTACKED YOU...
...AND FELL.
NOT BEFORE SCRATCHING ME WITH THAT DAMN BLACK DIAMOND.
NOT BEFORE I WAS PASSED ON TO YOU.
Huh. YOU KNOW WHAT YOU JUST MADE YOURSELF SOUND LIKE?
DO TELL.
AN INFECTION.

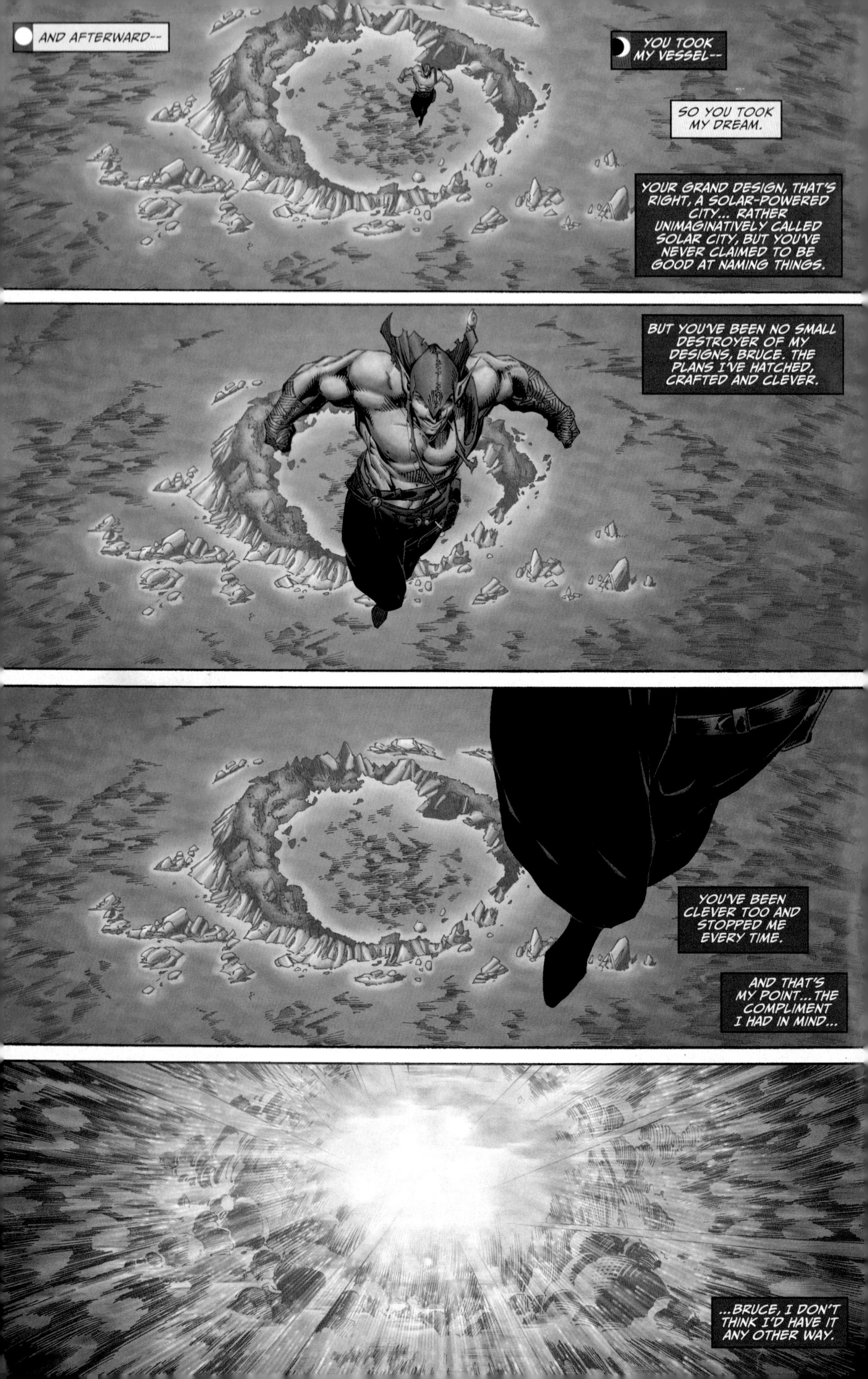
AND AFTERWARD--
YOU TOOK MY VESSEL--
SO YOU TOOK MY DREAM.
YOUR GRAND DESIGN, THAT'S RIGHT, A SOLAR-POWERED CITY... RATHER UNIMAGINATIVELY CALLED SOLAR CITY, BUT YOU'VE NEVER CLAIMED TO BE GOOD AT NAMING THINGS.
BUT YOU'VE BEEN NO SMALL DESTROYER OF MY DESIGNS, BRUCE. THE PLANS I'VE HATCHED, CRAFTED AND CLEVER.
YOU'VE BEEN CLEVER TOO AND STOPPED ME EVERY TIME.
AND THAT'S MY POINT...THE COMPLIMENT I HAD IN MIND...
...BRUCE, I DON'T THINK I'D HAVE IT ANY OTHER WAY.

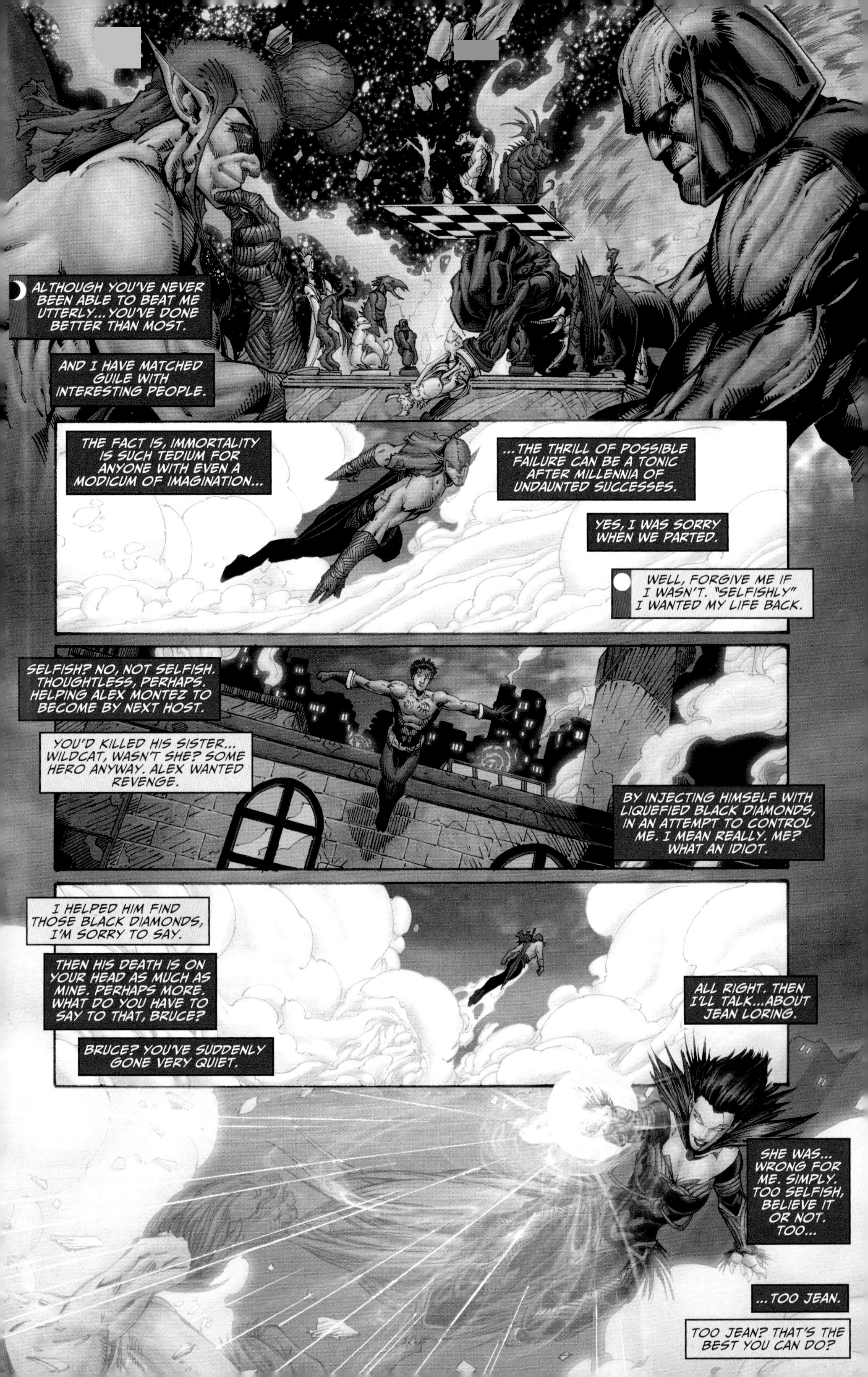
ALTHOUGH YOU'VE NEVER BEEN ABLE TO BEAT ME UTTERLY...YOU'VE DONE BETTER THAN MOST.
AND I HAVE MATCHED GUILE WITH INTERESTING PEOPLE.
THE FACT IS, IMMORTALITY IS SUCH TEDIUM FOR ANYONE WITH EVEN A MODICUM OF IMAGINATION...
...THE THRILL OF POSSIBLE FAILURE CAN BE A TONIC AFTER MILLENNIA OF UNDAUNTED SUCCESSES.
YES, I WAS SORRY WHEN WE PARTED.
WELL, FORGIVE ME IF I WASN'T. "SELFISHLY" I WANTED MY LIFE BACK.
SELFISH? NO, NOT SELFISH. THOUGHTLESS, PERHAPS. HELPING ALEX MONTEZ TO BECOME BY NEXT HOST.
YOU'D KILLED HIS SISTER... WILDCAT, WASN'T SHE? SOME HERO ANYWAY. ALEX WANTED REVENGE.
BY INJECTING HIMSELF WITH LIQUEFIED BLACK DIAMONDS, IN AN ATTEMPT TO CONTROL ME. I MEAN REALLY. ME? WHAT AN IDIOT.
I HELPED HIM FIND THOSE BLACK DIAMONDS, I'M SORRY TO SAY.
THEN HIS DEATH IS ON YOUR HEAD AS MUCH AS MINE. PERHAPS MORE. WHAT DO YOU HAVE TO SAY TO THAT, BRUCE?
BRUCE? YOU'VE SUDDENLY GONE VERY QUIET.
ALL RIGHT. THEN I'LL TALK...ABOUT JEAN LORING.
SHE WAS... WRONG FOR ME. SIMPLY. TOO SELFISH, BELIEVE IT OR NOT. TOO...
...TOO JEAN.
TOO JEAN? THAT'S THE BEST YOU CAN DO?

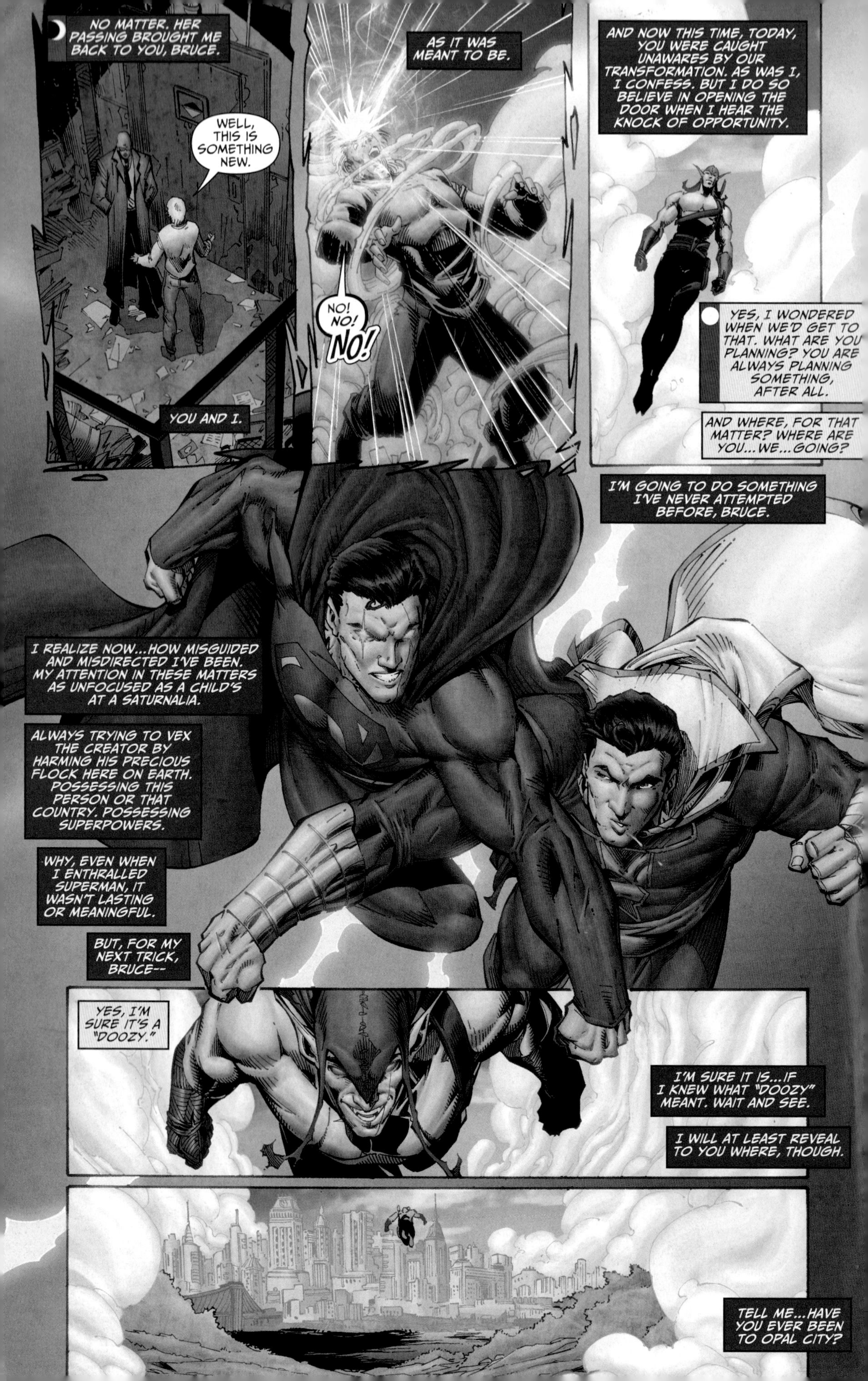
NO MATTER. HER PASSING BROUGHT ME BACK TO YOU, BRUCE.
WELL, THIS IS SOMETHING NEW.
YOU AND I.
AS IT WAS MEANT TO BE.
NO! NO! NO!
AND NOW THIS TIME, TODAY, YOU WERE CAUGHT UNAWARES BY OUR TRANSFORMATION. AS WAS I, I CONFESS. BUT I DO SO BELIEVE IN OPENING THE DOOR WHEN I HEAR THE KNOCK OF OPPORTUNITY.
YES, I WONDERED WHEN WE'D GET TO THAT. WHAT ARE YOU PLANNING? YOU ARE ALWAYS PLANNING SOMETHING, AFTER ALL.
AND WHERE, FOR THAT MATTER? WHERE ARE YOU...WE...GOING?
I'M GOING TO DO SOMETHING I'VE NEVER ATTEMPTED BEFORE, BRUCE.
I REALIZE NOW...HOW MISGUIDED AND MISDIRECTED I'VE BEEN. MY ATTENTION IN THESE MATTERS AS UNFOCUSED AS A CHILD'S AT A SATURNALIA.
ALWAYS TRYING TO VEX THE CREATOR BY HARMING HIS PRECIOUS FLOCK HERE ON EARTH. POSSESSING THIS PERSON OR THAT COUNTRY. POSSESSING SUPERPOWERS.
WHY, EVEN WHEN I ENTHRALLED SUPERMAN, IT WASN'T LASTING OR MEANINGFUL.
BUT, FOR MY NEXT TRICK, BRUCE--
YES, I'M SURE IT'S A "DOOZY."
I'M SURE IT IS...IF I KNEW WHAT "DOOZY" MEANT. WAIT AND SEE.
I WILL AT LEAST REVEAL TO YOU WHERE, THOUGH.
TELL ME...HAVE YOU EVER BEEN TO OPAL CITY?

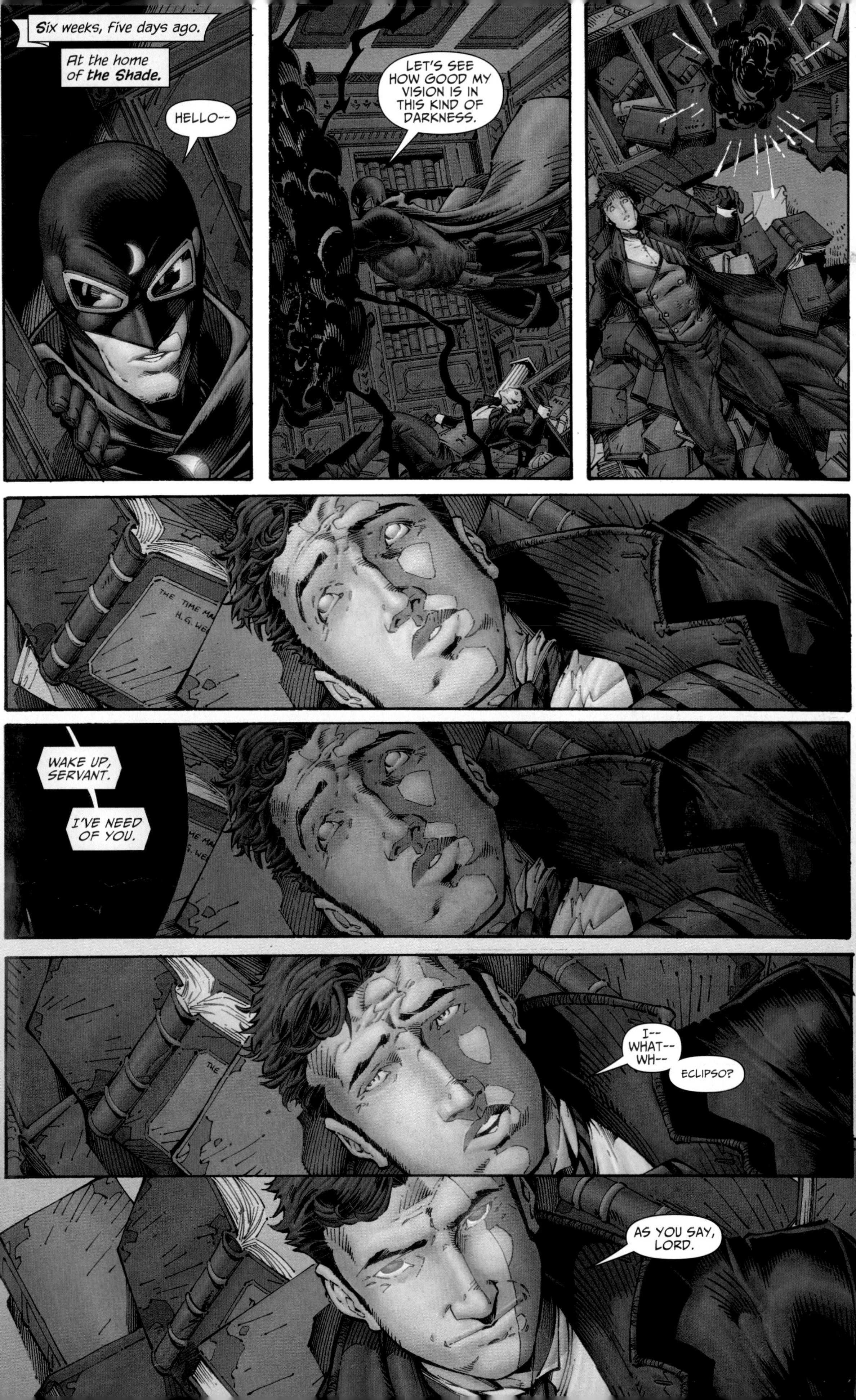

Six weeks, five days ago.
At the home of the Shade.
HELLO--
LET'S SEE HOW GOOD MY VISION IS IN THIS KIND OF DARKNESS.
THE TIME MA
H.G. WE
WAKE UP, SERVANT.
I'VE NEED OF YOU.
I-- WHAT-- WH--
ECLIPSO?
AS YOU SAY, LORD.

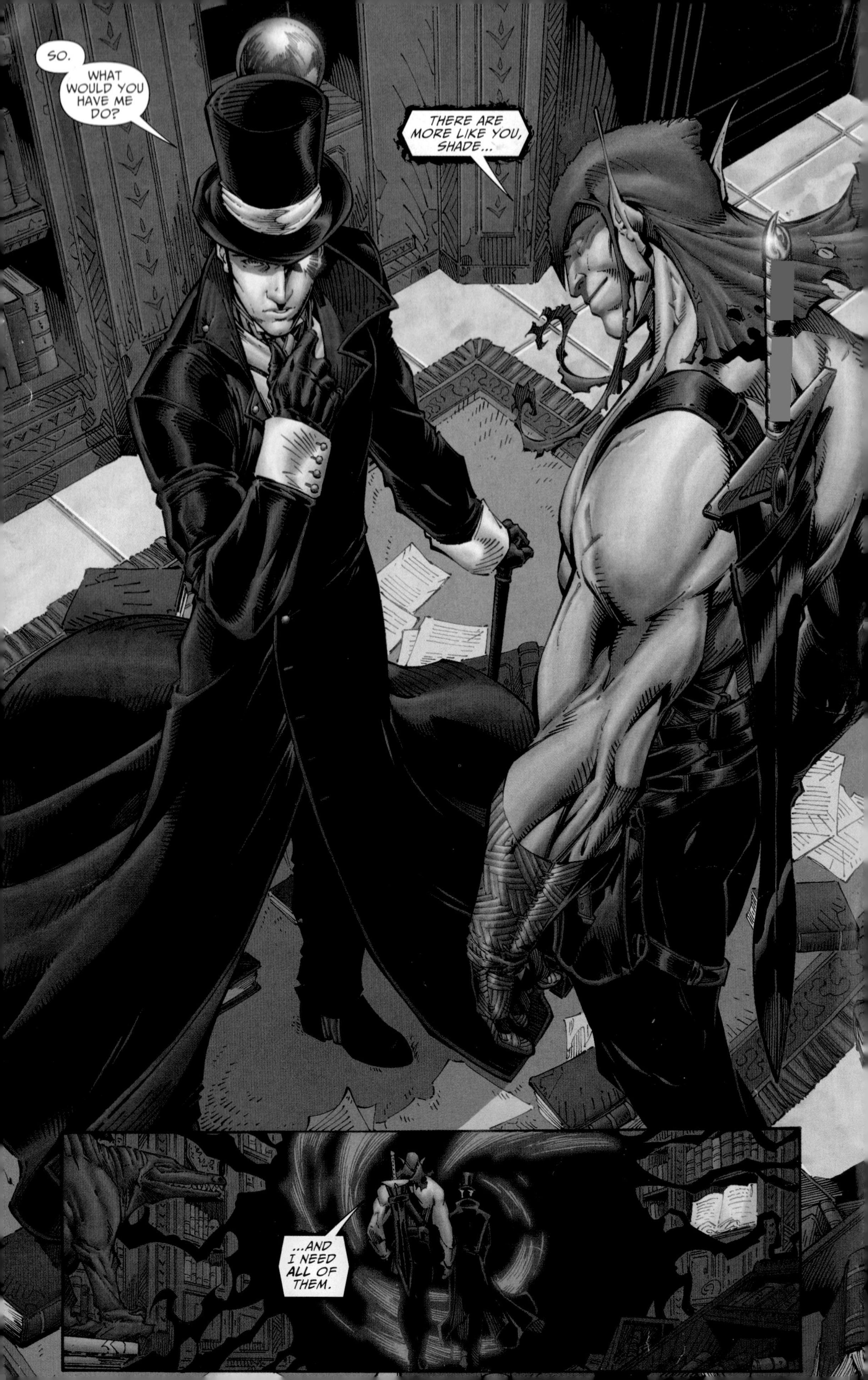
SO.
WHAT WOULD YOU HAVE ME DO?
THERE ARE MORE LIKE YOU, SHADE...
...AND I NEED ALL OF THEM.

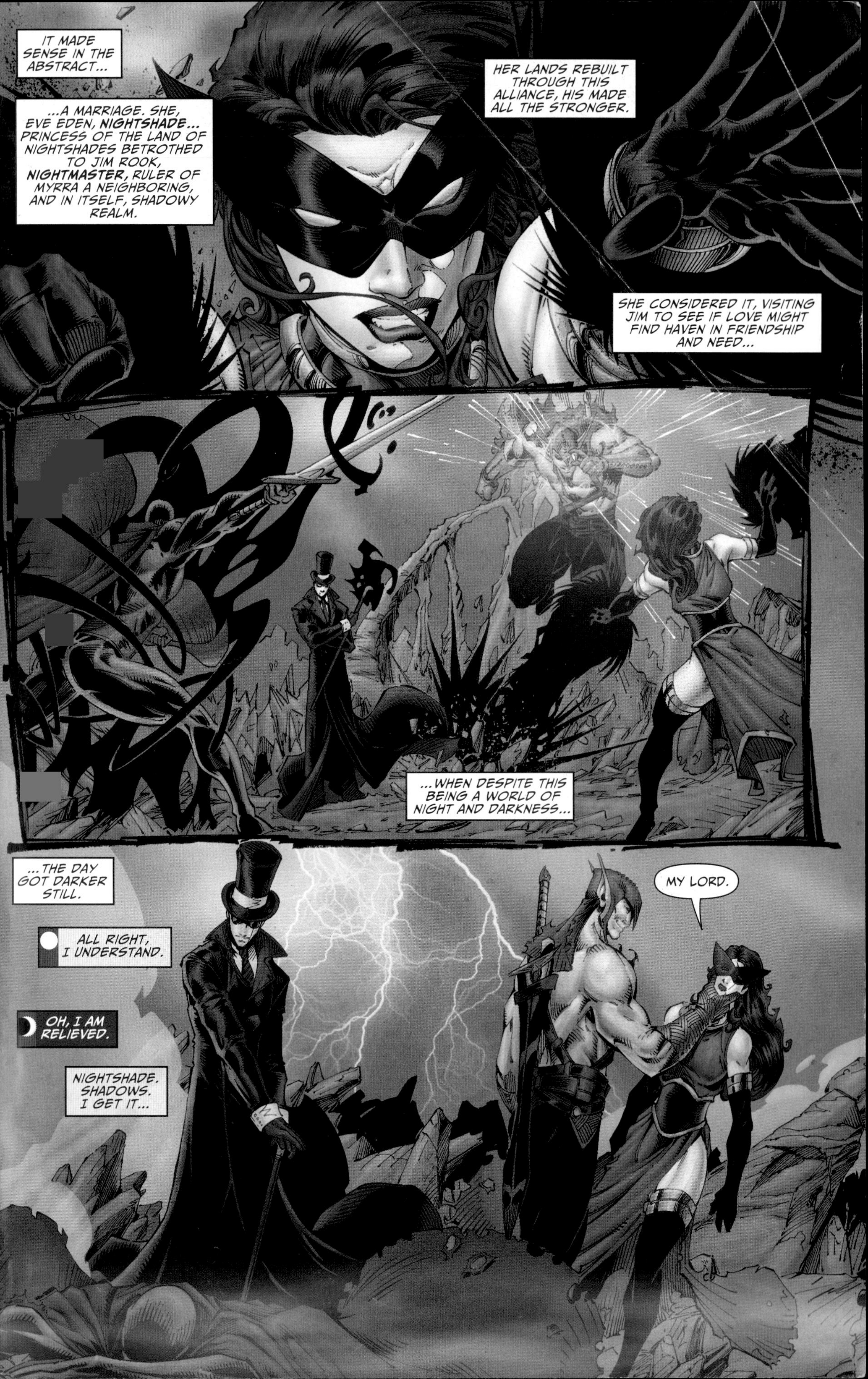
IT MADE SENSE IN THE ABSTRACT...
...A MARRIAGE. SHE, EVE EDEN, NIGHTSHADE... PRINCESS OF THE LAND OF NIGHTSHADES BETROTHED TO JIM ROOK, NIGHTMASTER, RULER OF MYRRA A NEIGHBORING, AND IN ITSELF, SHADOWY REALM.
HER LANDS REBUILT THROUGH THIS ALLIANCE, HIS MADE ALL THE STRONGER.
SHE CONSIDERED IT, VISITING JIM TO SEE IF LOVE MIGHT FIND HAVEN IN FRIENDSHIP AND NEED...
...WHEN DESPITE THIS BEING A WORLD OF NIGHT AND DARKNESS...
...THE DAY GOT DARKER STILL.
ALL RIGHT, I UNDERSTAND.
OH, I AM RELIEVED.
NIGHTSHADE. SHADOWS. I GET IT...
MY LORD.

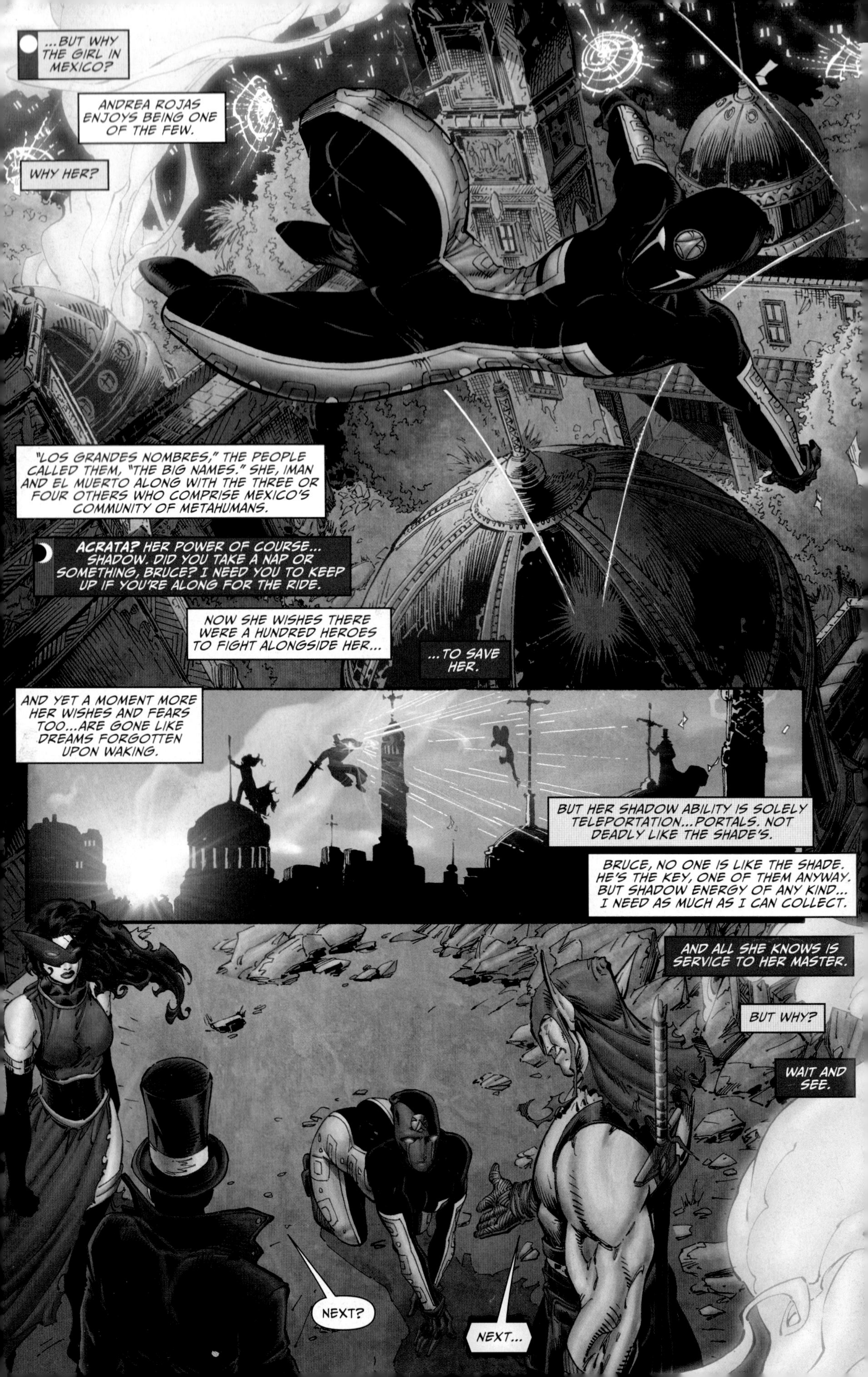
...BUT WHY THE GIRL IN MEXICO?
ANDREA ROJAS ENJOYS BEING ONE OF THE FEW.
WHY HER?
"LOS GRANDES NOMBRES," THE PEOPLE CALLED THEM, "THE BIG NAMES." SHE, IMAN AND EL MUERTO ALONG WITH THE THREE OR FOUR OTHERS WHO COMPRISE MEXICO'S COMMUNITY OF METAHUMANS.
ACRATA? HER POWER OF COURSE... SHADOW. DID YOU TAKE A NAP OR SOMETHING, BRUCE? I NEED YOU TO KEEP UP IF YOU'RE ALONG FOR THE RIDE.
NOW SHE WISHES THERE WERE A HUNDRED HEROES TO FIGHT ALONGSIDE HER...
...TO SAVE HER.
AND YET A MOMENT MORE HER WISHES AND FEARS TOO...ARE GONE LIKE DREAMS FORGOTTEN UPON WAKING.
BUT HER SHADOW ABILITY IS SOLELY TELEPORTATION...PORTALS. NOT DEADLY LIKE THE SHADE'S.
BRUCE, NO ONE IS LIKE THE SHADE. HE'S THE KEY, ONE OF THEM ANYWAY. BUT SHADOW ENERGY OF ANY KIND... I NEED AS MUCH AS I CAN COLLECT.
AND ALL SHE KNOWS IS SERVICE TO HER MASTER.
BUT WHY?
WAIT AND SEE.
NEXT?
NEXT...

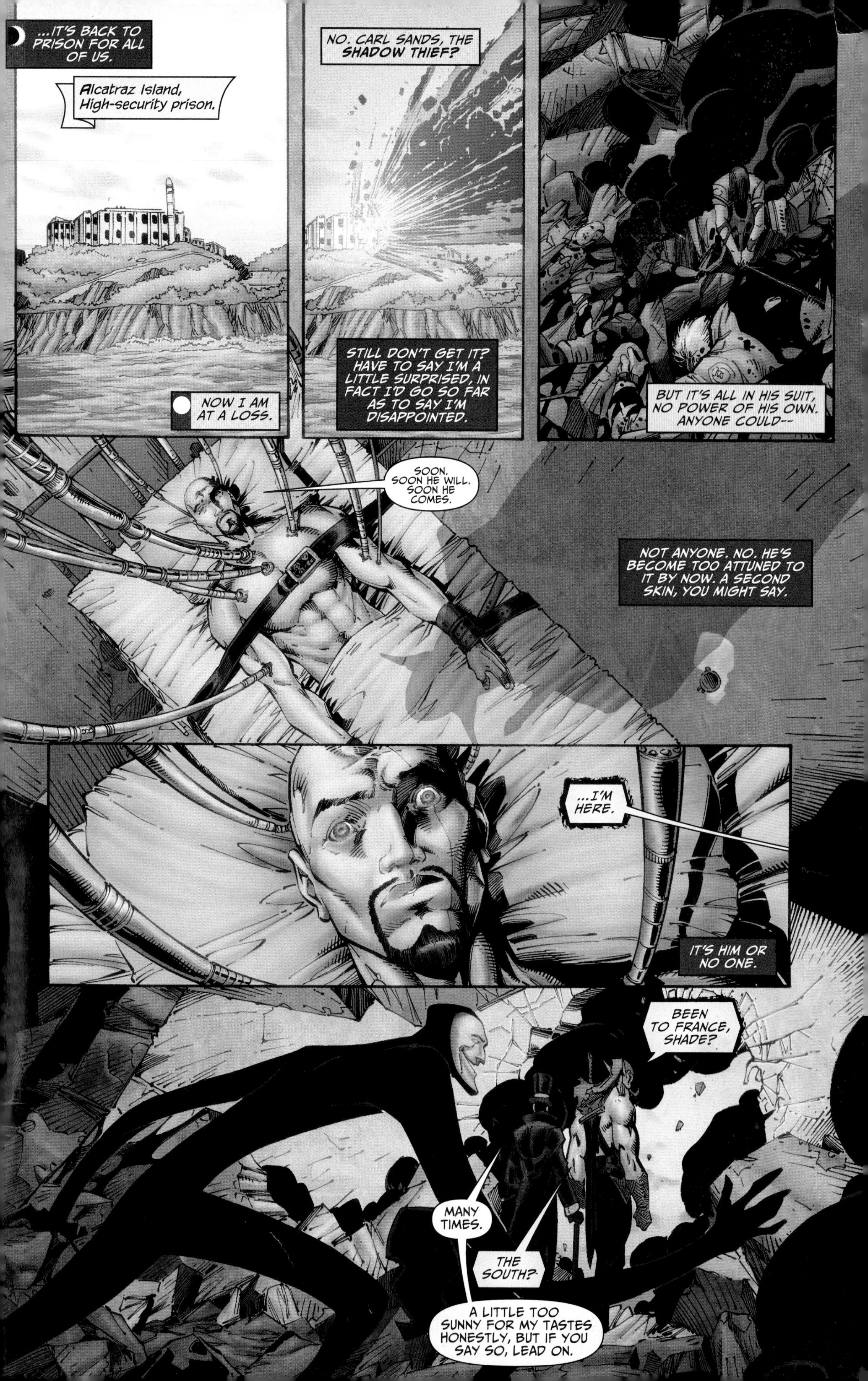
...IT'S BACK TO PRISON FOR ALL OF US.
Alcatraz Island, High-security prison.
NOW I AM AT A LOSS.
NO. CARL SANDS, THE SHADOW THIEF?
STILL DON'T GET IT? HAVE TO SAY I'M A LITTLE SURPRISED, IN FACT I'D GO SO FAR AS TO SAY I'M DISAPPOINTED.
BUT IT'S ALL IN HIS SUIT, NO POWER OF HIS OWN. ANYONE COULD--
SOON. SOON HE WILL. SOON HE COMES.
NOT ANYONE. NO. HE'S BECOME TOO ATTUNED TO IT BY NOW. A SECOND SKIN, YOU MIGHT SAY.
...I'M HERE.
IT'S HIM OR NO ONE.
BEEN TO FRANCE, SHADE?
MANY TIMES.
THE SOUTH?
A LITTLE TOO SUNNY FOR MY TASTES HONESTLY, BUT IF YOU SAY SO, LEAD ON.

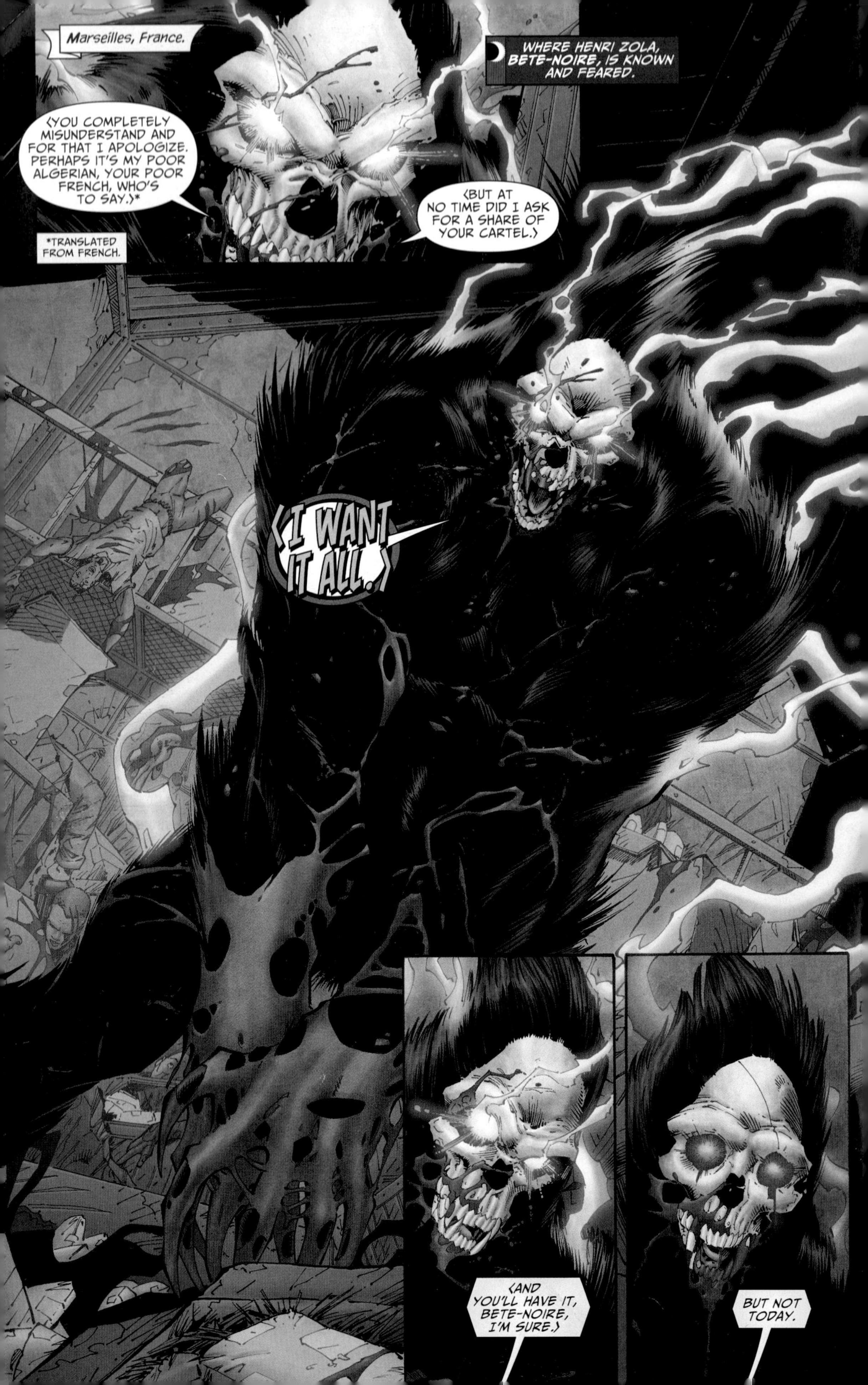
Marseilles, France.
WHERE HENRI ZOLA, BETE-NOIRE, IS KNOWN AND FEARED.
‹YOU COMPLETELY MISUNDERSTAND AND FOR THAT I APOLOGIZE. PERHAPS IT'S MY POOR ALGERIAN, YOUR POOR FRENCH, WHO'S TO SAY.›*
‹BUT AT NO TIME DID I ASK FOR A SHARE OF YOUR CARTEL.›
*TRANSLATED FROM FRENCH.
‹I WANT IT ALL.›
‹AND YOU'LL HAVE IT, BETE-NOIRE, I'M SURE.›
BUT NOT TODAY.

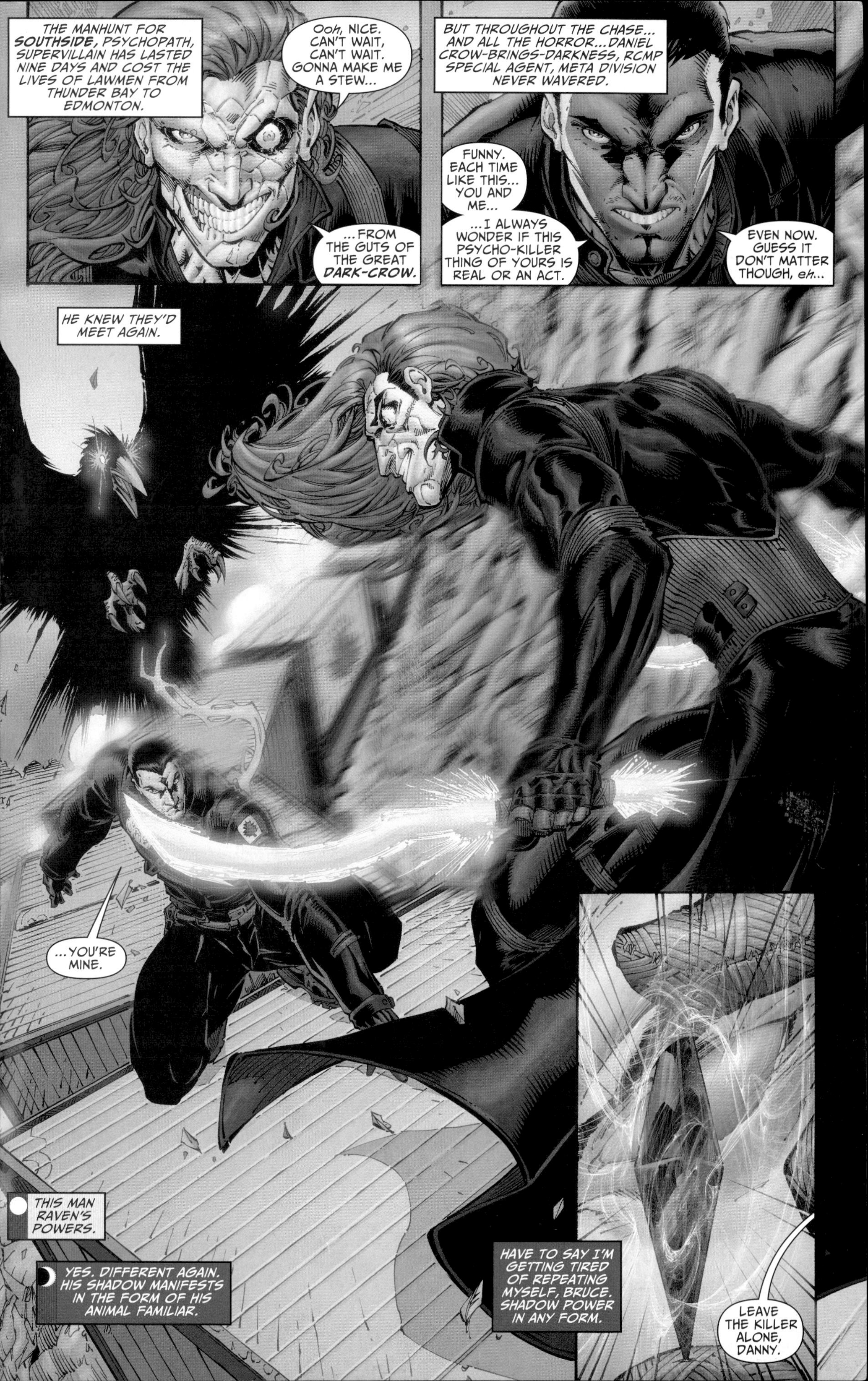
THE MANHUNT FOR SOUTHSIDE, PSYCHOPATH, SUPERVILLAIN HAS LASTED NINE DAYS AND COST THE LIVES OF LAWMEN FROM THUNDER BAY TO EDMONTON.
Ooh, NICE. CAN'T WAIT, CAN'T WAIT. GONNA MAKE ME A STEW...
...FROM THE GUTS OF THE GREAT DARK-CROW.
BUT THROUGHOUT THE CHASE... AND ALL THE HORROR...DANIEL CROW-BRINGS-DARKNESS, RCMP SPECIAL AGENT, META DIVISION NEVER WAVERED.
FUNNY. EACH TIME LIKE THIS... YOU AND ME...
...I ALWAYS WONDER IF THIS PSYCHO-KILLER THING OF YOURS IS REAL OR AN ACT.
EVEN NOW. GUESS IT DON'T MATTER THOUGH, eh...
HE KNEW THEY'D MEET AGAIN.
...YOU'RE MINE.
THIS MAN RAVEN'S POWERS.
YES. DIFFERENT AGAIN. HIS SHADOW MANIFESTS IN THE FORM OF HIS ANIMAL FAMILIAR.
HAVE TO SAY I'M GETTING TIRED OF REPEATING MYSELF, BRUCE. SHADOW POWER IN ANY FORM.
LEAVE THE KILLER ALONE, DANNY.

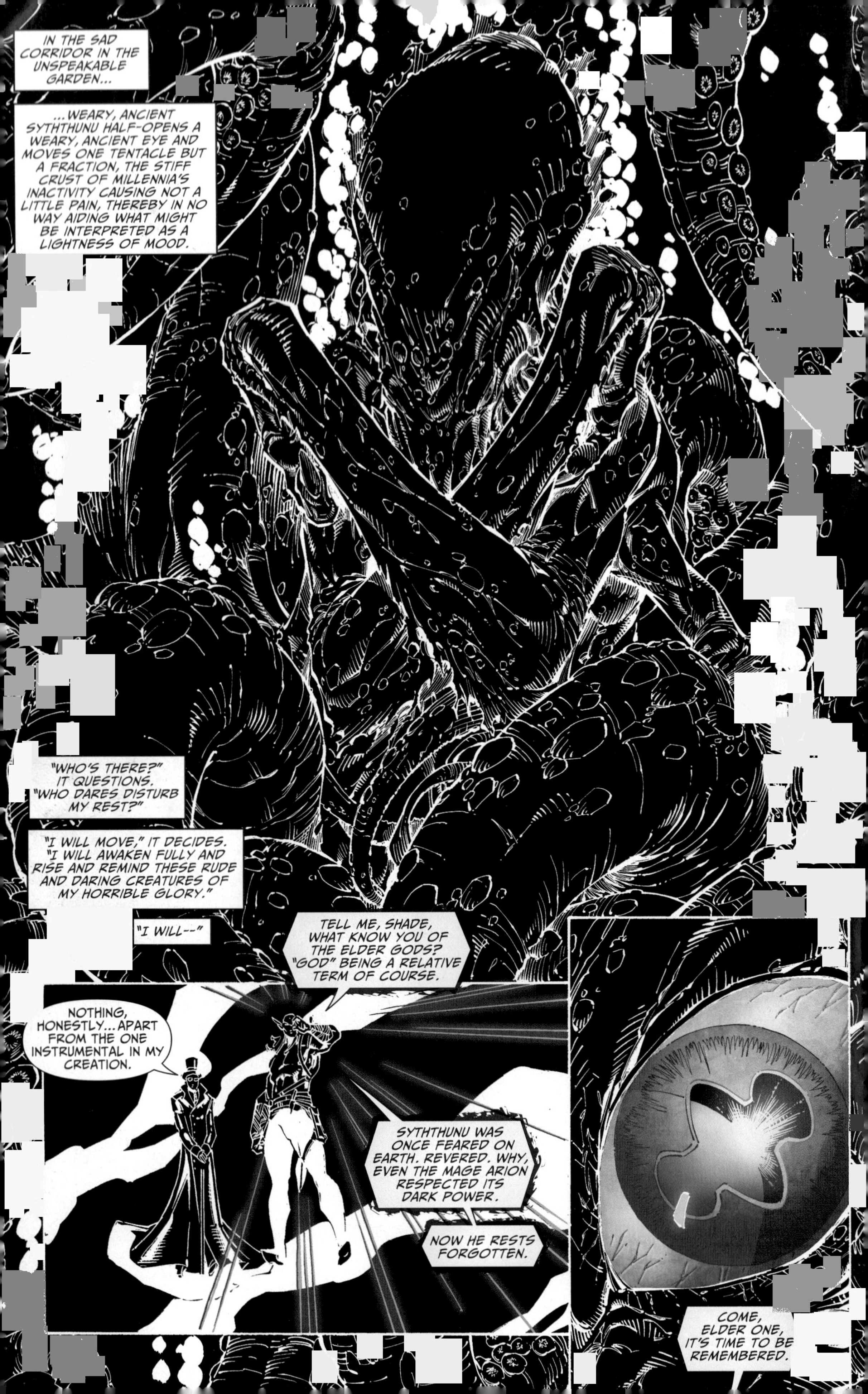
IN THE SAD CORRIDOR IN THE UNSPEAKABLE GARDEN...
...WEARY, ANCIENT SYTHTHUNU HALF-OPENS A WEARY, ANCIENT EYE AND MOVES ONE TENTACLE BUT A FRACTION, THE STIFF CRUST OF MILLENNIA'S INACTIVITY CAUSING NOT A LITTLE PAIN, THEREBY IN NO WAY AIDING WHAT MIGHT BE INTERPRETED AS A LIGHTNESS OF MOOD.
"WHO'S THERE?" IT QUESTIONS. "WHO DARES DISTURB MY REST?"
"I WILL MOVE," IT DECIDES. "I WILL AWAKEN FULLY AND RISE AND REMIND THESE RUDE AND DARING CREATURES OF MY HORRIBLE GLORY."
"I WILL--"
TELL ME, SHADE, WHAT KNOW YOU OF THE ELDER GODS? "GOD" BEING A RELATIVE TERM OF COURSE.
NOTHING, HONESTLY... APART FROM THE ONE INSTRUMENTAL IN MY CREATION.
SYTHTHUNU WAS ONCE FEARED ON EARTH. REVERED. WHY, EVEN THE MAGE ARION RESPECTED ITS DARK POWER.
NOW HE RESTS FORGOTTEN.
COME, ELDER ONE, IT'S TIME TO BE REMEMBERED.

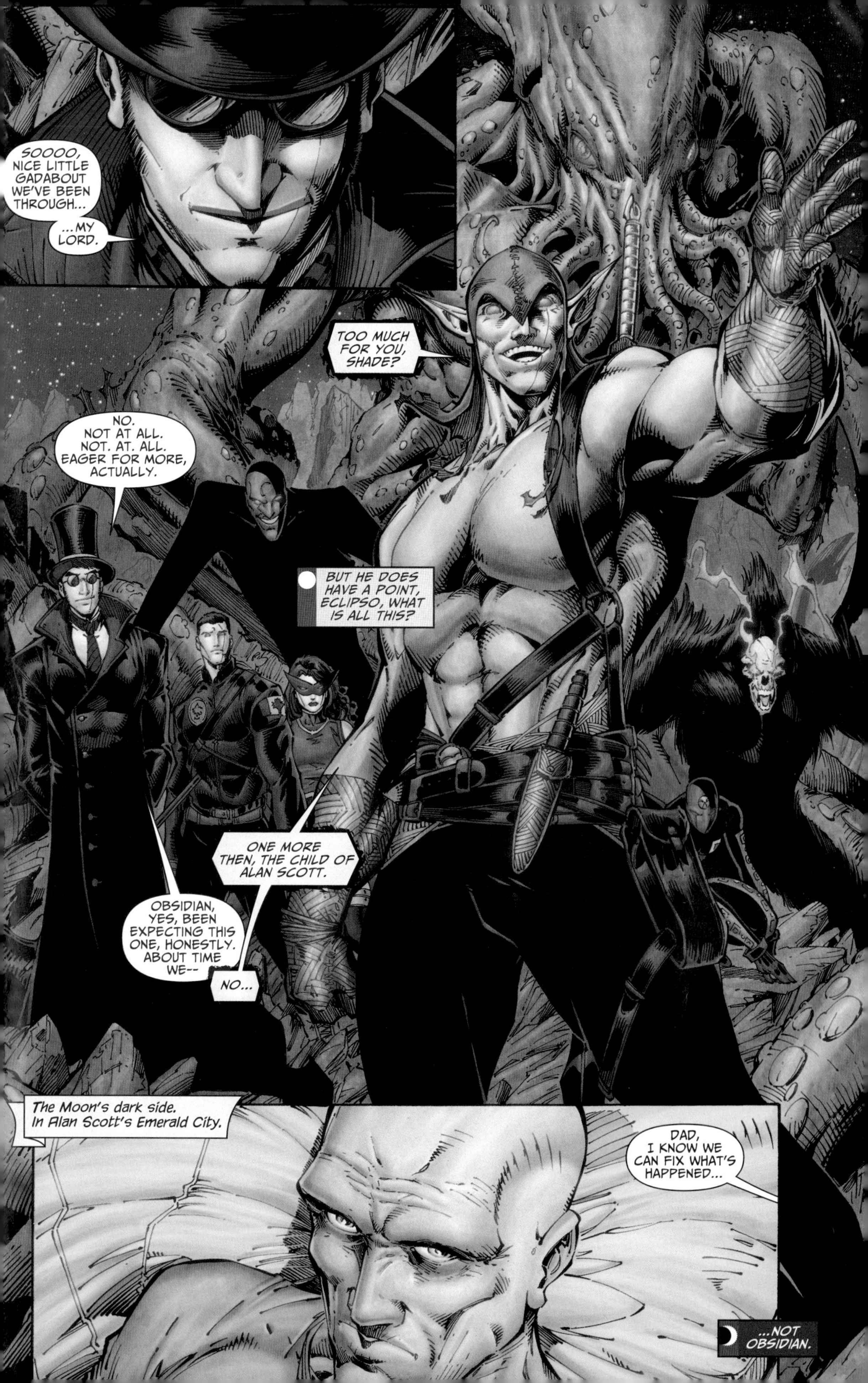
SOOOO, NICE LITTLE GADABOUT WE'VE BEEN THROUGH...
...MY LORD.
TOO MUCH FOR YOU, SHADE?
NO. NOT AT ALL. NOT. AT. ALL. EAGER FOR MORE, ACTUALLY.
BUT HE DOES HAVE A POINT, ECLIPSO, WHAT IS ALL THIS?
ONE MORE THEN, THE CHILD OF ALAN SCOTT.
OBSIDIAN, YES, BEEN EXPECTING THIS ONE, HONESTLY. ABOUT TIME WE--
NO...
The Moon's dark side. In Alan Scott's Emerald City.
DAD, I KNOW WE CAN FIX WHAT'S HAPPENED...
...NOT OBSIDIAN.

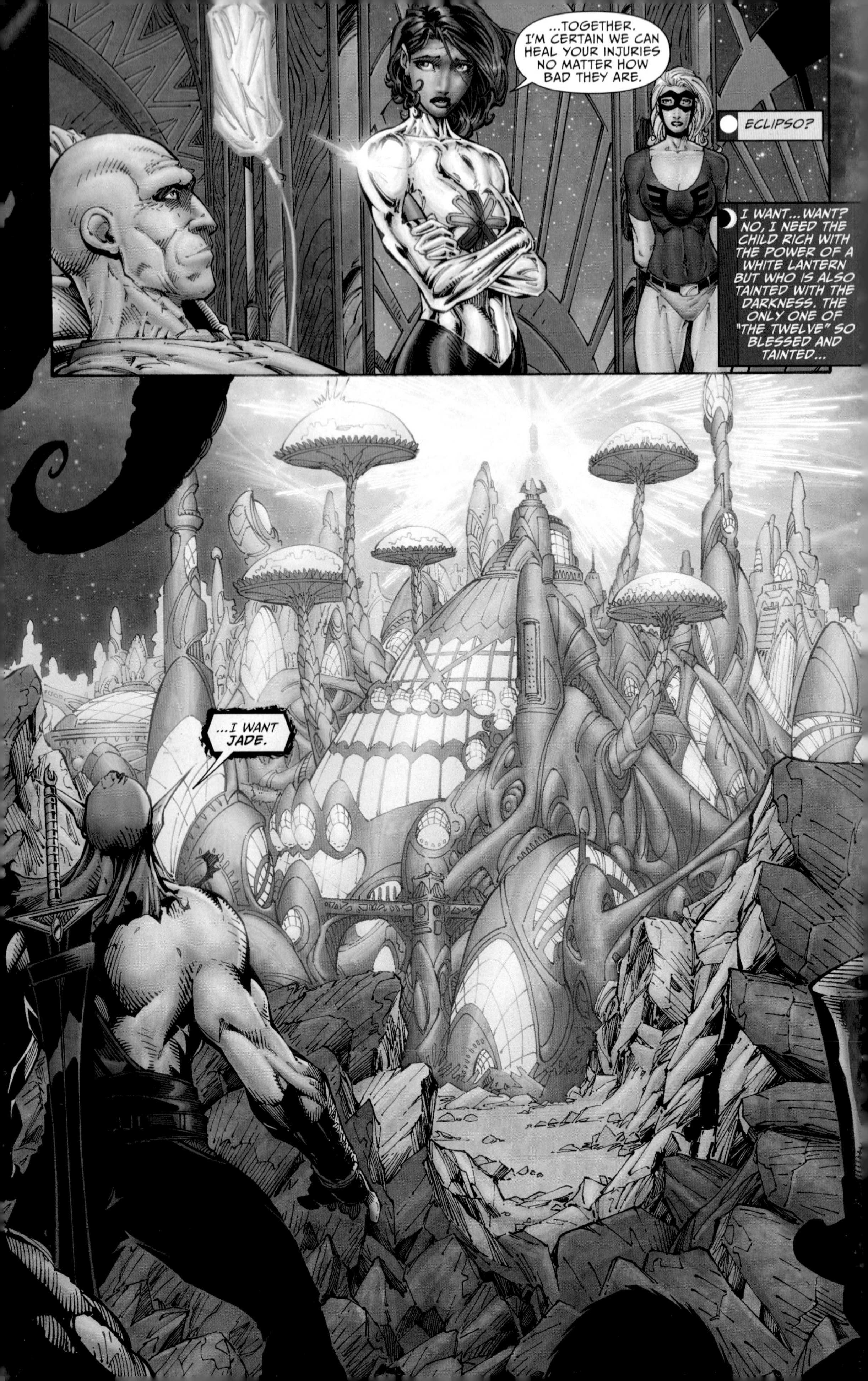
...TOGETHER. I'M CERTAIN WE CAN HEAL YOUR INJURIES NO MATTER HOW BAD THEY ARE.
ECLIPSO?
I WANT... WANT? NO, I NEED THE CHILD RICH WITH THE POWER OF A WHITE LANTERN BUT WHO IS ALSO TAINTED WITH THE DARKNESS. THE ONLY ONE OF "THE TWELVE" SO BLESSED AND TAINTED...
...I WANT JADE.

JUSTICE LEAGUE OF AMERICA 55
Cover by Brett Booth & Andrew Dalhouse

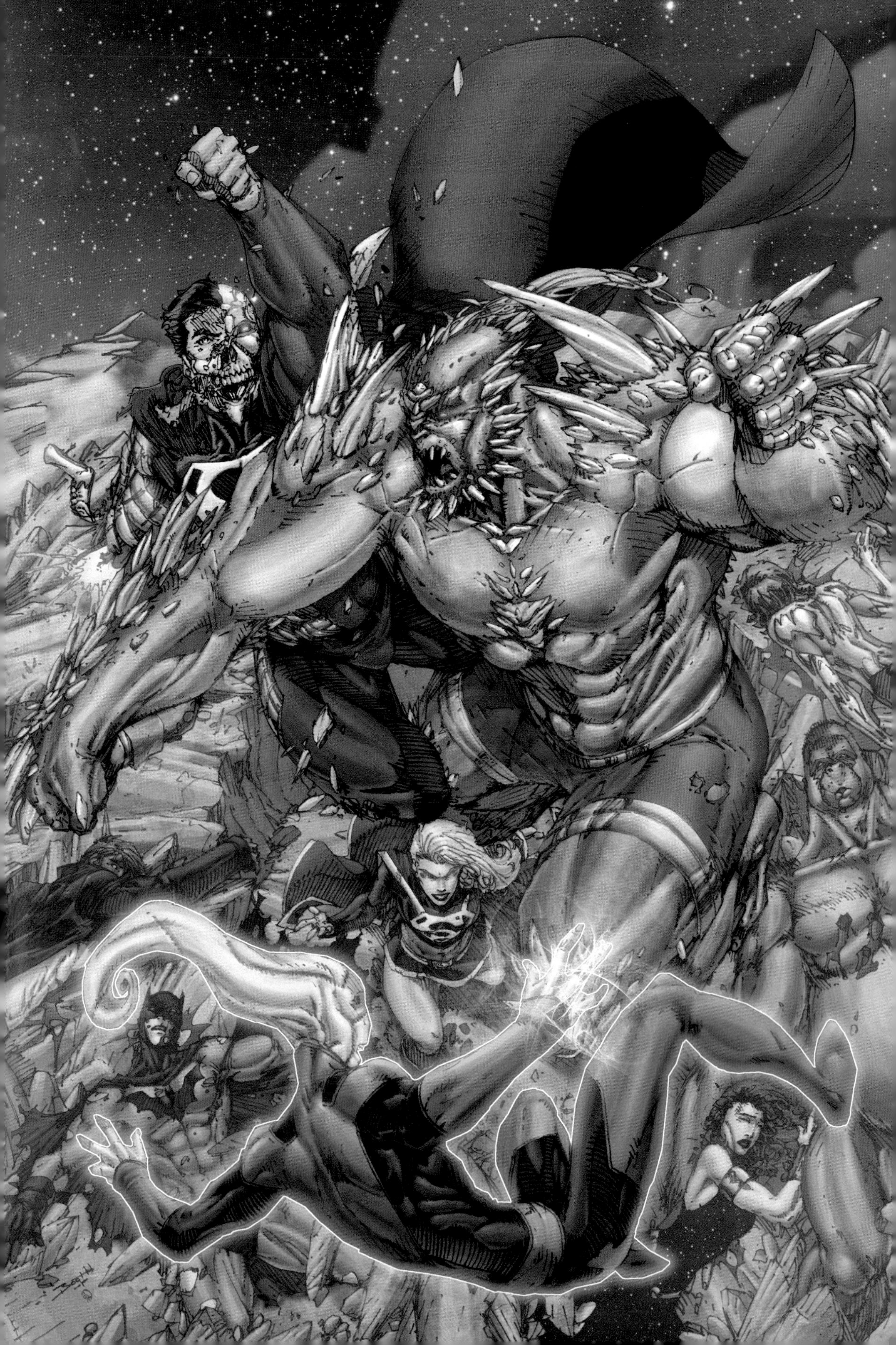

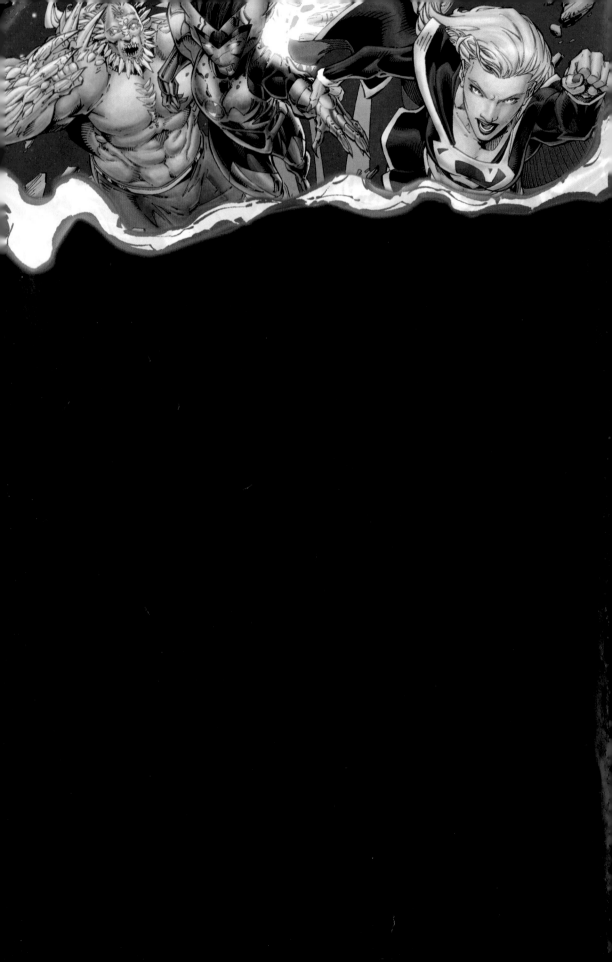

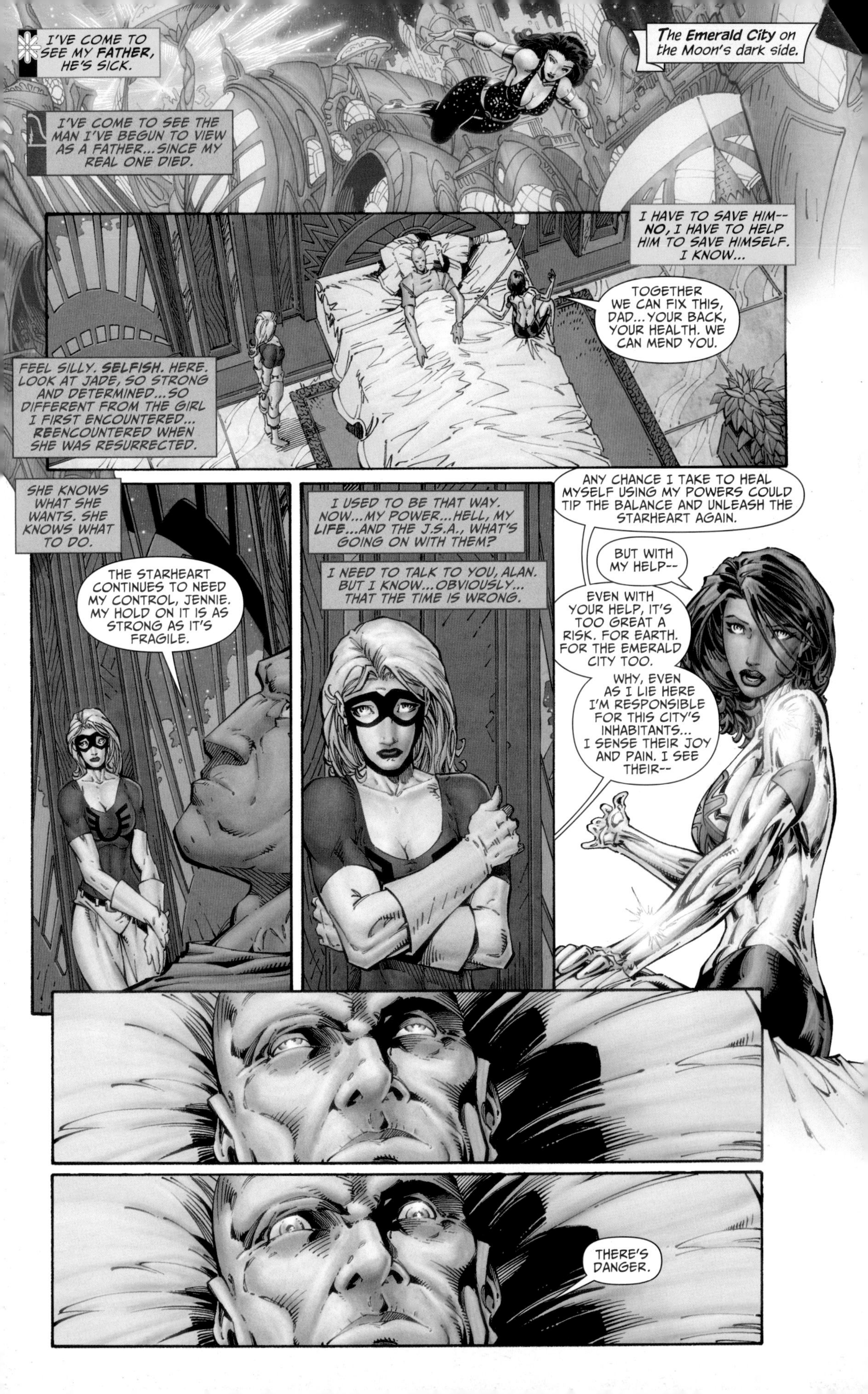

I'VE COME TO SEE MY FATHER, HE'S SICK.
The Emerald City on the Moon's dark side.
I'VE COME TO SEE THE MAN I'VE BEGUN TO VIEW AS A FATHER...SINCE MY REAL ONE DIED.
I HAVE TO SAVE HIM-- NO, I HAVE TO HELP HIM TO SAVE HIMSELF. I KNOW...
TOGETHER WE CAN FIX THIS, DAD...YOUR BACK, YOUR HEALTH. WE CAN MEND YOU.
FEEL SILLY. SELFISH. HERE. LOOK AT JADE, SO STRONG AND DETERMINED...SO DIFFERENT FROM THE GIRL I FIRST ENCOUNTERED... REENCOUNTERED WHEN SHE WAS RESURRECTED.
SHE KNOWS WHAT SHE WANTS. SHE KNOWS WHAT TO DO.
THE STARHEART CONTINUES TO NEED MY CONTROL, JENNIE. MY HOLD ON IT IS AS STRONG AS IT'S FRAGILE.
I USED TO BE THAT WAY. NOW...MY POWER...HELL, MY LIFE...AND THE J.S.A., WHAT'S GOING ON WITH THEM?
I NEED TO TALK TO YOU, ALAN. BUT I KNOW...OBVIOUSLY... THAT THE TIME IS WRONG.
ANY CHANCE I TAKE TO HEAL MYSELF USING MY POWERS COULD TIP THE BALANCE AND UNLEASH THE STARHEART AGAIN.
BUT WITH MY HELP--
EVEN WITH YOUR HELP, IT'S TOO GREAT A RISK. FOR EARTH. FOR THE EMERALD CITY TOO.
WHY, EVEN AS I LIE HERE I'M RESPONSIBLE FOR THIS CITY'S INHABITANTS... I SENSE THEIR JOY AND PAIN. I SEE THEIR--
THERE'S DANGER.

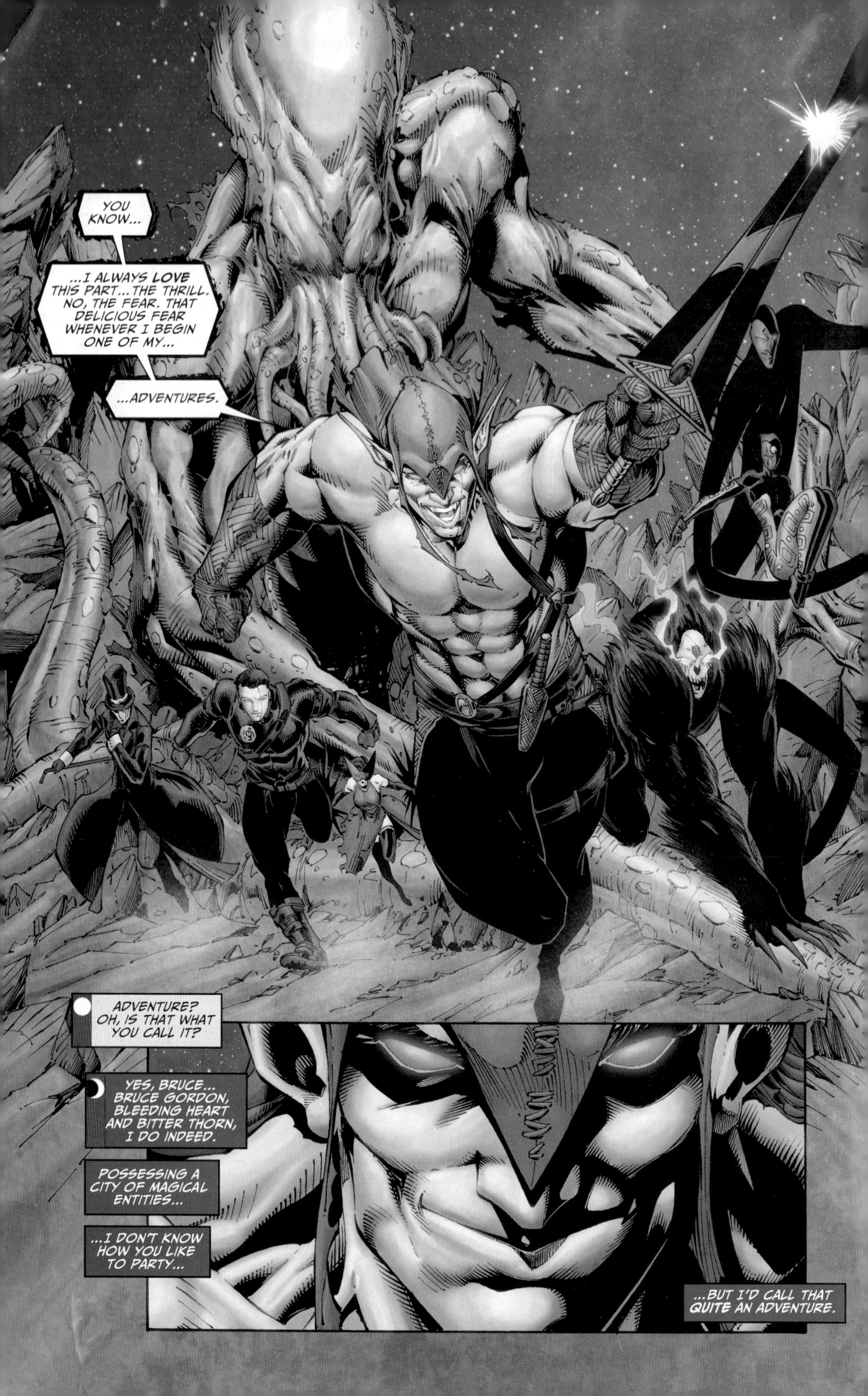
YOU KNOW...
...I ALWAYS LOVE THIS PART...THE THRILL. NO, THE FEAR. THAT DELICIOUS FEAR WHENEVER I BEGIN ONE OF MY...
...ADVENTURES.
ADVENTURE? OH, IS THAT WHAT YOU CALL IT?
YES, BRUCE... BRUCE GORDON, BLEEDING HEART AND BITTER THORN, I DO INDEED.
POSSESSING A CITY OF MAGICAL ENTITIES...
...I DON'T KNOW HOW YOU LIKE TO PARTY...
...BUT I'D CALL THAT QUITE AN ADVENTURE.

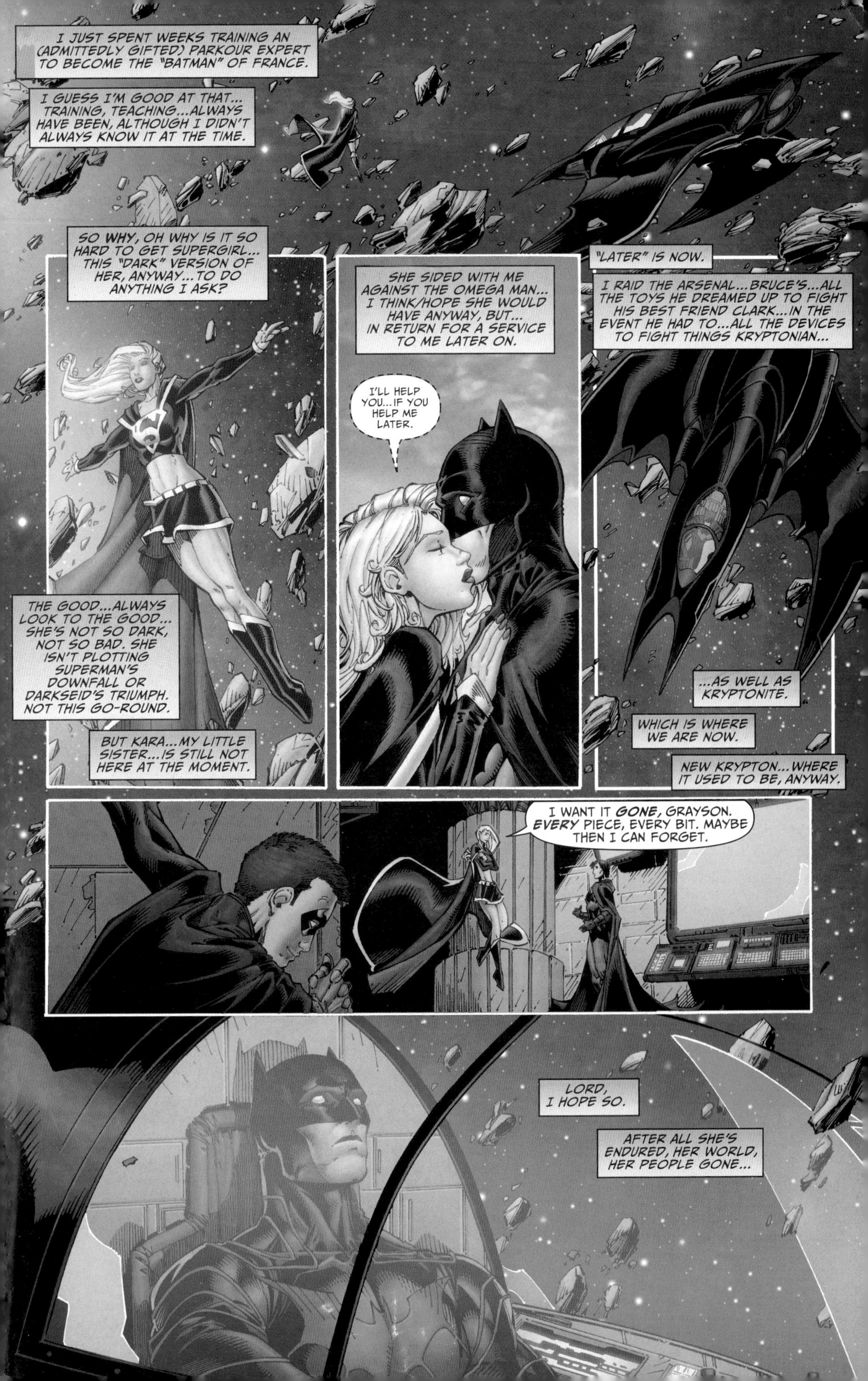
I JUST SPENT WEEKS TRAINING AN (ADMITTEDLY GIFTED) PARKOUR EXPERT TO BECOME THE "BATMAN" OF FRANCE.
I GUESS I'M GOOD AT THAT... TRAINING, TEACHING...ALWAYS HAVE BEEN, ALTHOUGH I DIDN'T ALWAYS KNOW IT AT THE TIME.
SO WHY, OH WHY IS IT SO HARD TO GET SUPERGIRL... THIS "DARK" VERSION OF HER, ANYWAY...TO DO ANYTHING I ASK?
THE GOOD...ALWAYS LOOK TO THE GOOD... SHE'S NOT SO DARK, NOT SO BAD. SHE ISN'T PLOTTING SUPERMAN'S DOWNFALL OR DARKSEID'S TRIUMPH. NOT THIS GO-ROUND.
BUT KARA...MY LITTLE SISTER...IS STILL NOT HERE AT THE MOMENT.
SHE SIDED WITH ME AGAINST THE OMEGA MAN... I THINK/HOPE SHE WOULD HAVE ANYWAY, BUT... IN RETURN FOR A SERVICE TO ME LATER ON.
I'LL HELP YOU...IF YOU HELP ME LATER.
"LATER" IS NOW.
I RAID THE ARSENAL...BRUCE'S...ALL THE TOYS HE DREAMED UP TO FIGHT HIS BEST FRIEND CLARK...IN THE EVENT HE HAD TO...ALL THE DEVICES TO FIGHT THINGS KRYPTONIAN...
...AS WELL AS KRYPTONITE.
WHICH IS WHERE WE ARE NOW.
NEW KRYPTON...WHERE IT USED TO BE, ANYWAY.
I WANT IT GONE, GRAYSON. EVERY PIECE, EVERY BIT. MAYBE THEN I CAN FORGET.
LORD, I HOPE SO.
AFTER ALL SHE'S ENDURED, HER WORLD, HER PEOPLE GONE...

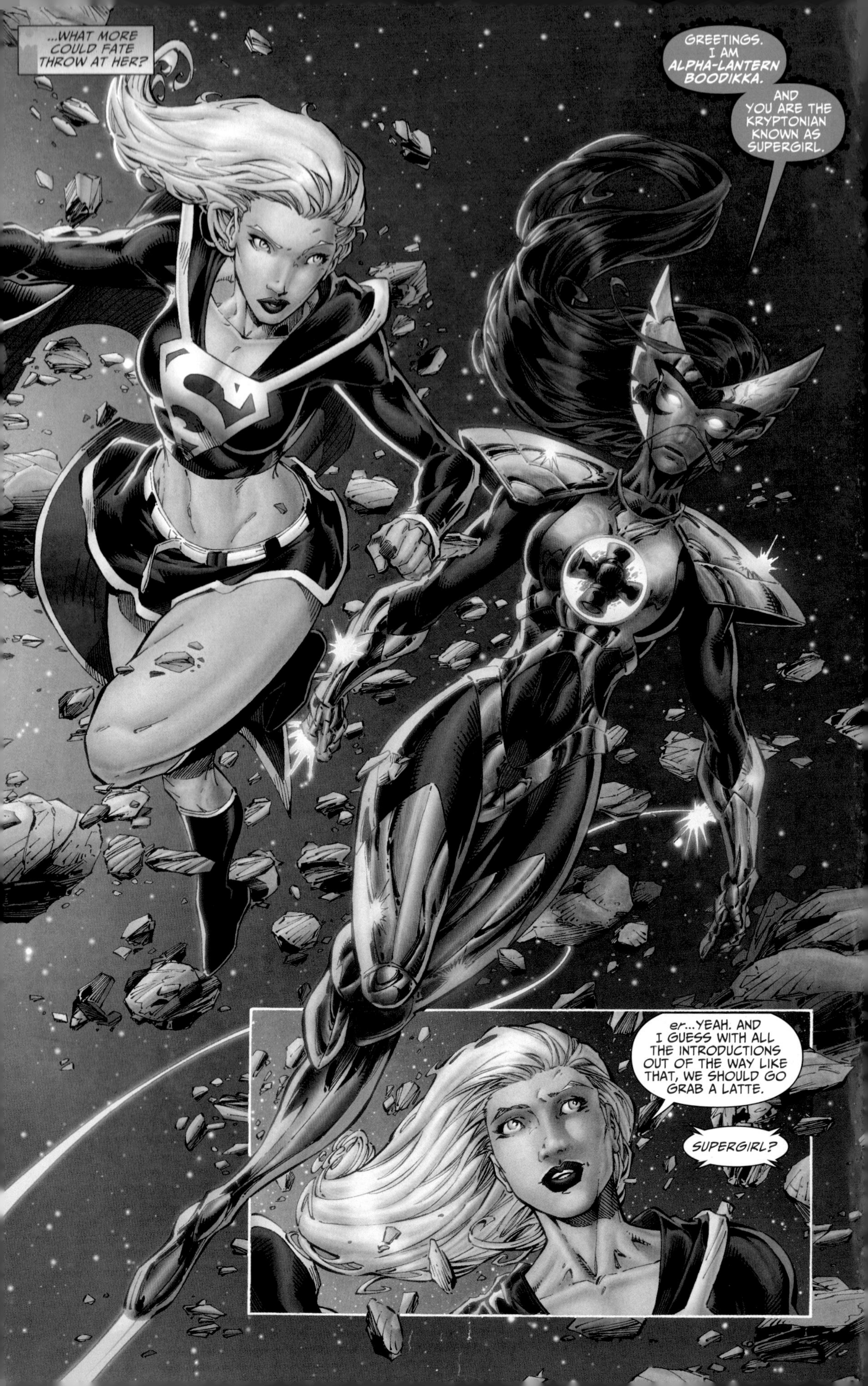
...WHAT MORE COULD FATE THROW AT HER?
GREETINGS. I AM ALPHA-LANTERN BOODIKKA.
AND YOU ARE THE KRYPTONIAN KNOWN AS SUPERGIRL.
er...YEAH. AND I GUESS WITH ALL THE INTRODUCTIONS OUT OF THE WAY LIKE THAT, WE SHOULD GO GRAB A LATTE.
SUPERGIRL?

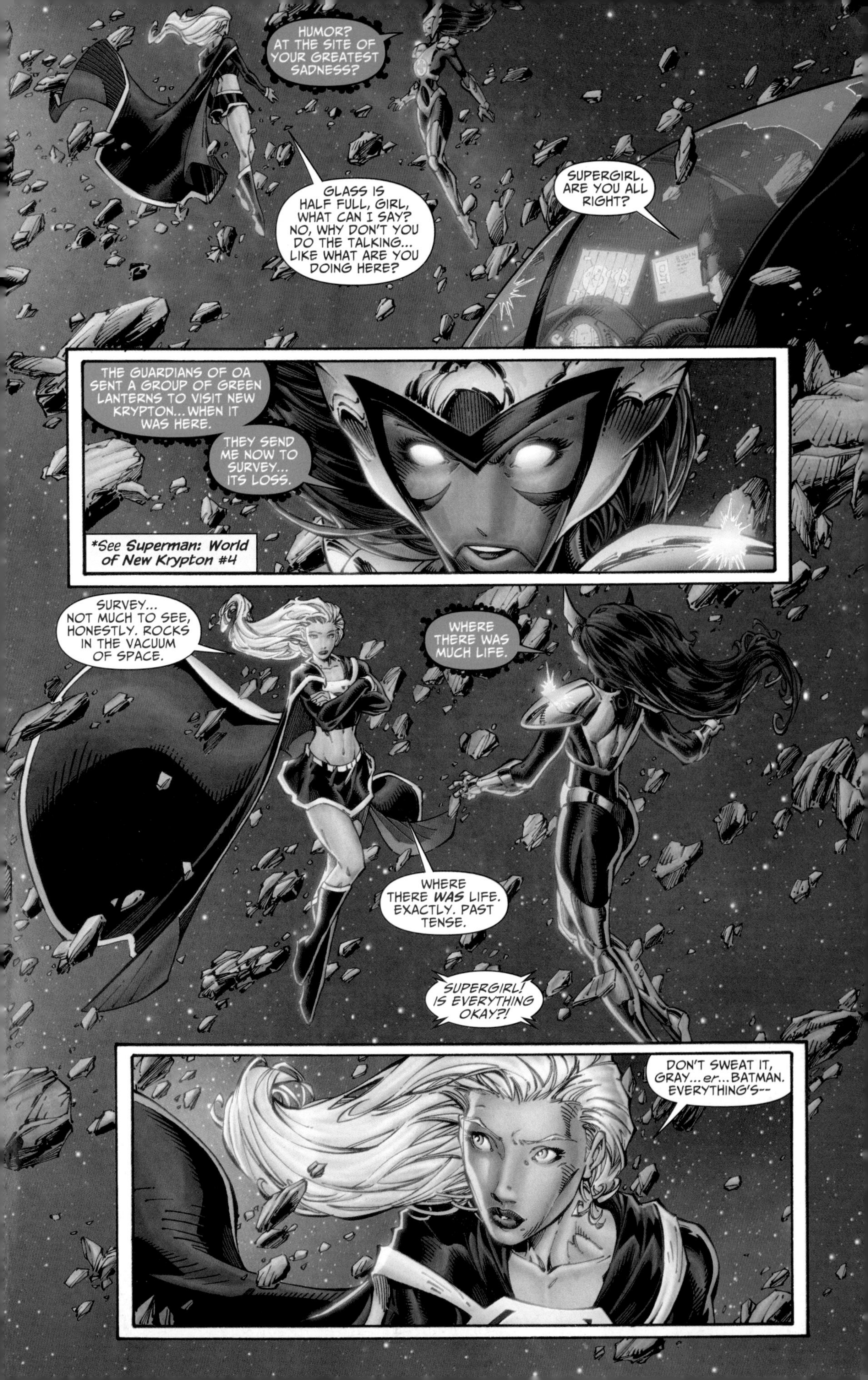
HUMOR? AT THE SITE OF YOUR GREATEST SADNESS?
GLASS IS HALF FULL, GIRL, WHAT CAN I SAY? NO, WHY DON'T YOU DO THE TALKING... LIKE WHAT ARE YOU DOING HERE?
SUPERGIRL. ARE YOU ALL RIGHT?
THE GUARDIANS OF OA SENT A GROUP OF GREEN LANTERNS TO VISIT NEW KRYPTON... WHEN IT WAS HERE.
THEY SEND ME NOW TO SURVEY... ITS LOSS.
*See Superman: World of New Krypton #4
SURVEY... NOT MUCH TO SEE, HONESTLY. ROCKS IN THE VACUUM OF SPACE.
WHERE THERE WAS MUCH LIFE.
WHERE THERE WAS LIFE. EXACTLY. PAST TENSE.
SUPERGIRL! IS EVERYTHING OKAY?!
DON'T SWEAT IT, GRAY... er... BATMAN. EVERYTHING'S--

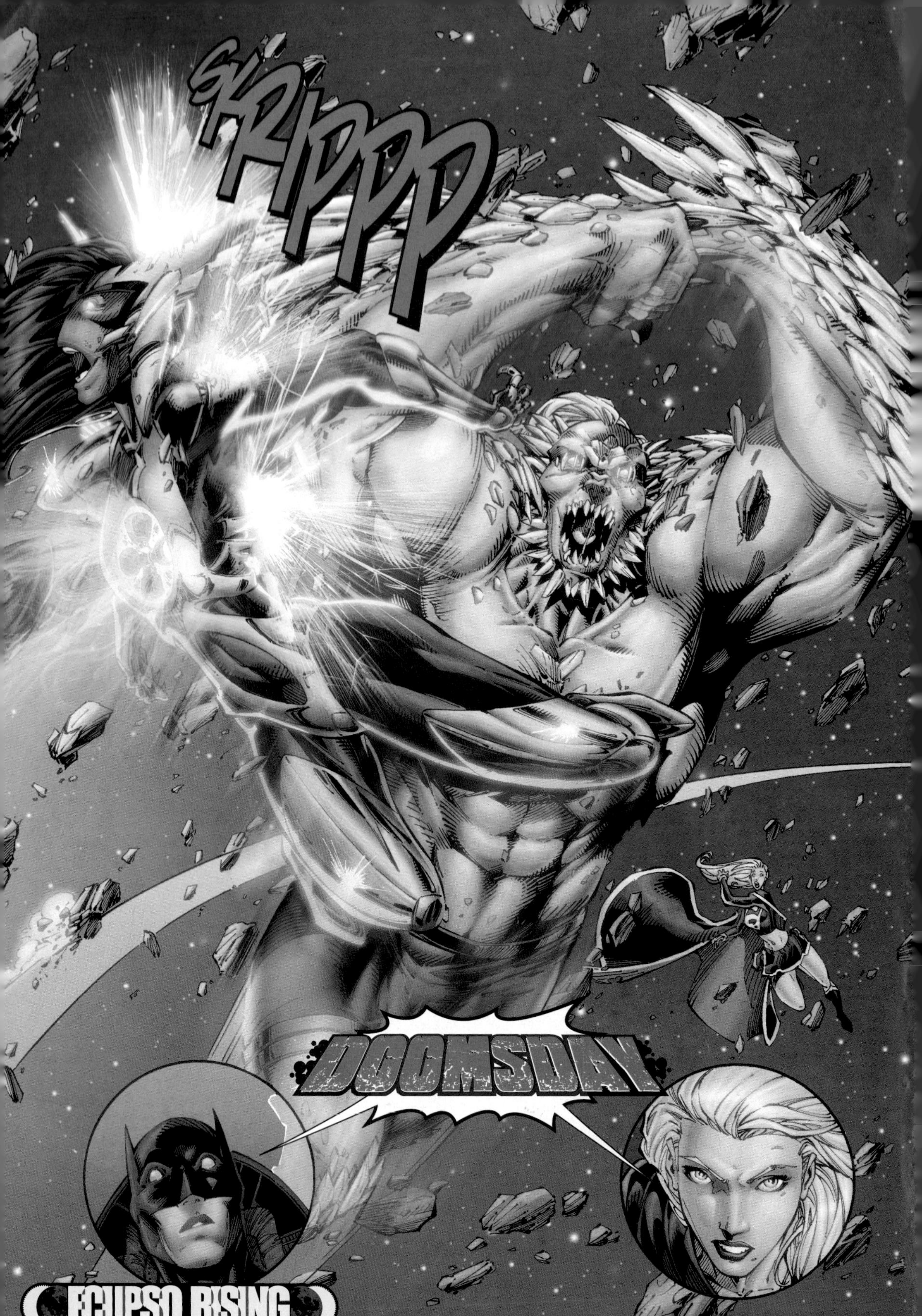
SKRIPPP
DOOMSDAY

ECLIPSO RISING

PART TWO: MAYHEM

writer: james robinson pencils: brett booth
inks: norm rapmund
colors: andrew dalhouse letters: rob leigh
cover: brett booth & andrew dalhouse
variant cover: dan jurgens, norm rapmund, & dalhouse
associate editor: rex ogle editor: eddie berganza

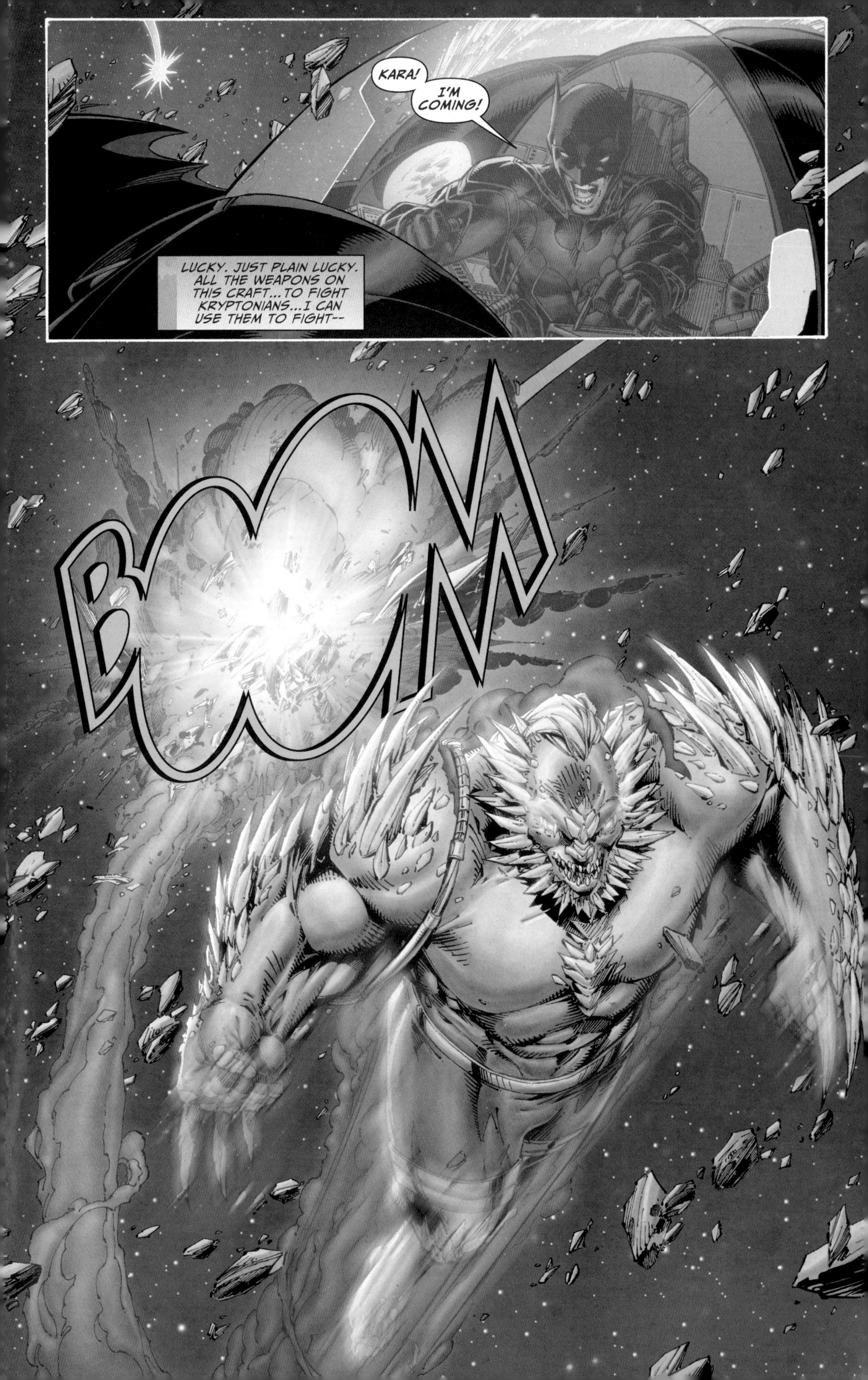
KARA!
I'M COMING!
LUCKY. JUST PLAIN LUCKY. ALL THE WEAPONS ON THIS CRAFT...TO FIGHT KRYPTONIANS...I CAN USE THEM TO FIGHT--
BOOM

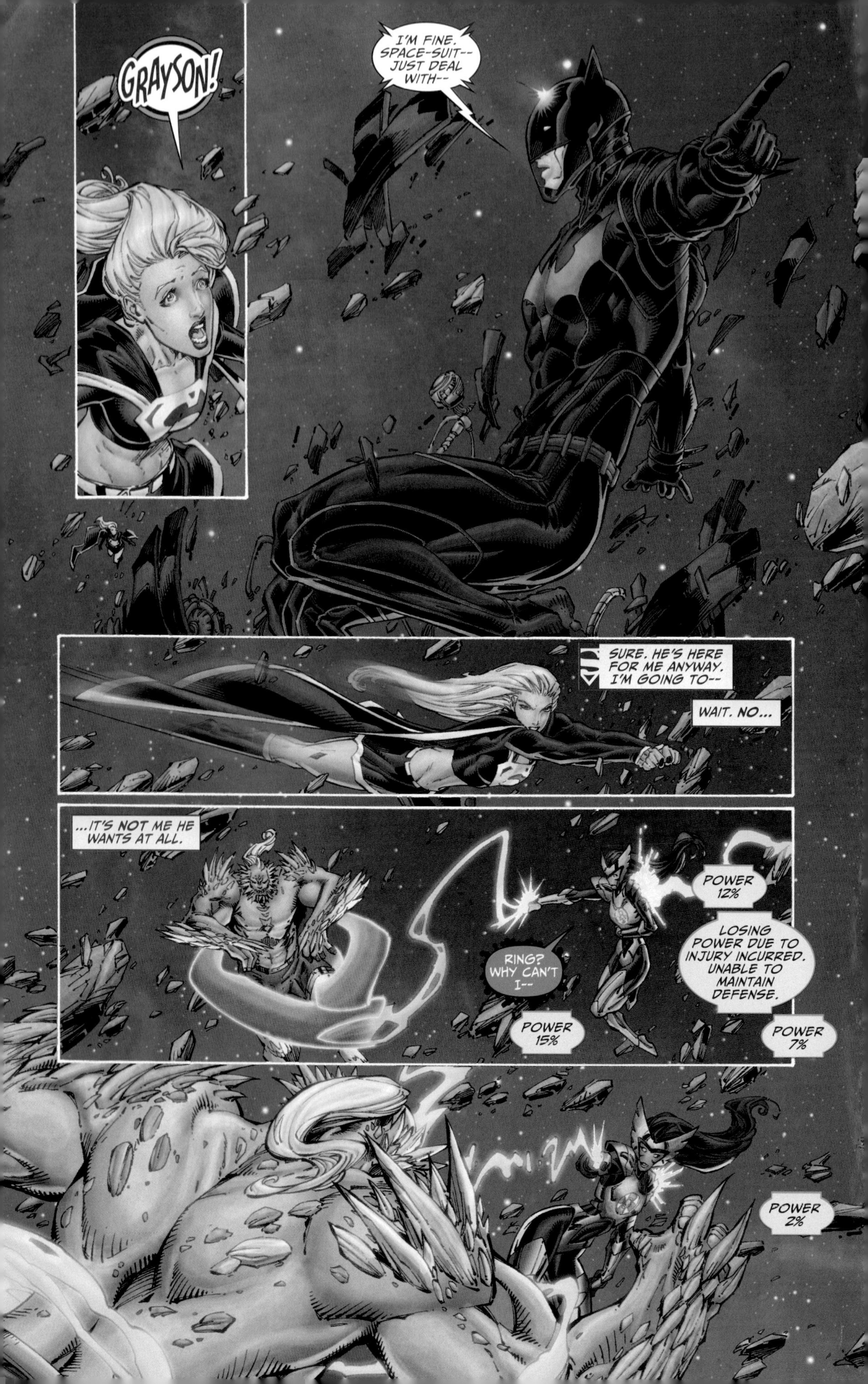
GRAYSON!
I'M FINE. SPACE-SUIT--JUST DEAL WITH--
SURE. HE'S HERE FOR ME ANYWAY. I'M GOING TO--
WAIT. NO...
...IT'S NOT ME HE WANTS AT ALL.
POWER 12%
LOSING POWER DUE TO INJURY INCURRED. UNABLE TO MAINTAIN DEFENSE.
RING? WHY CAN'T I--
POWER 15%
POWER 7%
POWER 2%

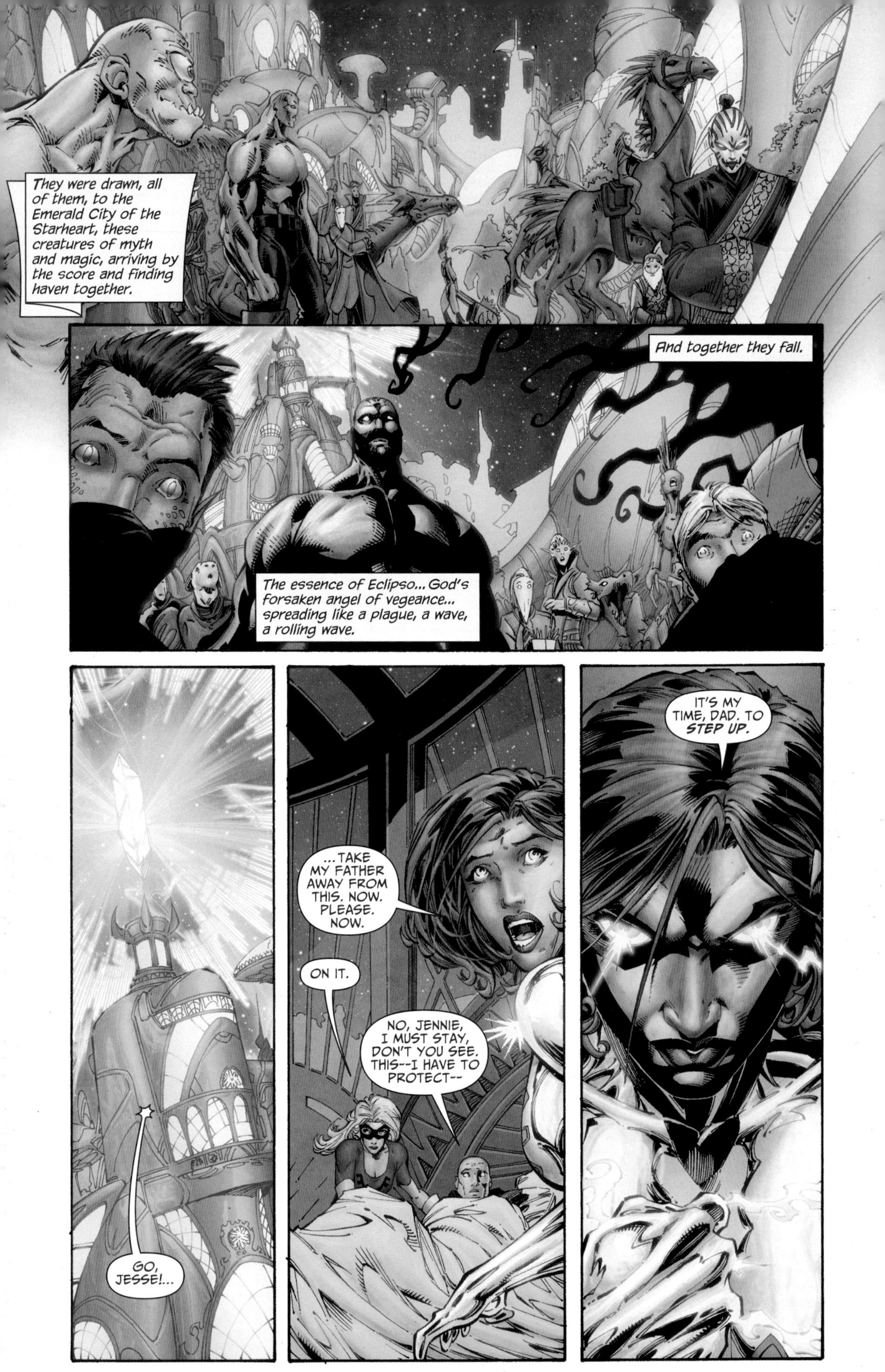
They were drawn, all of them, to the Emerald City of the Starheart, these creatures of myth and magic, arriving by the score and finding haven together.
And together they fall.
The essence of Eclipso... God's forsaken angel of vegeance... spreading like a plague, a wave, a rolling wave.
GO, JESSE!...
...TAKE MY FATHER AWAY FROM THIS. NOW. PLEASE. NOW.
ON IT.
NO, JENNIE, I MUST STAY, DON'T YOU SEE. THIS--I HAVE TO PROTECT--
IT'S MY TIME, DAD. TO STEP UP.

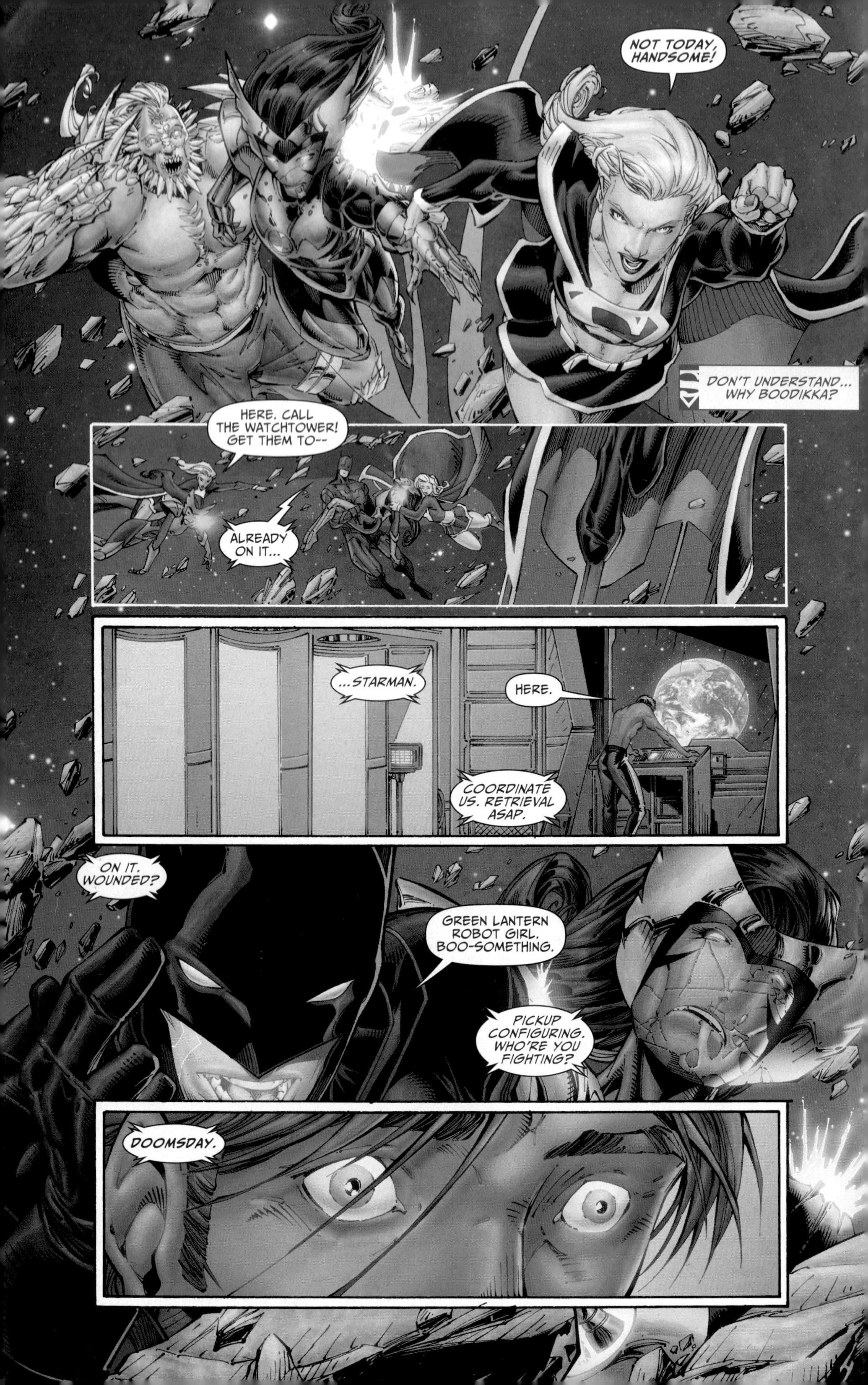
NOT TODAY, HANDSOME!
DON'T UNDERSTAND... WHY BOODIKKA?
HERE. CALL THE WATCHTOWER! GET THEM TO--
ALREADY ON IT...
...STARMAN.
HERE.
COORDINATE US. RETRIEVAL ASAP.
ON IT. WOUNDED?
GREEN LANTERN ROBOT GIRL. BOO-SOMETHING.
PICKUP CONFIGURING. WHO'RE YOU FIGHTING?
DOOMSDAY.

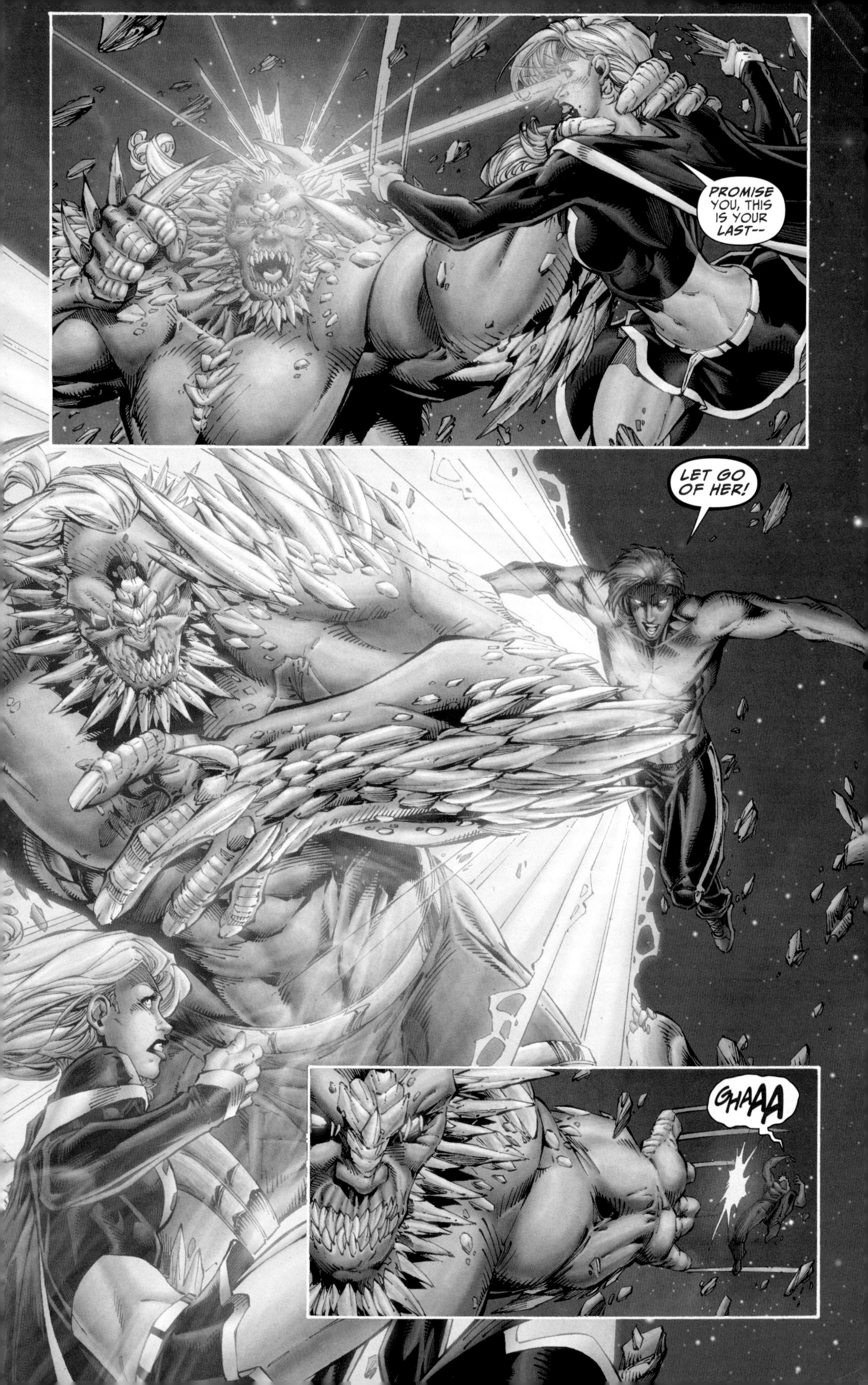
PROMISE YOU, THIS IS YOUR LAST--
LET GO OF HER!
GHAAA

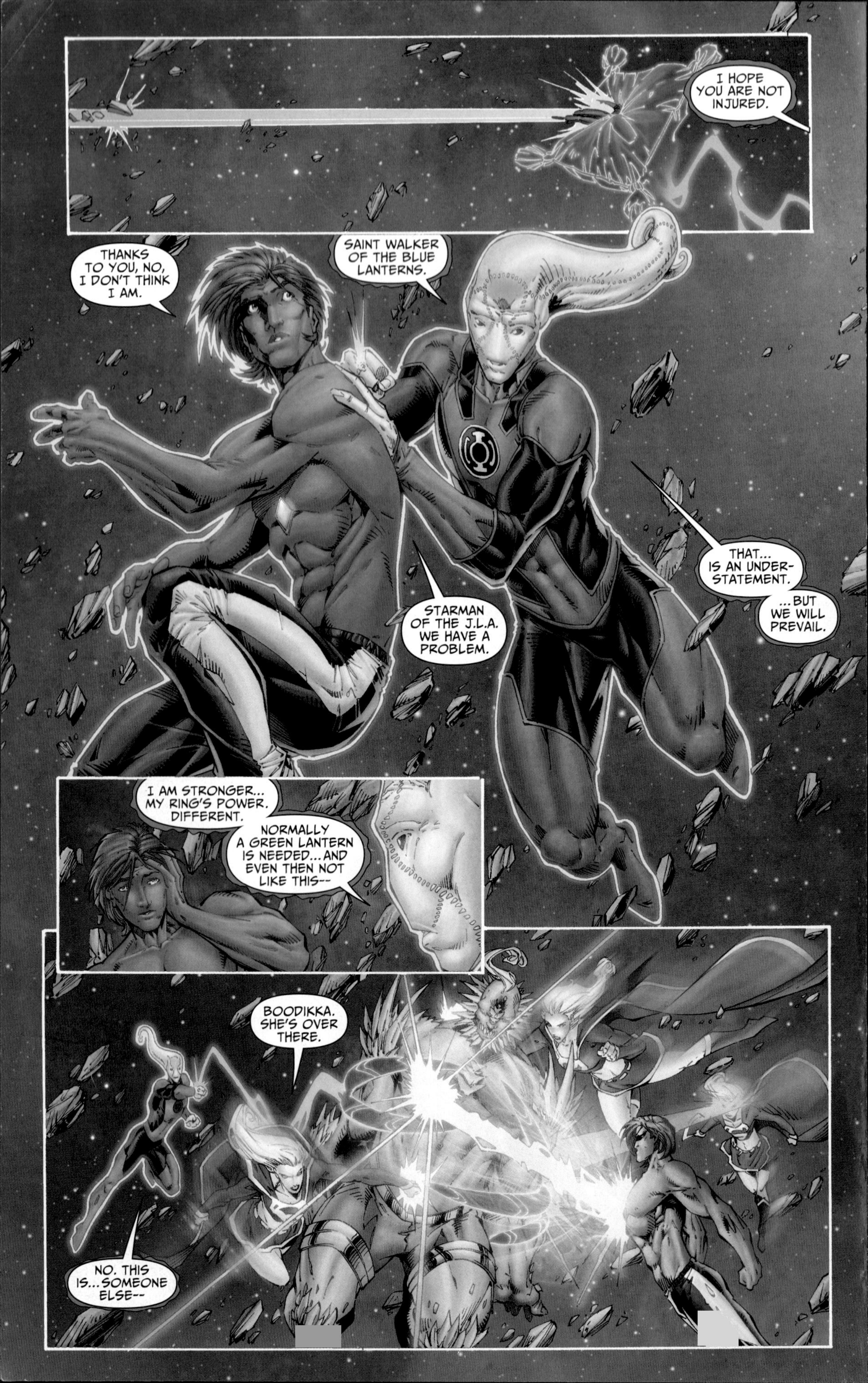
I HOPE YOU ARE NOT INJURED.
THANKS TO YOU, NO, I DON'T THINK I AM.
SAINT WALKER OF THE BLUE LANTERNS.
STARMAN OF THE J.L.A. WE HAVE A PROBLEM.
THAT... IS AN UNDER-STATEMENT.
...BUT WE WILL PREVAIL.
I AM STRONGER... MY RING'S POWER. DIFFERENT.
NORMALLY A GREEN LANTERN IS NEEDED...AND EVEN THEN NOT LIKE THIS--
BOODIKKA. SHE'S OVER THERE.
NO. THIS IS...SOMEONE ELSE--

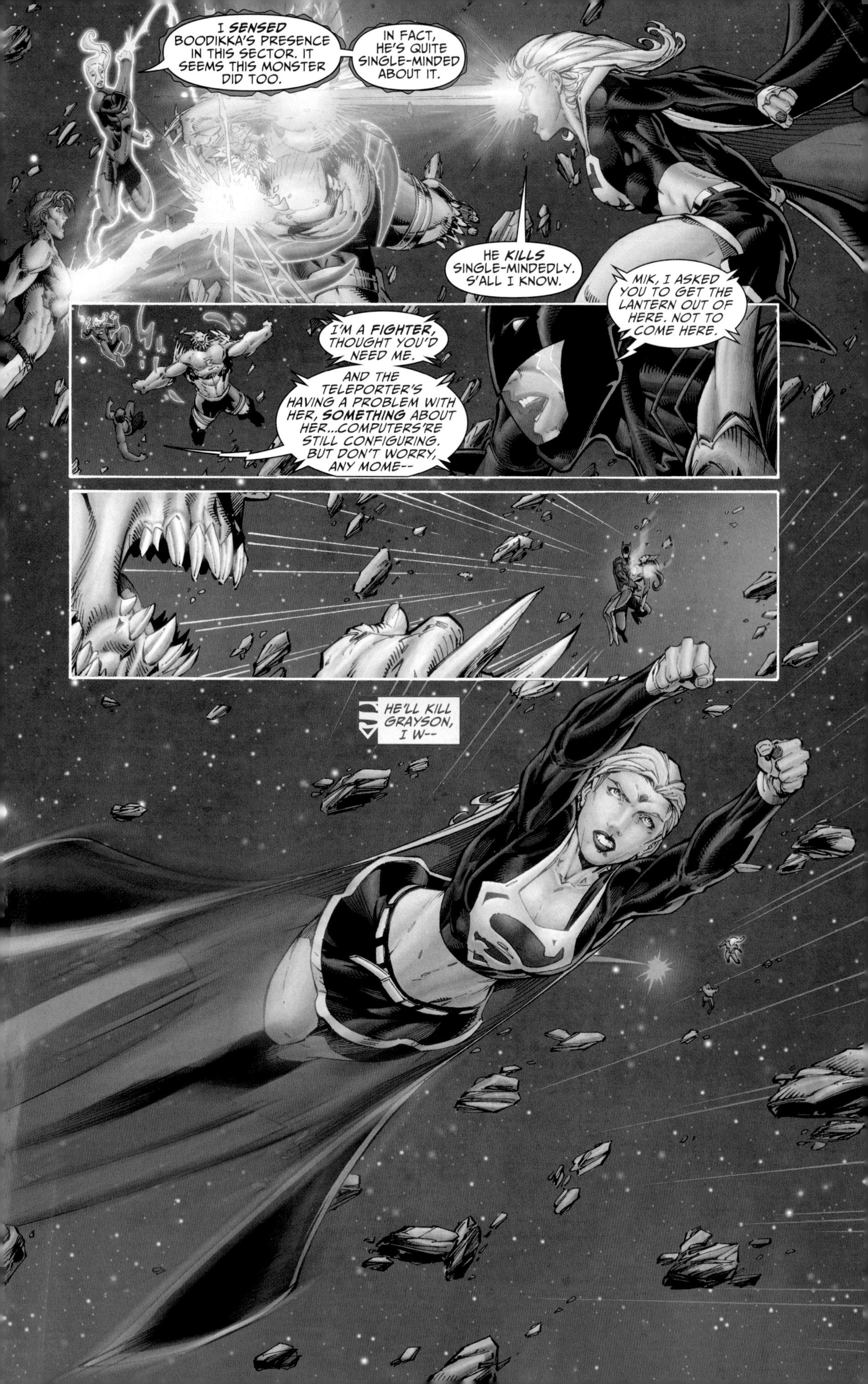
I SENSED BOODIKKA'S PRESENCE IN THIS SECTOR. IT SEEMS THIS MONSTER DID TOO.
IN FACT, HE'S QUITE SINGLE-MINDED ABOUT IT.
HE KILLS SINGLE-MINDEDLY. S'ALL I KNOW.
MIK, I ASKED YOU TO GET THE LANTERN OUT OF HERE. NOT TO COME HERE.
I'M A FIGHTER, THOUGHT YOU'D NEED ME.
AND THE TELEPORTER'S HAVING A PROBLEM WITH HER, SOMETHING ABOUT HER...COMPUTERS'RE STILL CONFIGURING. BUT DON'T WORRY, ANY MOME--
HE'LL KILL GRAYSON, I W--

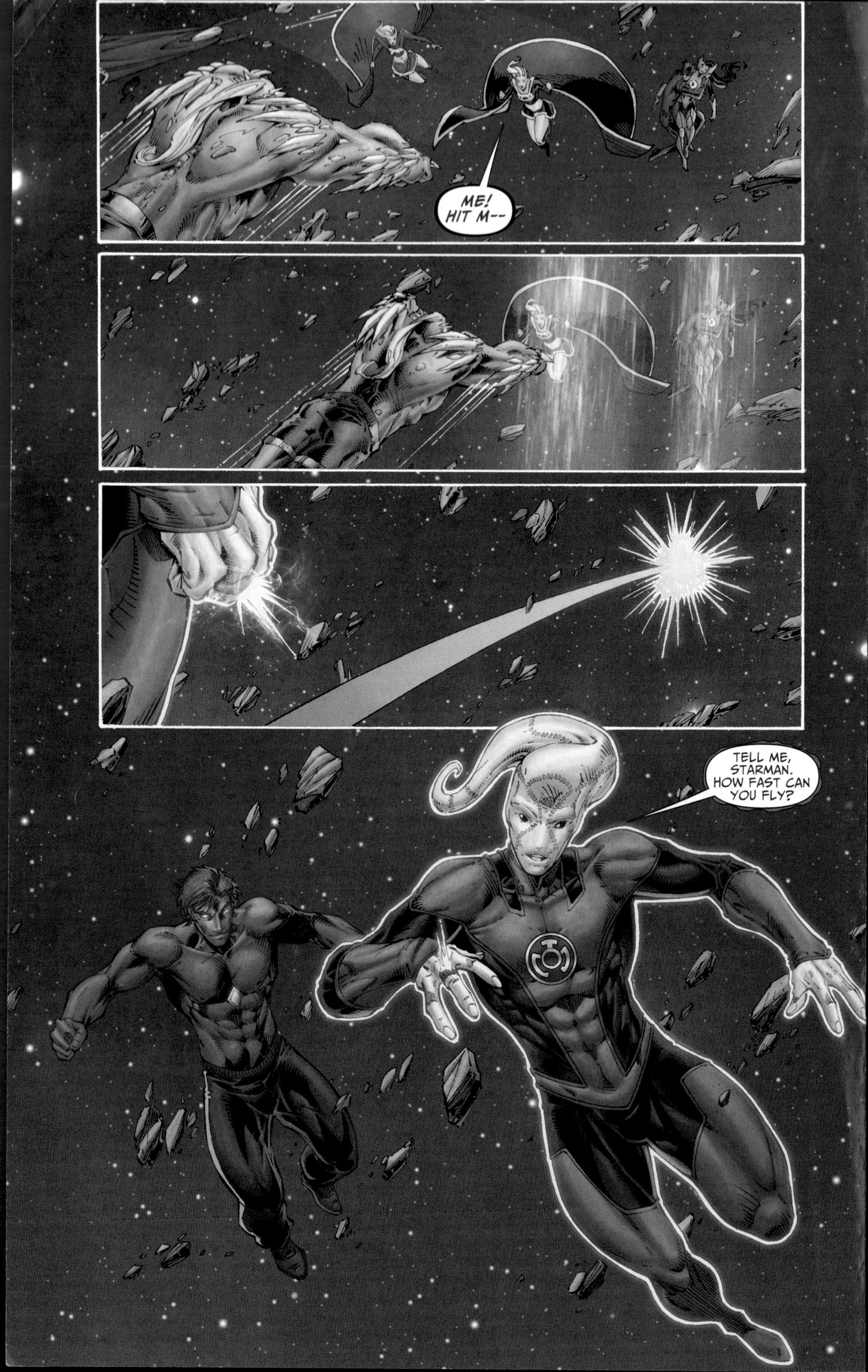
ME! HIT M--
TELL ME, STARMAN. HOW FAST CAN YOU FLY?

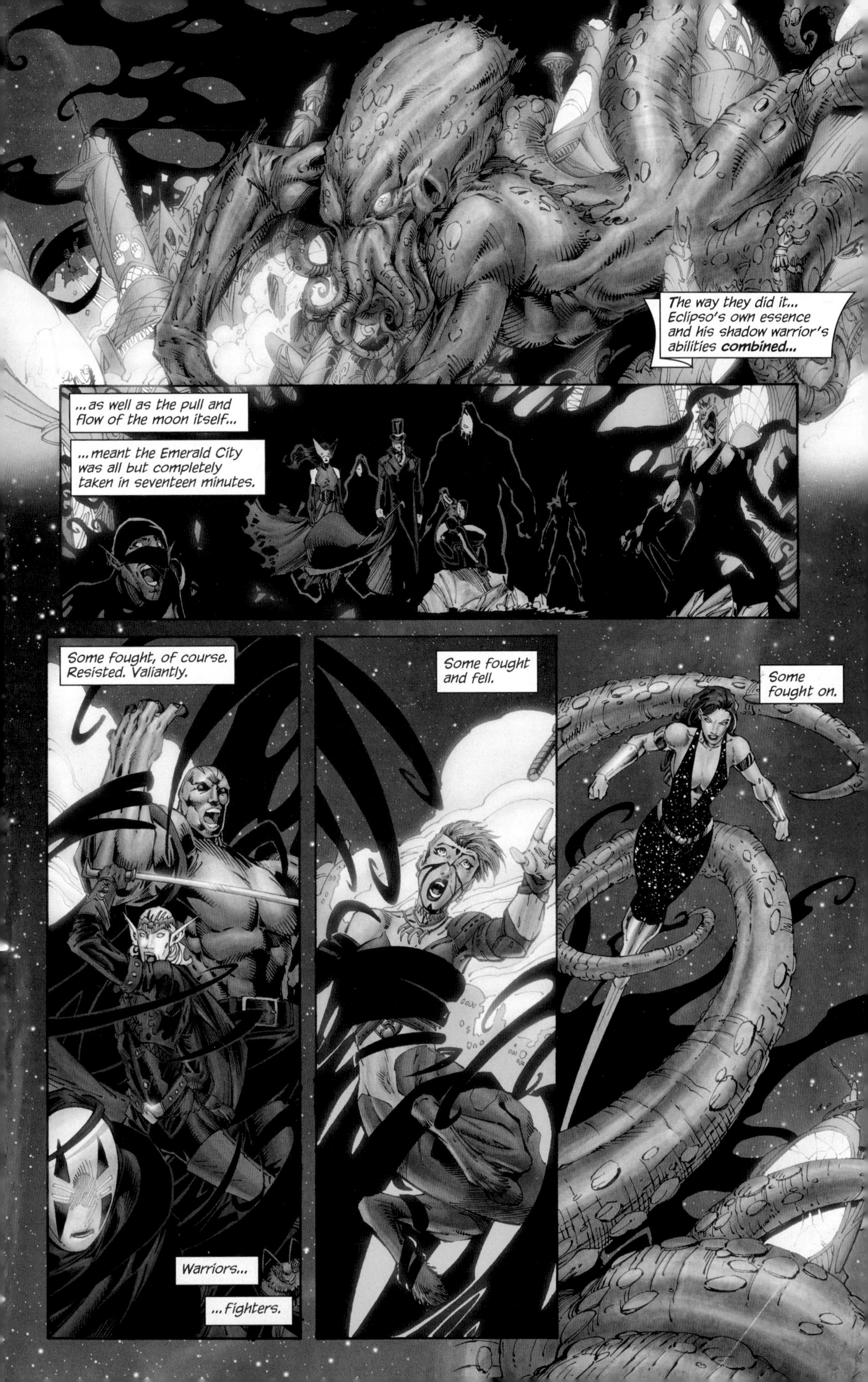
The way they did it... Eclipso's own essence and his shadow warrior's abilities **combined...**
...as well as the pull and flow of the moon itself...
...meant the Emerald City was all but completely taken in seventeen minutes.
Some fought, of course. Resisted. Valiantly.
Warriors...
...Fighters.
Some fought and fell.
Some fought on.

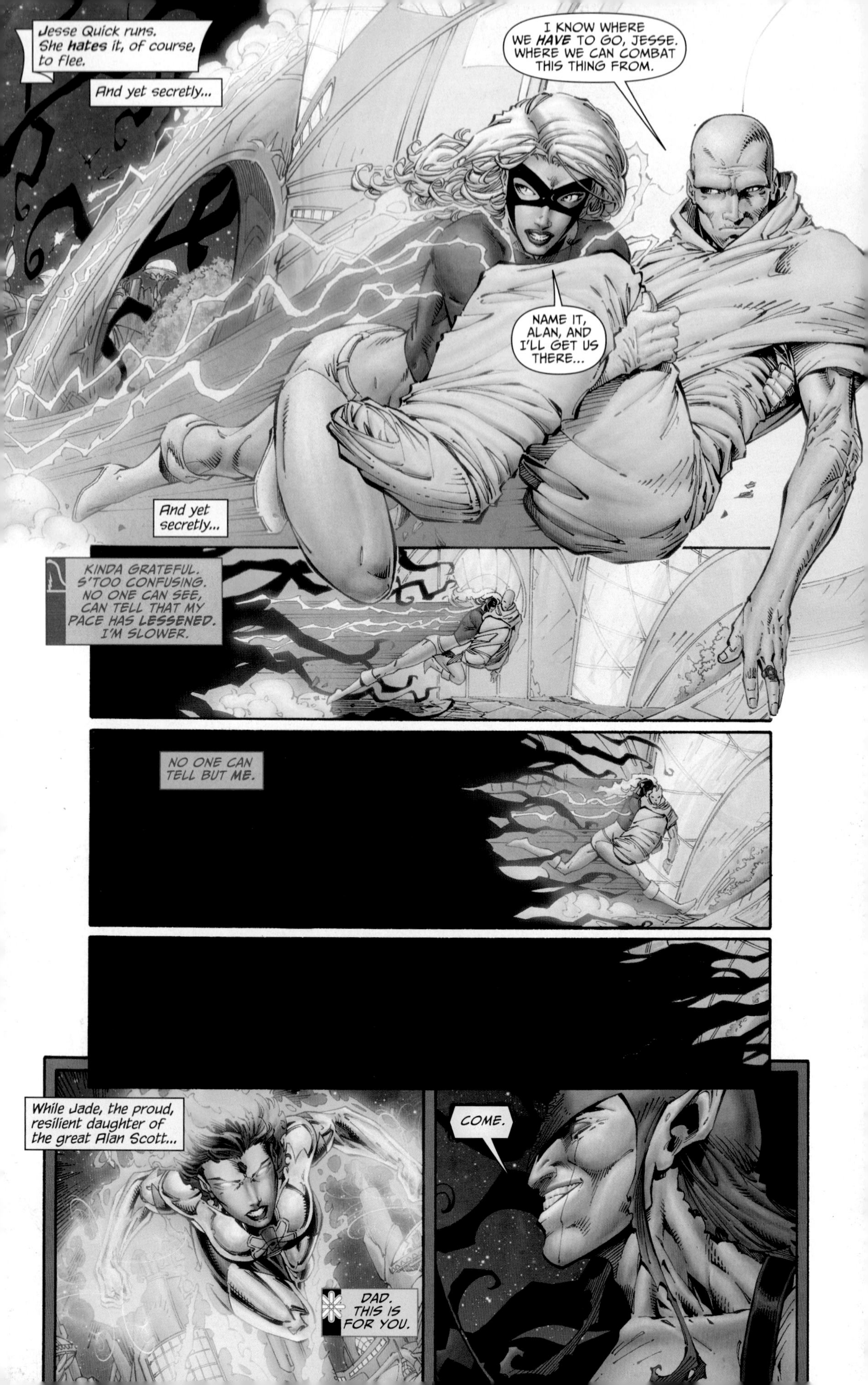
Jesse Quick runs. She hates it, of course, to flee.
And yet secretly...
I KNOW WHERE WE HAVE TO GO, JESSE. WHERE WE CAN COMBAT THIS THING FROM.
NAME IT, ALAN, AND I'LL GET US THERE...
And yet secretly...
KINDA GRATEFUL. S'TOO CONFUSING. NO ONE CAN SEE, CAN TELL THAT MY PACE HAS LESSENED. I'M SLOWER.
NO ONE CAN TELL BUT ME.
While Jade, the proud, resilient daughter of the great Alan Scott...
DAD. THIS IS FOR YOU.
COME.

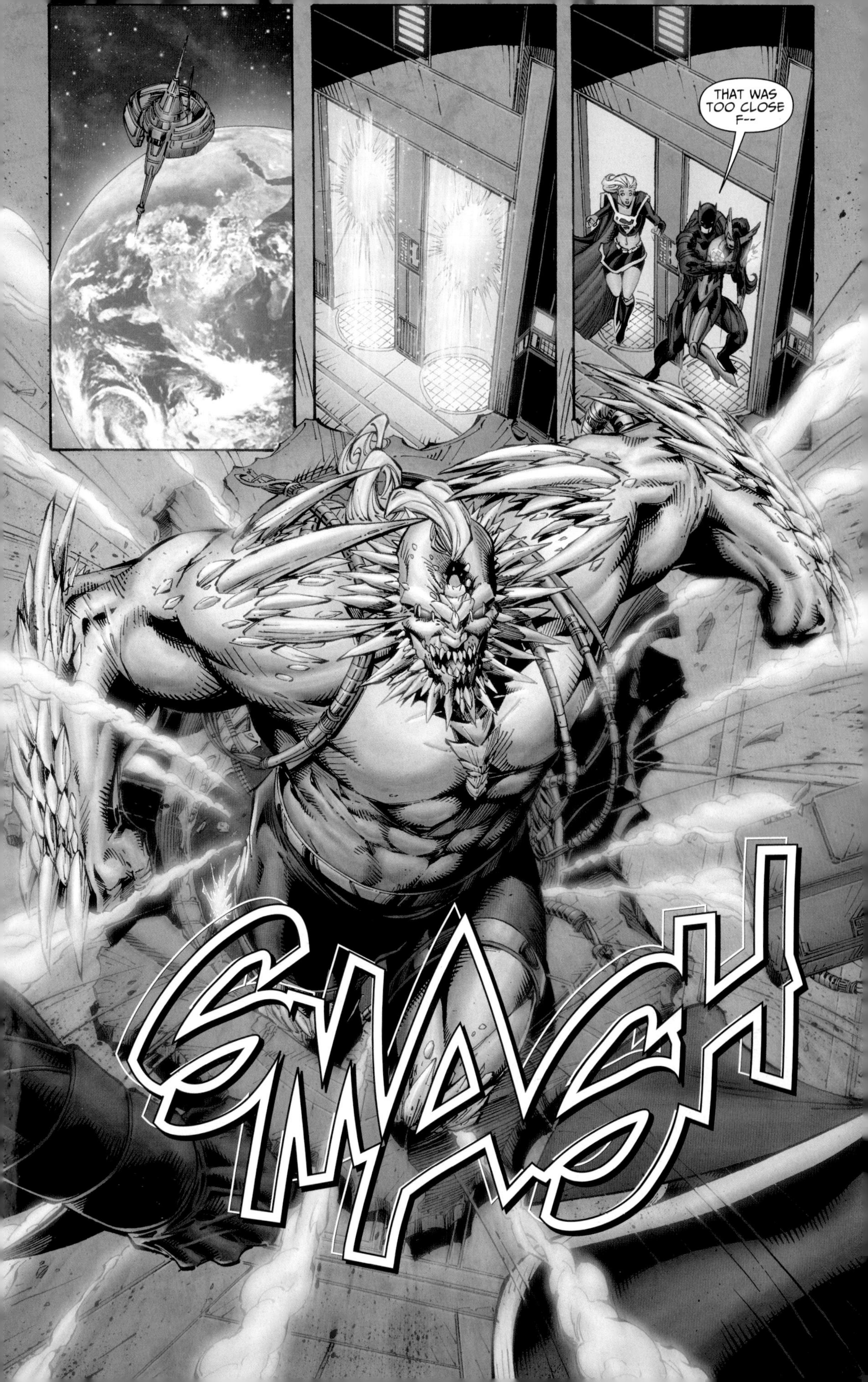
THAT WAS TOO CLOSE F--
SMASH

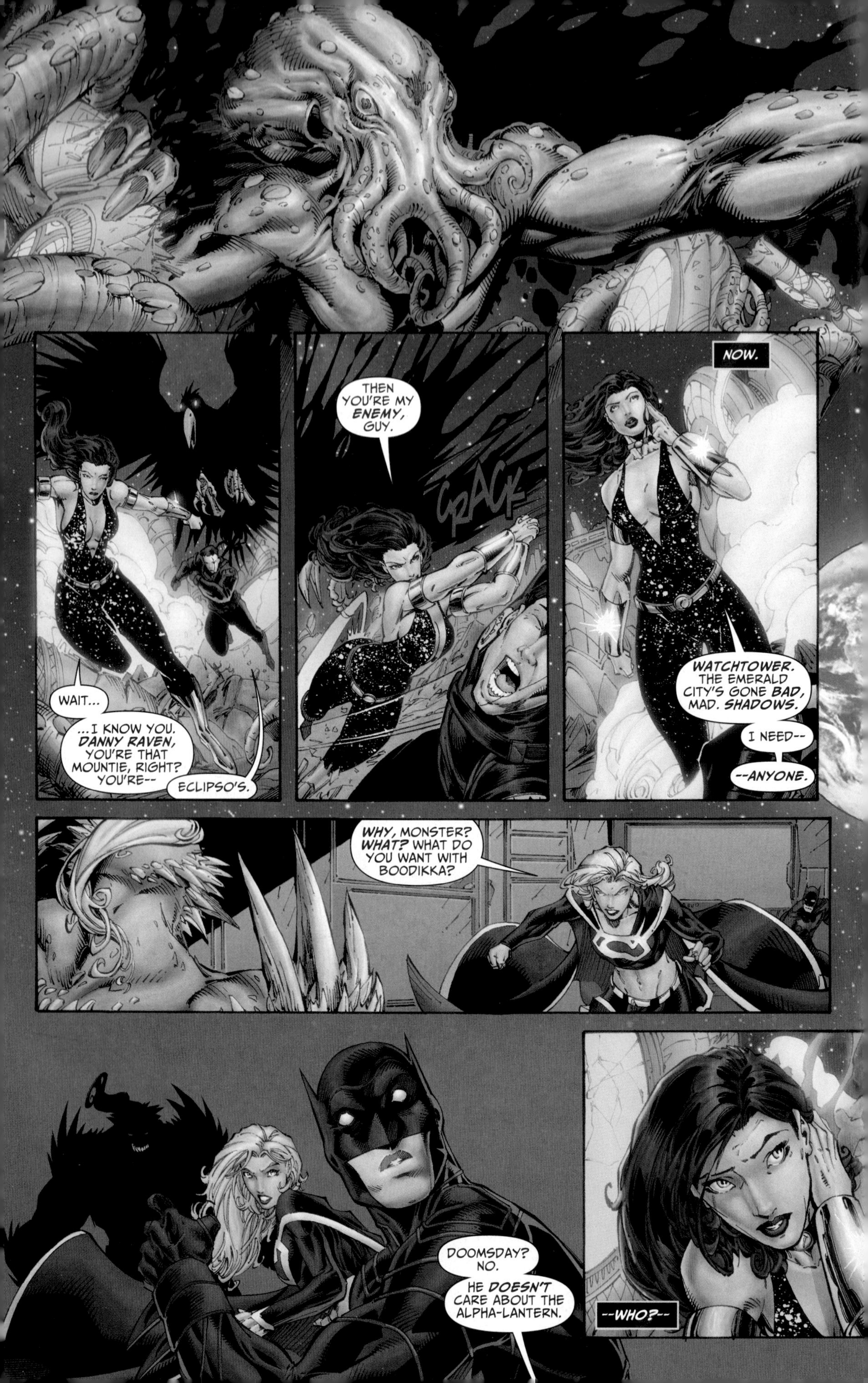

THEN YOU'RE MY ENEMY, GUY.
CRACK
NOW.
WAIT...
...I KNOW YOU. DANNY RAVEN, YOU'RE THAT MOUNTIE, RIGHT? YOU'RE--
ECLIPSO'S.
WATCHTOWER. THE EMERALD CITY'S GONE BAD, MAD. SHADOWS.
I NEED--
--ANYONE.
WHY, MONSTER? WHAT? WHAT DO YOU WANT WITH BOODIKKA?
DOOMSDAY? NO.
HE DOESN'T CARE ABOUT THE ALPHA-LANTERN.
--WHO?--

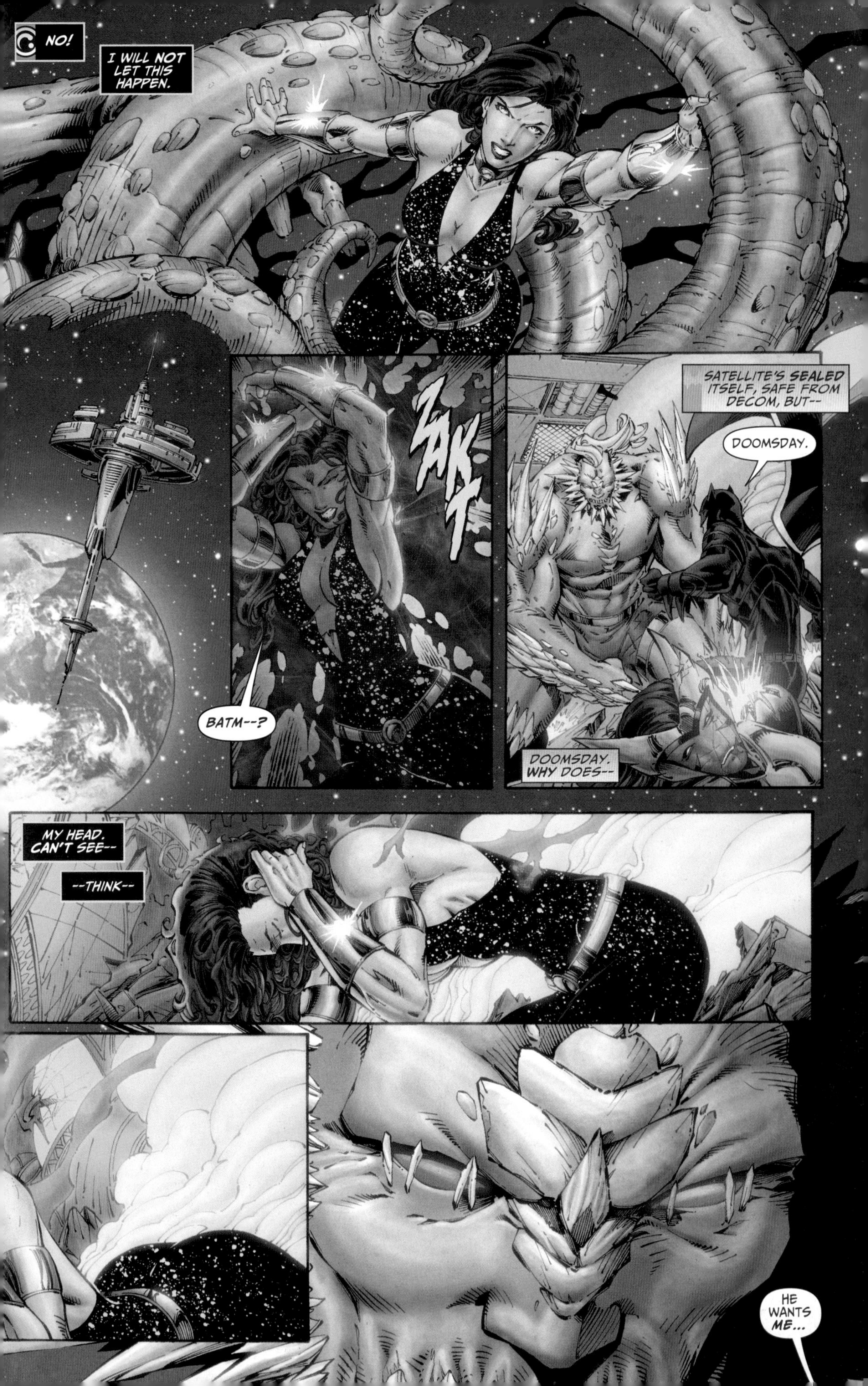
NO!
I WILL NOT LET THIS HAPPEN.
ZAKT
BATM--?
SATELLITE'S SEALED ITSELF, SAFE FROM DECOM, BUT--
DOOMSDAY.
DOOMSDAY. WHY DOES--
MY HEAD. CAN'T SEE--
--THINK--
HE WANTS ME...

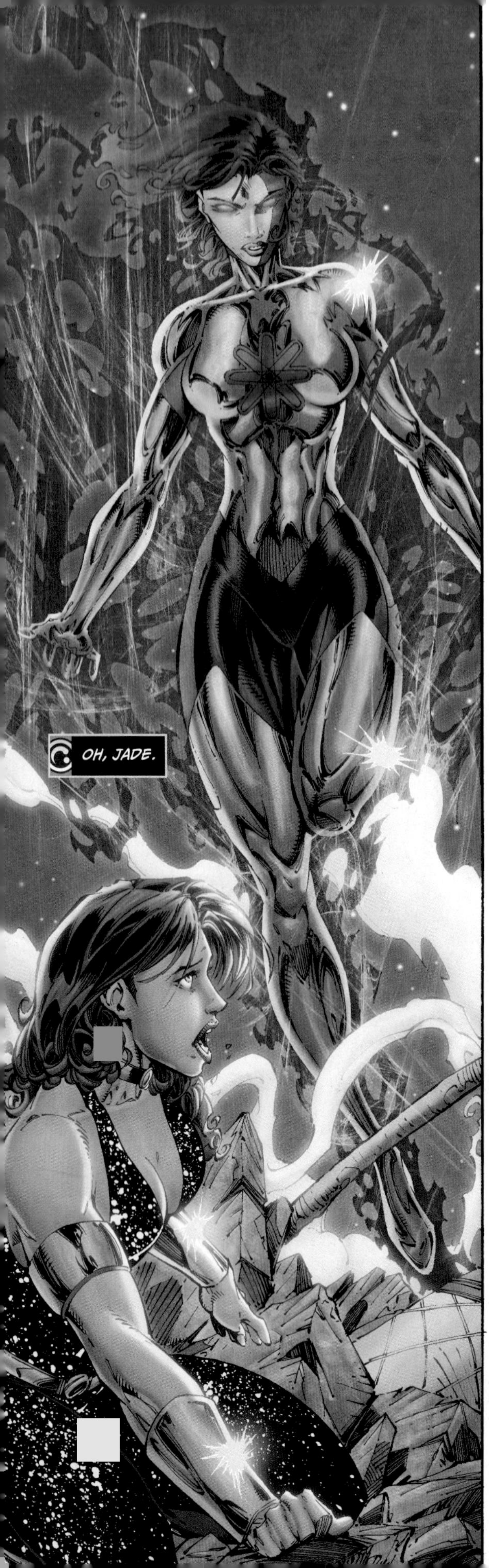
OH, JADE.

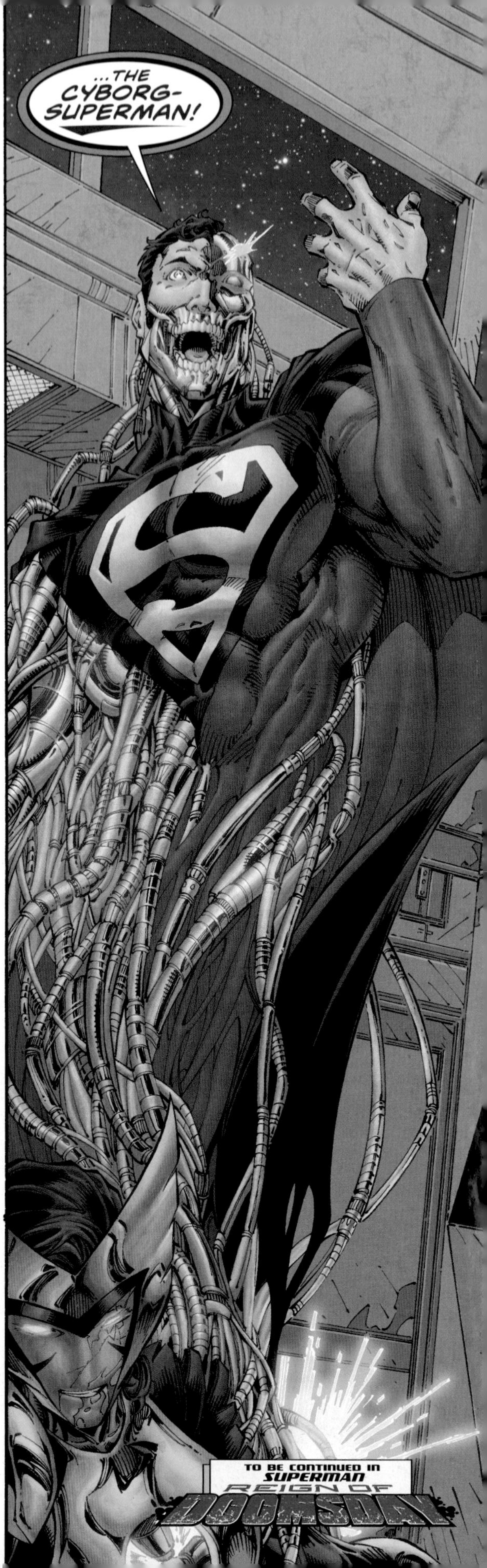
...THE CYBORG-SUPERMAN!
TO BE CONTINUED IN
SUPERMAN
REIGN OF
DOOMSDAY

JUSTICE LEAGUE OF AMERICA 56
Cover by Brett Booth, Norm Rapmund & Andrew Dalhouse

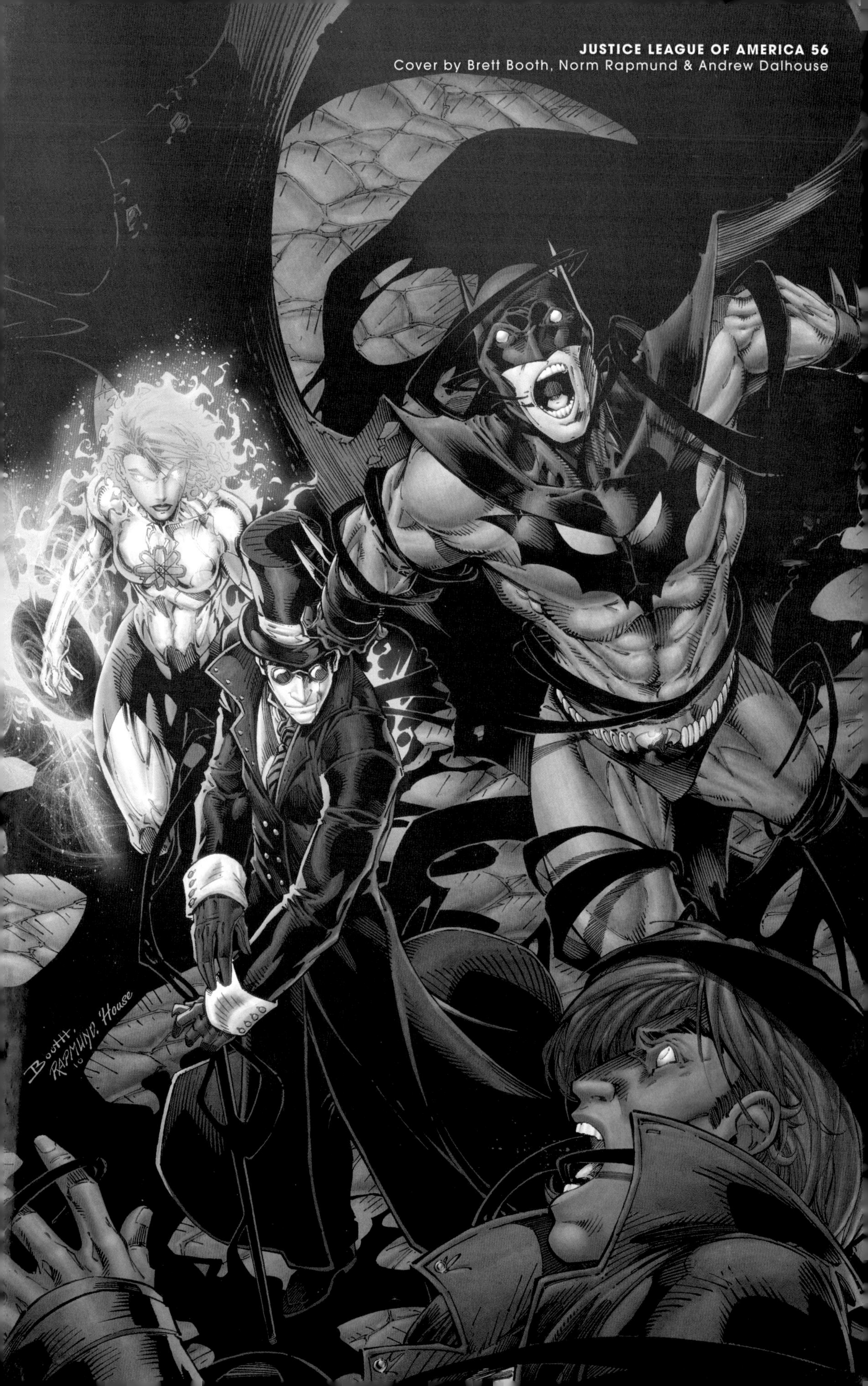

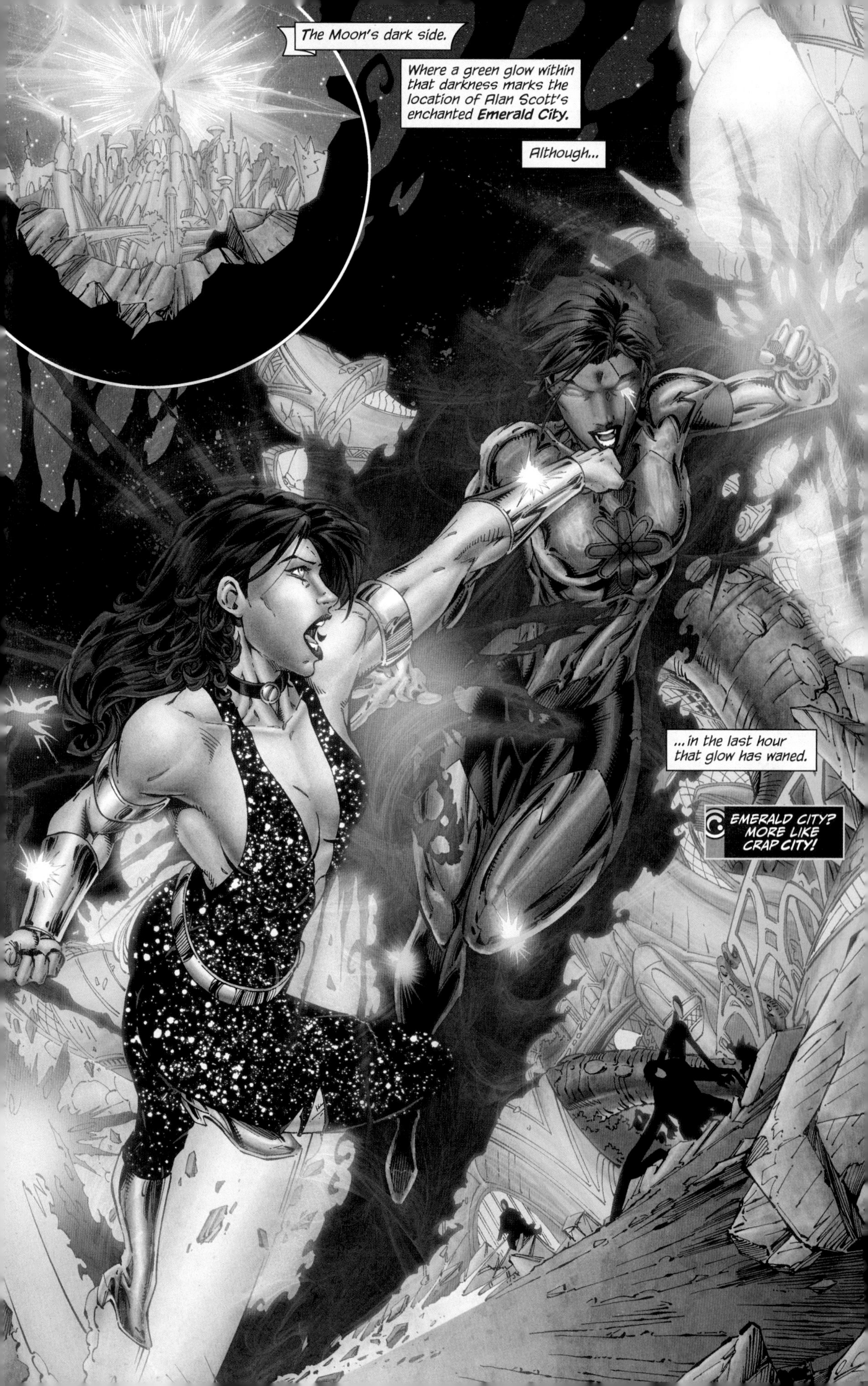
The Moon's dark side.
Where a green glow within that darkness marks the location of Alan Scott's enchanted **Emerald City.**
Although...
...in the last hour that glow has waned.
EMERALD CITY? MORE LIKE CRAP CITY!

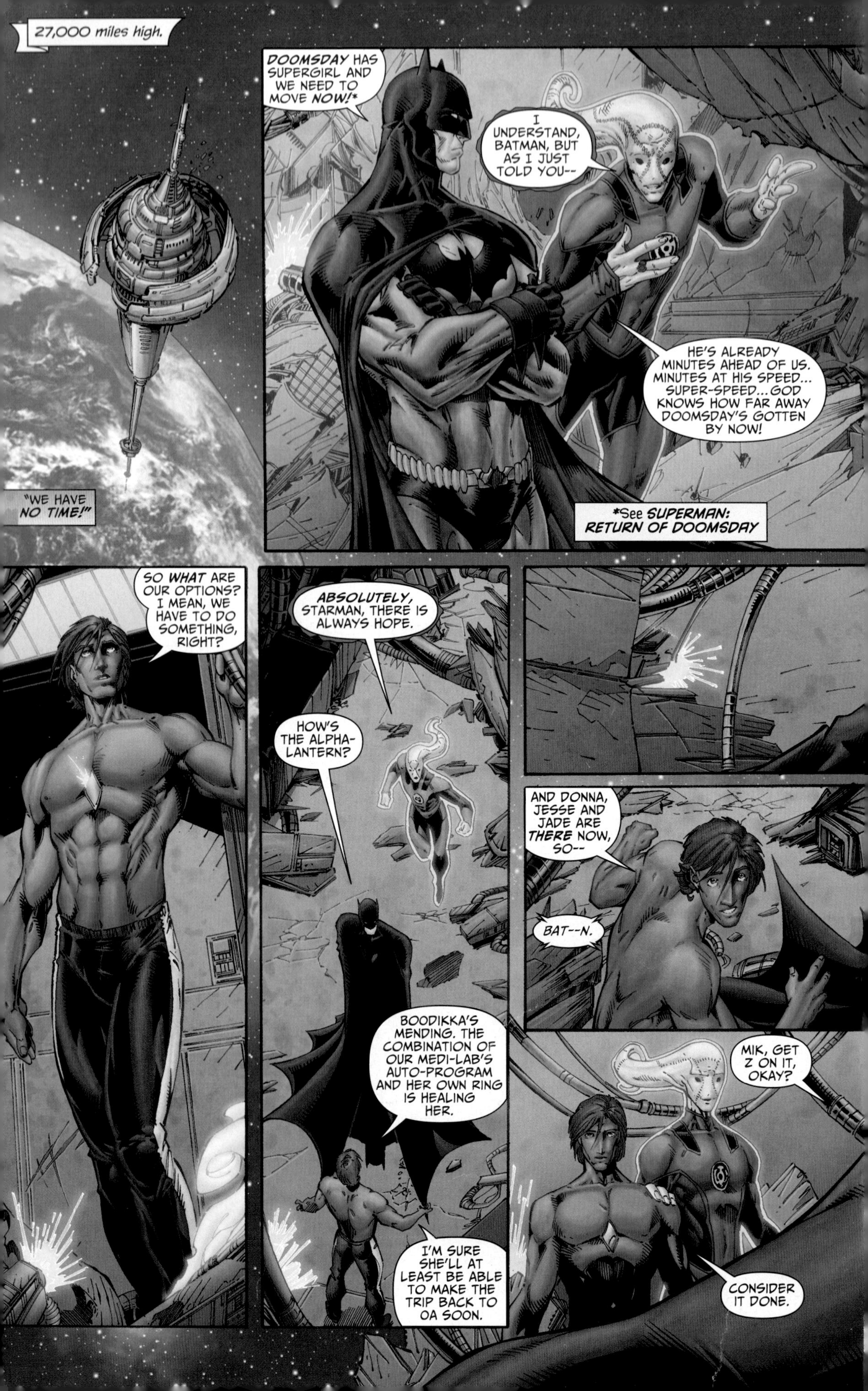
27,000 miles high.
"WE HAVE NO TIME!"
DOOMSDAY HAS SUPERGIRL AND WE NEED TO MOVE NOW!*
I UNDERSTAND, BATMAN, BUT AS I JUST TOLD YOU--
HE'S ALREADY MINUTES AHEAD OF US. MINUTES AT HIS SPEED... SUPER-SPEED...GOD KNOWS HOW FAR AWAY DOOMSDAY'S GOTTEN BY NOW!
*See SUPERMAN: RETURN OF DOOMSDAY
SO WHAT ARE OUR OPTIONS? I MEAN, WE HAVE TO DO SOMETHING, RIGHT?
ABSOLUTELY, STARMAN, THERE IS ALWAYS HOPE.
HOW'S THE ALPHA-LANTERN?
BOODIKKA'S MENDING. THE COMBINATION OF OUR MEDI-LAB'S AUTO-PROGRAM AND HER OWN RING IS HEALING HER.
I'M SURE SHE'LL AT LEAST BE ABLE TO MAKE THE TRIP BACK TO OA SOON.
AND DONNA, JESSE AND JADE ARE THERE NOW, SO--
BAT--N.
MIK, GET Z ON IT, OKAY?
CONSIDER IT DONE.

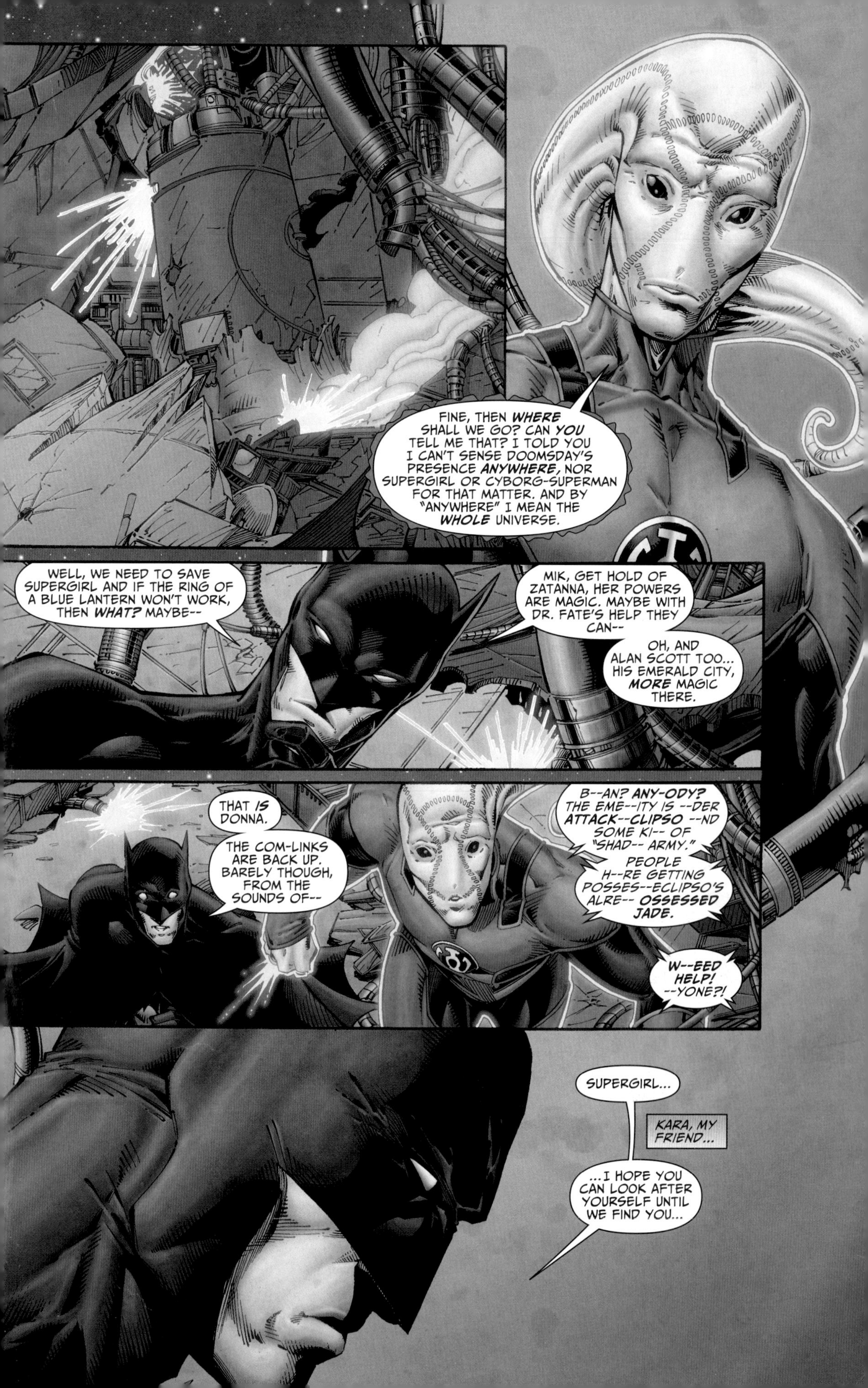

FINE, THEN WHERE SHALL WE GO? CAN YOU TELL ME THAT? I TOLD YOU I CAN'T SENSE DOOMSDAY'S PRESENCE ANYWHERE, NOR SUPERGIRL OR CYBORG-SUPERMAN FOR THAT MATTER. AND BY "ANYWHERE" I MEAN THE WHOLE UNIVERSE.
WELL, WE NEED TO SAVE SUPERGIRL AND IF THE RING OF A BLUE LANTERN WON'T WORK, THEN WHAT? MAYBE--
MIK, GET HOLD OF ZATANNA, HER POWERS ARE MAGIC. MAYBE WITH DR. FATE'S HELP THEY CAN--
OH, AND ALAN SCOTT TOO... HIS EMERALD CITY, MORE MAGIC THERE.
THAT IS DONNA.
THE COM-LINKS ARE BACK UP. BARELY THOUGH, FROM THE SOUNDS OF--
B--AN? ANY-ODY? THE EME--ITY IS --DER ATTACK--CLIPSO --ND SOME KI-- OF "SHAD-- ARMY."
PEOPLE H--RE GETTING POSSES--ECLIPSO'S ALRE-- OSSESSED JADE.
W--EED HELP! --YONE?!
SUPERGIRL...
KARA, MY FRIEND...
...I HOPE YOU CAN LOOK AFTER YOURSELF UNTIL WE FIND YOU...

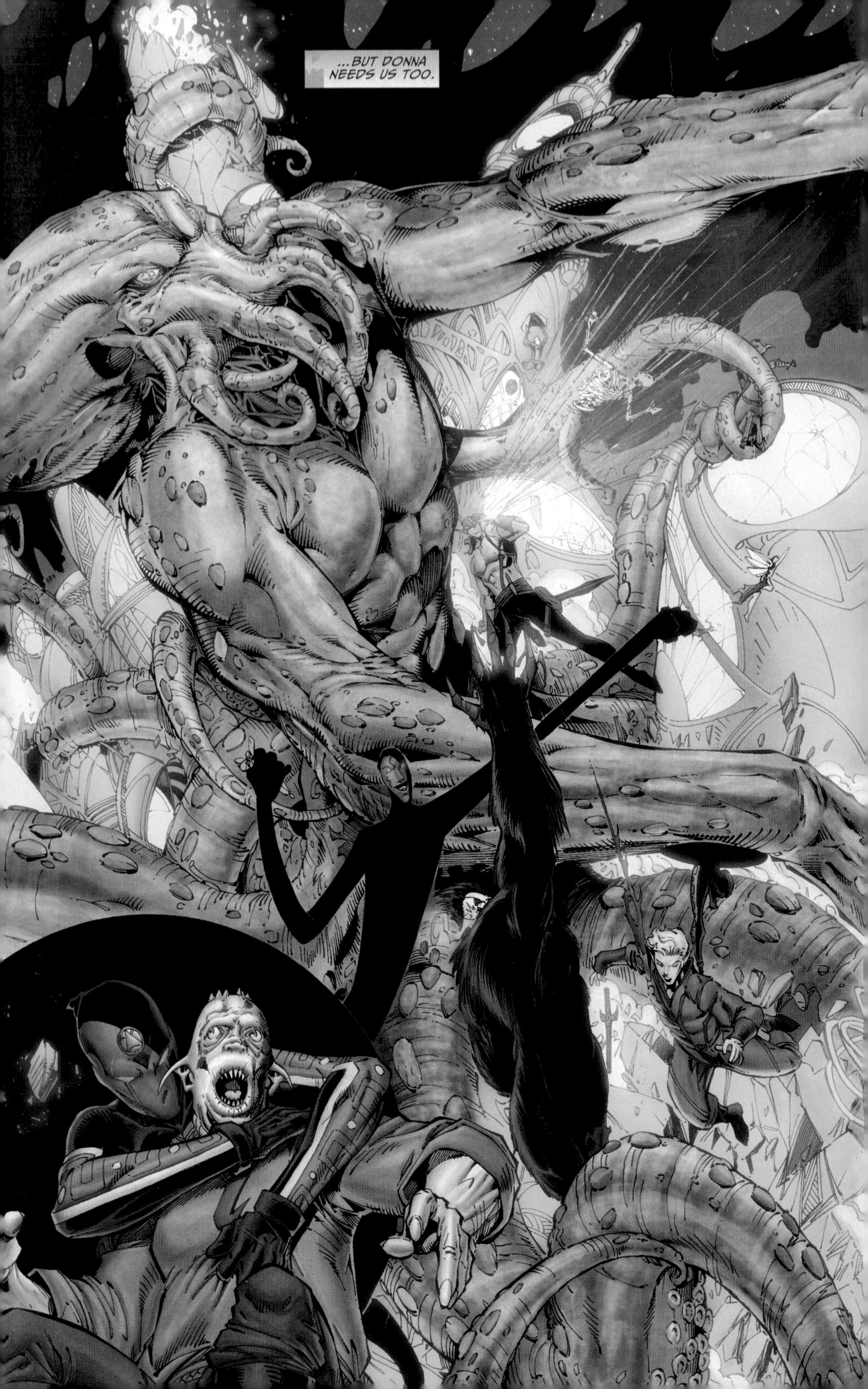
...BUT DONNA NEEDS US TOO.

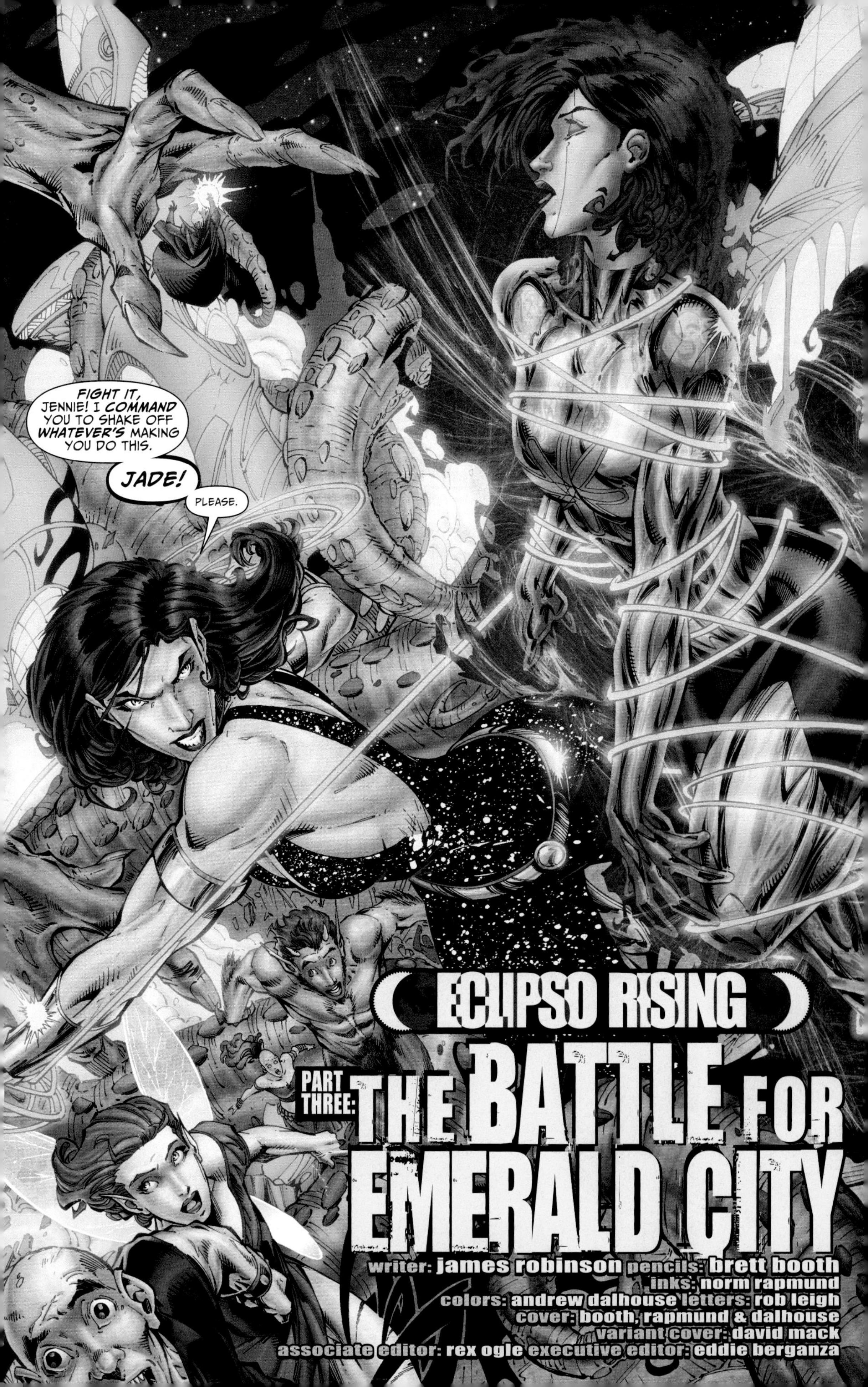

FIGHT IT, JENNIE! I COMMAND YOU TO SHAKE OFF WHATEVER'S MAKING YOU DO THIS.
JADE!
PLEASE.
ECLIPSO RISING
PART THREE: THE BATTLE FOR EMERALD CITY
writer: james robinson pencils: brett booth
inks: norm rapmund
colors: andrew dalhouse letters: rob leigh
cover: booth, rapmund & dalhouse
variant cover: david mack
associate editor: rex ogle executive editor: eddie berganza

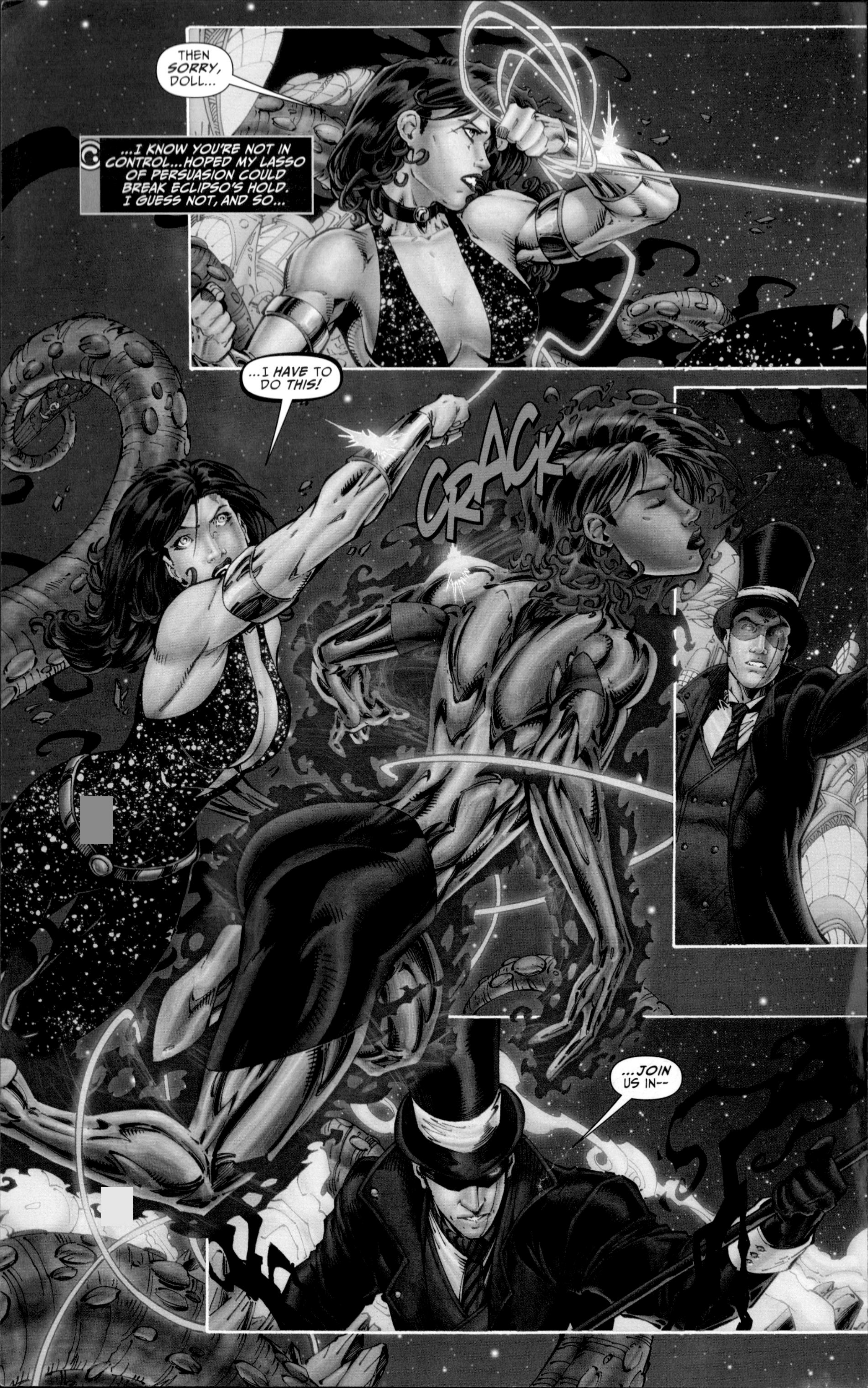

THEN SORRY, DOLL...
...I KNOW YOU'RE NOT IN CONTROL...HOPED MY LASSO OF PERSUASION COULD BREAK ECLIPSO'S HOLD. I GUESS NOT, AND SO...
...I HAVE TO DO THIS!
CRACK
...JOIN US IN--

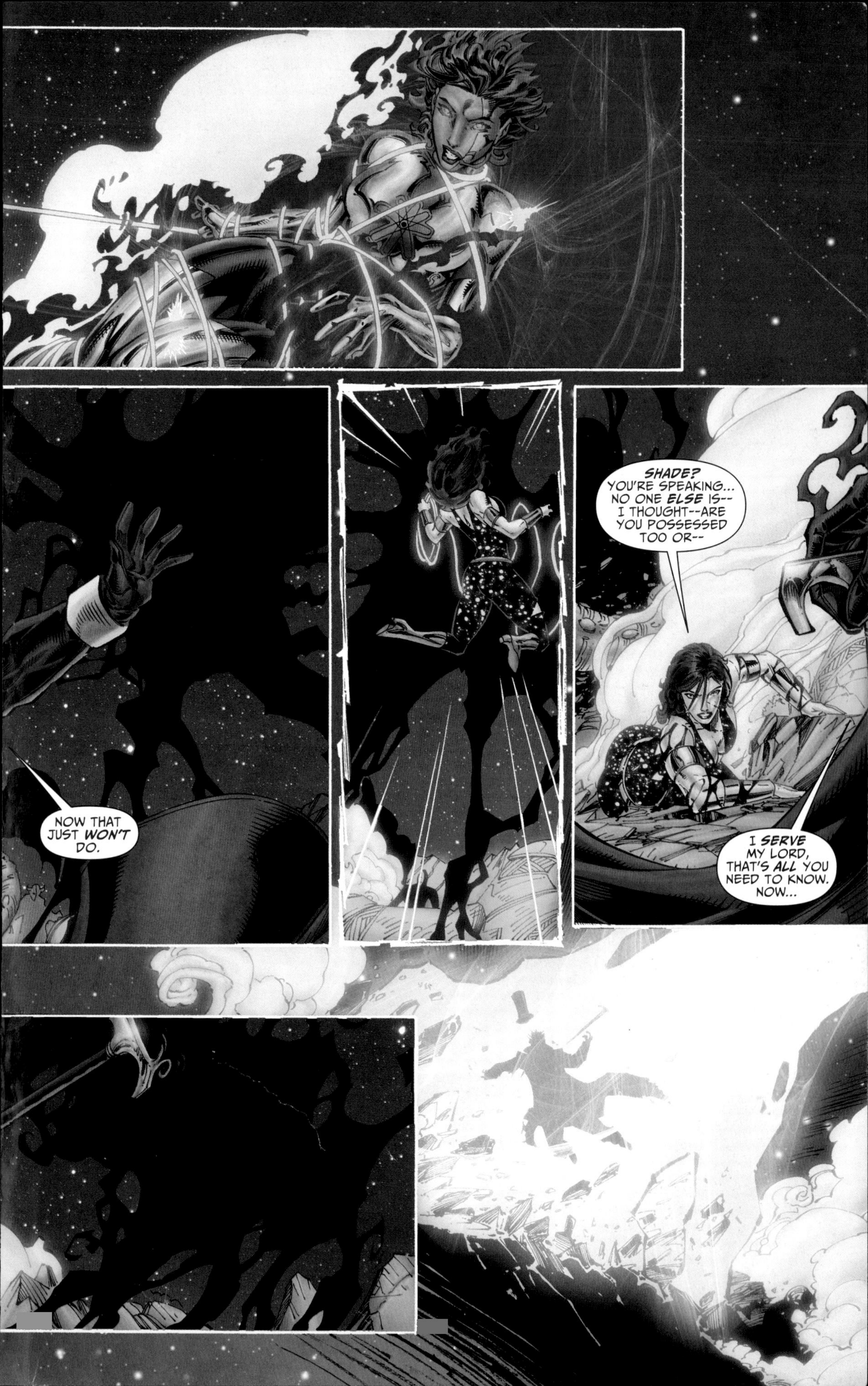
NOW THAT JUST WON'T DO.
SHADE? YOU'RE SPEAKING... NO ONE ELSE IS-- I THOUGHT--ARE YOU POSSESSED TOO OR--
I SERVE MY LORD, THAT'S ALL YOU NEED TO KNOW. NOW...

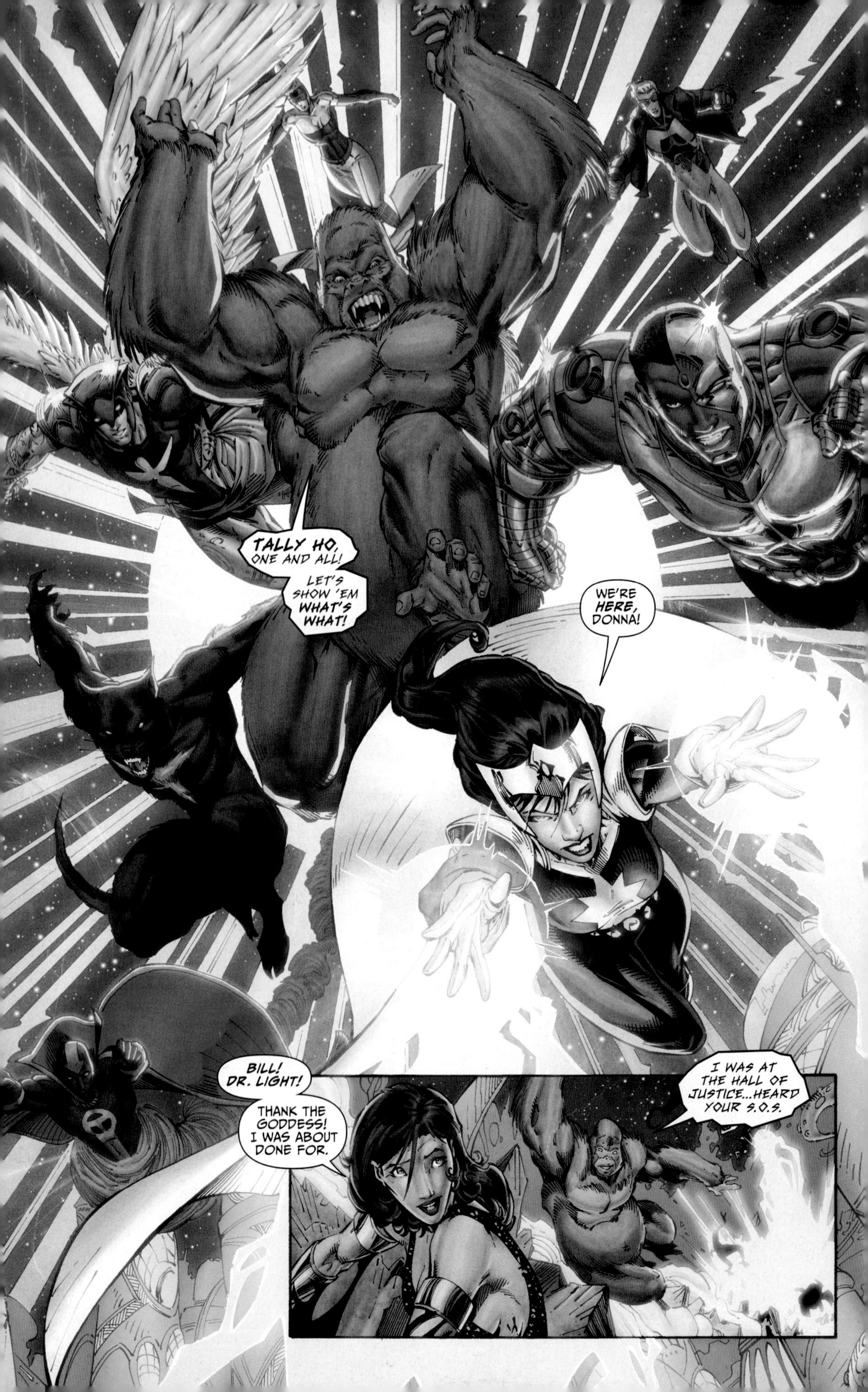
TALLY HO, ONE AND ALL!
LET'S SHOW 'EM WHAT'S WHAT!
WE'RE HERE, DONNA!
BILL! DR. LIGHT!
THANK THE GODDESS! I WAS ABOUT DONE FOR.
I WAS AT THE HALL OF JUSTICE...HEARD YOUR S.O.S.

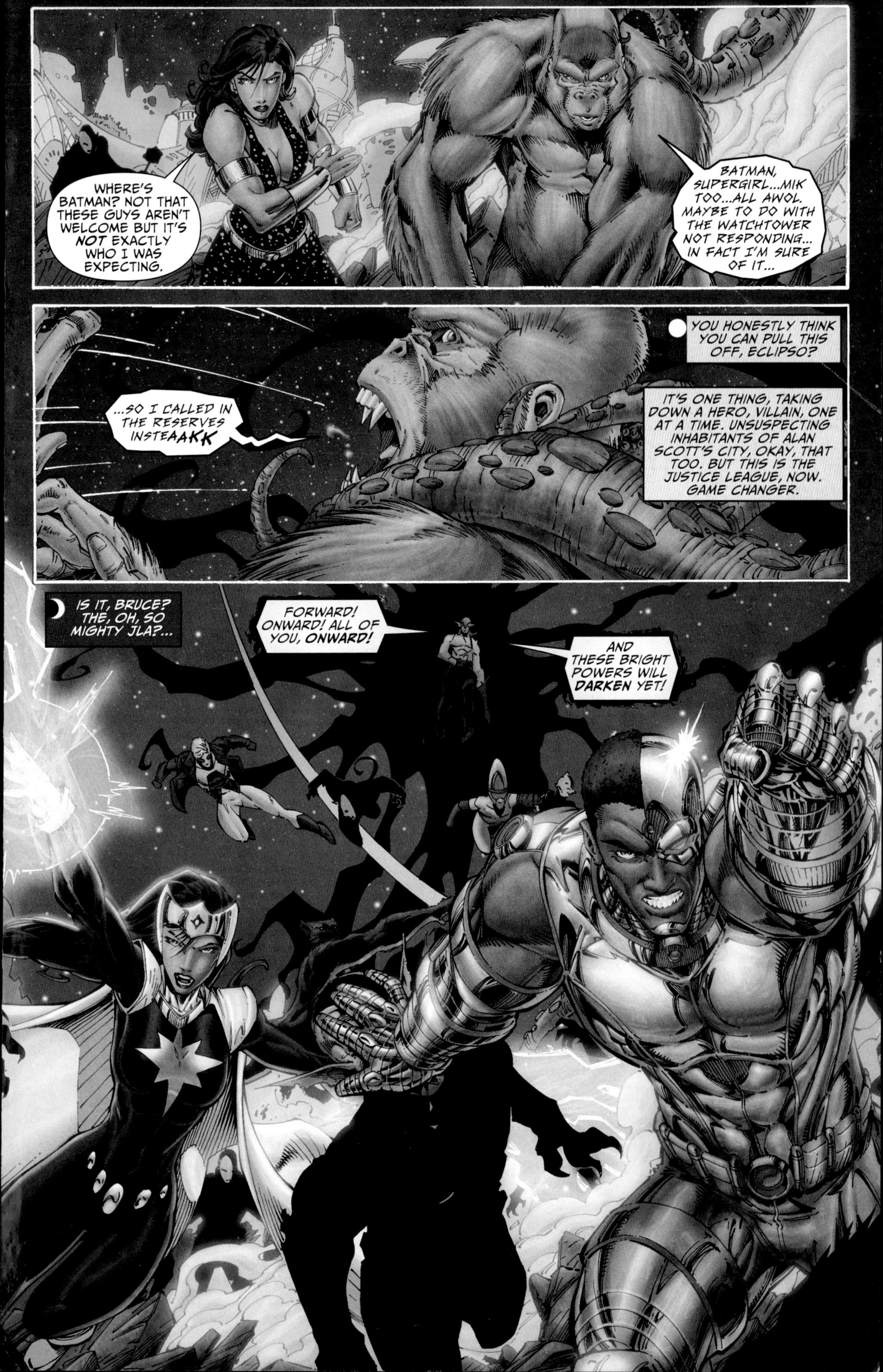
WHERE'S BATMAN? NOT THAT THESE GUYS AREN'T WELCOME BUT IT'S NOT EXACTLY WHO I WAS EXPECTING.
BATMAN, SUPERGIRL...MIK TOO...ALL AWOL. MAYBE TO DO WITH THE WATCHTOWER NOT RESPONDING... IN FACT I'M SURE OF IT...
...SO I CALLED IN THE RESERVES INSTEAAKK
YOU HONESTLY THINK YOU CAN PULL THIS OFF, ECLIPSO?
IT'S ONE THING, TAKING DOWN A HERO, VILLAIN, ONE AT A TIME. UNSUSPECTING INHABITANTS OF ALAN SCOTT'S CITY, OKAY, THAT TOO. BUT THIS IS THE JUSTICE LEAGUE, NOW. GAME CHANGER.
IS IT, BRUCE? THE, OH, SO MIGHTY JLA?...
FORWARD! ONWARD! ALL OF YOU, ONWARD!
AND THESE BRIGHT POWERS WILL DARKEN YET!

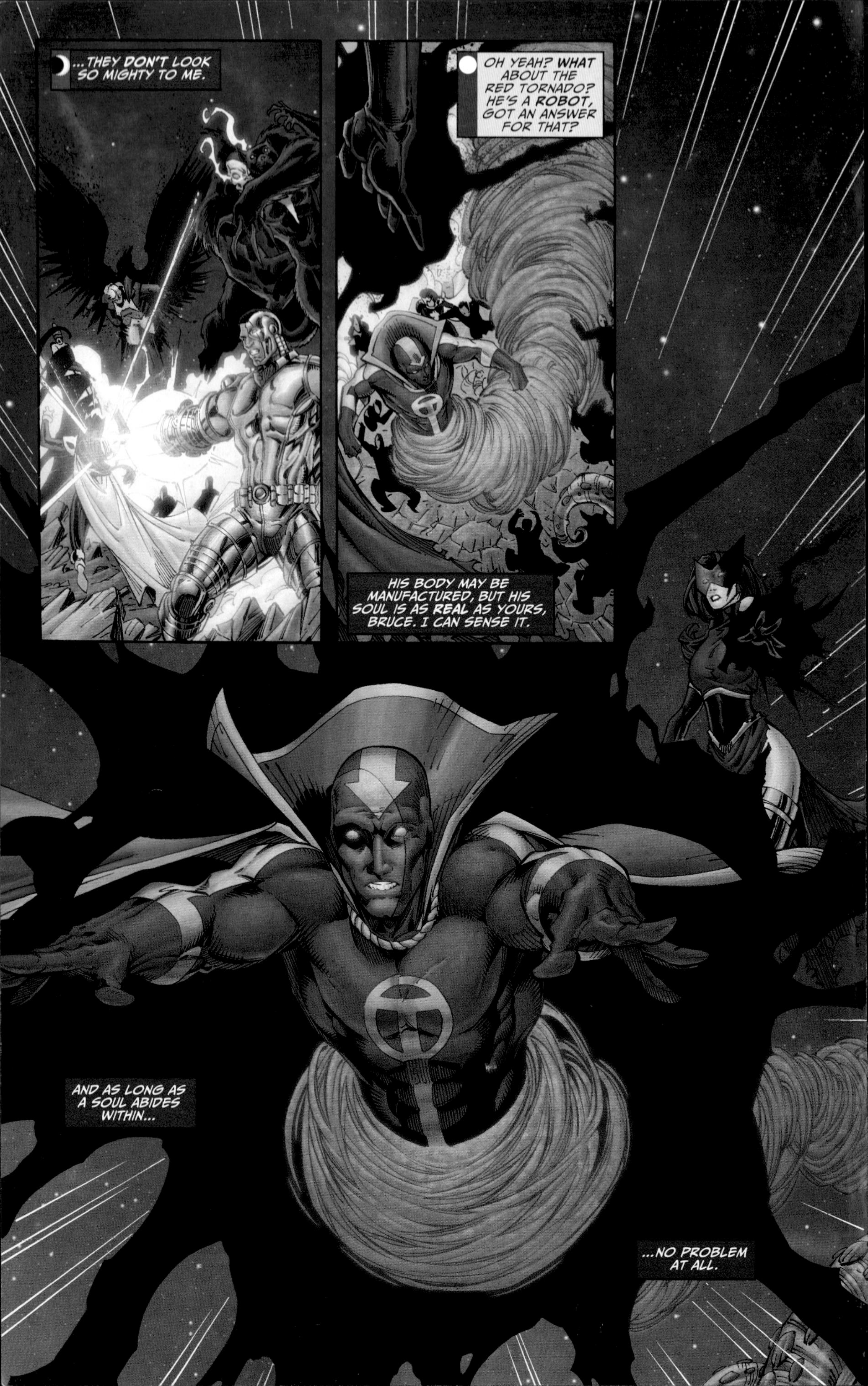
...THEY DON'T LOOK SO MIGHTY TO ME.
OH YEAH? WHAT ABOUT THE RED TORNADO? HE'S A ROBOT, GOT AN ANSWER FOR THAT?
HIS BODY MAY BE MANUFACTURED, BUT HIS SOUL IS AS REAL AS YOURS, BRUCE. I CAN SENSE IT.
AND AS LONG AS A SOUL ABIDES WITHIN...
...NO PROBLEM AT ALL.

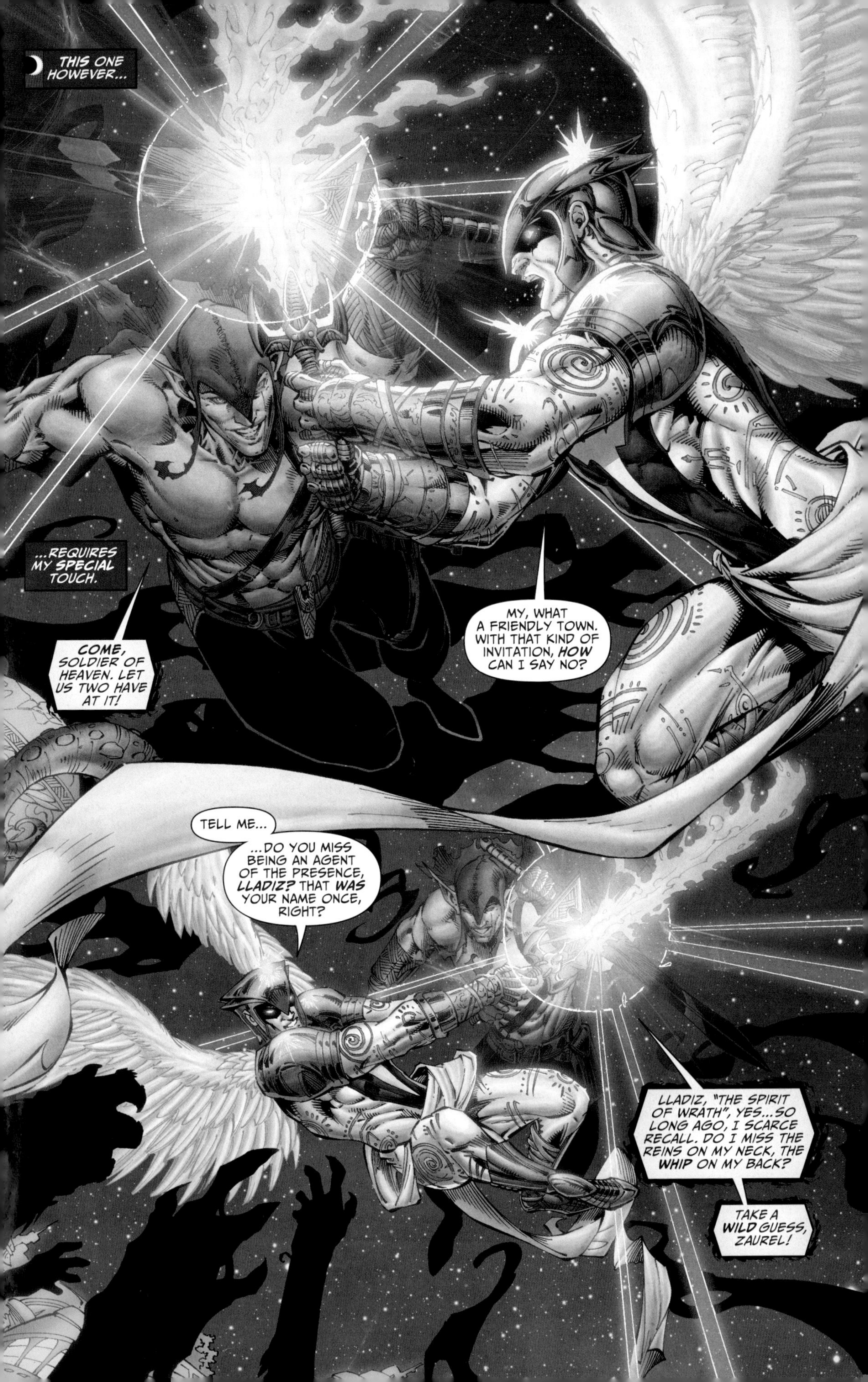

THIS ONE HOWEVER...
...REQUIRES MY SPECIAL TOUCH.
COME, SOLDIER OF HEAVEN. LET US TWO HAVE AT IT!
MY, WHAT A FRIENDLY TOWN. WITH THAT KIND OF INVITATION, HOW CAN I SAY NO?
TELL ME...
...DO YOU MISS BEING AN AGENT OF THE PRESENCE, LLADIZ? THAT WAS YOUR NAME ONCE, RIGHT?
LLADIZ, "THE SPIRIT OF WRATH", YES...SO LONG AGO, I SCARCE RECALL. DO I MISS THE REINS ON MY NECK, THE WHIP ON MY BACK?
TAKE A WILD GUESS, ZAUREL!

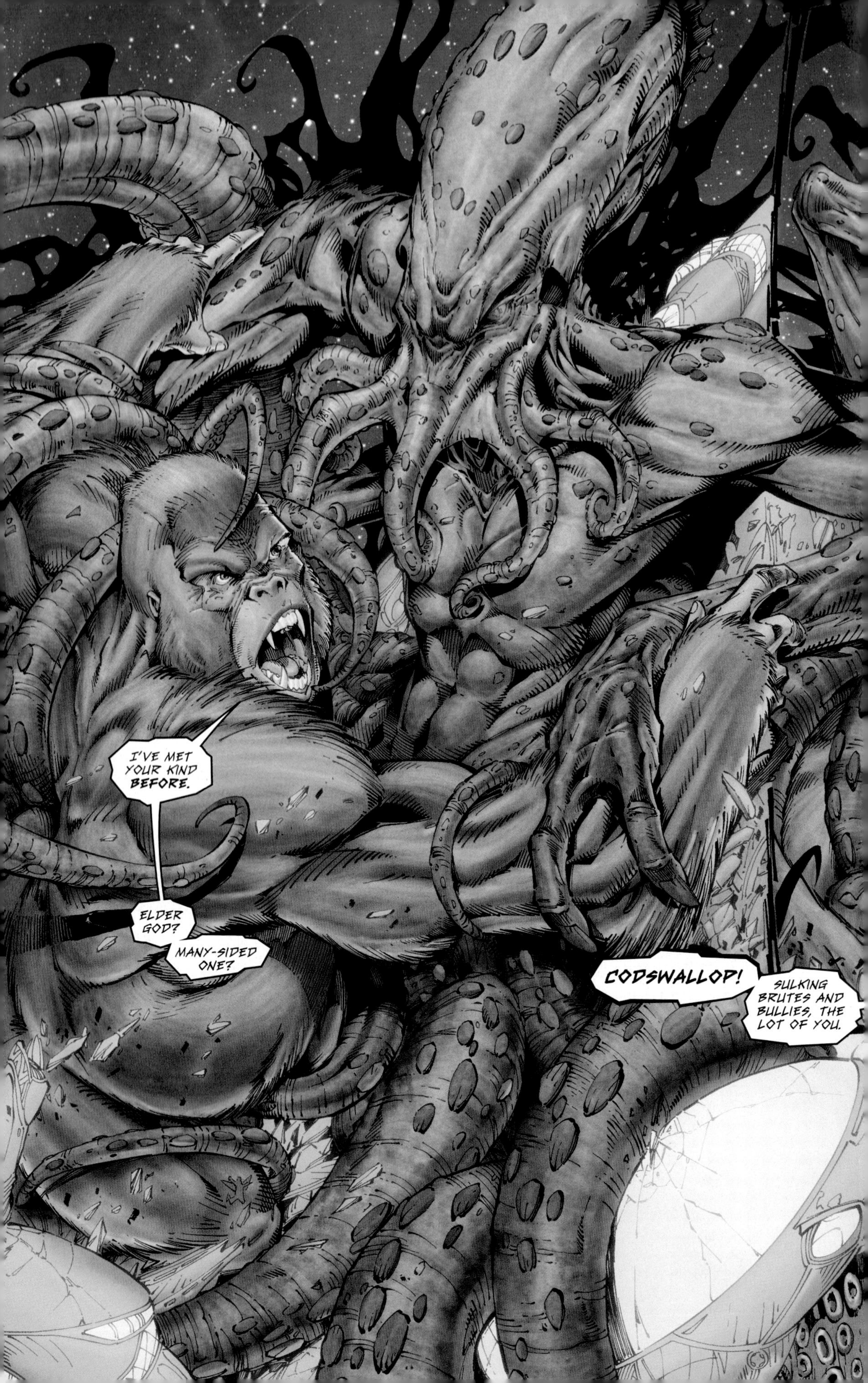
I'VE MET YOUR KIND **BEFORE**.
ELDER GOD?
MANY-SIDED ONE?
CODSWALLOP!
SULKING BRUTES AND BULLIES, THE LOT OF YOU.

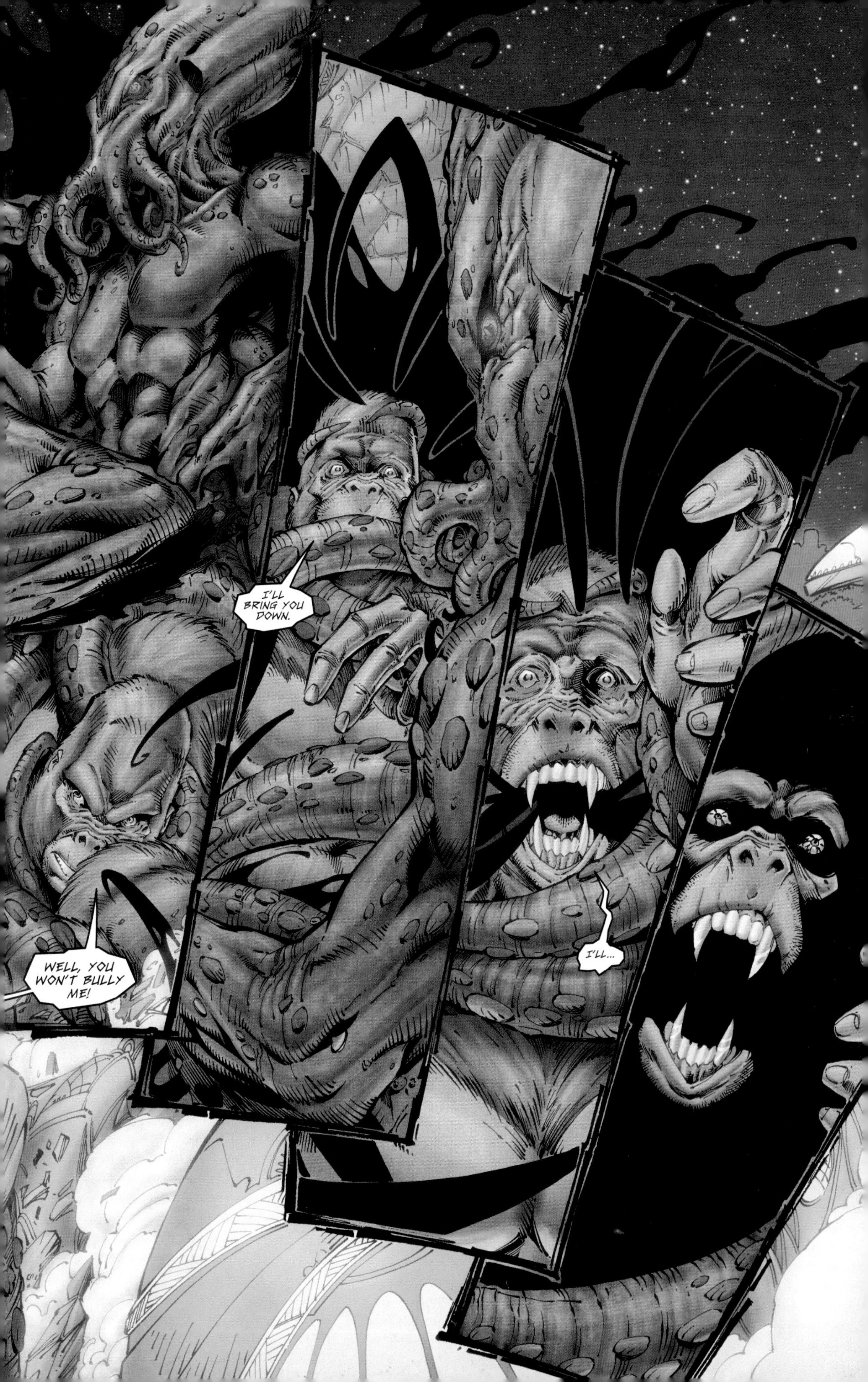
I'LL BRING YOU DOWN.
WELL, YOU WON'T BULLY ME!
I'LL...

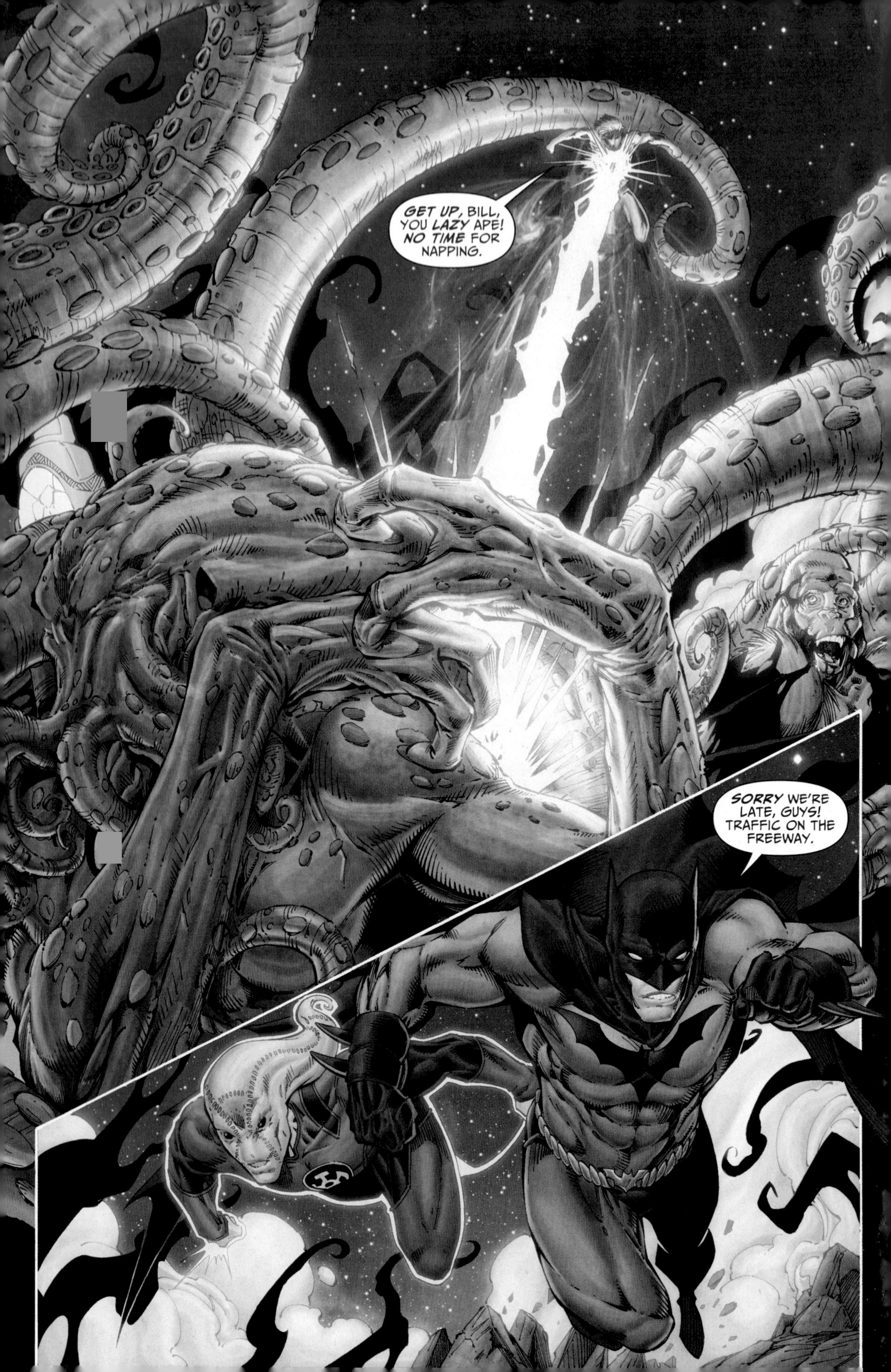
GET UP, BILL, YOU LAZY APE! NO TIME FOR NAPPING.
SORRY WE'RE LATE, GUYS! TRAFFIC ON THE FREEWAY.

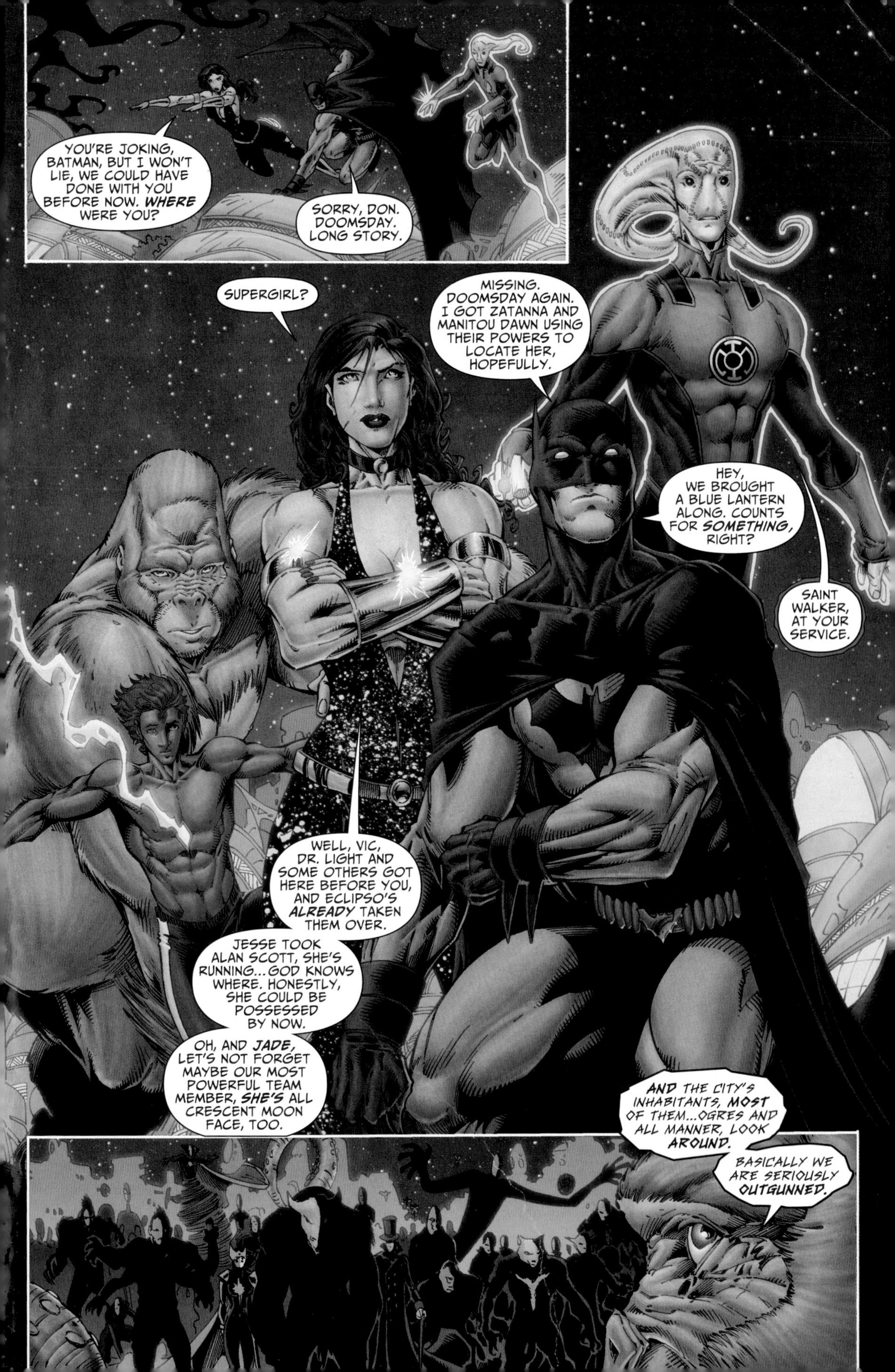
YOU'RE JOKING, BATMAN, BUT I WON'T LIE, WE COULD HAVE DONE WITH YOU BEFORE NOW. WHERE WERE YOU?
SORRY, DON. DOOMSDAY. LONG STORY.
SUPERGIRL?
MISSING. DOOMSDAY AGAIN. I GOT ZATANNA AND MANITOU DAWN USING THEIR POWERS TO LOCATE HER, HOPEFULLY.
HEY, WE BROUGHT A BLUE LANTERN ALONG. COUNTS FOR SOMETHING, RIGHT?
SAINT WALKER, AT YOUR SERVICE.
WELL, VIC, DR. LIGHT AND SOME OTHERS GOT HERE BEFORE YOU, AND ECLIPSO'S ALREADY TAKEN THEM OVER.
JESSE TOOK ALAN SCOTT, SHE'S RUNNING...GOD KNOWS WHERE. HONESTLY, SHE COULD BE POSSESSED BY NOW.
OH, AND JADE, LET'S NOT FORGET MAYBE OUR MOST POWERFUL TEAM MEMBER, SHE'S ALL CRESCENT MOON FACE, TOO.
AND THE CITY'S INHABITANTS, MOST OF THEM...OGRES AND ALL MANNER, LOOK AROUND.
BASICALLY WE ARE SERIOUSLY OUTGUNNED.

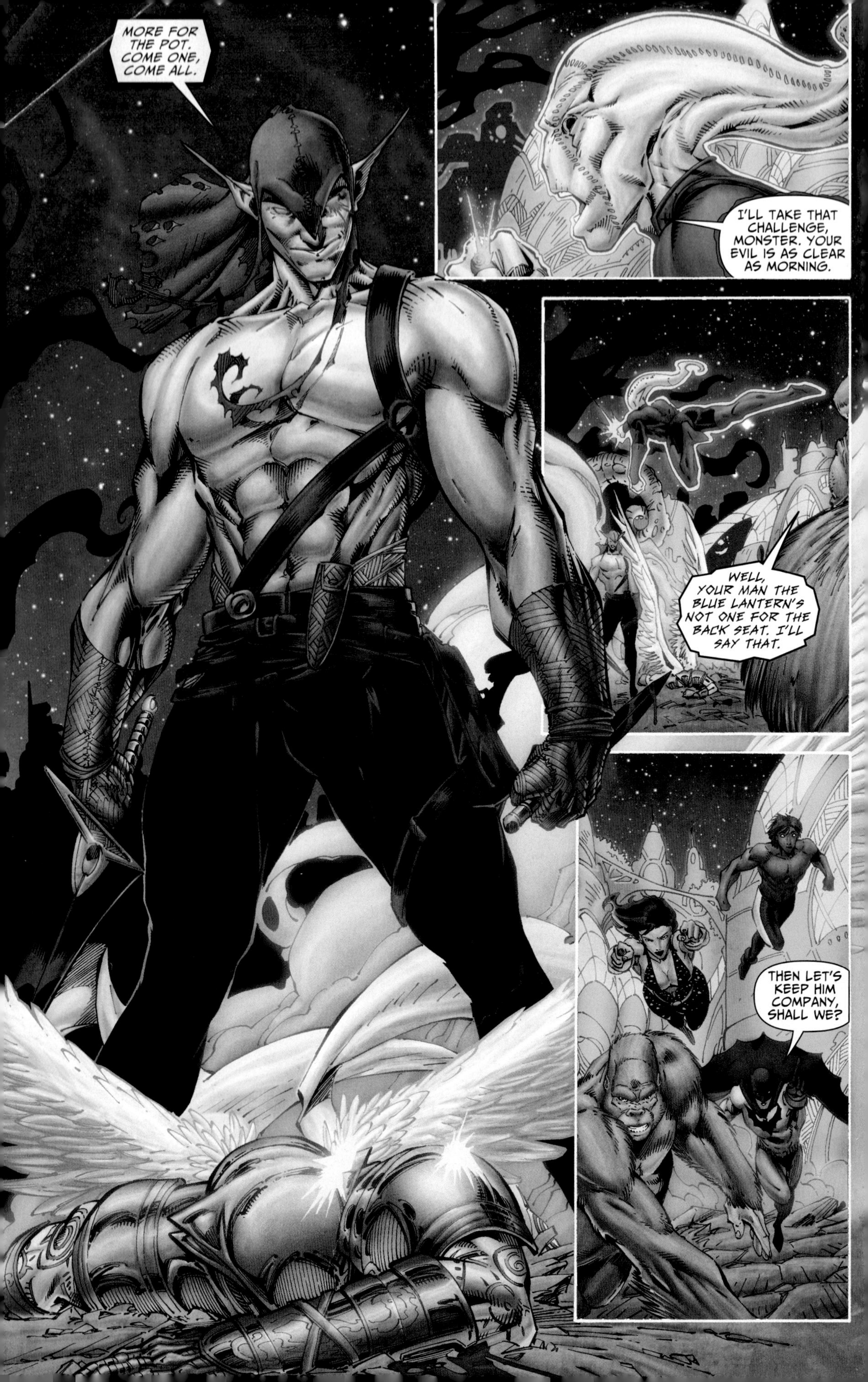
MORE FOR THE POT. COME ONE, COME ALL.
I'LL TAKE THAT CHALLENGE, MONSTER. YOUR EVIL IS AS CLEAR AS MORNING.
WELL, YOUR MAN THE BLUE LANTERN'S NOT ONE FOR THE BACK SEAT. I'LL SAY THAT.
THEN LET'S KEEP HIM COMPANY, SHALL WE?

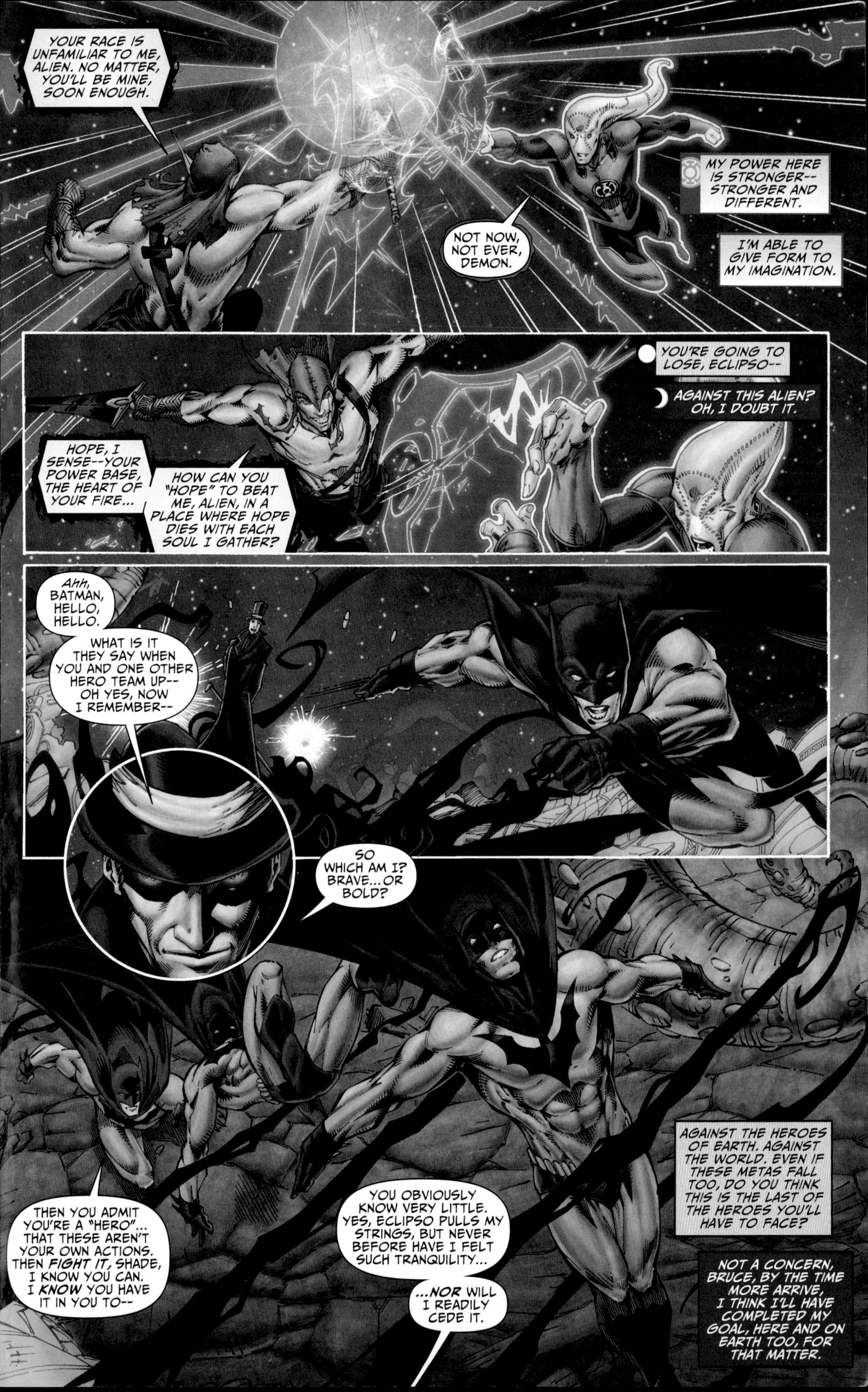
YOUR RACE IS UNFAMILIAR TO ME, ALIEN. NO MATTER, YOU'LL BE MINE, SOON ENOUGH.
NOT NOW, NOT EVER, DEMON.
MY POWER HERE IS STRONGER-- STRONGER AND DIFFERENT.
I'M ABLE TO GIVE FORM TO MY IMAGINATION.
YOU'RE GOING TO LOSE, ECLIPSO--
AGAINST THIS ALIEN? OH, I DOUBT IT.
HOPE, I SENSE--YOUR POWER BASE, THE HEART OF YOUR FIRE...
HOW CAN YOU "HOPE" TO BEAT ME, ALIEN, IN A PLACE WHERE HOPE DIES WITH EACH SOUL I GATHER?
Ahh, BATMAN, HELLO, HELLO.
WHAT IS IT THEY SAY WHEN YOU AND ONE OTHER HERO TEAM UP-- OH YES, NOW I REMEMBER--
SO WHICH AM I? BRAVE...OR BOLD?
THEN YOU ADMIT YOU'RE A "HERO"... THAT THESE AREN'T YOUR OWN ACTIONS. THEN FIGHT IT, SHADE, I KNOW YOU CAN. I KNOW YOU HAVE IT IN YOU TO--
YOU OBVIOUSLY KNOW VERY LITTLE. YES, ECLIPSO PULLS MY STRINGS, BUT NEVER BEFORE HAVE I FELT SUCH TRANQUILITY...
...NOR WILL I READILY CEDE IT.
AGAINST THE HEROES OF EARTH. AGAINST THE WORLD. EVEN IF THESE METAS FALL TOO, DO YOU THINK THIS IS THE LAST OF THE HEROES YOU'LL HAVE TO FACE?
NOT A CONCERN, BRUCE, BY THE TIME MORE ARRIVE, I THINK I'LL HAVE COMPLETED MY GOAL, HERE AND ON EARTH TOO, FOR THAT MATTER.

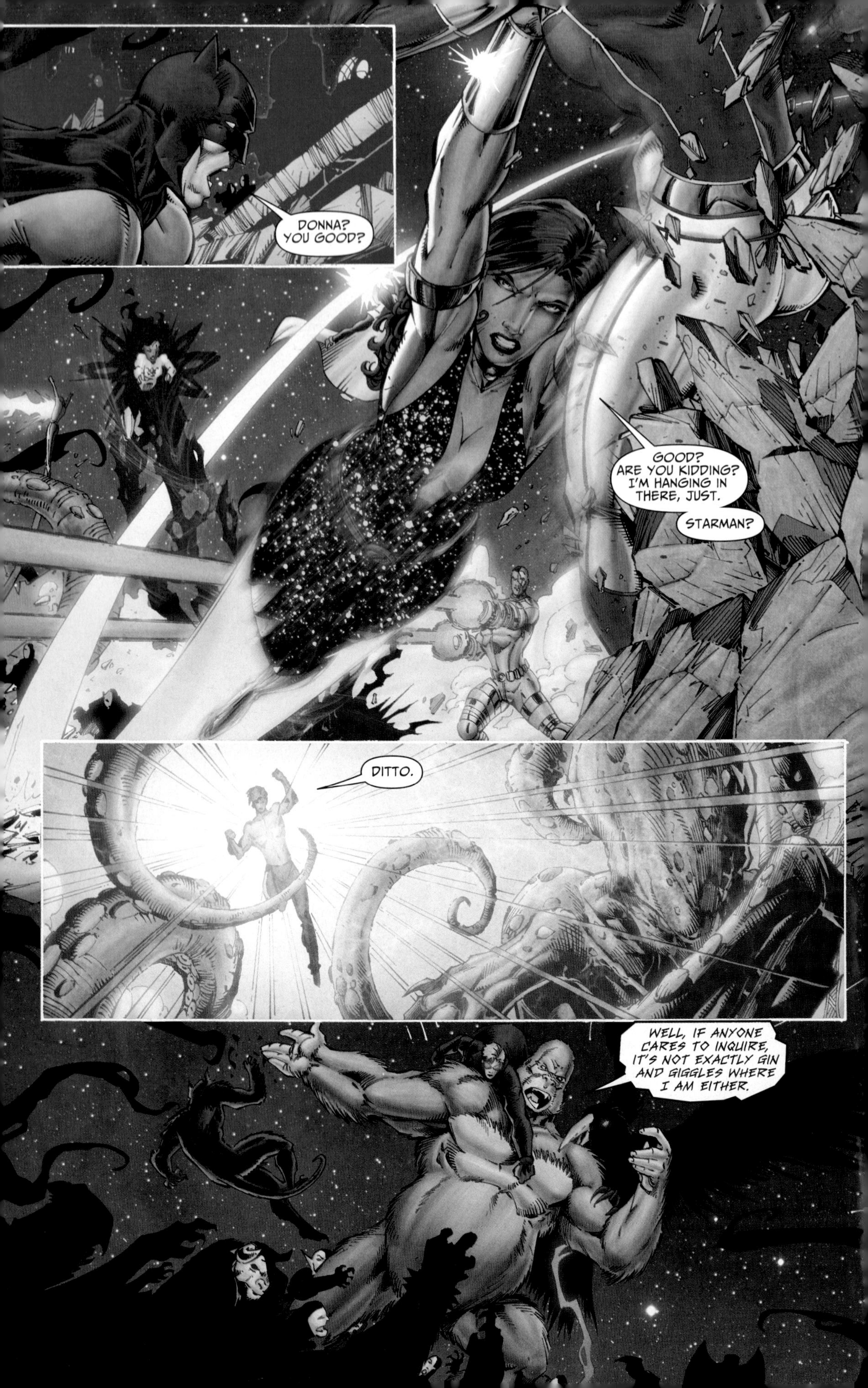
DONNA? YOU GOOD?
GOOD? ARE YOU KIDDING? I'M HANGING IN THERE, JUST.
STARMAN?
DITTO.
WELL, IF ANYONE CARES TO INQUIRE, IT'S NOT EXACTLY GIN AND GIGGLES WHERE I AM EITHER.

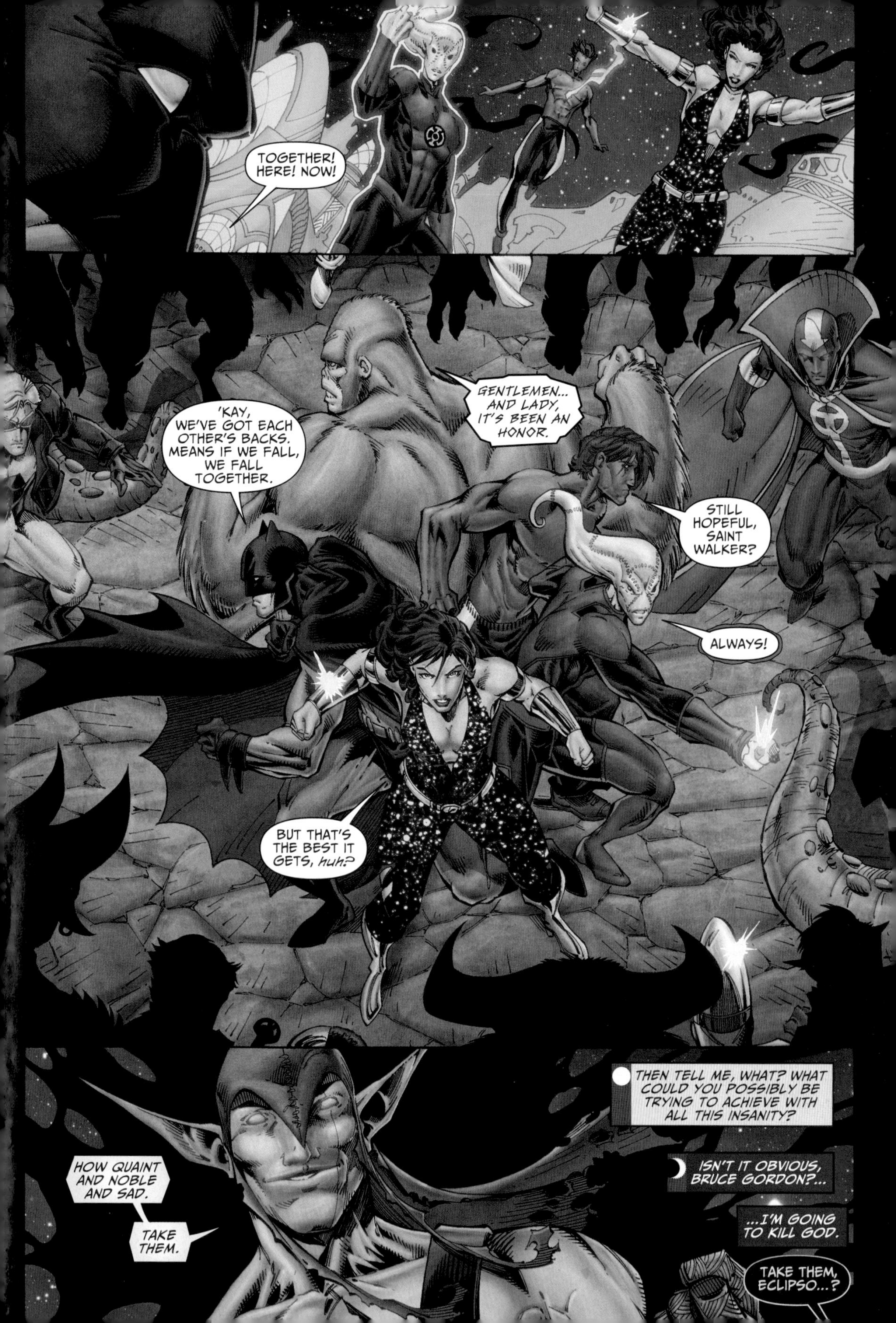
TOGETHER! HERE! NOW!
GENTLEMEN... AND LADY, IT'S BEEN AN HONOR.
'KAY, WE'VE GOT EACH OTHER'S BACKS. MEANS IF WE FALL, WE FALL TOGETHER.
STILL HOPEFUL, SAINT WALKER?
ALWAYS!
BUT THAT'S THE BEST IT GETS, huh?
THEN TELL ME, WHAT? WHAT COULD YOU POSSIBLY BE TRYING TO ACHIEVE WITH ALL THIS INSANITY?
ISN'T IT OBVIOUS, BRUCE GORDON?...
...I'M GOING TO KILL GOD.
HOW QUAINT AND NOBLE AND SAD.
TAKE THEM.
TAKE THEM, ECLIPSO...?

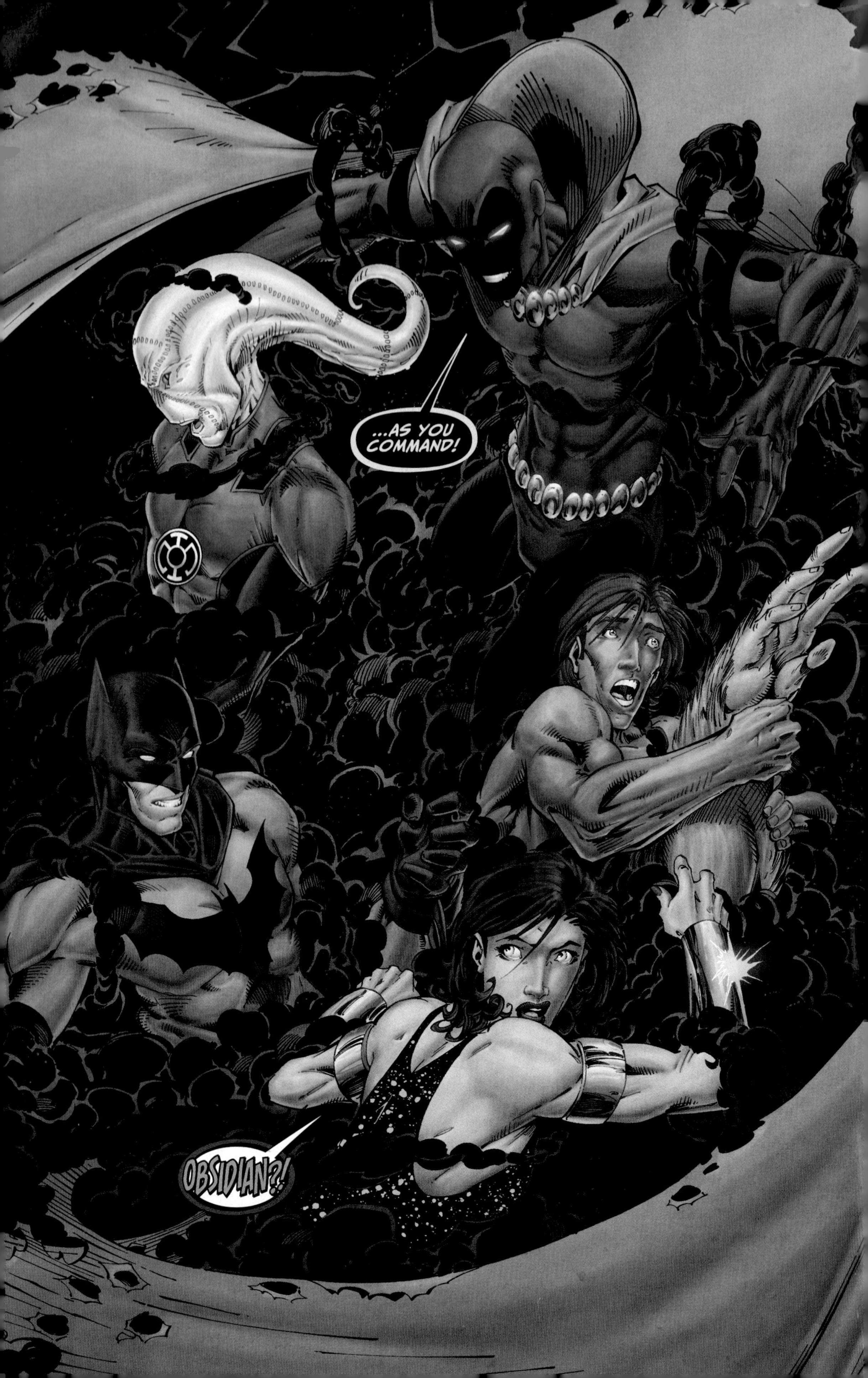
...AS YOU COMMAND!
OBSIDIAN?!

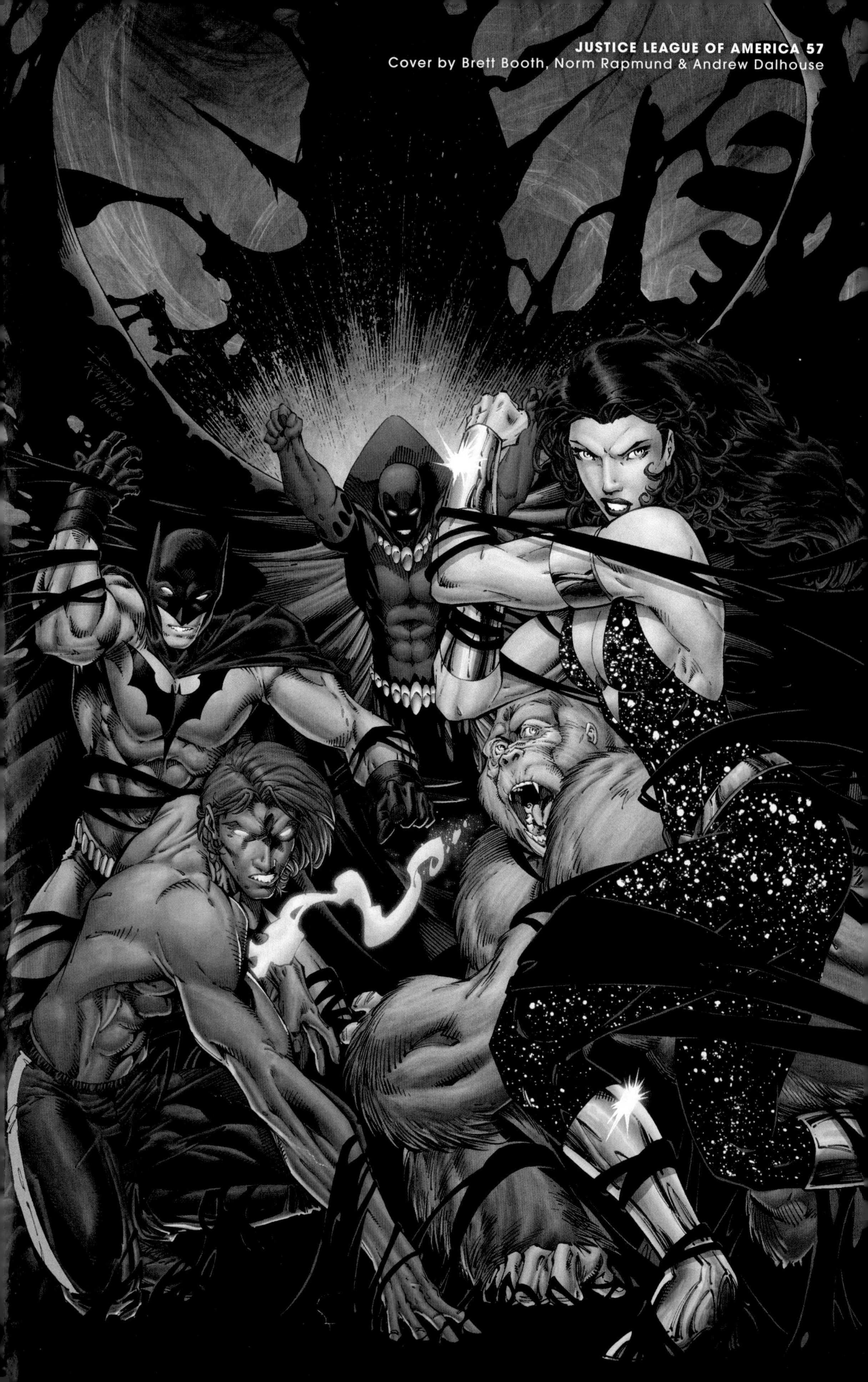

JUSTICE LEAGUE OF AMERICA 57
Cover by Brett Booth, Norm Rapmund & Andrew Dalhouse

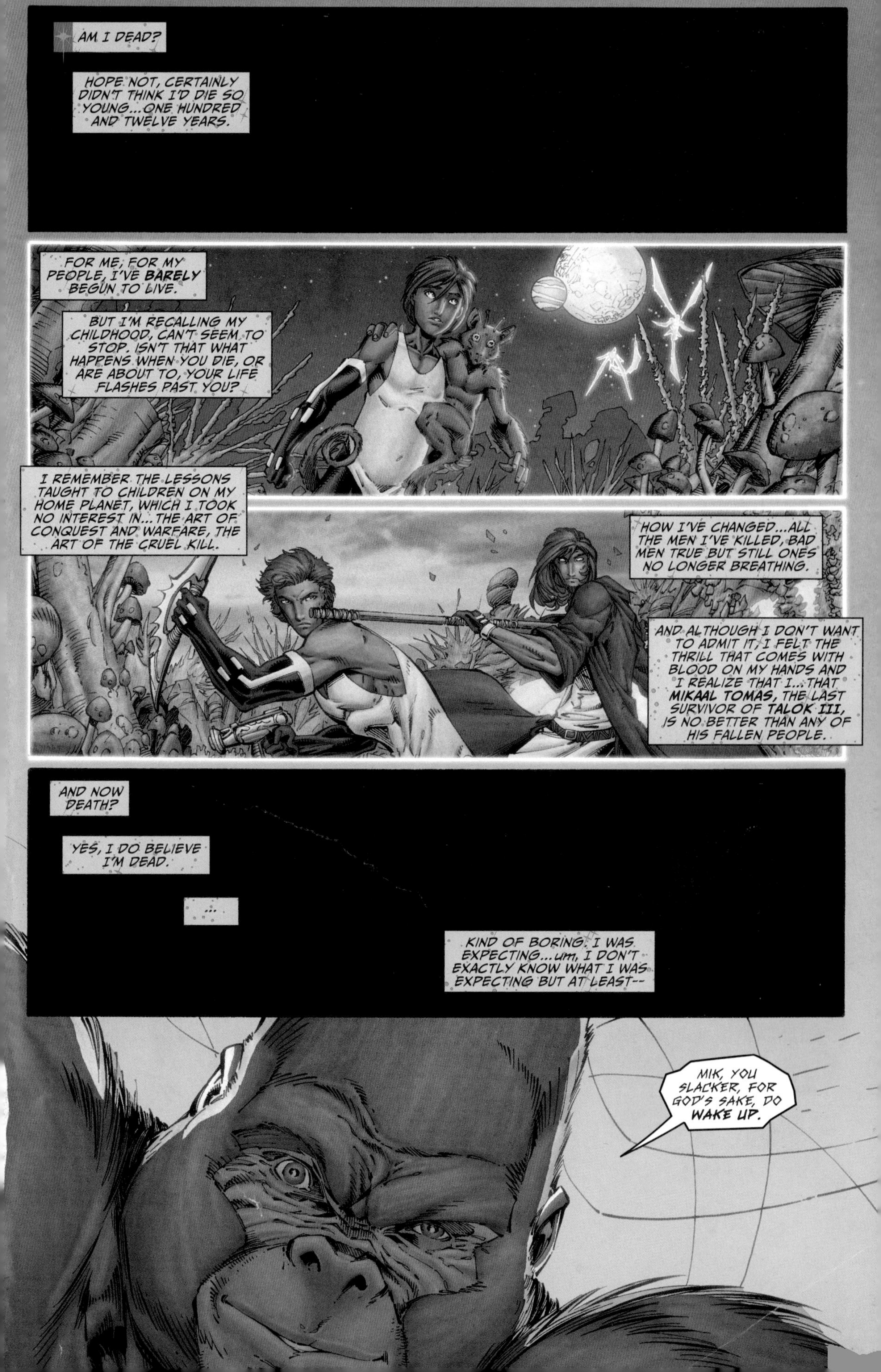
AM I DEAD?
HOPE NOT, CERTAINLY DIDN'T THINK I'D DIE SO YOUNG...ONE HUNDRED AND TWELVE YEARS.
FOR ME, FOR MY PEOPLE, I'VE BARELY BEGUN TO LIVE.
BUT I'M RECALLING MY CHILDHOOD, CAN'T SEEM TO STOP. ISN'T THAT WHAT HAPPENS WHEN YOU DIE, OR ARE ABOUT TO, YOUR LIFE FLASHES PAST YOU?
I REMEMBER THE LESSONS TAUGHT TO CHILDREN ON MY HOME PLANET, WHICH I TOOK NO INTEREST IN...THE ART OF CONQUEST AND WARFARE, THE ART OF THE CRUEL KILL.
HOW I'VE CHANGED...ALL THE MEN I'VE KILLED, BAD MEN TRUE BUT STILL ONES NO LONGER BREATHING.
AND ALTHOUGH I DON'T WANT TO ADMIT IT, I FELT THE THRILL THAT COMES WITH BLOOD ON MY HANDS AND I REALIZE THAT I...THAT MIKAAL TOMAS, THE LAST SURVIVOR OF TALOK III, IS NO BETTER THAN ANY OF HIS FALLEN PEOPLE.
AND NOW DEATH?
YES, I DO BELIEVE I'M DEAD.
...
KIND OF BORING. I WAS EXPECTING...um, I DON'T EXACTLY KNOW WHAT I WAS EXPECTING BUT AT LEAST--
MIK, YOU SLACKER, FOR GOD'S SAKE, DO WAKE UP.

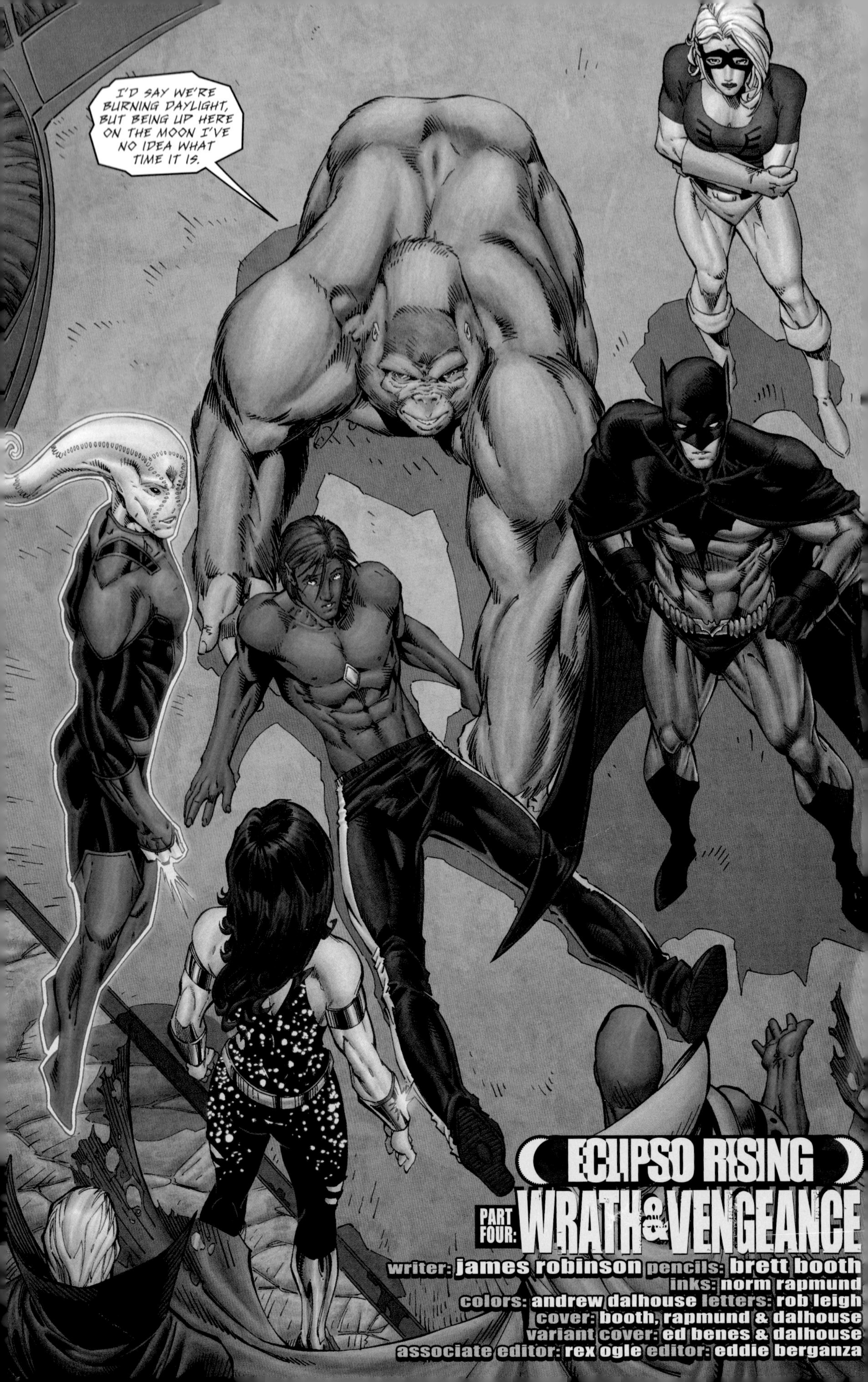
I'D SAY WE'RE BURNING DAYLIGHT, BUT BEING UP HERE ON THE MOON I'VE NO IDEA WHAT TIME IT IS.
ECLIPSO RISING
PART FOUR: WRATH & VENGEANCE
writer: james robinson pencils: brett booth
inks: norm rapmund
colors: andrew dalhouse letters: rob leigh
cover: booth, rapmund & dalhouse
variant cover: ed benes & dalhouse
associate editor: rex ogle editor: eddie berganza

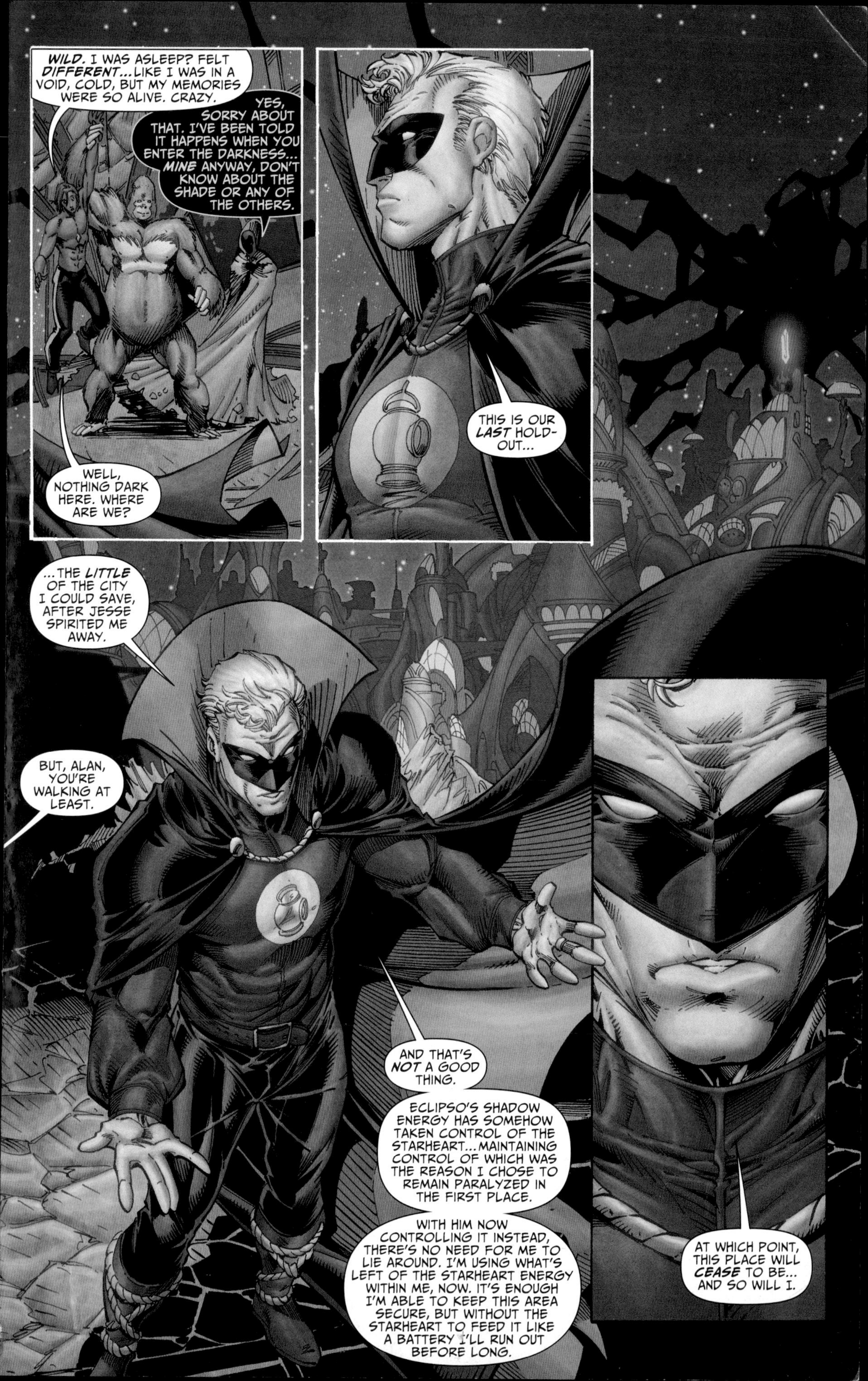
WILD. I WAS ASLEEP? FELT DIFFERENT...LIKE I WAS IN A VOID, COLD, BUT MY MEMORIES WERE SO ALIVE. CRAZY.
YES, SORRY ABOUT THAT. I'VE BEEN TOLD IT HAPPENS WHEN YOU ENTER THE DARKNESS... MINE ANYWAY, DON'T KNOW ABOUT THE SHADE OR ANY OF THE OTHERS.
WELL, NOTHING DARK HERE. WHERE ARE WE?
THIS IS OUR LAST HOLD-OUT...
...THE LITTLE OF THE CITY I COULD SAVE, AFTER JESSE SPIRITED ME AWAY.
BUT, ALAN, YOU'RE WALKING AT LEAST.
AND THAT'S NOT A GOOD THING.
ECLIPSO'S SHADOW ENERGY HAS SOMEHOW TAKEN CONTROL OF THE STARHEART...MAINTAINING CONTROL OF WHICH WAS THE REASON I CHOSE TO REMAIN PARALYZED IN THE FIRST PLACE.
WITH HIM NOW CONTROLLING IT INSTEAD, THERE'S NO NEED FOR ME TO LIE AROUND. I'M USING WHAT'S LEFT OF THE STARHEART ENERGY WITHIN ME, NOW. IT'S ENOUGH I'M ABLE TO KEEP THIS AREA SECURE, BUT WITHOUT THE STARHEART TO FEED IT LIKE A BATTERY I'LL RUN OUT BEFORE LONG.
AT WHICH POINT, THIS PLACE WILL CEASE TO BE... AND SO WILL I.

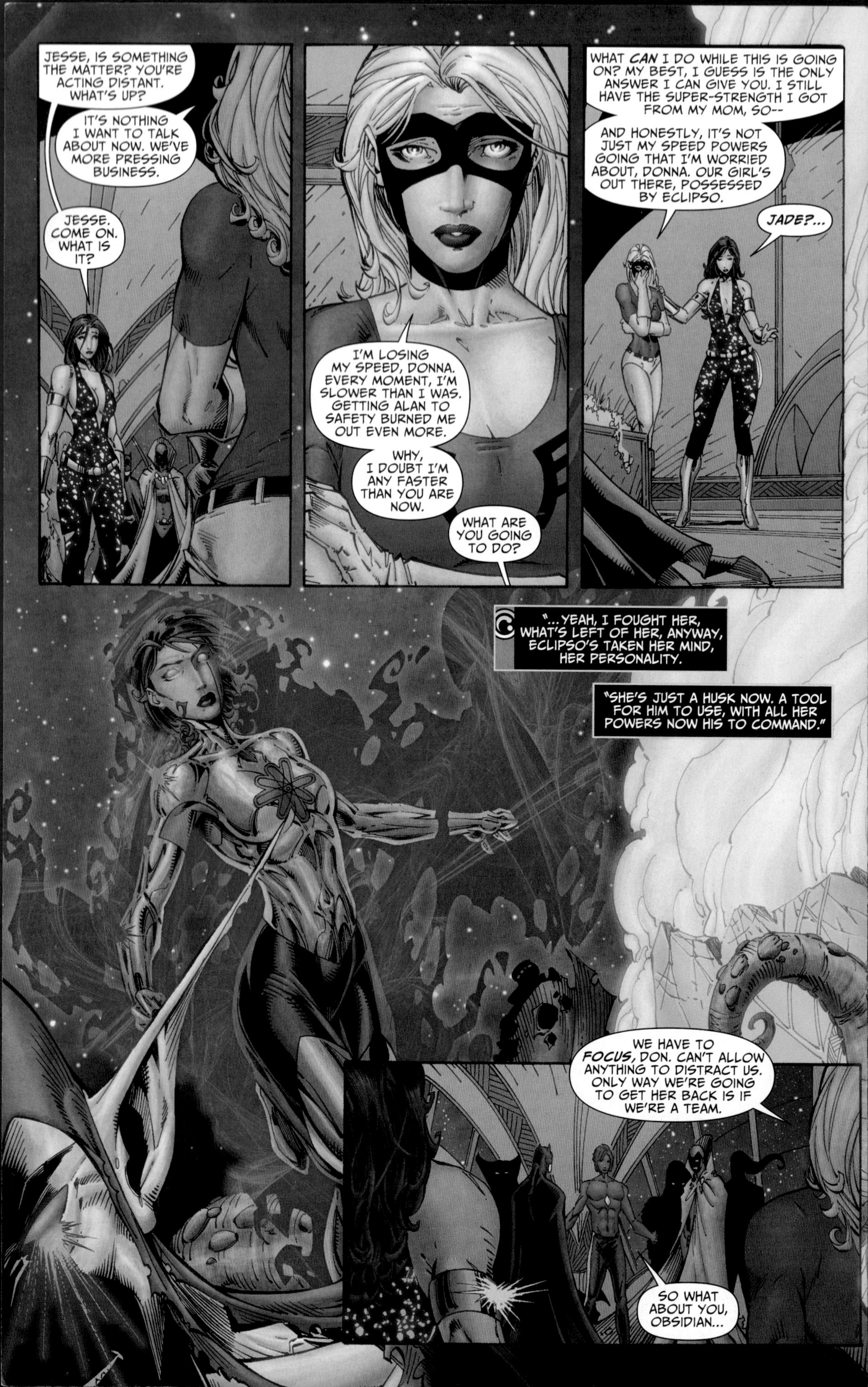

JESSE, IS SOMETHING THE MATTER? YOU'RE ACTING DISTANT. WHAT'S UP?
IT'S NOTHING I WANT TO TALK ABOUT NOW. WE'VE MORE PRESSING BUSINESS.
JESSE. COME ON. WHAT IS IT?
I'M LOSING MY SPEED, DONNA. EVERY MOMENT, I'M SLOWER THAN I WAS. GETTING ALAN TO SAFETY BURNED ME OUT EVEN MORE.
WHY, I DOUBT I'M ANY FASTER THAN YOU ARE NOW.
WHAT ARE YOU GOING TO DO?
WHAT CAN I DO WHILE THIS IS GOING ON? MY BEST, I GUESS IS THE ONLY ANSWER I CAN GIVE YOU. I STILL HAVE THE SUPER-STRENGTH I GOT FROM MY MOM, SO--
AND HONESTLY, IT'S NOT JUST MY SPEED POWERS GOING THAT I'M WORRIED ABOUT, DONNA. OUR GIRL'S OUT THERE, POSSESSED BY ECLIPSO.
JADE?...
"...YEAH, I FOUGHT HER, WHAT'S LEFT OF HER, ANYWAY, ECLIPSO'S TAKEN HER MIND, HER PERSONALITY.
"SHE'S JUST A HUSK NOW. A TOOL FOR HIM TO USE, WITH ALL HER POWERS NOW HIS TO COMMAND."
WE HAVE TO FOCUS, DON. CAN'T ALLOW ANYTHING TO DISTRACT US. ONLY WAY WE'RE GOING TO GET HER BACK IS IF WE'RE A TEAM.
SO WHAT ABOUT YOU, OBSIDIAN...

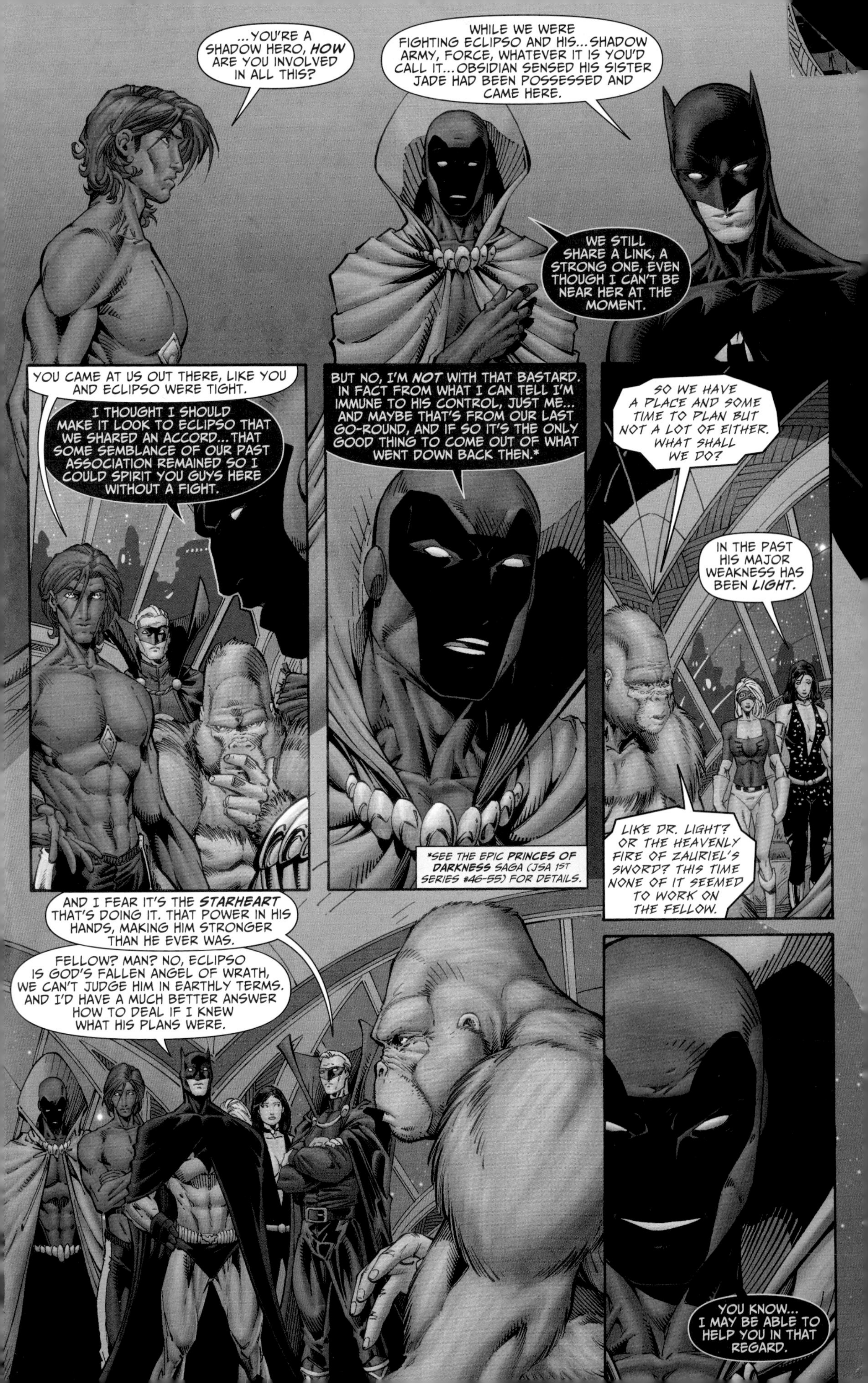
...YOU'RE A SHADOW HERO, HOW ARE YOU INVOLVED IN ALL THIS?
WHILE WE WERE FIGHTING ECLIPSO AND HIS...SHADOW ARMY, FORCE, WHATEVER IT IS YOU'D CALL IT...OBSIDIAN SENSED HIS SISTER JADE HAD BEEN POSSESSED AND CAME HERE.
WE STILL SHARE A LINK, A STRONG ONE, EVEN THOUGH I CAN'T BE NEAR HER AT THE MOMENT.
YOU CAME AT US OUT THERE, LIKE YOU AND ECLIPSO WERE TIGHT.
I THOUGHT I SHOULD MAKE IT LOOK TO ECLIPSO THAT WE SHARED AN ACCORD...THAT SOME SEMBLANCE OF OUR PAST ASSOCIATION REMAINED SO I COULD SPIRIT YOU GUYS HERE WITHOUT A FIGHT.
BUT NO, I'M NOT WITH THAT BASTARD. IN FACT FROM WHAT I CAN TELL I'M IMMUNE TO HIS CONTROL, JUST ME... AND MAYBE THAT'S FROM OUR LAST GO-ROUND, AND IF SO IT'S THE ONLY GOOD THING TO COME OUT OF WHAT WENT DOWN BACK THEN.*
*SEE THE EPIC PRINCES OF DARKNESS SAGA (JSA 1ST SERIES #46-55) FOR DETAILS.
SO WE HAVE A PLACE AND SOME TIME TO PLAN BUT NOT A LOT OF EITHER. WHAT SHALL WE DO?
IN THE PAST HIS MAJOR WEAKNESS HAS BEEN LIGHT.
LIKE DR. LIGHT? OR THE HEAVENLY FIRE OF ZAURIEL'S SWORD? THIS TIME NONE OF IT SEEMED TO WORK ON THE FELLOW.
AND I FEAR IT'S THE STARHEART THAT'S DOING IT. THAT POWER IN HIS HANDS, MAKING HIM STRONGER THAN HE EVER WAS.
FELLOW? MAN? NO, ECLIPSO IS GOD'S FALLEN ANGEL OF WRATH, WE CAN'T JUDGE HIM IN EARTHLY TERMS. AND I'D HAVE A MUCH BETTER ANSWER HOW TO DEAL IF I KNEW WHAT HIS PLANS WERE.
YOU KNOW... I MAY BE ABLE TO HELP YOU IN THAT REGARD.

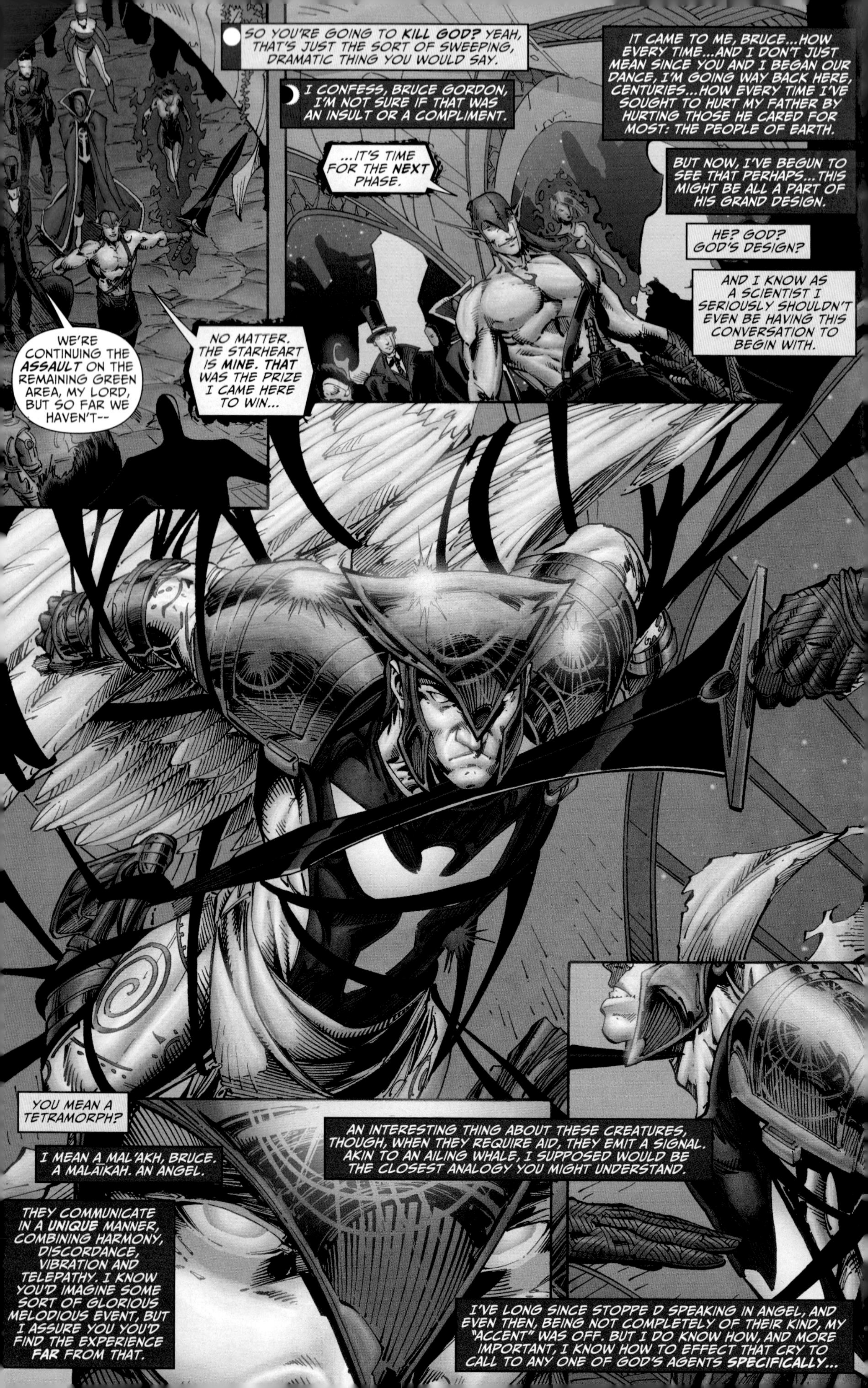

SO YOU'RE GOING TO KILL GOD? YEAH, THAT'S JUST THE SORT OF SWEEPING, DRAMATIC THING YOU WOULD SAY.
I CONFESS, BRUCE GORDON, I'M NOT SURE IF THAT WAS AN INSULT OR A COMPLIMENT.
IT CAME TO ME, BRUCE...HOW EVERY TIME...AND I DON'T JUST MEAN SINCE YOU AND I BEGAN OUR DANCE, I'M GOING WAY BACK HERE, CENTURIES...HOW EVERY TIME I'VE SOUGHT TO HURT MY FATHER BY HURTING THOSE HE CARED FOR MOST: THE PEOPLE OF EARTH.
BUT NOW, I'VE BEGUN TO SEE THAT PERHAPS...THIS MIGHT BE ALL A PART OF HIS GRAND DESIGN.
HE? GOD? GOD'S DESIGN?
AND I KNOW AS A SCIENTIST I SERIOUSLY SHOULDN'T EVEN BE HAVING THIS CONVERSATION TO BEGIN WITH.
WE'RE CONTINUING THE ASSAULT ON THE REMAINING GREEN AREA, MY LORD, BUT SO FAR WE HAVEN'T--
NO MATTER. THE STARHEART IS MINE. THAT WAS THE PRIZE I CAME HERE TO WIN...
...IT'S TIME FOR THE NEXT PHASE.
YOU MEAN A TETRAMORPH?
I MEAN A MAL'AKH, BRUCE. A MALAIKAH. AN ANGEL.
THEY COMMUNICATE IN A UNIQUE MANNER, COMBINING HARMONY, DISCORDANCE, VIBRATION AND TELEPATHY. I KNOW YOU'D IMAGINE SOME SORT OF GLORIOUS MELODIOUS EVENT, BUT I ASSURE YOU YOU'D FIND THE EXPERIENCE FAR FROM THAT.
AN INTERESTING THING ABOUT THESE CREATURES, THOUGH, WHEN THEY REQUIRE AID, THEY EMIT A SIGNAL. AKIN TO AN AILING WHALE, I SUPPOSED WOULD BE THE CLOSEST ANALOGY YOU MIGHT UNDERSTAND.
I'VE LONG SINCE STOPPE D SPEAKING IN ANGEL, AND EVEN THEN, BEING NOT COMPLETELY OF THEIR KIND, MY "ACCENT" WAS OFF. BUT I DO KNOW HOW, AND MORE IMPORTANT, I KNOW HOW TO EFFECT THAT CRY TO CALL TO ANY ONE OF GOD'S AGENTS SPECIFICALLY...

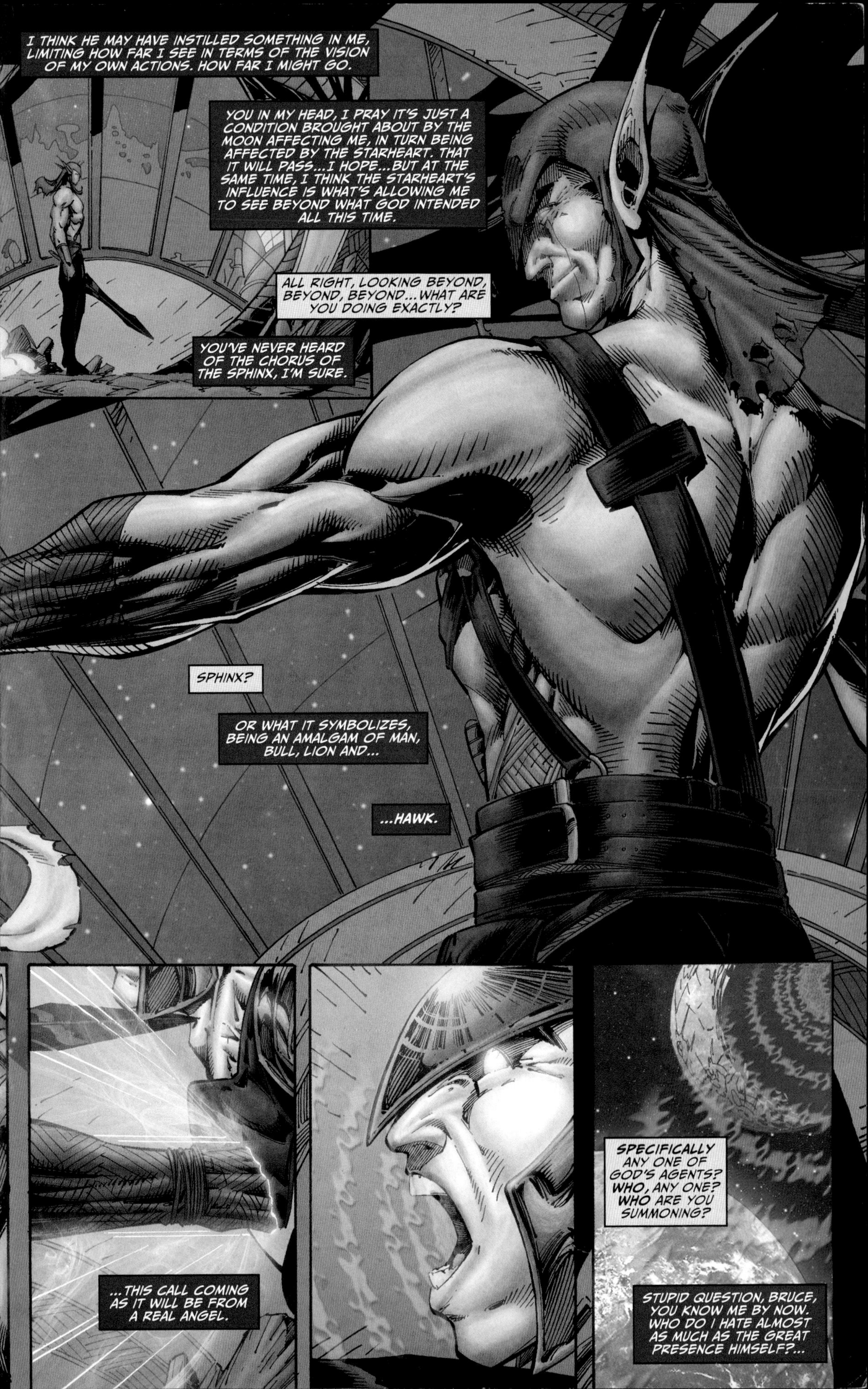
I THINK HE MAY HAVE INSTILLED SOMETHING IN ME, LIMITING HOW FAR I SEE IN TERMS OF THE VISION OF MY OWN ACTIONS. HOW FAR I MIGHT GO.
YOU IN MY HEAD, I PRAY IT'S JUST A CONDITION BROUGHT ABOUT BY THE MOON AFFECTING ME, IN TURN BEING AFFECTED BY THE STARHEART. THAT IT WILL PASS...I HOPE...BUT AT THE SAME TIME, I THINK THE STARHEART'S INFLUENCE IS WHAT'S ALLOWING ME TO SEE BEYOND WHAT GOD INTENDED ALL THIS TIME.
ALL RIGHT, LOOKING BEYOND, BEYOND, BEYOND...WHAT ARE YOU DOING EXACTLY?
YOU'VE NEVER HEARD OF THE CHORUS OF THE SPHINX, I'M SURE.
SPHINX?
OR WHAT IT SYMBOLIZES, BEING AN AMALGAM OF MAN, BULL, LION AND...
...HAWK.
...THIS CALL COMING AS IT WILL BE FROM A REAL ANGEL.
SPECIFICALLY ANY ONE OF GOD'S AGENTS? WHO, ANY ONE? WHO ARE YOU SUMMONING?
STUPID QUESTION, BRUCE, YOU KNOW ME BY NOW. WHO DO I HATE ALMOST AS MUCH AS THE GREAT PRESENCE HIMSELF?...

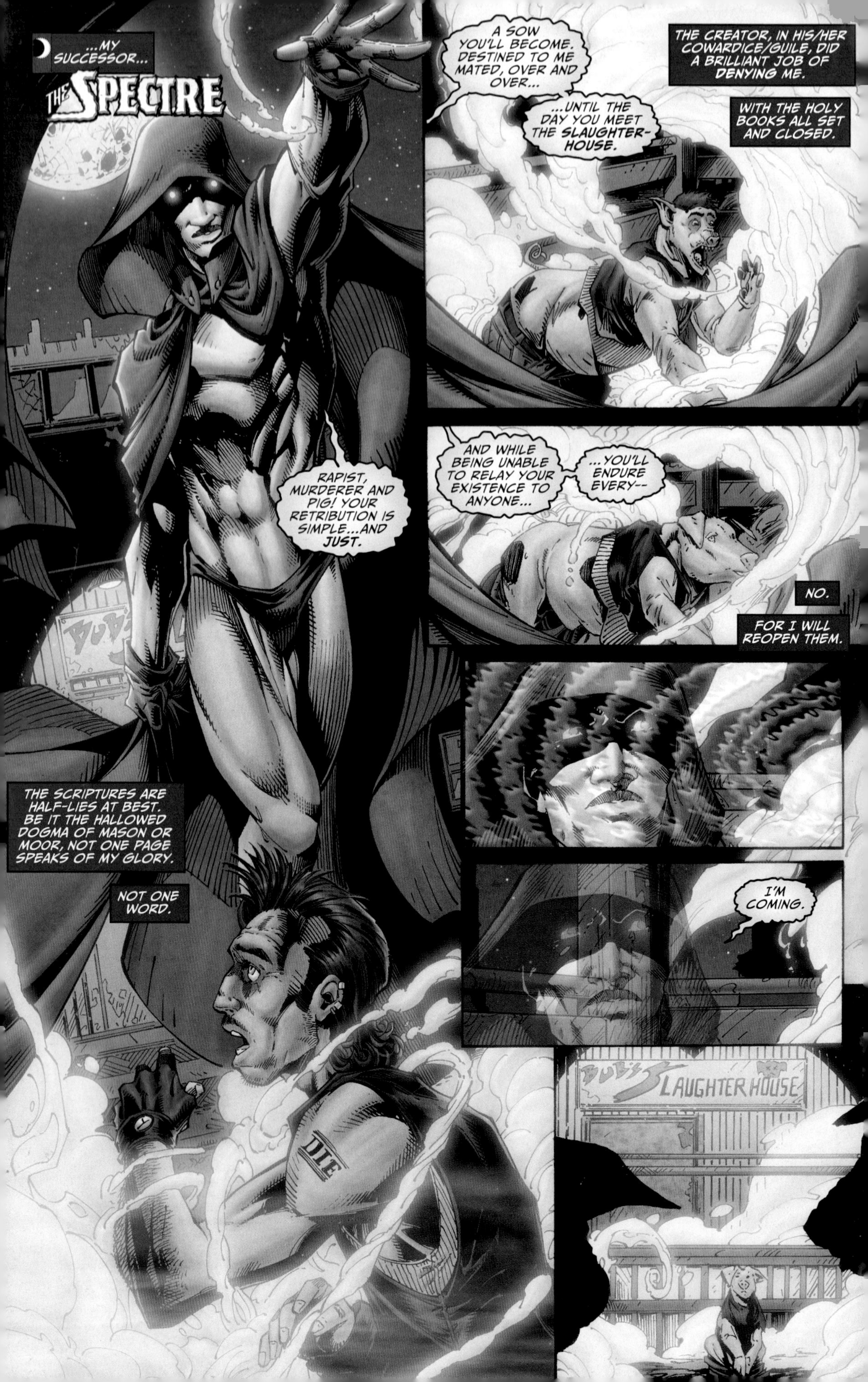
...MY SUCCESSOR...
THE SPECTRE
RAPIST, MURDERER AND PIG! YOUR RETRIBUTION IS SIMPLE...AND JUST.
THE SCRIPTURES ARE HALF-LIES AT BEST. BE IT THE HALLOWED DOGMA OF MASON OR MOOR, NOT ONE PAGE SPEAKS OF MY GLORY.
NOT ONE WORD.
DIE
A SOW YOU'LL BECOME. DESTINED TO ME MATED, OVER AND OVER...
...UNTIL THE DAY YOU MEET THE SLAUGHTER-HOUSE.
THE CREATOR, IN HIS/HER COWARDICE/GUILE, DID A BRILLIANT JOB OF DENYING ME.
WITH THE HOLY BOOKS ALL SET AND CLOSED.
AND WHILE BEING UNABLE TO RELAY YOUR EXISTENCE TO ANYONE...
...YOU'LL ENDURE EVERY--
NO.
FOR I WILL REOPEN THEM.
I'M COMING.
SLAUGHTER HOUSE

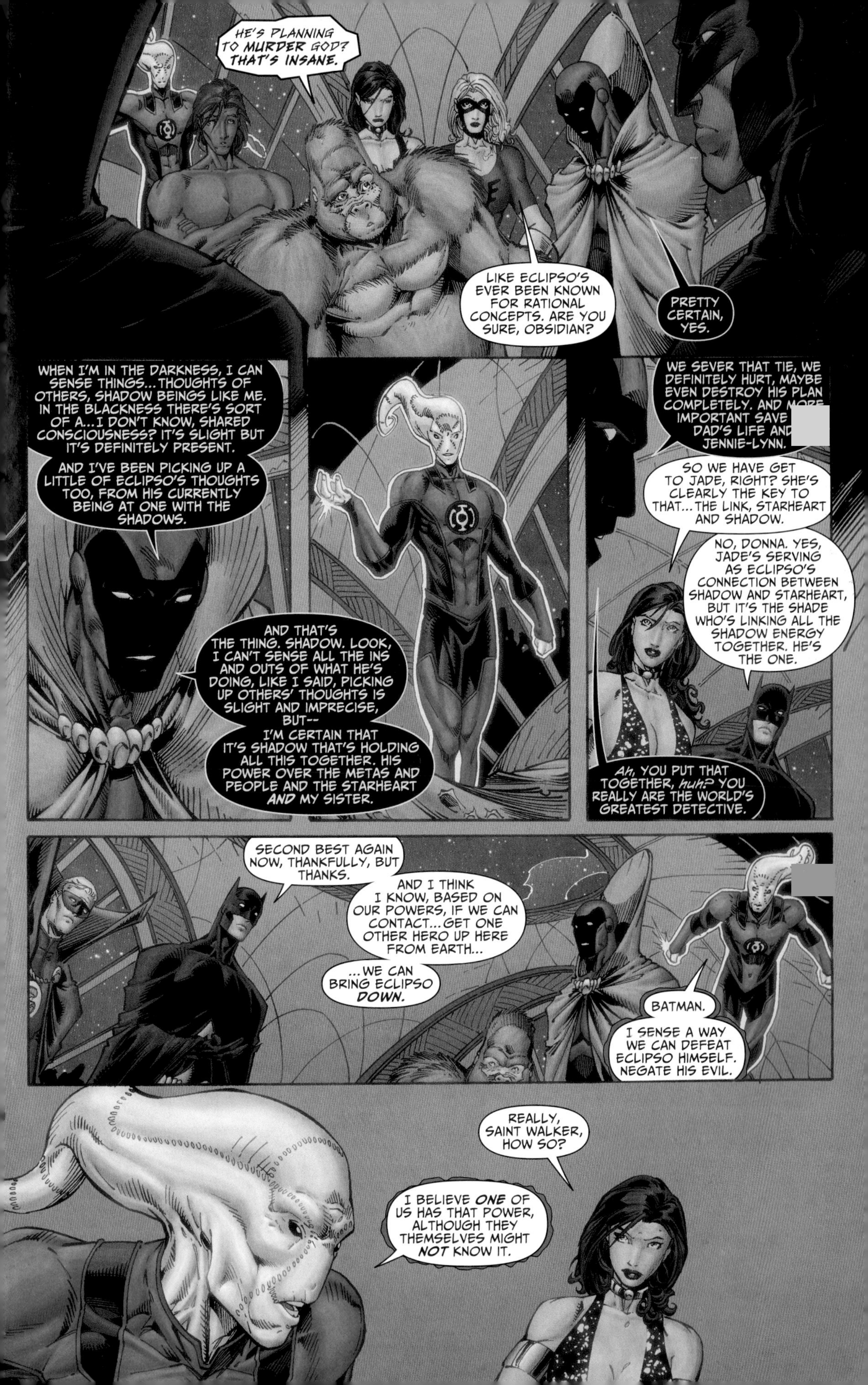

HE'S PLANNING TO MURDER GOD? THAT'S INSANE.
LIKE ECLIPSO'S EVER BEEN KNOWN FOR RATIONAL CONCEPTS. ARE YOU SURE, OBSIDIAN?
PRETTY CERTAIN, YES.
WHEN I'M IN THE DARKNESS, I CAN SENSE THINGS...THOUGHTS OF OTHERS, SHADOW BEINGS LIKE ME. IN THE BLACKNESS THERE'S SORT OF A...I DON'T KNOW, SHARED CONSCIOUSNESS? IT'S SLIGHT BUT IT'S DEFINITELY PRESENT.
AND I'VE BEEN PICKING UP A LITTLE OF ECLIPSO'S THOUGHTS TOO, FROM HIS CURRENTLY BEING AT ONE WITH THE SHADOWS.
AND THAT'S THE THING. SHADOW. LOOK, I CAN'T SENSE ALL THE INS AND OUTS OF WHAT HE'S DOING, LIKE I SAID, PICKING UP OTHERS' THOUGHTS IS SLIGHT AND IMPRECISE, BUT--
I'M CERTAIN THAT IT'S SHADOW THAT'S HOLDING ALL THIS TOGETHER. HIS POWER OVER THE METAS AND PEOPLE AND THE STARHEART AND MY SISTER.
WE SEVER THAT TIE, WE DEFINITELY HURT, MAYBE EVEN DESTROY HIS PLAN COMPLETELY. AND MORE IMPORTANT SAVE DAD'S LIFE AND JENNIE-LYNN.
SO WE HAVE GET TO JADE, RIGHT? SHE'S CLEARLY THE KEY TO THAT...THE LINK, STARHEART AND SHADOW.
NO, DONNA. YES, JADE'S SERVING AS ECLIPSO'S CONNECTION BETWEEN SHADOW AND STARHEART, BUT IT'S THE SHADE WHO'S LINKING ALL THE SHADOW ENERGY TOGETHER. HE'S THE ONE.
Ah, YOU PUT THAT TOGETHER, huh? YOU REALLY ARE THE WORLD'S GREATEST DETECTIVE.
SECOND BEST AGAIN NOW, THANKFULLY, BUT THANKS.
AND I THINK I KNOW, BASED ON OUR POWERS, IF WE CAN CONTACT...GET ONE OTHER HERO UP HERE FROM EARTH...
...WE CAN BRING ECLIPSO DOWN.
BATMAN.
I SENSE A WAY WE CAN DEFEAT ECLIPSO HIMSELF. NEGATE HIS EVIL.
REALLY, SAINT WALKER, HOW SO?
I BELIEVE ONE OF US HAS THAT POWER, ALTHOUGH THEY THEMSELVES MIGHT NOT KNOW IT.

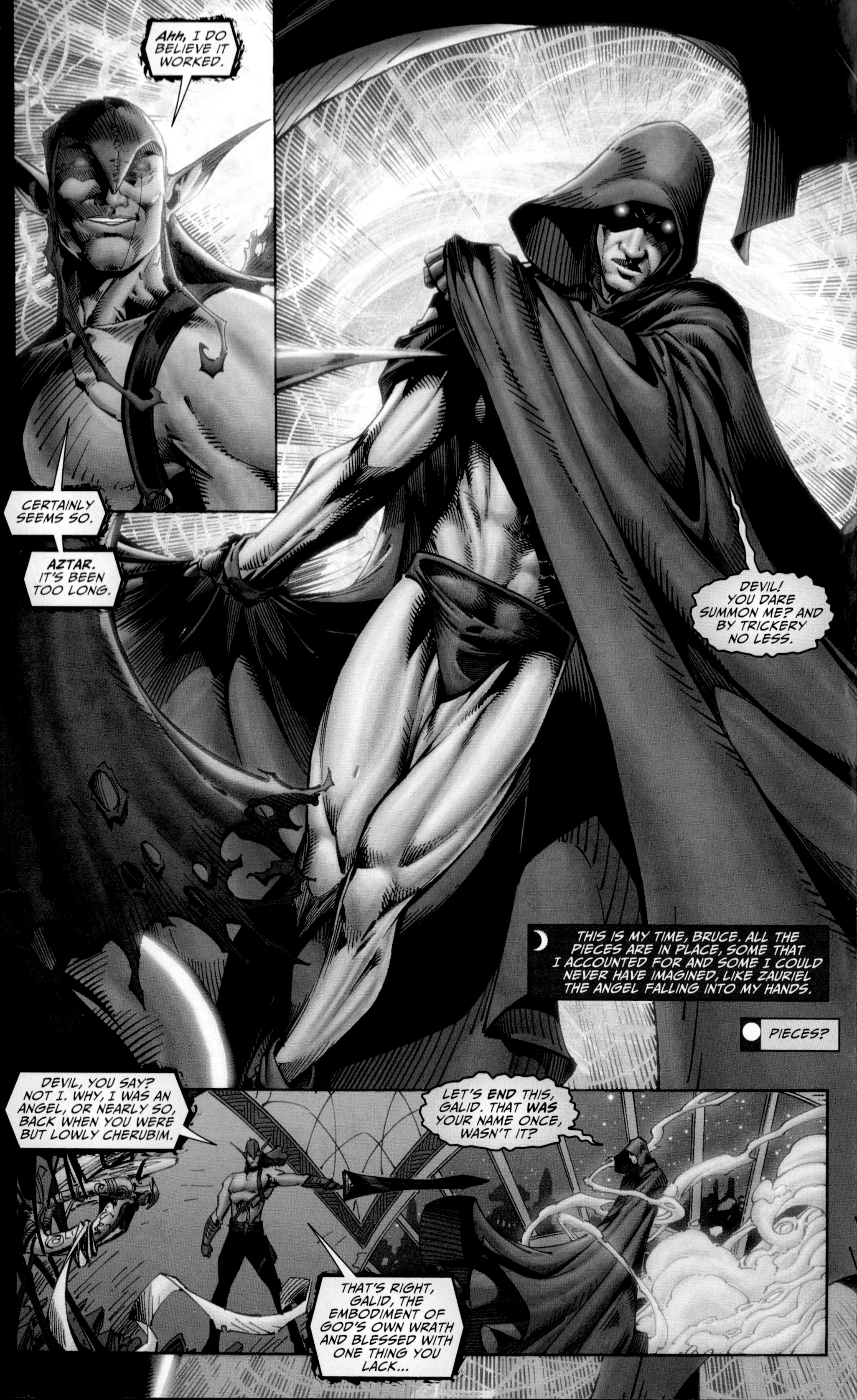
AHH, I DO BELIEVE IT WORKED.
CERTAINLY SEEMS SO.
AZTAR. IT'S BEEN TOO LONG.
DEVIL! YOU DARE SUMMON ME? AND BY TRICKERY NO LESS.
THIS IS MY TIME, BRUCE. ALL THE PIECES ARE IN PLACE, SOME THAT I ACCOUNTED FOR AND SOME I COULD NEVER HAVE IMAGINED, LIKE ZAURIEL THE ANGEL FALLING INTO MY HANDS.
PIECES?
DEVIL, YOU SAY? NOT I. WHY, I WAS AN ANGEL, OR NEARLY SO, BACK WHEN YOU WERE BUT LOWLY CHERUBIM.
LET'S END THIS, GALID. THAT WAS YOUR NAME ONCE, WASN'T IT?
THAT'S RIGHT, GALID, THE EMBODIMENT OF GOD'S OWN WRATH AND BLESSED WITH ONE THING YOU LACK...

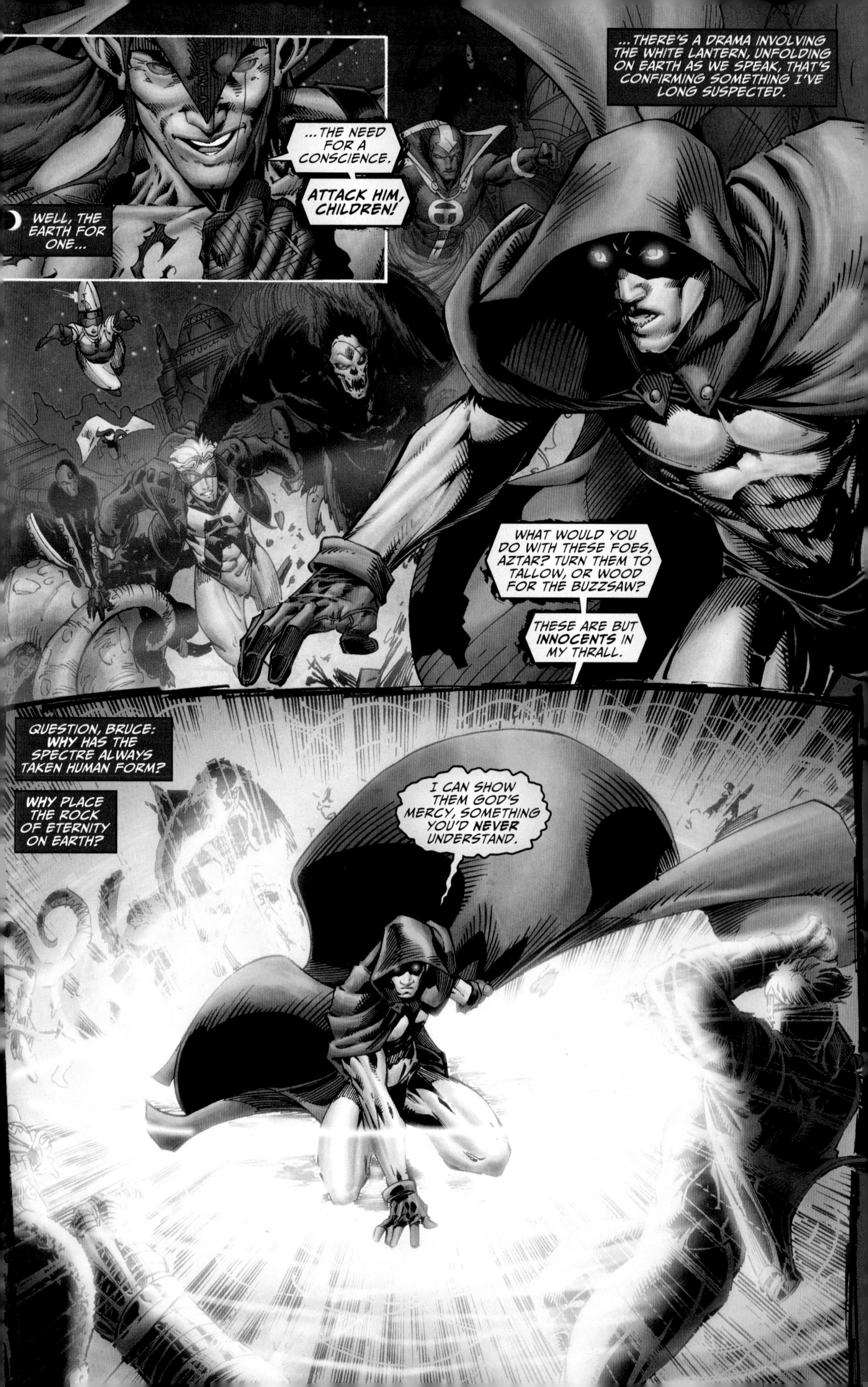
...THERE'S A DRAMA INVOLVING THE WHITE LANTERN, UNFOLDING ON EARTH AS WE SPEAK, THAT'S CONFIRMING SOMETHING I'VE LONG SUSPECTED.
WELL, THE EARTH FOR ONE...
...THE NEED FOR A CONSCIENCE.
ATTACK HIM, CHILDREN!
WHAT WOULD YOU DO WITH THESE FOES, AZTAR? TURN THEM TO TALLOW, OR WOOD FOR THE BUZZSAW?
THESE ARE BUT INNOCENTS IN MY THRALL.
QUESTION, BRUCE: WHY HAS THE SPECTRE ALWAYS TAKEN HUMAN FORM?
WHY PLACE THE ROCK OF ETERNITY ON EARTH?
I CAN SHOW THEM GOD'S MERCY, SOMETHING YOU'D NEVER UNDERSTAND.

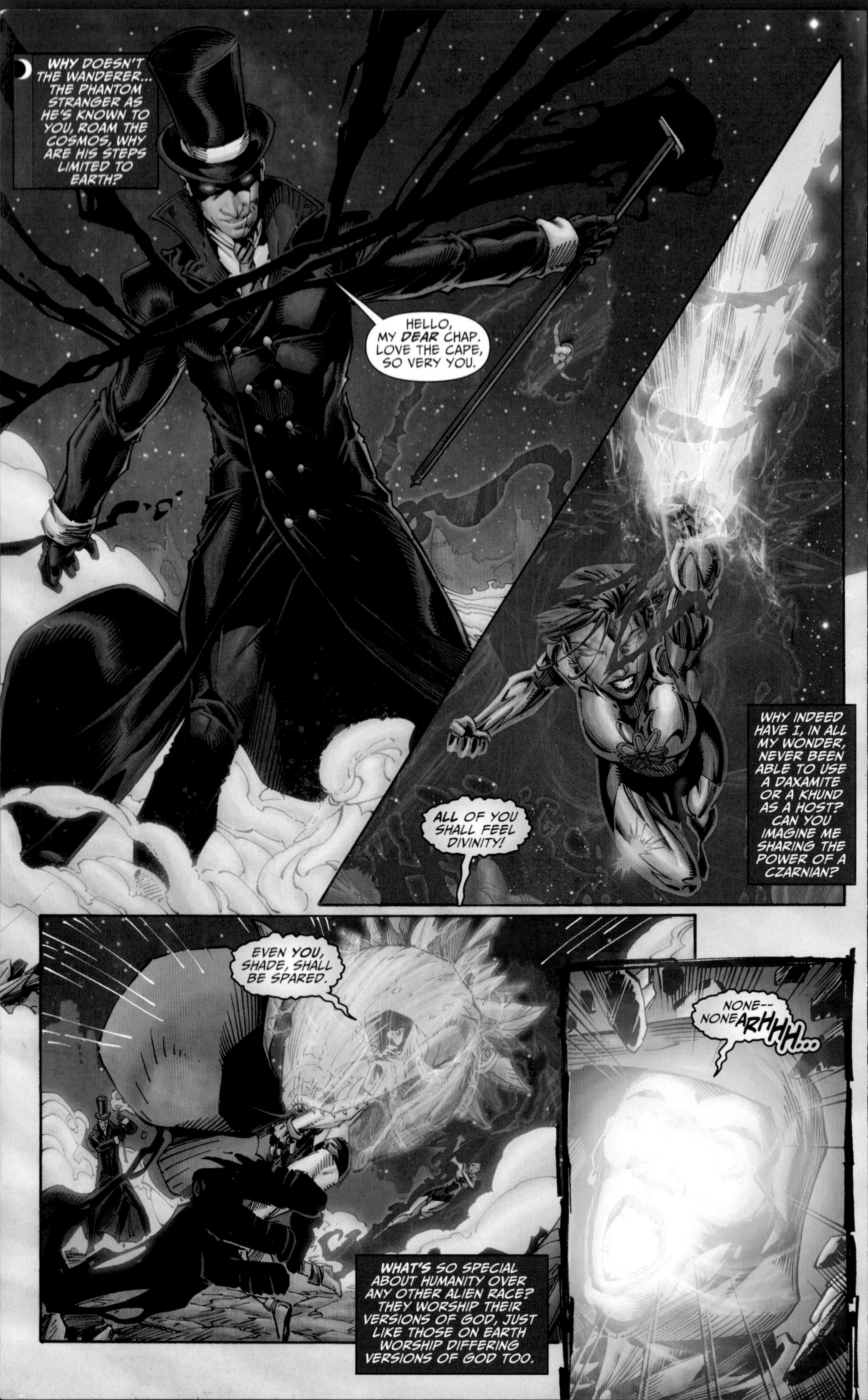
WHY DOESN'T THE WANDERER... THE PHANTOM STRANGER AS HE'S KNOWN TO YOU, ROAM THE COSMOS, WHY ARE HIS STEPS LIMITED TO EARTH?
HELLO, MY DEAR CHAP. LOVE THE CAPE, SO VERY YOU.
WHY INDEED HAVE I, IN ALL MY WONDER, NEVER BEEN ABLE TO USE A DAXAMITE OR A KHUND AS A HOST? CAN YOU IMAGINE ME SHARING THE POWER OF A CZARNIAN?
ALL OF YOU SHALL FEEL DIVINITY!
EVEN YOU, SHADE, SHALL BE SPARED.
WHAT'S SO SPECIAL ABOUT HUMANITY OVER ANY OTHER ALIEN RACE? THEY WORSHIP THEIR VERSIONS OF GOD, JUST LIKE THOSE ON EARTH WORSHIP DIFFERING VERSIONS OF GOD TOO.
NONE-- NONE ARHHH...

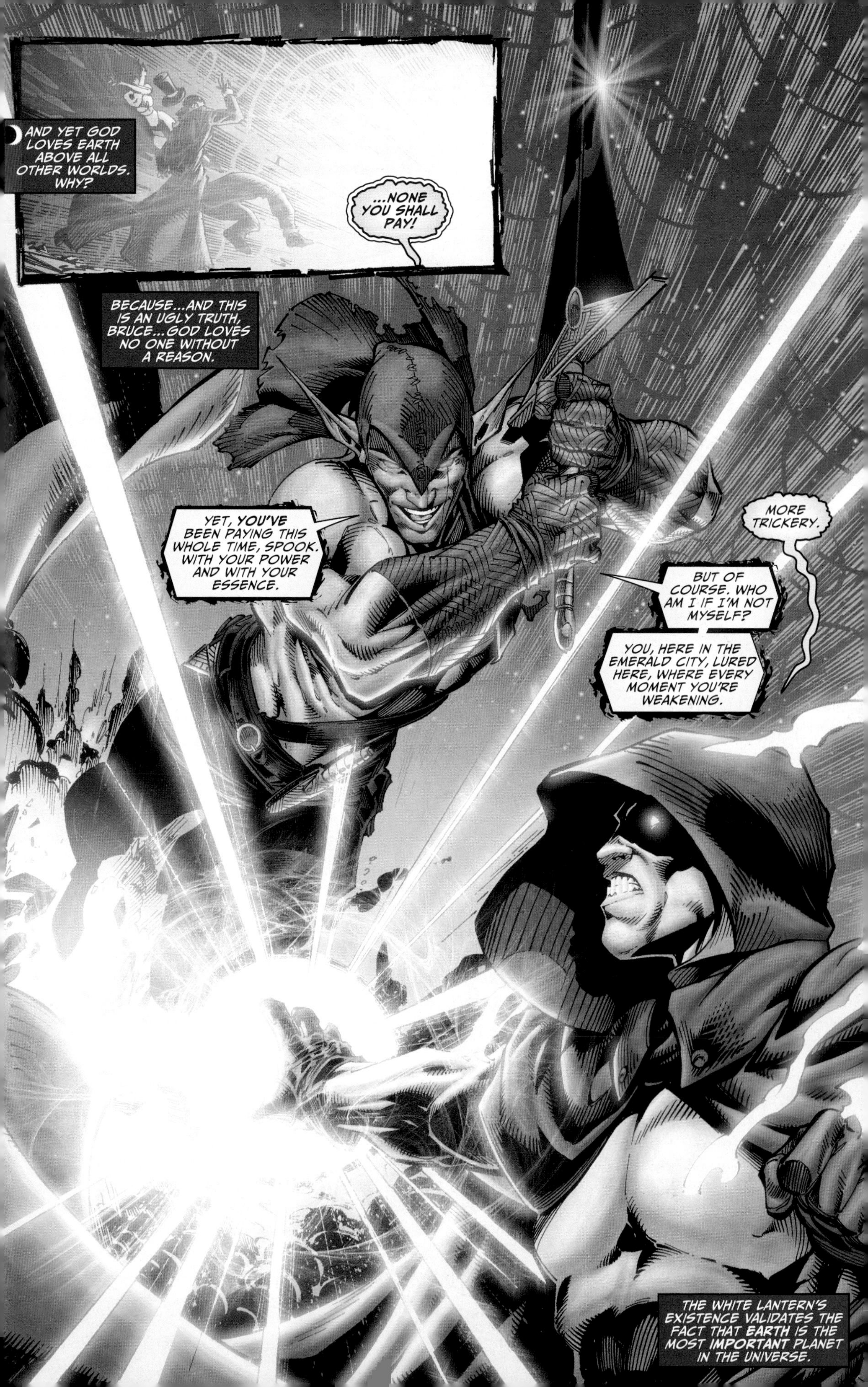
AND YET GOD LOVES EARTH ABOVE ALL OTHER WORLDS. WHY?
...NONE YOU SHALL PAY!
BECAUSE...AND THIS IS AN UGLY TRUTH, BRUCE...GOD LOVES NO ONE WITHOUT A REASON.
YET, YOU'VE BEEN PAYING THIS WHOLE TIME, SPOOK. WITH YOUR POWER AND WITH YOUR ESSENCE.
MORE TRICKERY.
BUT OF COURSE. WHO AM I IF I'M NOT MYSELF?
YOU, HERE IN THE EMERALD CITY, LURED HERE, WHERE EVERY MOMENT YOU'RE WEAKENING.
THE WHITE LANTERN'S EXISTENCE VALIDATES THE FACT THAT EARTH IS THE MOST IMPORTANT PLANET IN THE UNIVERSE.

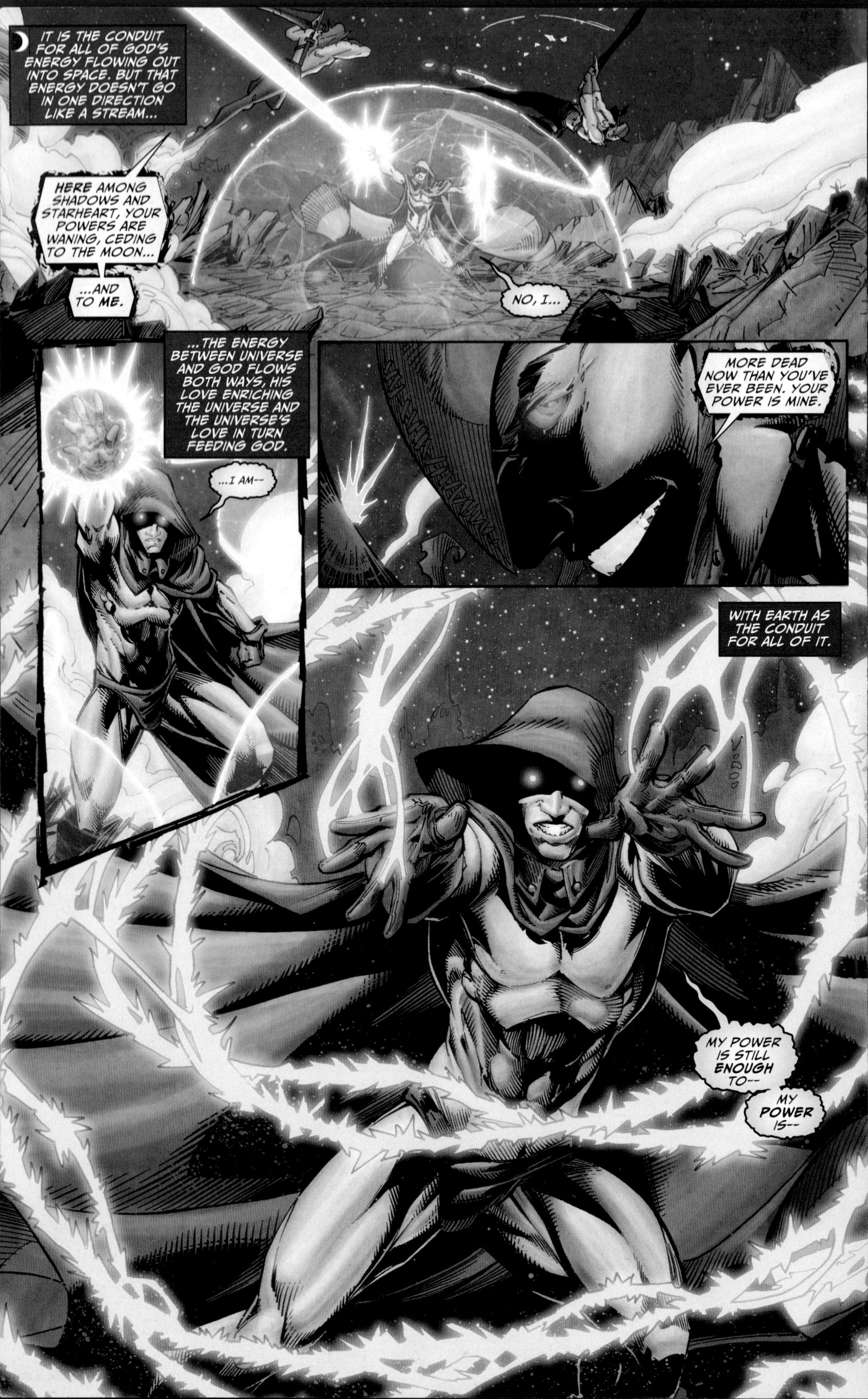
IT IS THE CONDUIT FOR ALL OF GOD'S ENERGY FLOWING OUT INTO SPACE. BUT THAT ENERGY DOESN'T GO IN ONE DIRECTION LIKE A STREAM...
HERE AMONG SHADOWS AND STARHEART, YOUR POWERS ARE WANING, CEDING TO THE MOON...
...AND TO ME.
NO, I...
...THE ENERGY BETWEEN UNIVERSE AND GOD FLOWS BOTH WAYS, HIS LOVE ENRICHING THE UNIVERSE AND THE UNIVERSE'S LOVE IN TURN FEEDING GOD.
...I AM--
MORE DEAD NOW THAN YOU'VE EVER BEEN. YOUR POWER IS MINE.
WITH EARTH AS THE CONDUIT FOR ALL OF IT.
MY POWER IS STILL ENOUGH TO--
MY POWER IS--

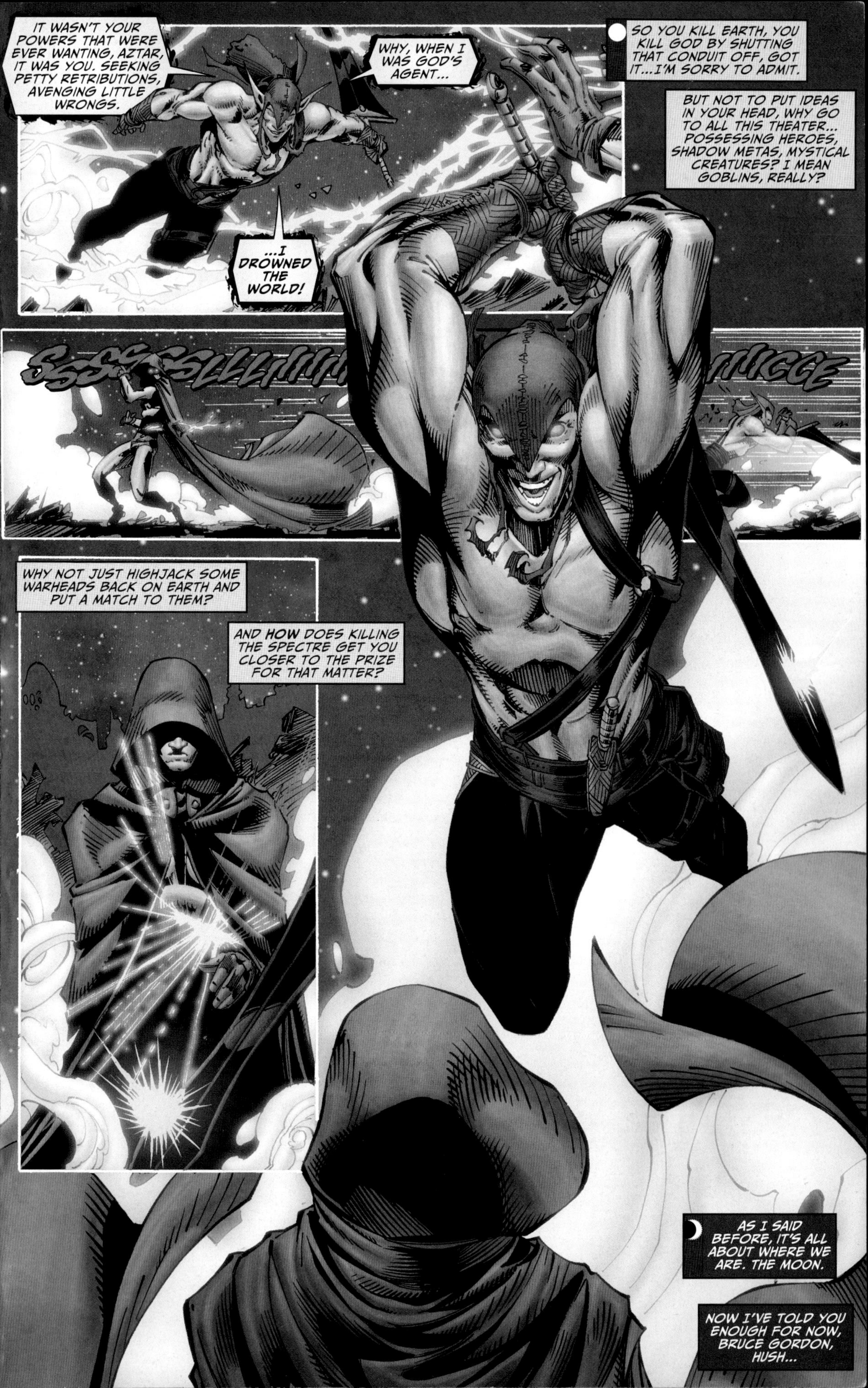
IT WASN'T YOUR POWERS THAT WERE EVER WANTING, AZTAR, IT WAS YOU. SEEKING PETTY RETRIBUTIONS, AVENGING LITTLE WRONGS.
WHY, WHEN I WAS GOD'S AGENT...
...I DROWNED THE WORLD!
SO YOU KILL EARTH, YOU KILL GOD BY SHUTTING THAT CONDUIT OFF, GOT IT...I'M SORRY TO ADMIT.
BUT NOT TO PUT IDEAS IN YOUR HEAD, WHY GO TO ALL THIS THEATER... POSSESSING HEROES, SHADOW METAS, MYSTICAL CREATURES? I MEAN GOBLINS, REALLY?
SSSSSLLLIIIIII...IIICCE
WHY NOT JUST HIGHJACK SOME WARHEADS BACK ON EARTH AND PUT A MATCH TO THEM?
AND HOW DOES KILLING THE SPECTRE GET YOU CLOSER TO THE PRIZE FOR THAT MATTER?
AS I SAID BEFORE, IT'S ALL ABOUT WHERE WE ARE. THE MOON.
NOW I'VE TOLD YOU ENOUGH FOR NOW, BRUCE GORDON, HUSH...

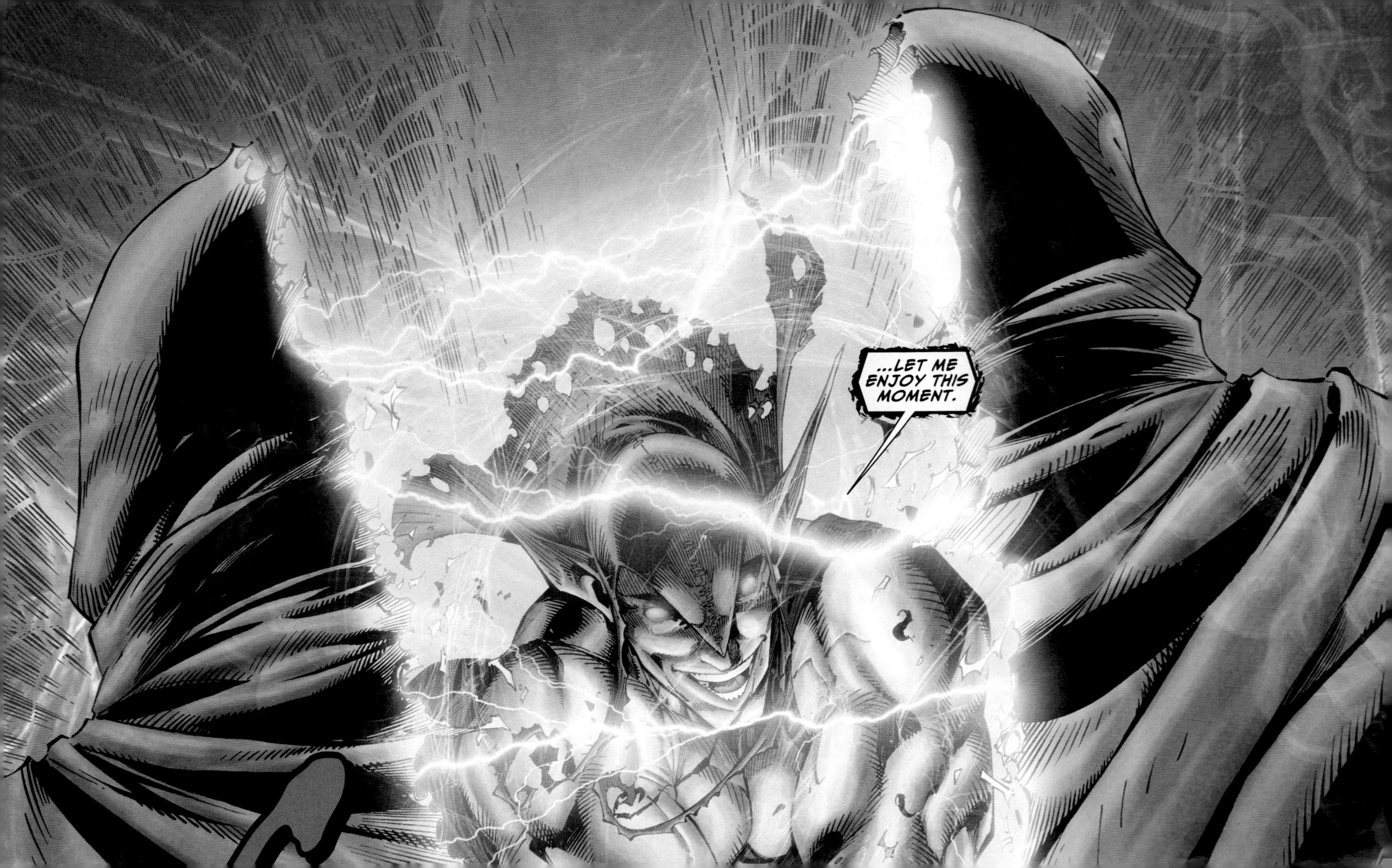
...LET ME ENJOY THIS MOMENT.

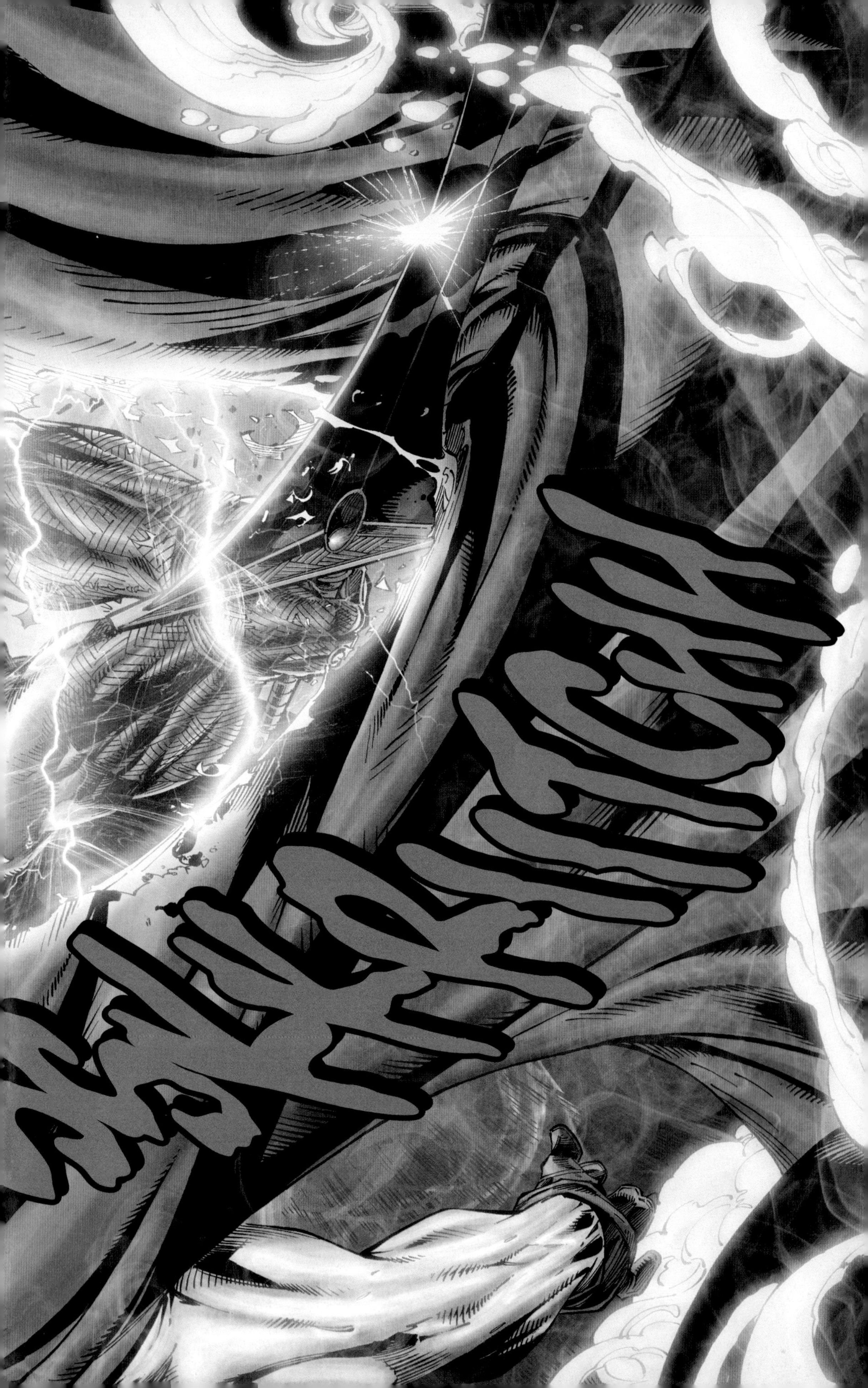
SHKRTCH

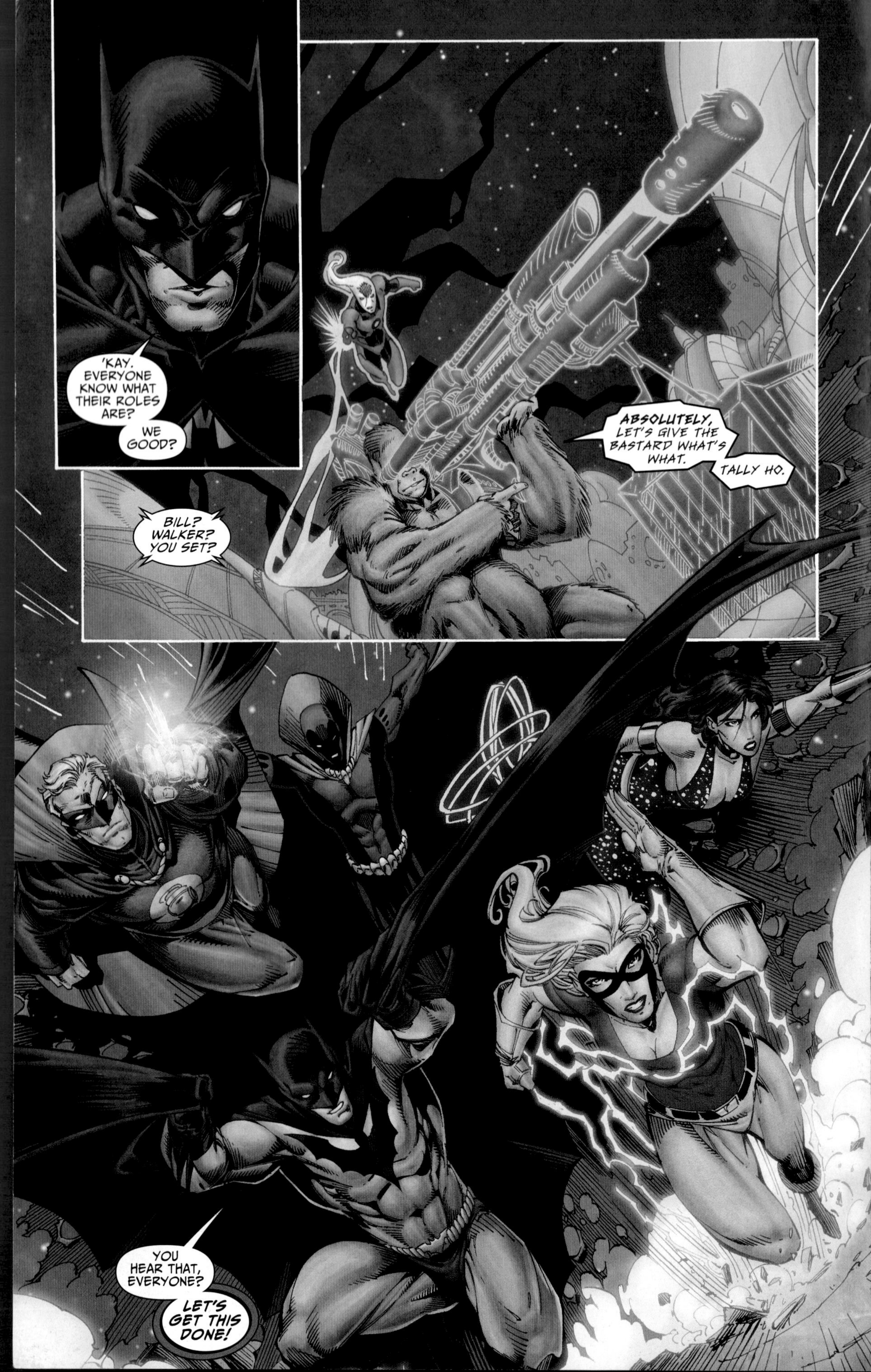
'KAY. EVERYONE KNOW WHAT THEIR ROLES ARE?
WE GOOD?
BILL? WALKER? YOU SET?
ABSOLUTELY, LET'S GIVE THE BASTARD WHAT'S WHAT.
TALLY HO.
YOU HEAR THAT, EVERYONE?
LET'S GET THIS DONE!

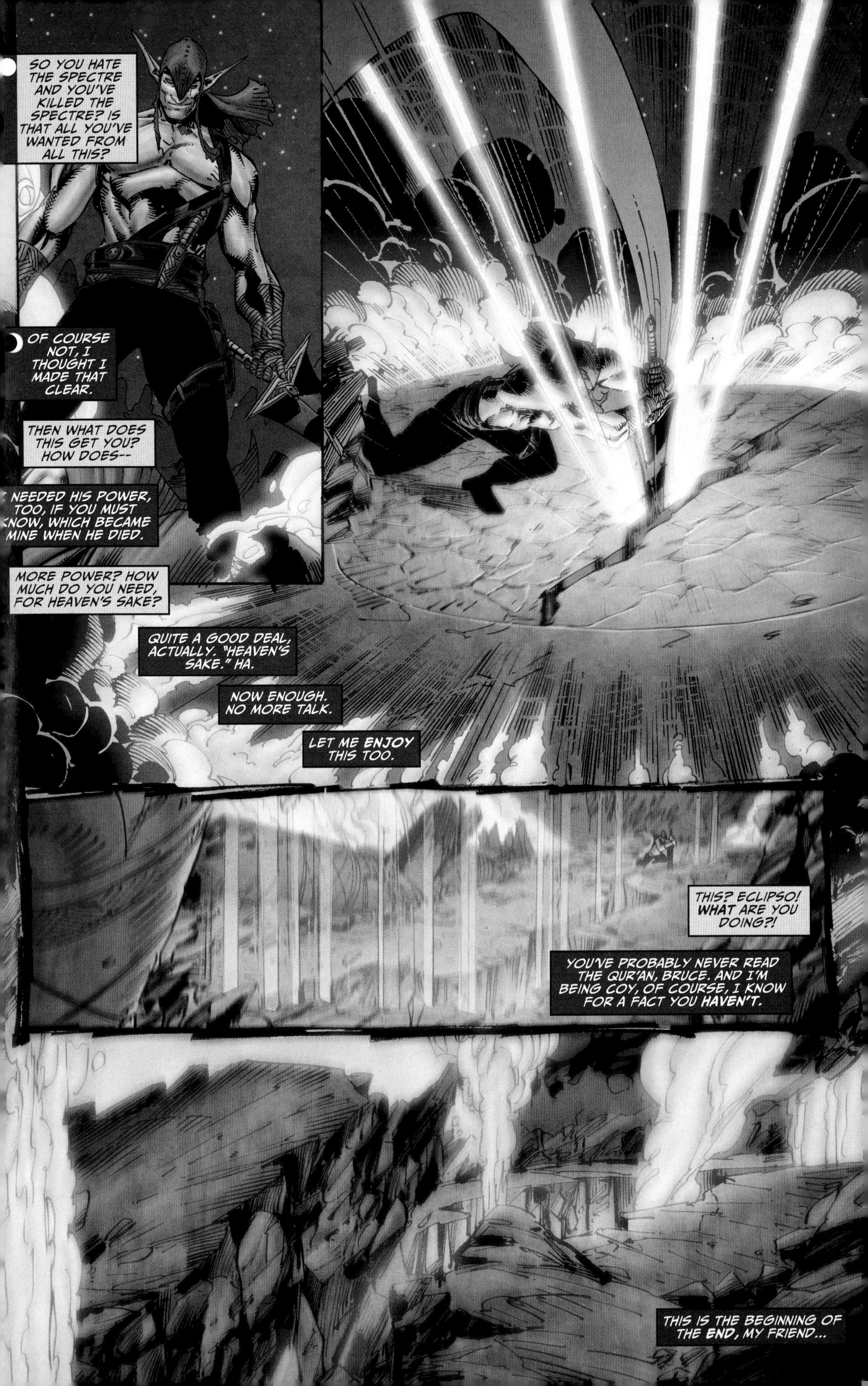
SO YOU HATE THE SPECTRE AND YOU'VE KILLED THE SPECTRE? IS THAT ALL YOU'VE WANTED FROM ALL THIS?
OF COURSE NOT, I THOUGHT I MADE THAT CLEAR.
THEN WHAT DOES THIS GET YOU? HOW DOES--
NEEDED HIS POWER, TOO, IF YOU MUST KNOW, WHICH BECAME MINE WHEN HE DIED.
MORE POWER? HOW MUCH DO YOU NEED, FOR HEAVEN'S SAKE?
QUITE A GOOD DEAL, ACTUALLY. "HEAVEN'S SAKE." HA.
NOW ENOUGH. NO MORE TALK.
LET ME ENJOY THIS TOO.
THIS? ECLIPSO! WHAT ARE YOU DOING?!
YOU'VE PROBABLY NEVER READ THE QUR'AN, BRUCE. AND I'M BEING COY, OF COURSE, I KNOW FOR A FACT YOU HAVEN'T.
THIS IS THE BEGINNING OF THE END, MY FRIEND...

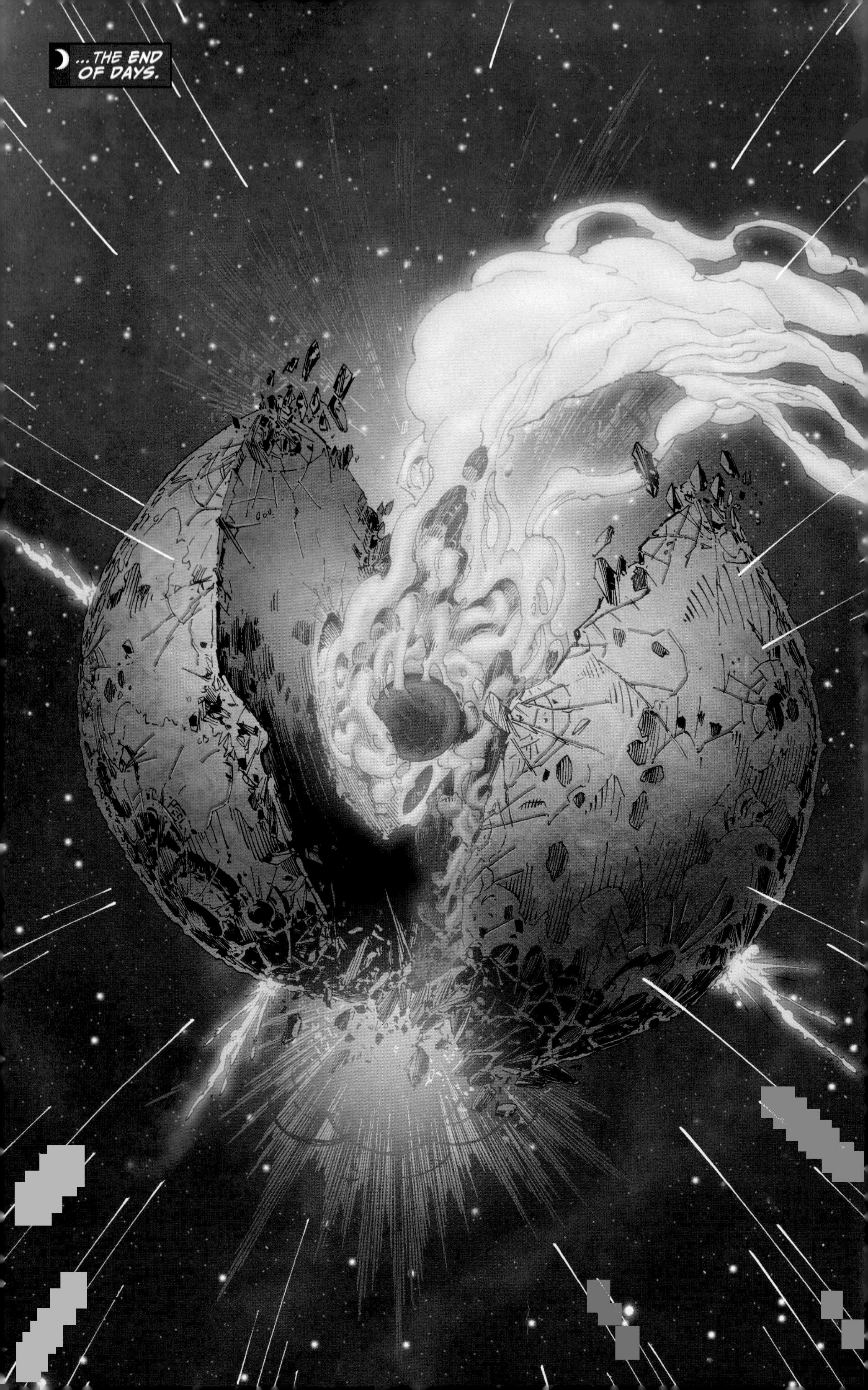
...THE END OF DAYS.

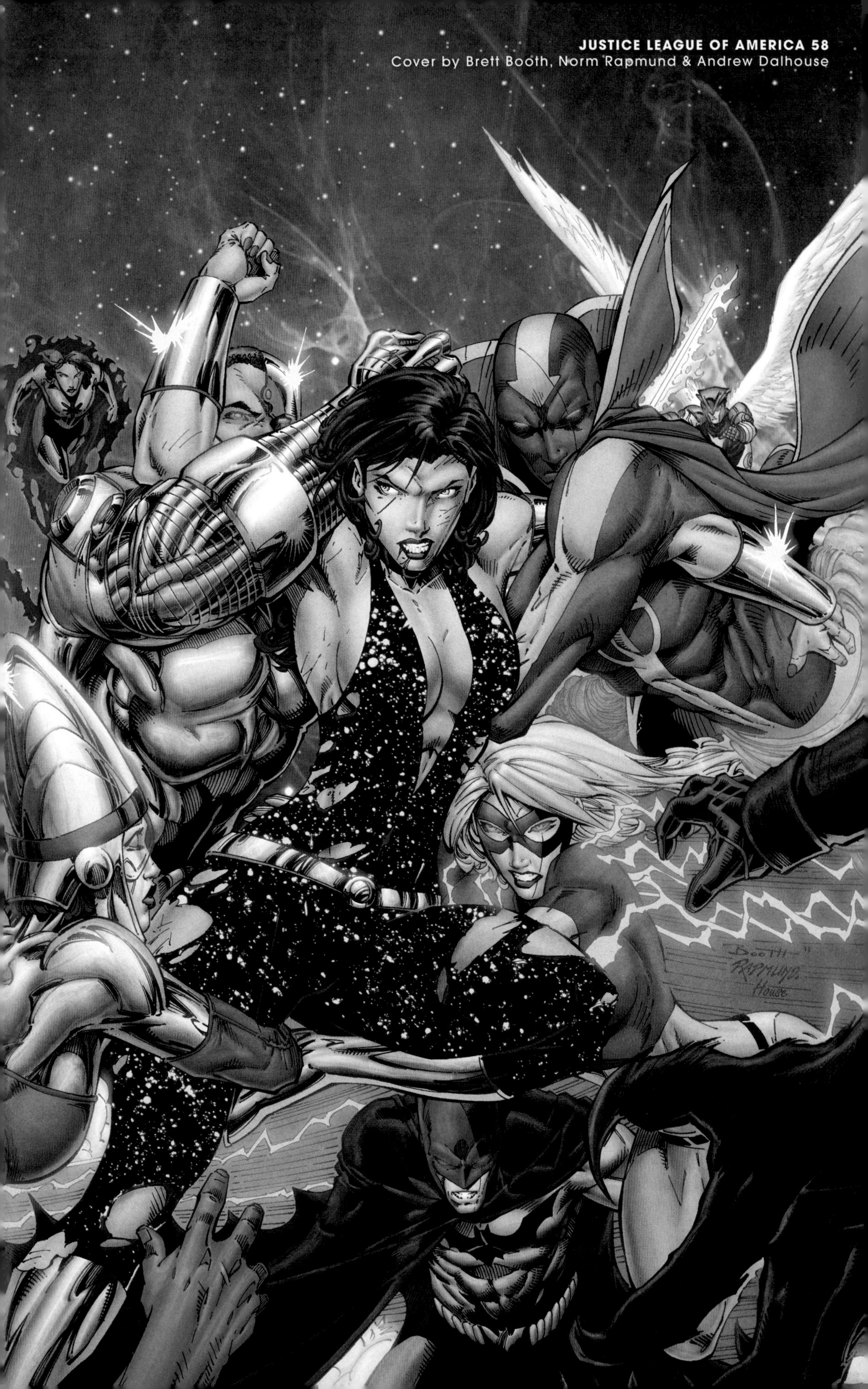
Booth
Rapmund
House

JUSTICE LEAGUE OF AMERICA 58
Cover by Brett Booth, Norm Rapmund & Andrew Dalhouse

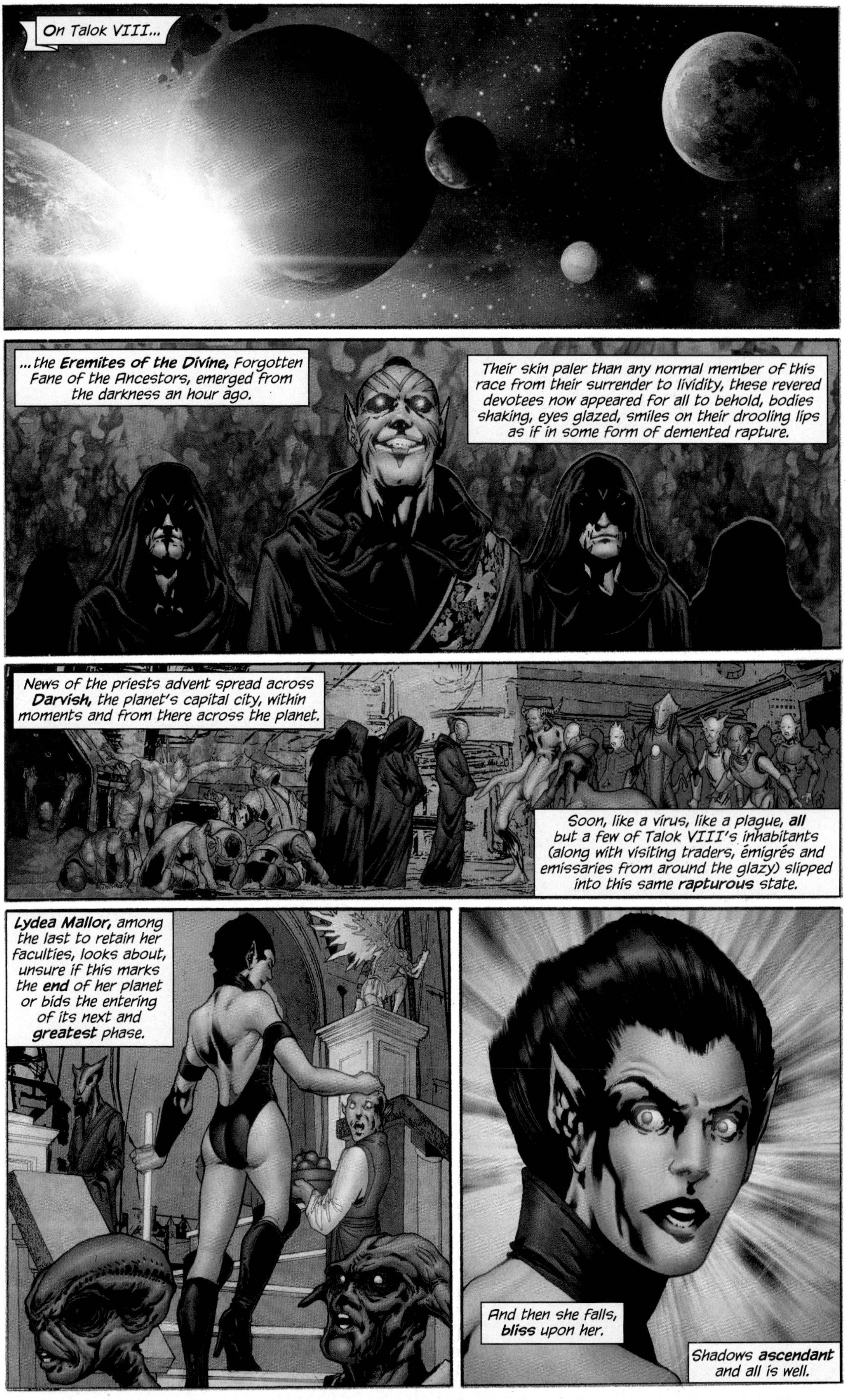

On Talok VIII...
...the **Eremites of the Divine,** Forgotten Fane of the Ancestors, emerged from the darkness an hour ago.
Their skin paler than any normal member of this race from their surrender to lividity, these revered devotees now appeared for all to behold, bodies shaking, eyes glazed, smiles on their drooling lips as if in some form of demented rapture.
News of the priests advent spread across **Darvish,** the planet's capital city, within moments and from there across the planet.
Soon, like a virus, like a plague, **all** but a few of Talok VIII's inhabitants (along with visiting traders, émigrés and emissaries from around the glazy) slipped into this same **rapturous** state.
Lydea Mallor, among the last to retain her faculties, looks about, unsure if this marks the **end** of her planet or bids the entering of its next and **greatest** phase.
And then she falls, **bliss** upon her.
Shadows **ascendant** and all is well.

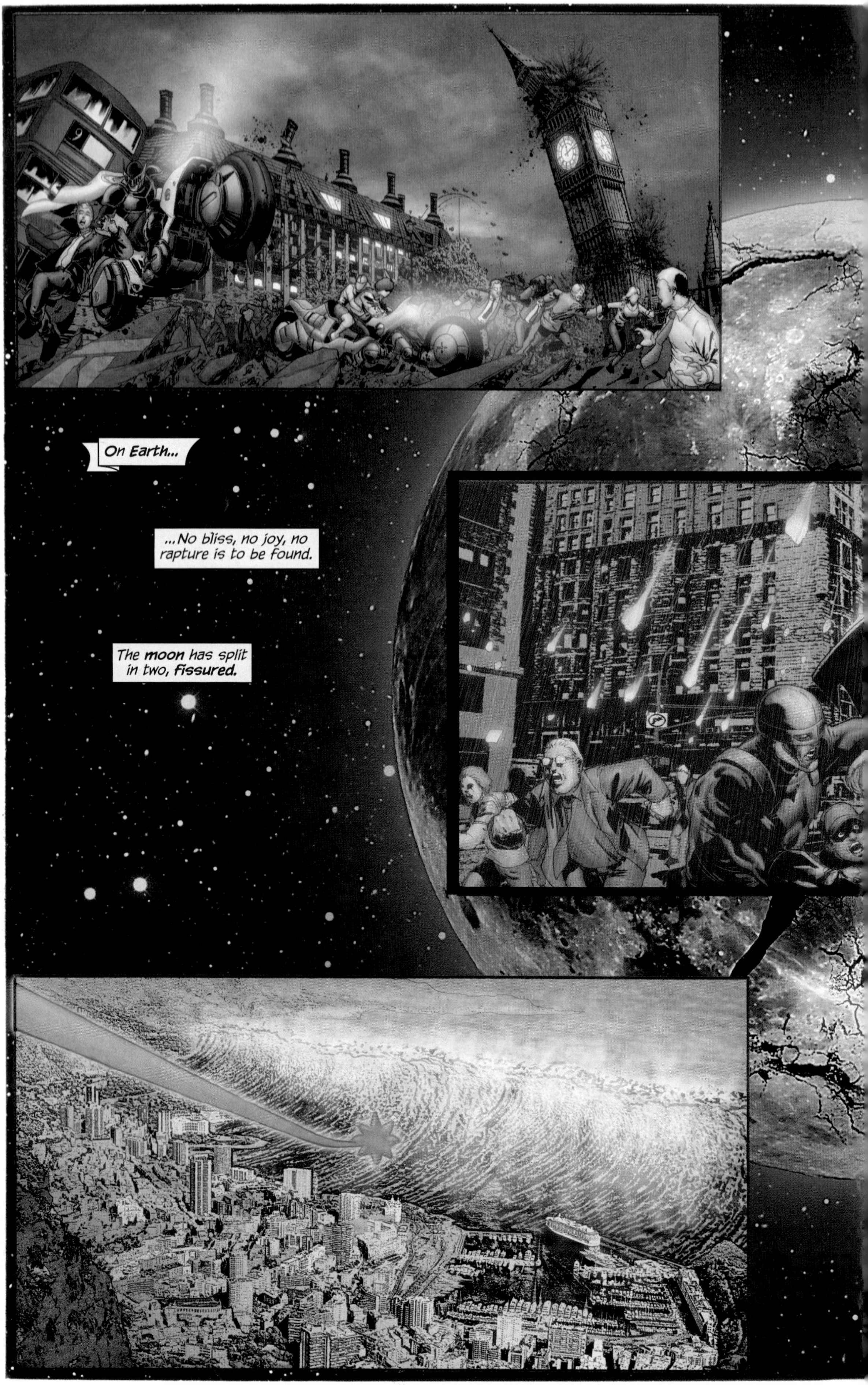
On Earth...
...No bliss, no joy, no rapture is to be found.
The moon has split in two, fissured.

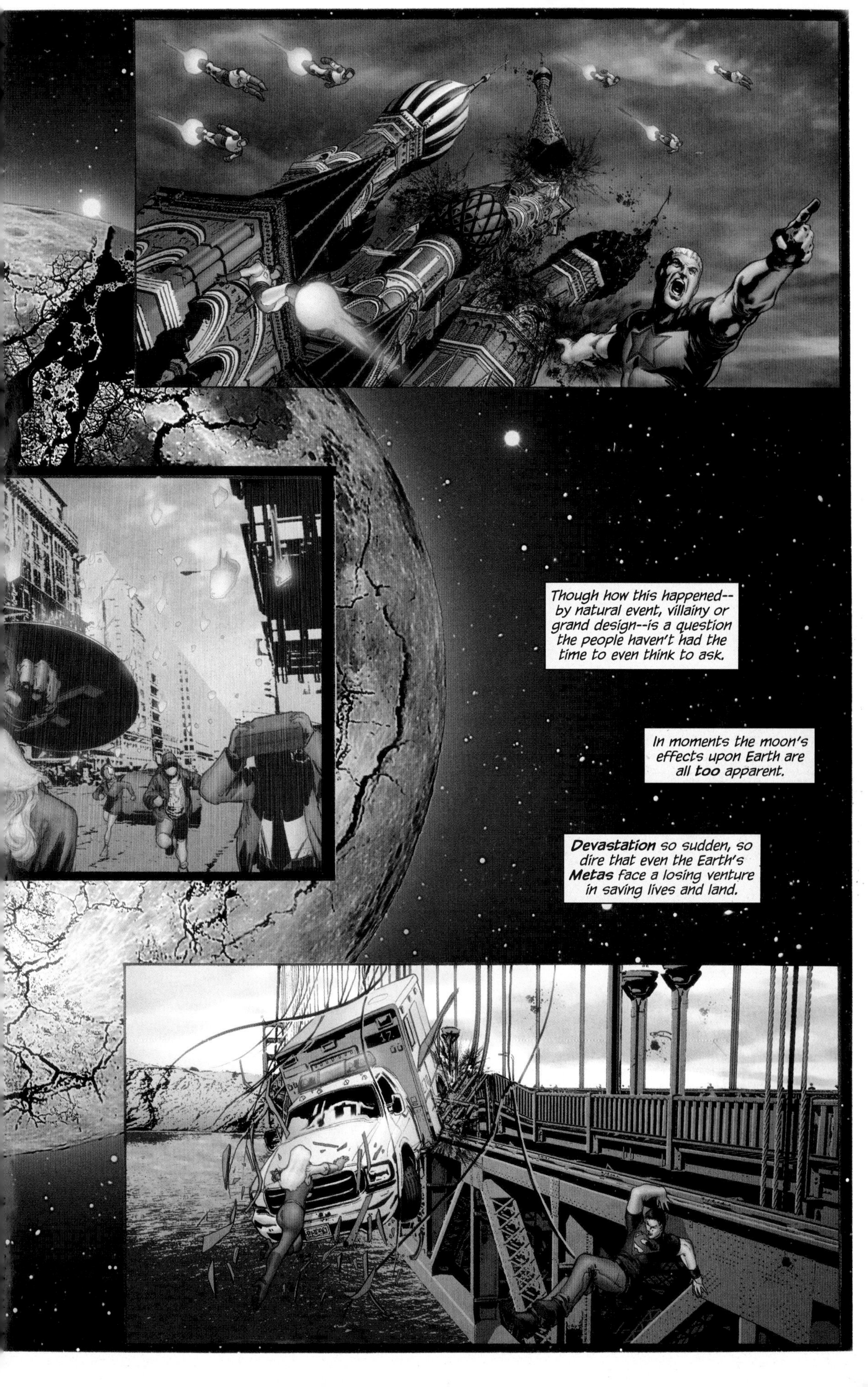
Though how this happened--by natural event, villainy or grand design--is a question the people haven't had the time to even think to ask.
In moments the moon's effects upon Earth are all **too** apparent.
Devastation so sudden, so dire that even the Earth's **Metas** face a losing venture in saving lives and land.

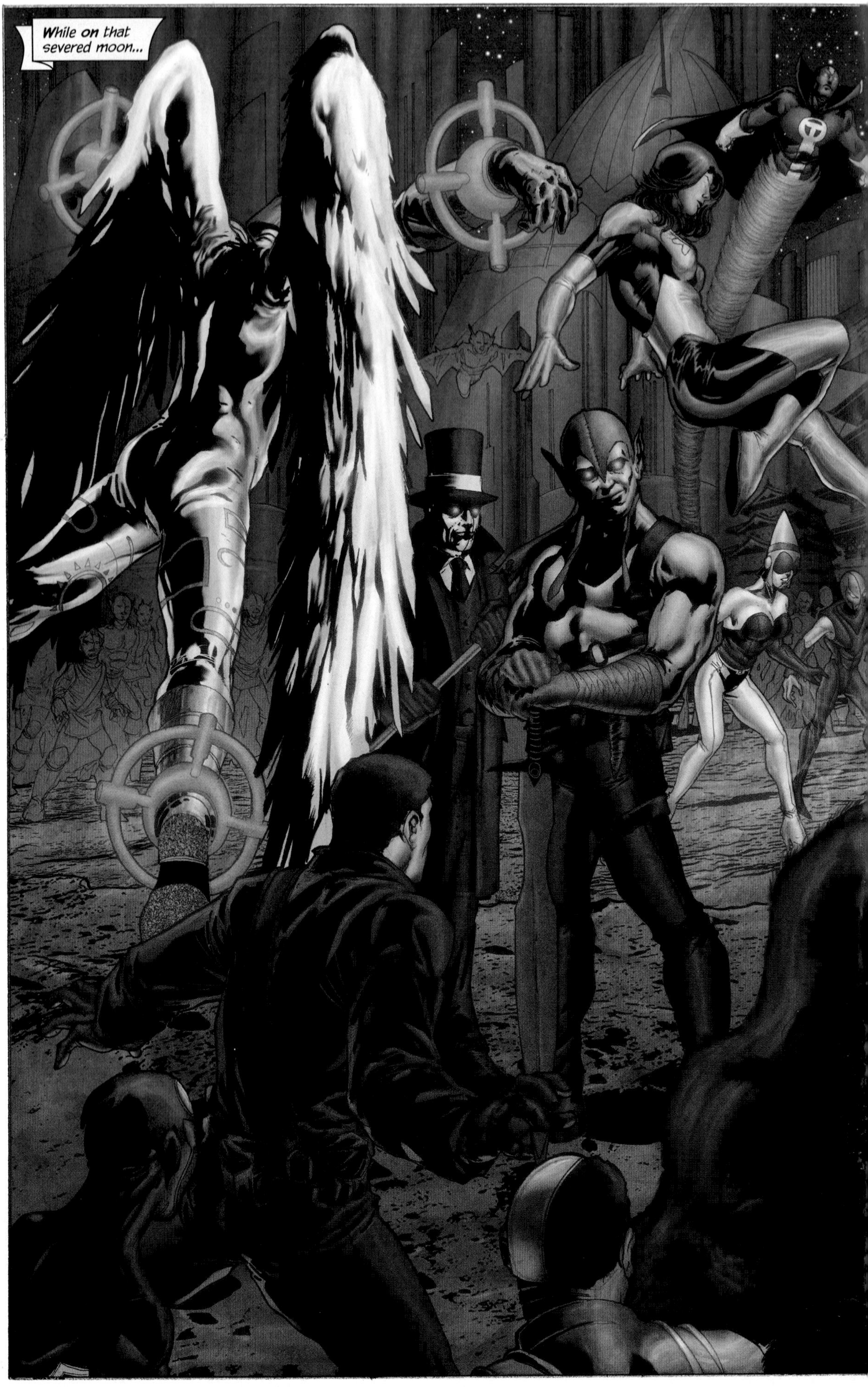
While on that severed moon...

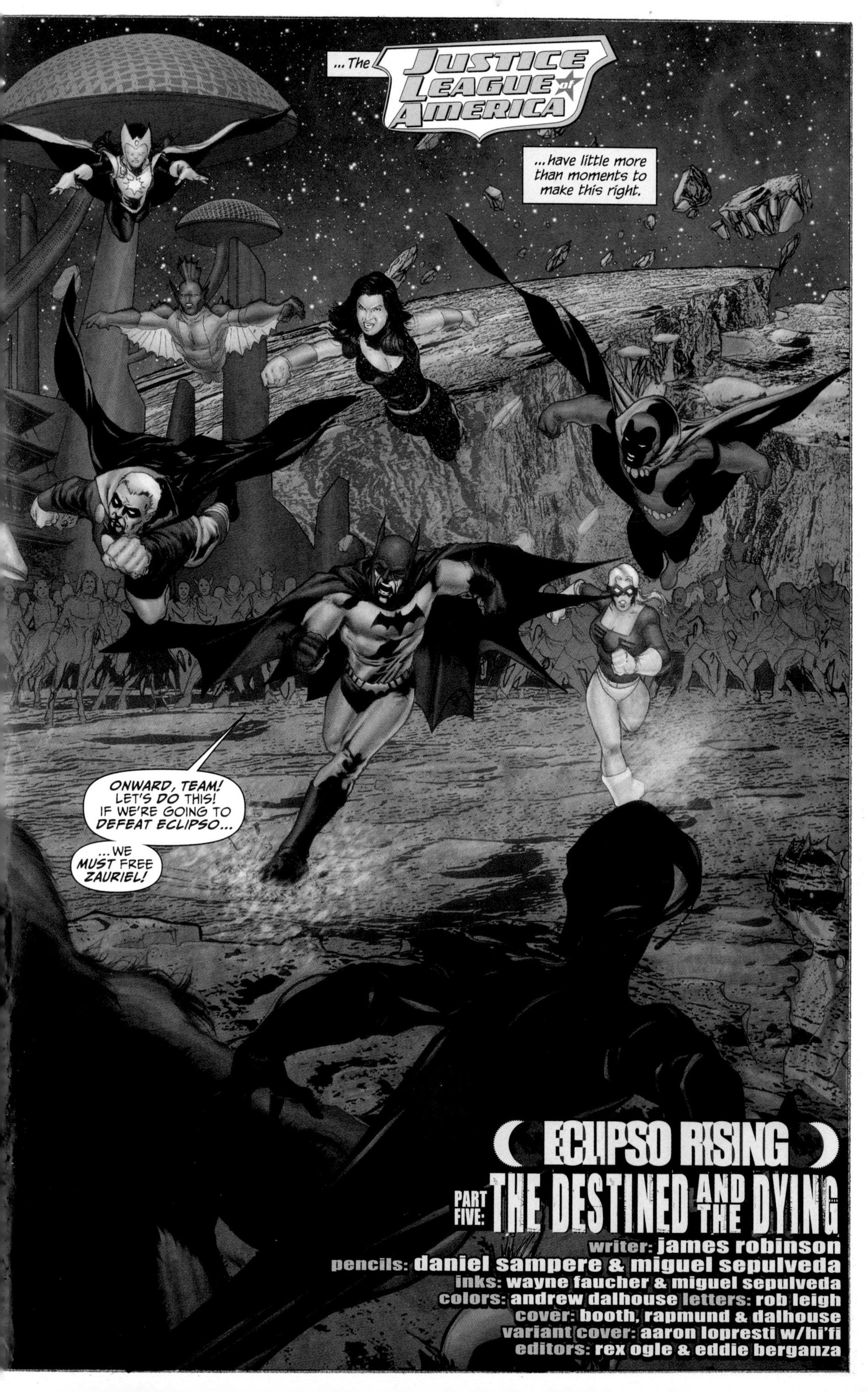
...The JUSTICE LEAGUE of AMERICA
...have little more than moments to make this right.
ONWARD, TEAM! LET'S DO THIS! IF WE'RE GOING TO DEFEAT ECLIPSO...
...WE MUST FREE ZAURIEL!
ECLIPSO RISING
PART FIVE: THE DESTINED AND THE DYING...
writer: james robinson
pencils: daniel sampere & miguel sepulveda
inks: wayne faucher & miguel sepulveda
colors: andrew dalhouse letters: rob leigh
cover: booth, rapmund & dalhouse
variant cover: aaron lopresti w/hi'fi
editors: rex ogle & eddie berganza

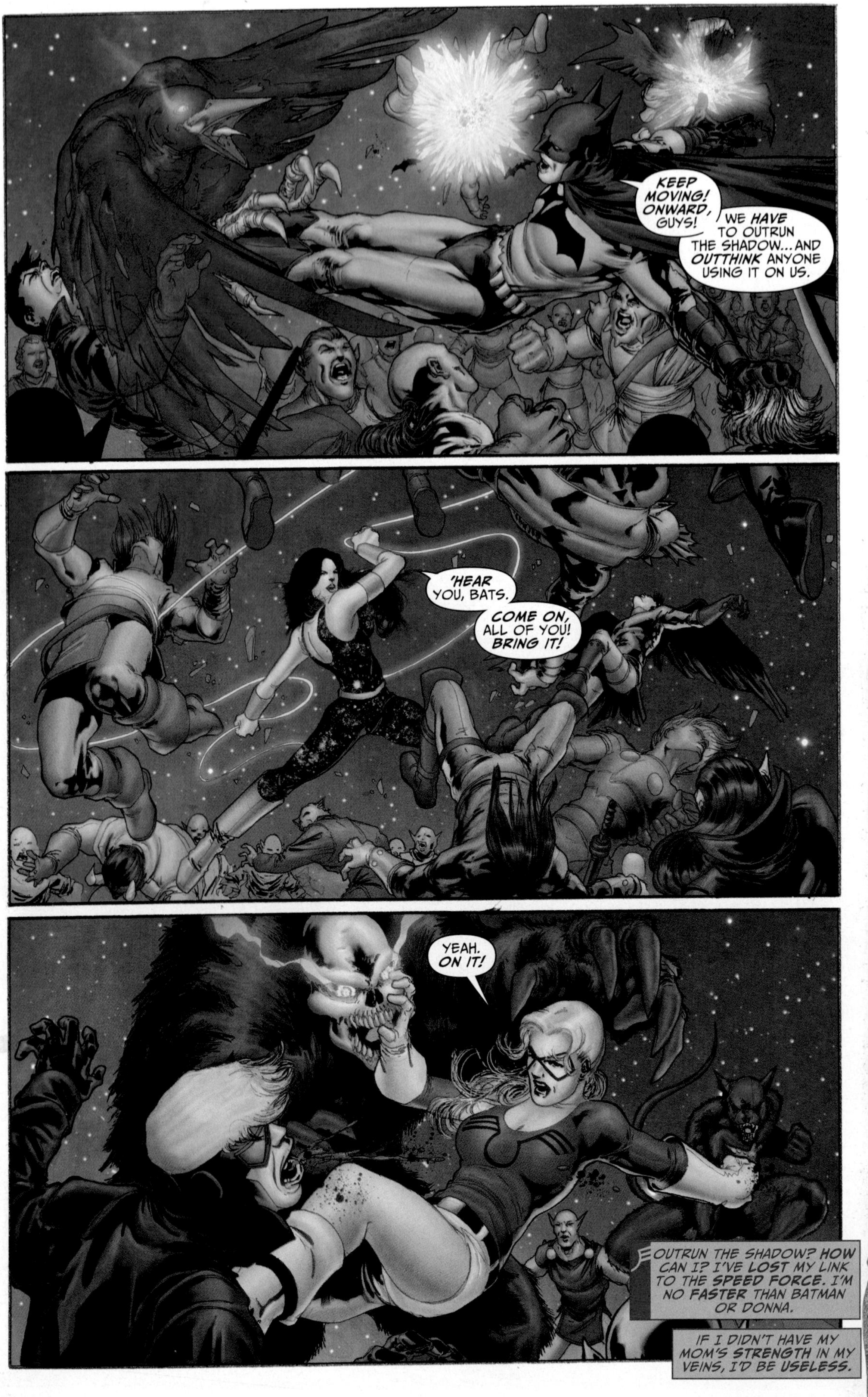
KEEP MOVING! ONWARD, GUYS!
WE HAVE TO OUTRUN THE SHADOW...AND OUTTHINK ANYONE USING IT ON US.
'HEAR YOU, BATS.
COME ON, ALL OF YOU! BRING IT!
YEAH. ON IT!
OUTRUN THE SHADOW? HOW CAN I? I'VE LOST MY LINK TO THE SPEED FORCE. I'M NO FASTER THAN BATMAN OR DONNA.
IF I DIDN'T HAVE MY MOM'S STRENGTH IN MY VEINS, I'D BE USELESS.

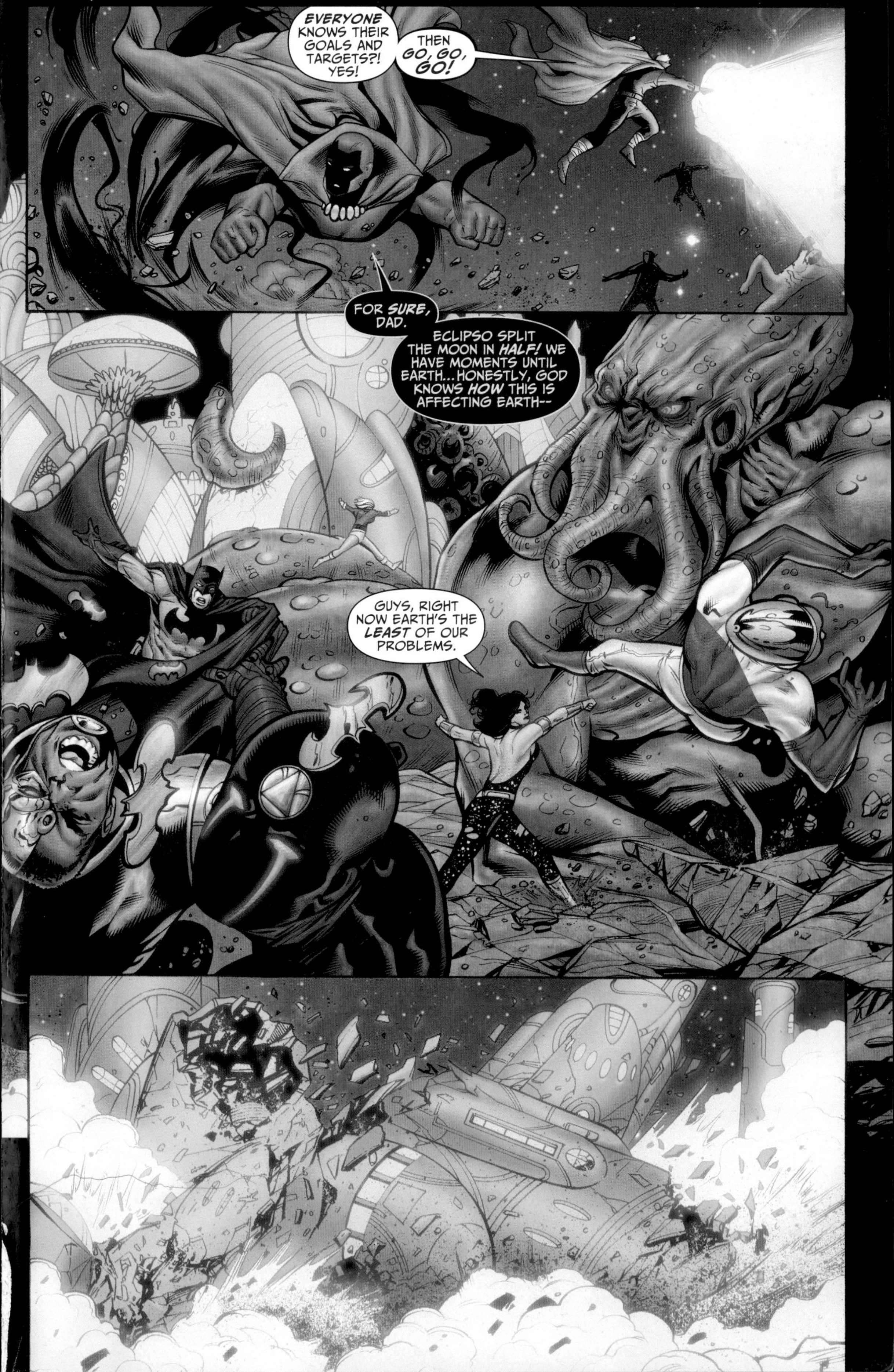
EVERYONE KNOWS THEIR GOALS AND TARGETS?! YES!
THEN GO, GO, GO!
FOR SURE, DAD.
ECLIPSO SPLIT THE MOON IN HALF! WE HAVE MOMENTS UNTIL EARTH...HONESTLY, GOD KNOWS HOW THIS IS AFFECTING EARTH--
GUYS, RIGHT NOW EARTH'S THE LEAST OF OUR PROBLEMS.

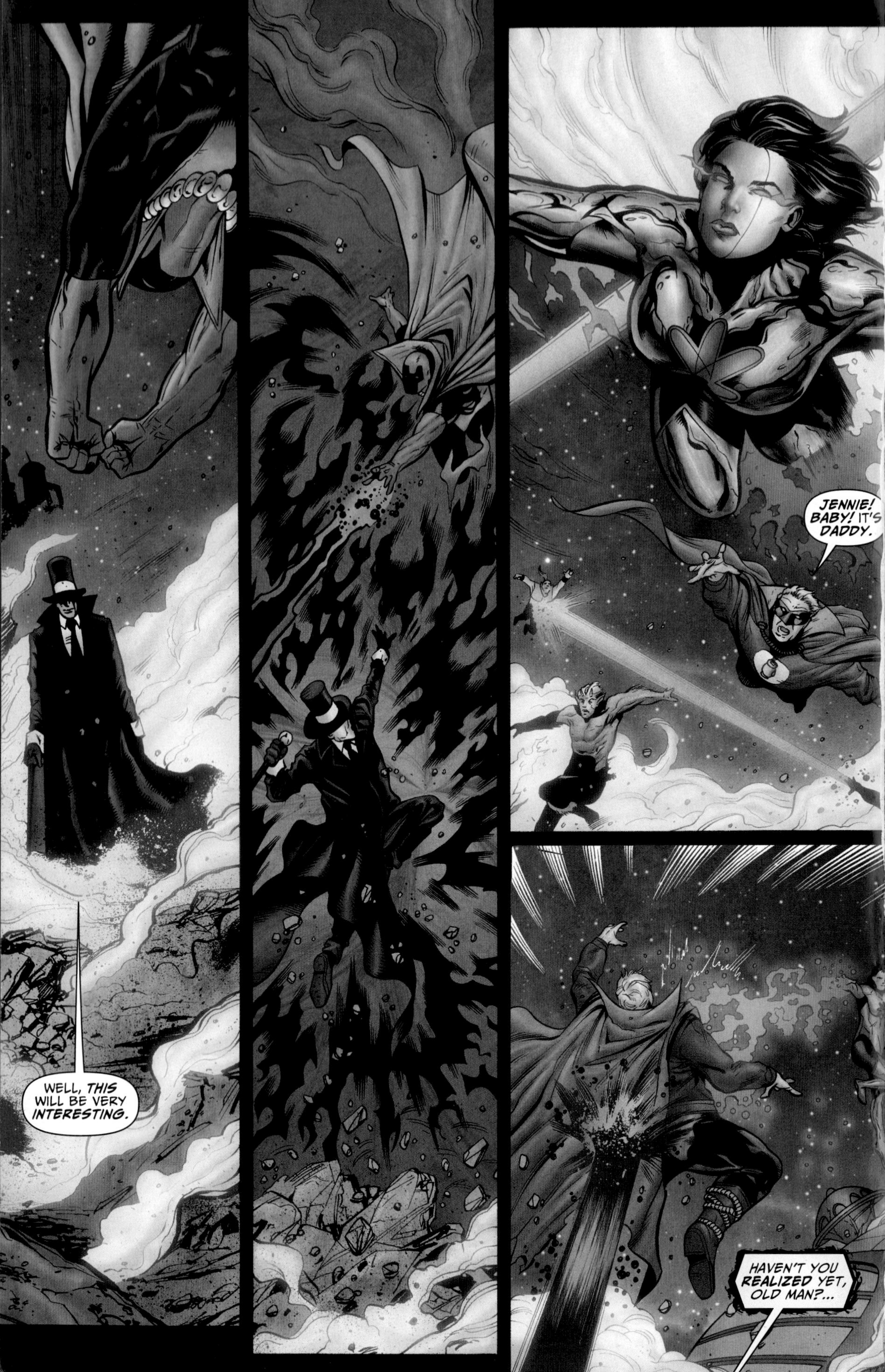
WELL, THIS WILL BE VERY INTERESTING.
JENNIE! BABY! IT'S DADDY.
HAVEN'T YOU REALIZED YET, OLD MAN?...

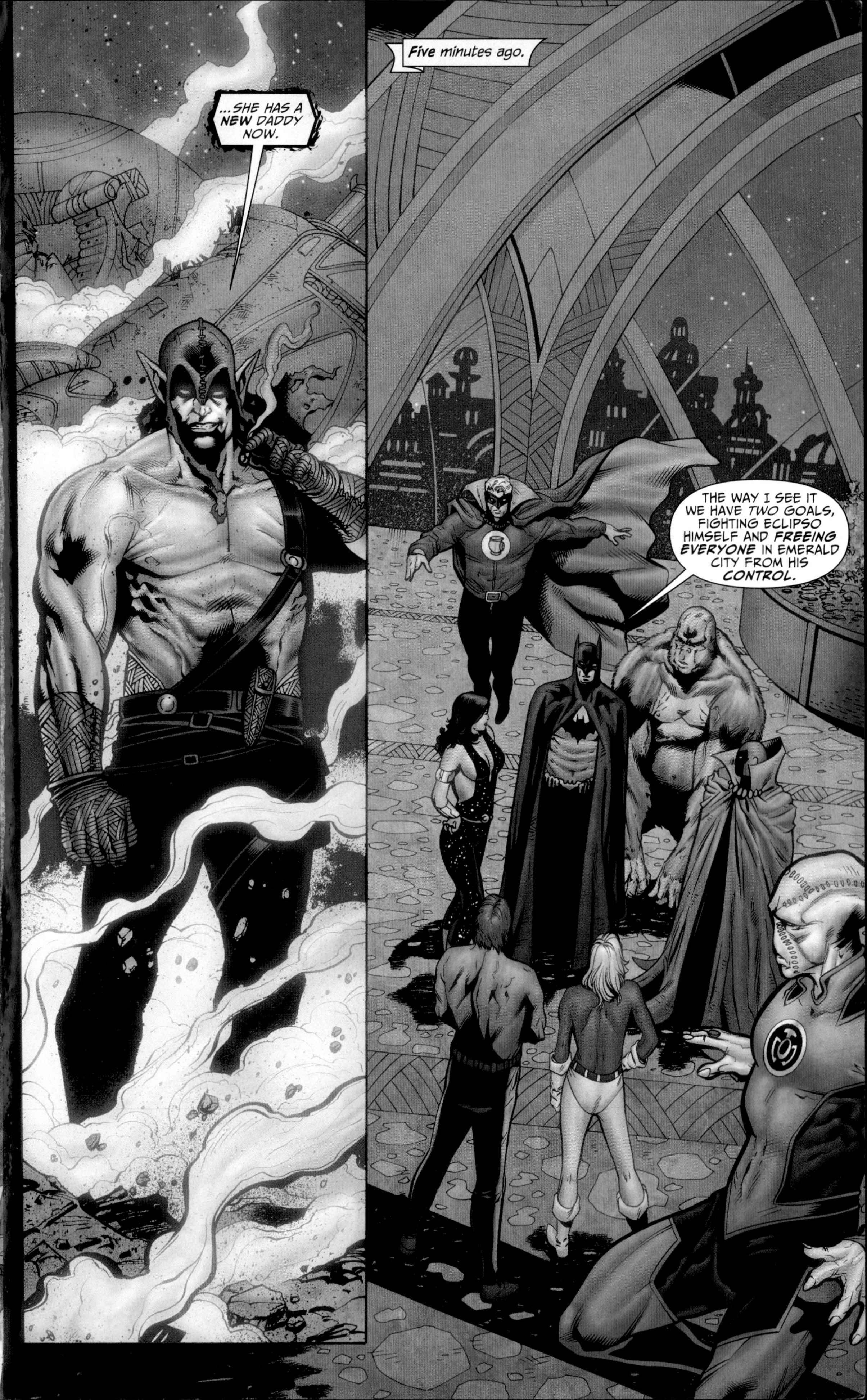
...SHE HAS A NEW DADDY NOW.
Five minutes ago.
THE WAY I SEE IT WE HAVE TWO GOALS, FIGHTING ECLIPSO HIMSELF AND FREEING EVERYONE IN EMERALD CITY FROM HIS CONTROL.

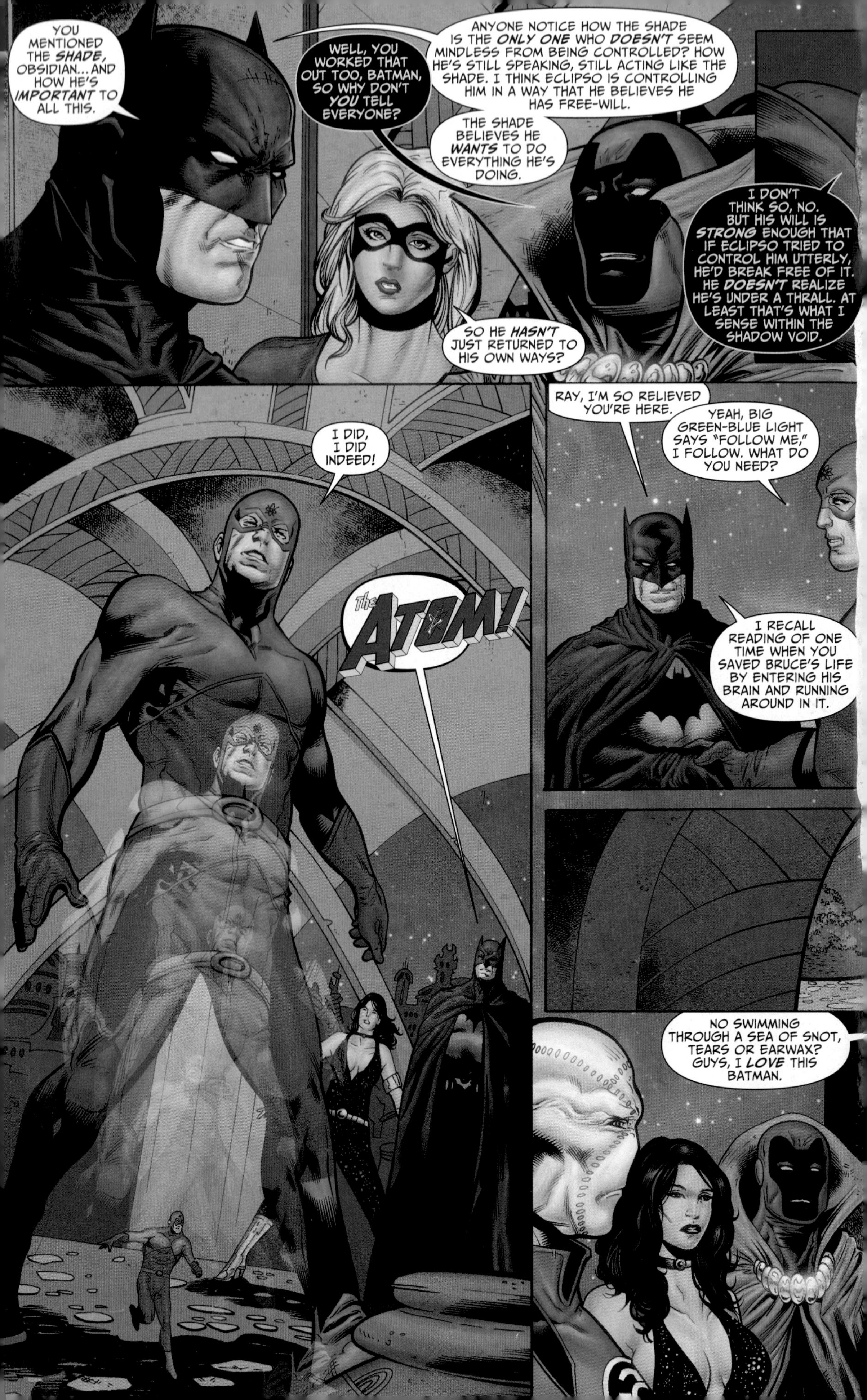
YOU MENTIONED THE SHADE, OBSIDIAN...AND HOW HE'S IMPORTANT TO ALL THIS.
WELL, YOU WORKED THAT OUT TOO, BATMAN, SO WHY DON'T YOU TELL EVERYONE?
ANYONE NOTICE HOW THE SHADE IS THE ONLY ONE WHO DOESN'T SEEM MINDLESS FROM BEING CONTROLLED? HOW HE'S STILL SPEAKING, STILL ACTING LIKE THE SHADE. I THINK ECLIPSO IS CONTROLLING HIM IN A WAY THAT HE BELIEVES HE HAS FREE-WILL.
THE SHADE BELIEVES HE WANTS TO DO EVERYTHING HE'S DOING.
SO HE HASN'T JUST RETURNED TO HIS OWN WAYS?
I DON'T THINK SO, NO. BUT HIS WILL IS STRONG ENOUGH THAT IF ECLIPSO TRIED TO CONTROL HIM UTTERLY, HE'D BREAK FREE OF IT. HE DOESN'T REALIZE HE'S UNDER A THRALL. AT LEAST THAT'S WHAT I SENSE WITHIN THE SHADOW VOID.
I DID, I DID INDEED!
The ATOM!
RAY, I'M SO RELIEVED YOU'RE HERE.
YEAH, BIG GREEN-BLUE LIGHT SAYS "FOLLOW ME," I FOLLOW. WHAT DO YOU NEED?
I RECALL READING OF ONE TIME WHEN YOU SAVED BRUCE'S LIFE BY ENTERING HIS BRAIN AND RUNNING AROUND IN IT.
NO SWIMMING THROUGH A SEA OF SNOT, TEARS OR EARWAX? GUYS, I LOVE THIS BATMAN.

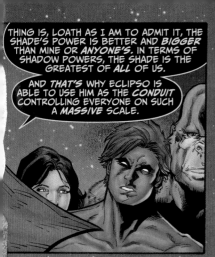

THING IS, LOATH AS I AM TO ADMIT IT, THE SHADE'S POWER IS BETTER AND *BIGGER* THAN MINE OR *ANYONE'S.* IN TERMS OF SHADOW POWERS, THE SHADE IS THE GREATEST OF *ALL* OF US.

AND *THAT'S* WHY ECLIPSO IS ABLE TO USE HIM AS THE *CONDUIT* CONTROLLING EVERYONE ON SUCH A *MASSIVE* SCALE.

SO IF WE *FREE* THE SHADE, WE FREE *EVERYONE.* BUT *HOW?*

FOLLOWING BATMAN'S ORDER I SENT A *SUMMONS* TO EARTH FOR ONE OF YOUR HEROES...*ALTHOUGH* WITH EVERYTHING HAPPENING THERE I CAN BUT HOPE THAT HE GOT THE SIGNAL.

HE WAS BRAIN-DEAD, SURE, I KICK-STARTED SOME NEURONS. LONG TIME AGO.

EDITORS NOTE: WAY BACK IN *BRAVE & THE BOLD* #115 (1ST SERIES).

THEN WHAT I NEED IS FOR YOU TO DO SOMETHING LIKE THAT AGAIN. I WANT YOU TO ENTER THE BRAIN OF THE SHADE AND ACT AS A GUIDE FOR ONE OF OUR TEAM.

WHO?

THE ONE WHOSE LIGHT SHINES *BRIGHTEST,* MIKAAL.

ME AND STARMAN, *huh?* SURE. I CAN JERRY-RIG THE WHITE DWARF STAR IN MY BELT TO SHRINK THE PAIR OF US. THEN WE JUST HAVE TO SNEAK INTO HIS HEAD.

YEAH, ABOUT THAT, I DON'T WANT TO RISK SHOWING OUR HAND, SO IT *WON'T* BE YOUR NORMAL ROUTE INTO SOMEONE'S SKULL.

SO WHAT IS OUR ROUTE?

BILL, YOU'RE GOOD WITH A *RIFLE,* RIGHT?

WELL, AS "CONGO" BILL, I CERTAINLY FIRED ONE OFTEN ENOUGH, AND MY FATHER WAS A GAMEKEEPER.

DON'T GET THE LINK, BUDDY.

SCOTTISH GAMEKEEPERS *INVENTED* SNIPING, MIK. LOOK IT UP.

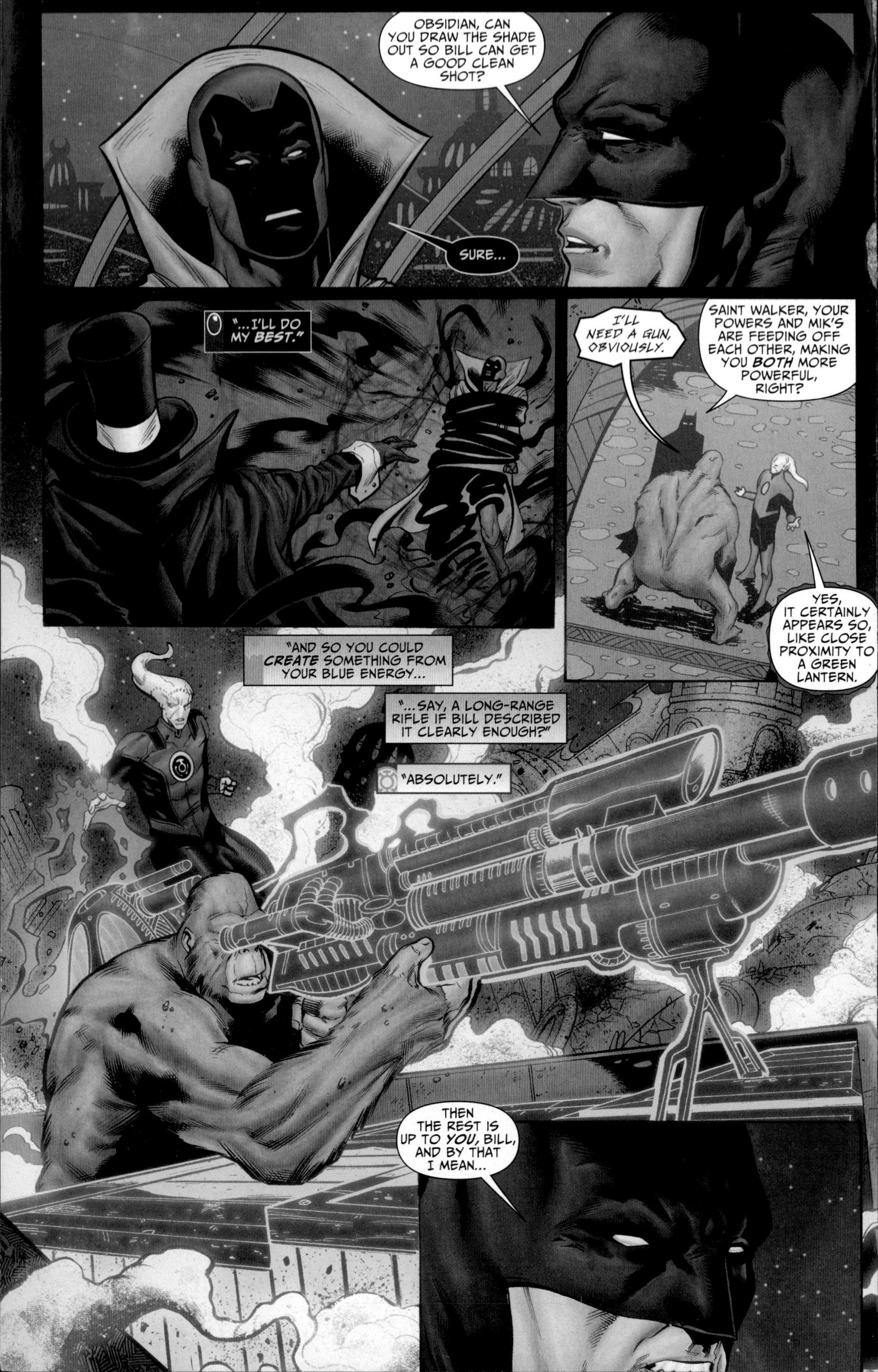
OBSIDIAN, CAN YOU DRAW THE SHADE OUT SO BILL CAN GET A GOOD CLEAN SHOT?
SURE...
"...I'LL DO MY BEST."
I'LL NEED A GUN, OBVIOUSLY.
SAINT WALKER, YOUR POWERS AND MIK'S ARE FEEDING OFF EACH OTHER, MAKING YOU BOTH MORE POWERFUL, RIGHT?
YES, IT CERTAINLY APPEARS SO, LIKE CLOSE PROXIMITY TO A GREEN LANTERN.
"AND SO YOU COULD CREATE SOMETHING FROM YOUR BLUE ENERGY...
"...SAY, A LONG-RANGE RIFLE IF BILL DESCRIBED IT CLEARLY ENOUGH?"
"ABSOLUTELY."
THEN THE REST IS UP TO YOU, BILL, AND BY THAT I MEAN...

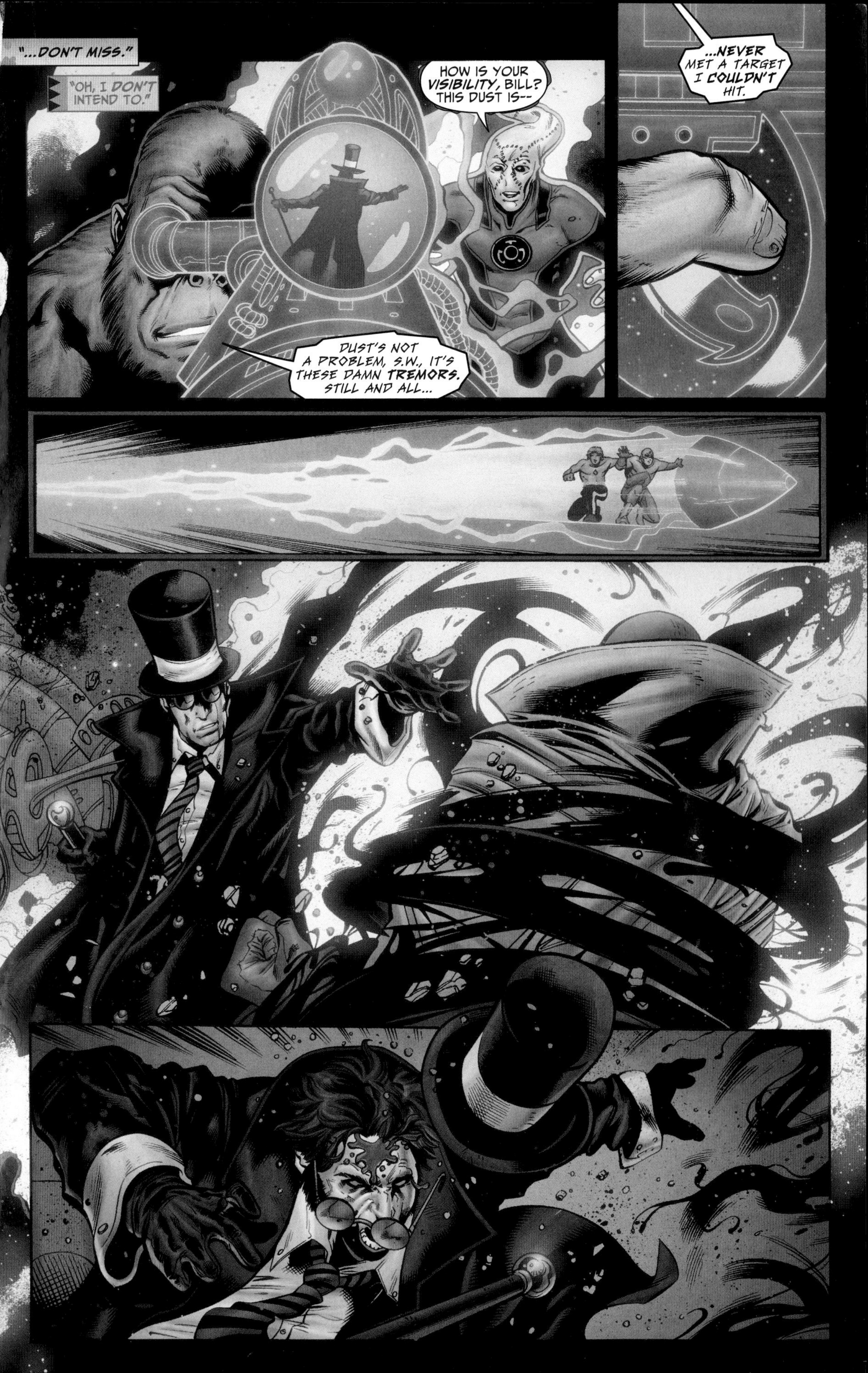
"...DON'T MISS."
"OH, I DON'T INTEND TO."
HOW IS YOUR VISIBILITY, BILL? THIS DUST IS--
DUST'S NOT A PROBLEM, S.W., IT'S THESE DAMN TREMORS. STILL AND ALL...
...NEVER MET A TARGET I COULDN'T HIT.

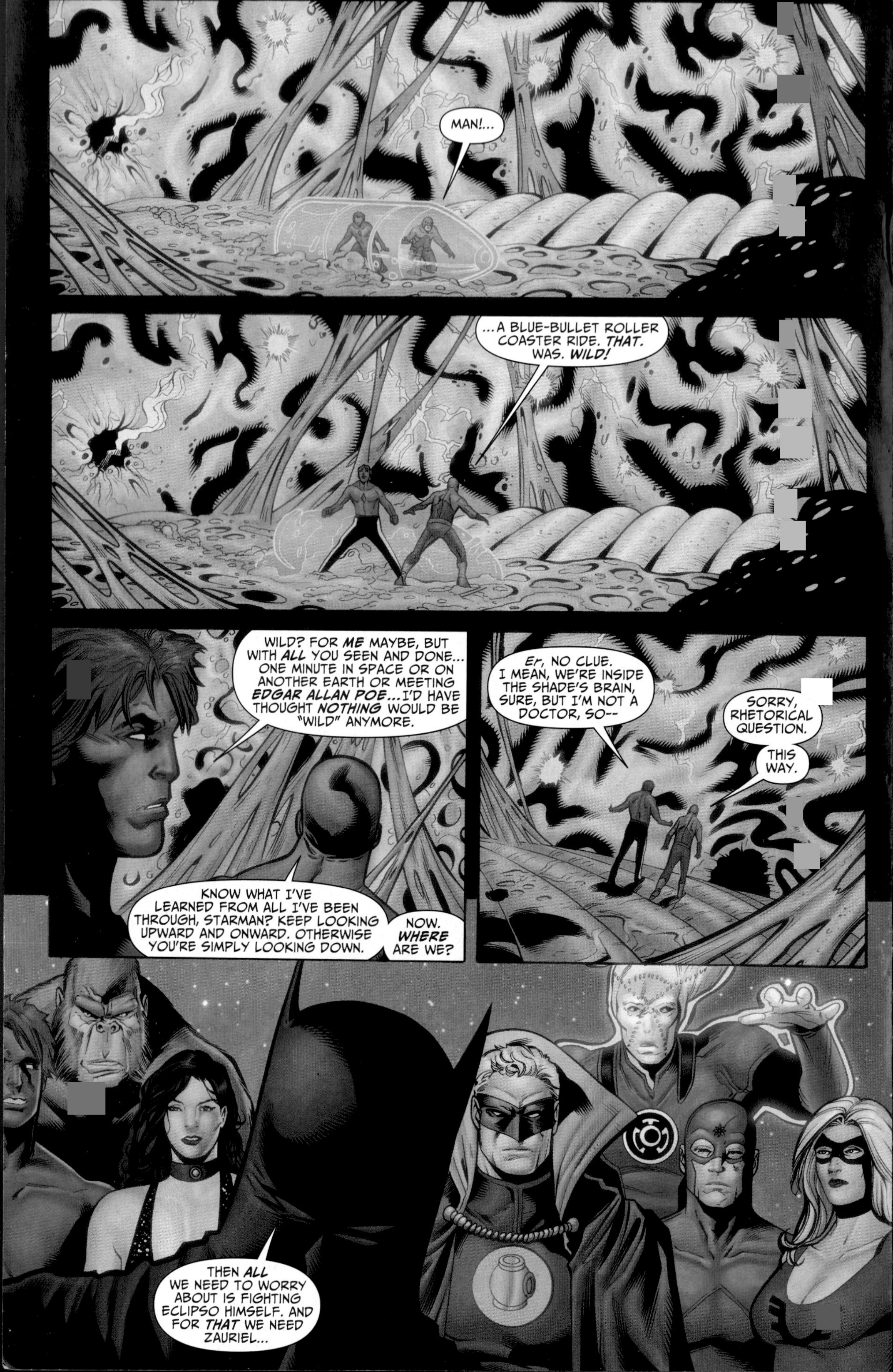
MAN!...
...A BLUE-BULLET ROLLER COASTER RIDE. THAT. WAS. WILD!
WILD? FOR ME MAYBE, BUT WITH ALL YOU SEEN AND DONE... ONE MINUTE IN SPACE OR ON ANOTHER EARTH OR MEETING EDGAR ALLAN POE...I'D HAVE THOUGHT NOTHING WOULD BE "WILD" ANYMORE.
KNOW WHAT I'VE LEARNED FROM ALL I'VE BEEN THROUGH, STARMAN? KEEP LOOKING UPWARD AND ONWARD. OTHERWISE YOU'RE SIMPLY LOOKING DOWN.
NOW. WHERE ARE WE?
Er, NO CLUE. I MEAN, WE'RE INSIDE THE SHADE'S BRAIN, SURE, BUT I'M NOT A DOCTOR, SO--
SORRY, RHETORICAL QUESTION.
THIS WAY.
THEN ALL WE NEED TO WORRY ABOUT IS FIGHTING ECLIPSO HIMSELF. AND FOR THAT WE NEED ZAURIEL...

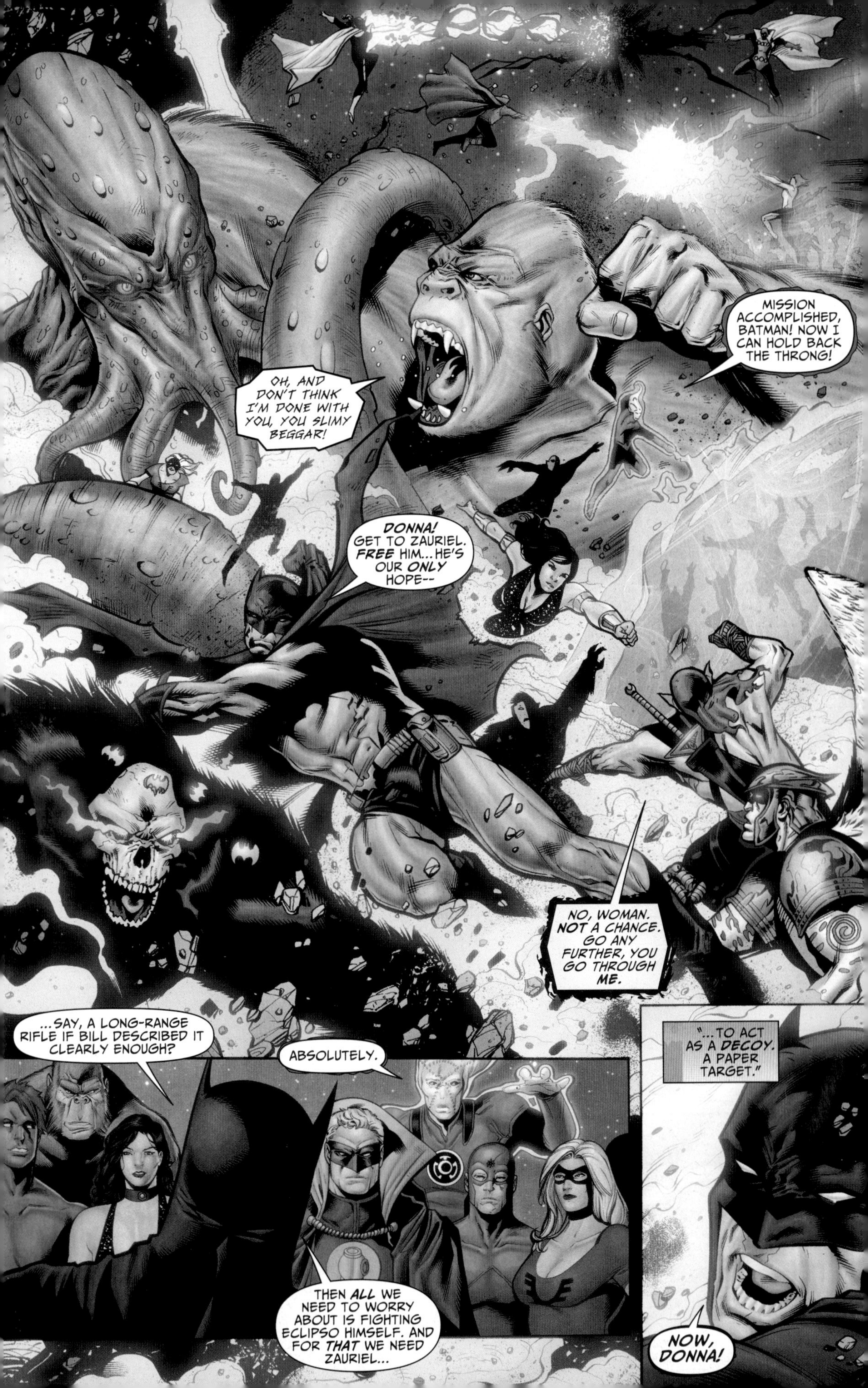
MISSION ACCOMPLISHED, BATMAN! NOW I CAN HOLD BACK THE THRONG!
OH, AND DON'T THINK I'M DONE WITH YOU, YOU SLIMY BEGGAR!
DONNA! GET TO ZAURIEL. FREE HIM... HE'S OUR ONLY HOPE--
NO, WOMAN. NOT A CHANCE. GO ANY FURTHER, YOU GO THROUGH ME.
...SAY, A LONG-RANGE RIFLE IF BILL DESCRIBED IT CLEARLY ENOUGH?
ABSOLUTELY.
THEN ALL WE NEED TO WORRY ABOUT IS FIGHTING ECLIPSO HIMSELF. AND FOR THAT WE NEED ZAURIEL...
"...TO ACT AS A DECOY. A PAPER TARGET."
NOW, DONNA!

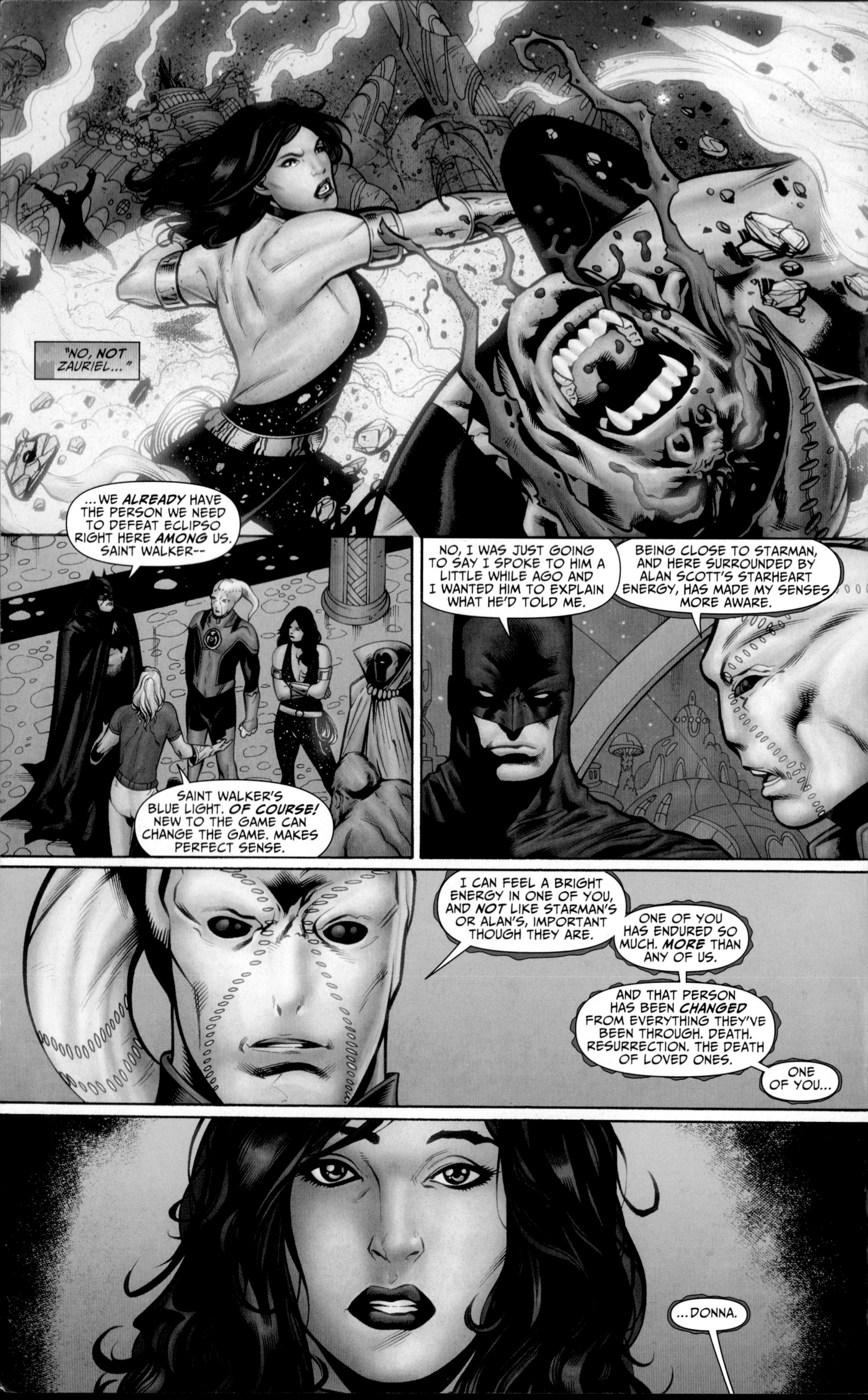
"NO, NOT ZAURIEL..."
...WE ALREADY HAVE THE PERSON WE NEED TO DEFEAT ECLIPSO RIGHT HERE AMONG US. SAINT WALKER--
SAINT WALKER'S BLUE LIGHT. OF COURSE! NEW TO THE GAME CAN CHANGE THE GAME. MAKES PERFECT SENSE.
NO, I WAS JUST GOING TO SAY I SPOKE TO HIM A LITTLE WHILE AGO AND I WANTED HIM TO EXPLAIN WHAT HE'D TOLD ME.
BEING CLOSE TO STARMAN, AND HERE SURROUNDED BY ALAN SCOTT'S STARHEART ENERGY, HAS MADE MY SENSES MORE AWARE.
I CAN FEEL A BRIGHT ENERGY IN ONE OF YOU, AND NOT LIKE STARMAN'S OR ALAN'S, IMPORTANT THOUGH THEY ARE.
ONE OF YOU HAS ENDURED SO MUCH. MORE THAN ANY OF US.
AND THAT PERSON HAS BEEN CHANGED FROM EVERYTHING THEY'VE BEEN THROUGH. DEATH. RESURRECTION. THE DEATH OF LOVED ONES.
ONE OF YOU...
...DONNA.

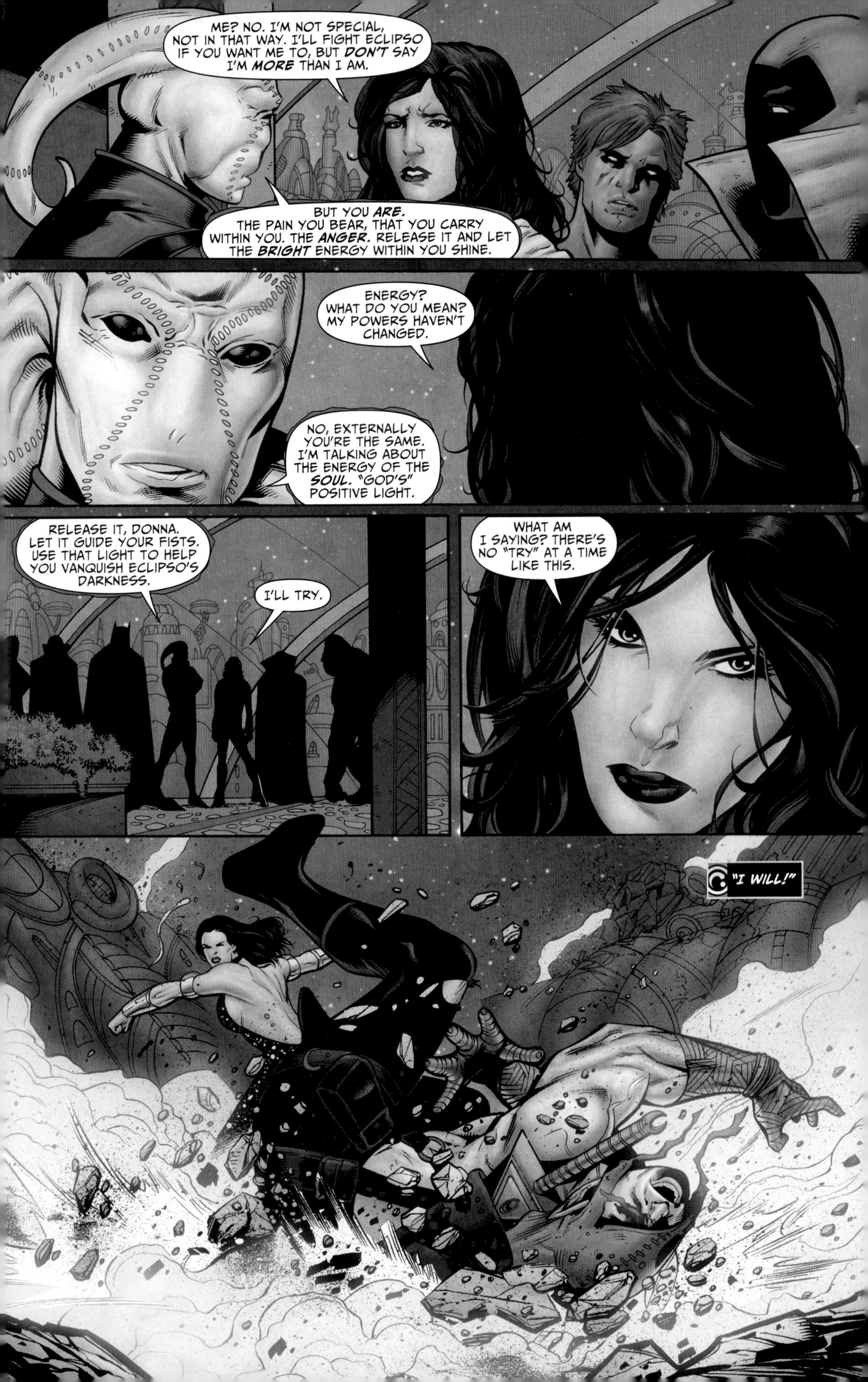
ME? NO. I'M NOT SPECIAL, NOT IN THAT WAY. I'LL FIGHT ECLIPSO IF YOU WANT ME TO, BUT DON'T SAY I'M MORE THAN I AM.
BUT YOU ARE. THE PAIN YOU BEAR, THAT YOU CARRY WITHIN YOU. THE ANGER. RELEASE IT AND LET THE BRIGHT ENERGY WITHIN YOU SHINE.
ENERGY? WHAT DO YOU MEAN? MY POWERS HAVEN'T CHANGED.
NO, EXTERNALLY YOU'RE THE SAME. I'M TALKING ABOUT THE ENERGY OF THE SOUL. "GOD'S" POSITIVE LIGHT.
RELEASE IT, DONNA. LET IT GUIDE YOUR FISTS. USE THAT LIGHT TO HELP YOU VANQUISH ECLIPSO'S DARKNESS.
I'LL TRY.
WHAT AM I SAYING? THERE'S NO "TRY" AT A TIME LIKE THIS.
"I WILL!"

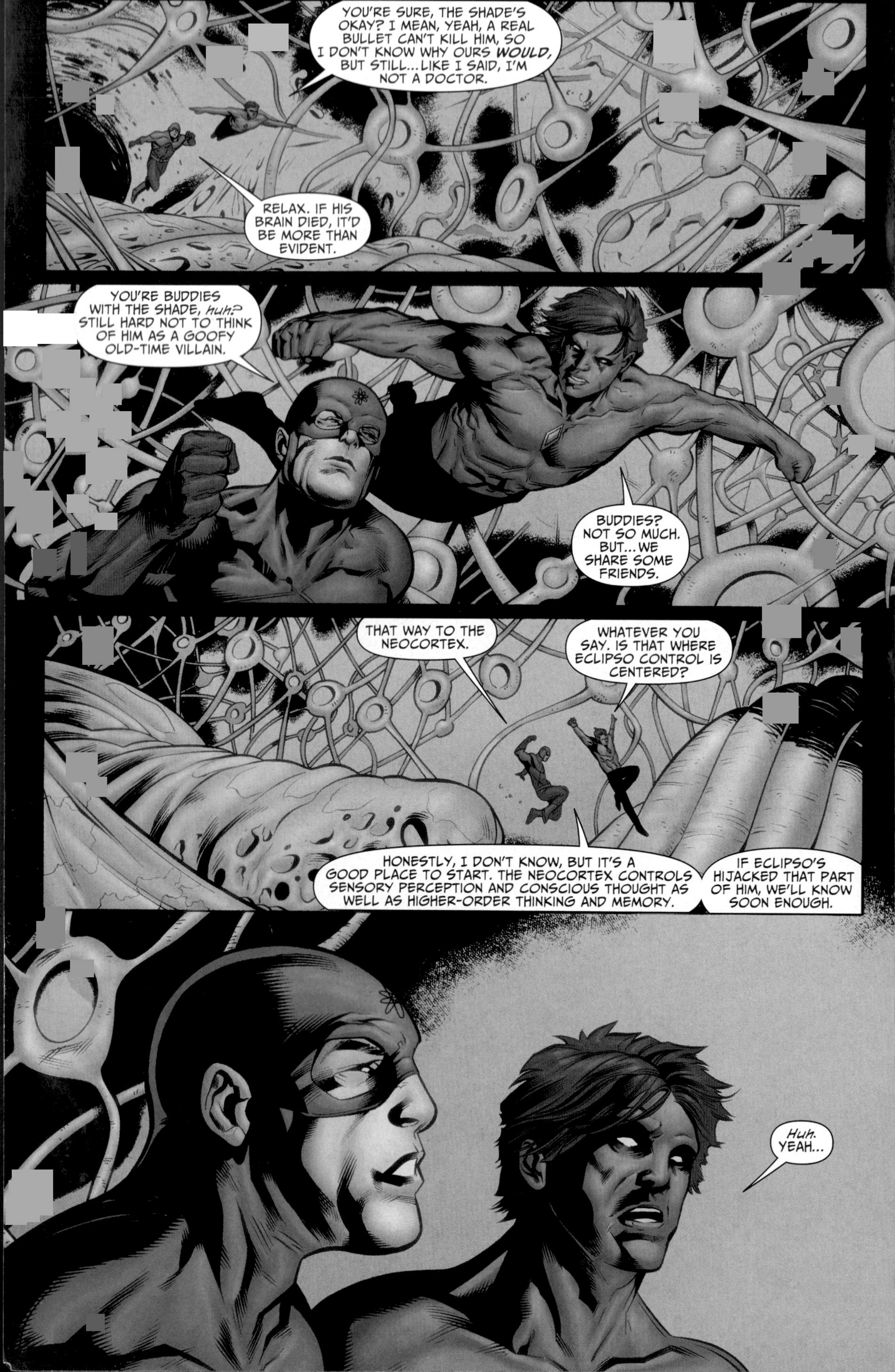
YOU'RE SURE, THE SHADE'S OKAY? I MEAN, YEAH, A REAL BULLET CAN'T KILL HIM, SO I DON'T KNOW WHY OURS *WOULD*, BUT STILL... LIKE I SAID, I'M NOT A DOCTOR.
RELAX. IF HIS BRAIN DIED, IT'D BE MORE THAN EVIDENT.
YOU'RE BUDDIES WITH THE SHADE, *huh?* STILL HARD NOT TO THINK OF HIM AS A GOOFY OLD-TIME VILLAIN.
BUDDIES? NOT SO MUCH. BUT... WE SHARE SOME FRIENDS.
THAT WAY TO THE NEOCORTEX.
WHATEVER YOU SAY. IS THAT WHERE ECLIPSO CONTROL IS CENTERED?
HONESTLY, I DON'T KNOW, BUT IT'S A GOOD PLACE TO START. THE NEOCORTEX CONTROLS SENSORY PERCEPTION AND CONSCIOUS THOUGHT AS WELL AS HIGHER-ORDER THINKING AND MEMORY.
IF ECLIPSO'S HIJACKED THAT PART OF HIM, WE'LL KNOW SOON ENOUGH.
Huh. YEAH...

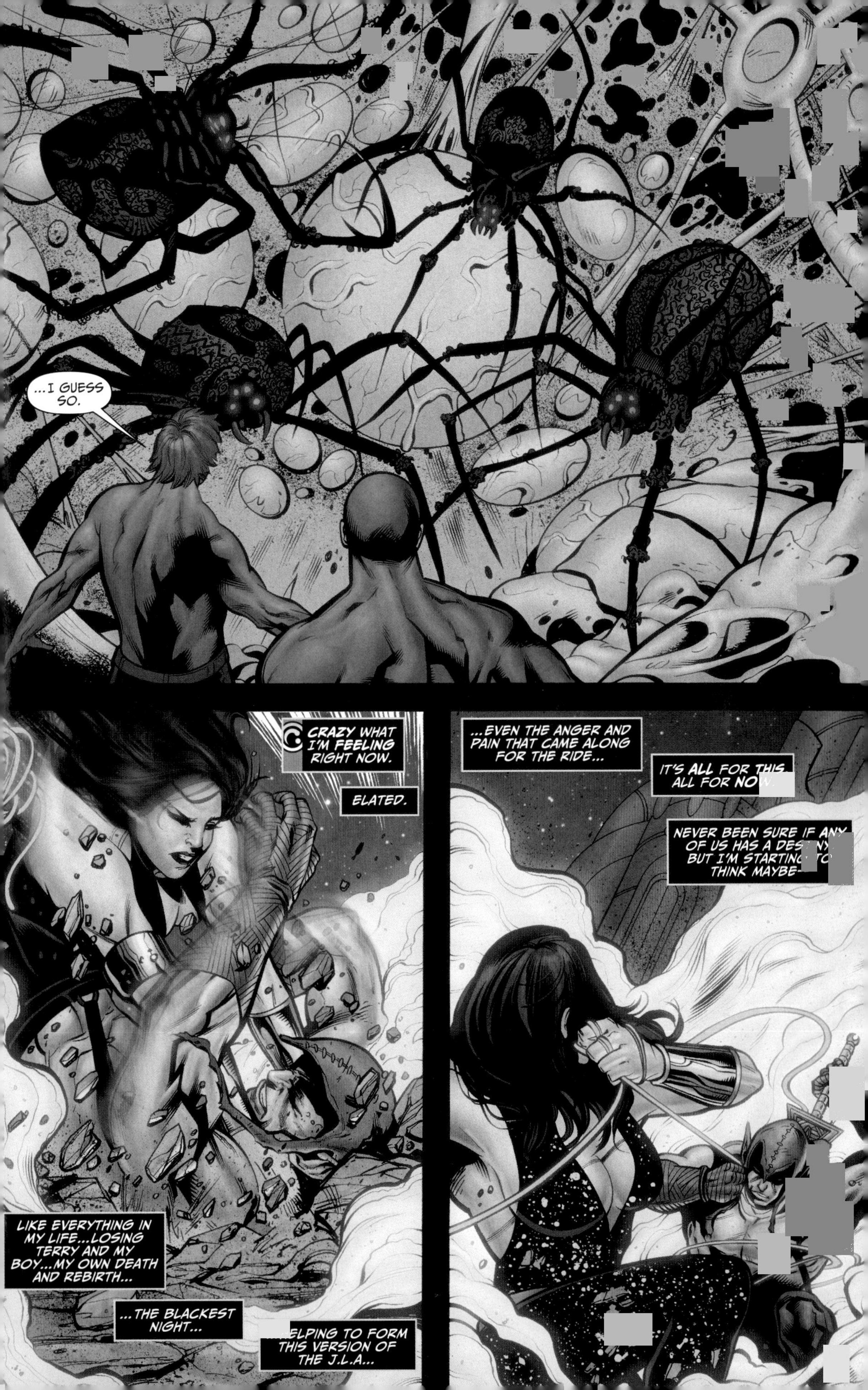
...I GUESS SO.
CRAZY WHAT I'M FEELING RIGHT NOW.
ELATED.
LIKE EVERYTHING IN MY LIFE...LOSING TERRY AND MY BOY...MY OWN DEATH AND REBIRTH...
...THE BLACKEST NIGHT...
...HELPING TO FORM THIS VERSION OF THE J.L.A...
...EVEN THE ANGER AND PAIN THAT CAME ALONG FOR THE RIDE...
IT'S ALL FOR THIS. ALL FOR NOW.
NEVER BEEN SURE IF ANY OF US HAS A DESTINY, BUT I'M STARTING TO THINK MAYBE--

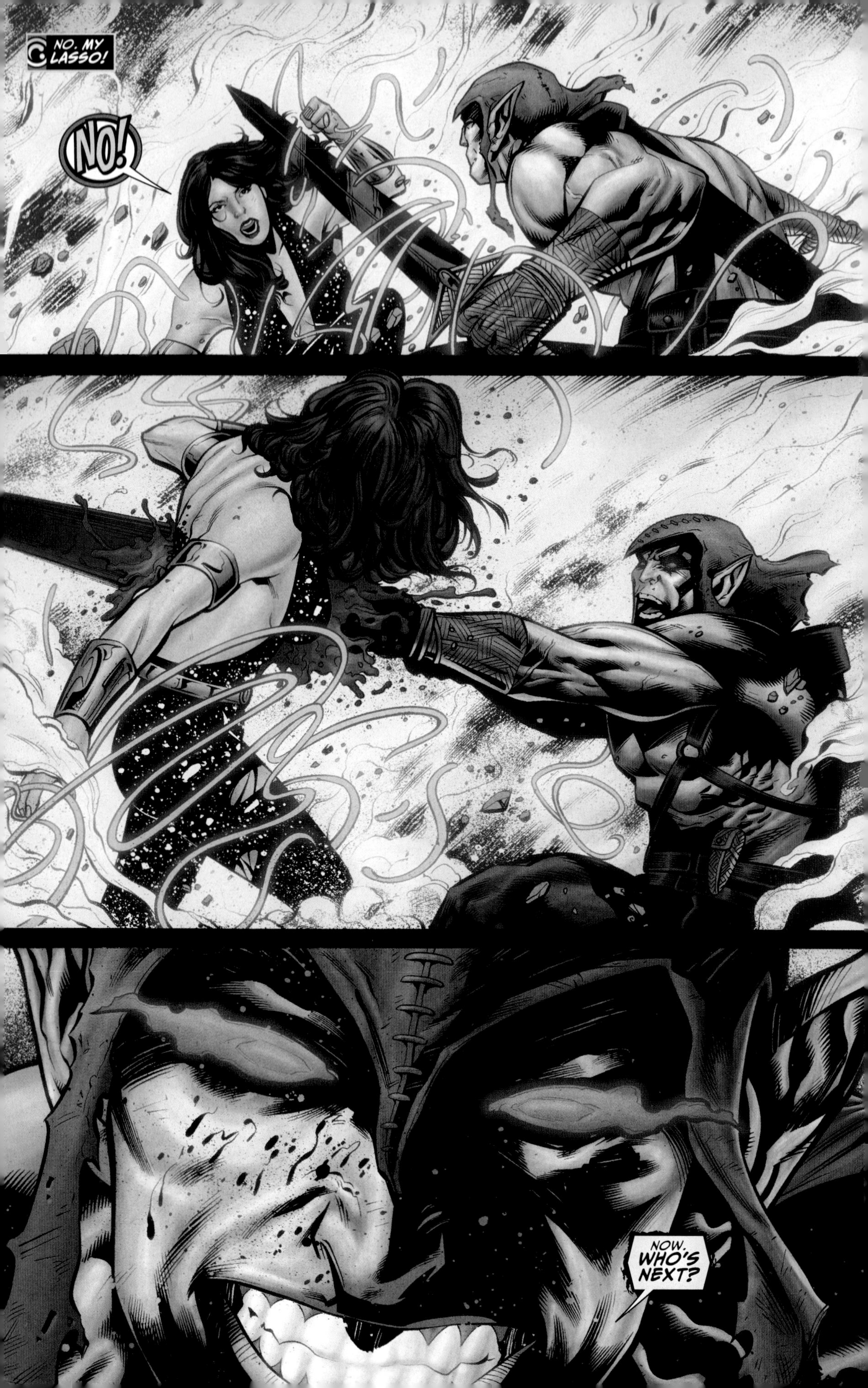
NO. MY LASSO!
NO!
NOW. WHO'S NEXT?

JUSTICE LEAGUE OF AMERICA 59
Cover by Brett Booth, Norm Rapmund & Andrew Dalhouse

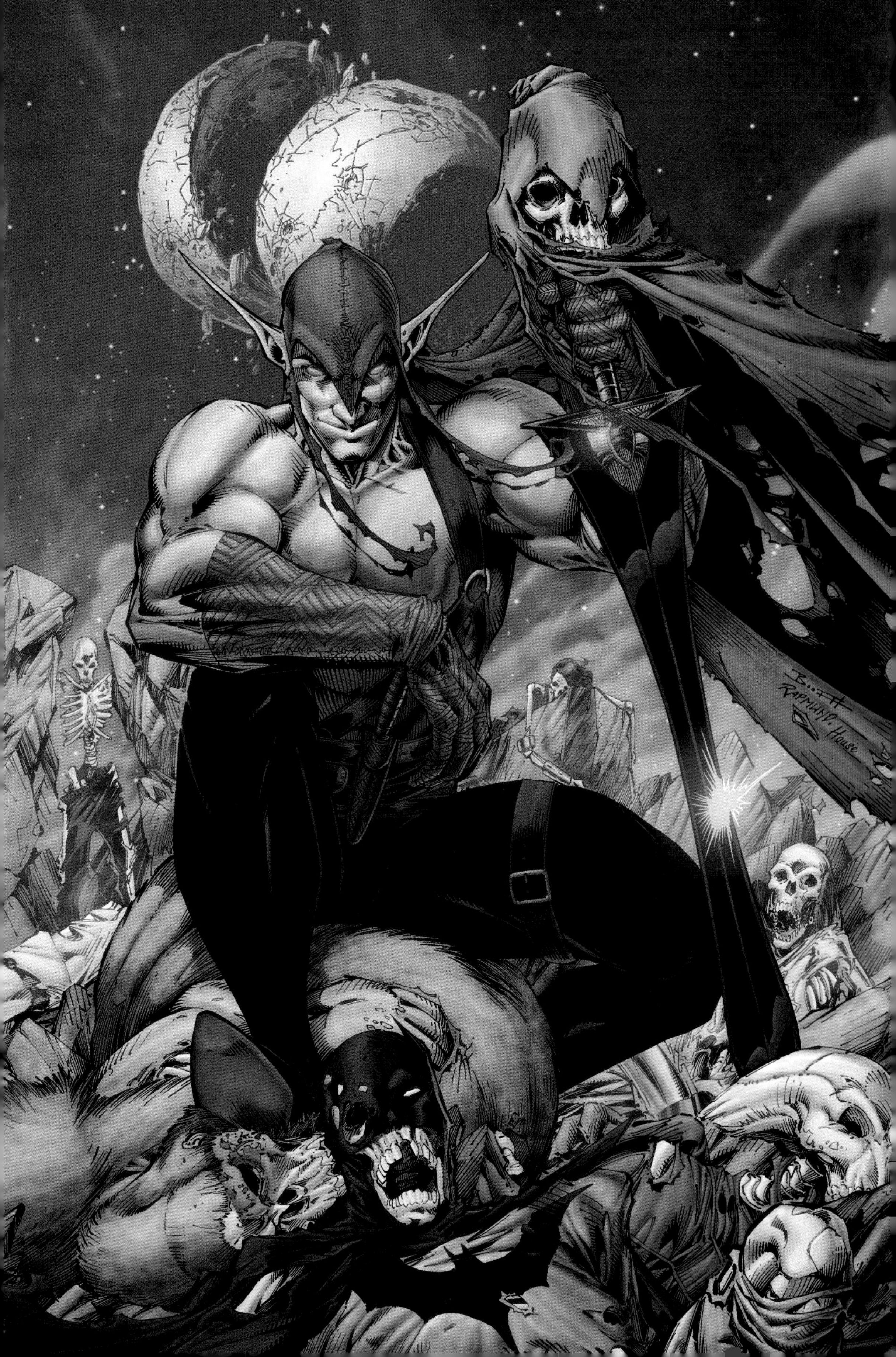

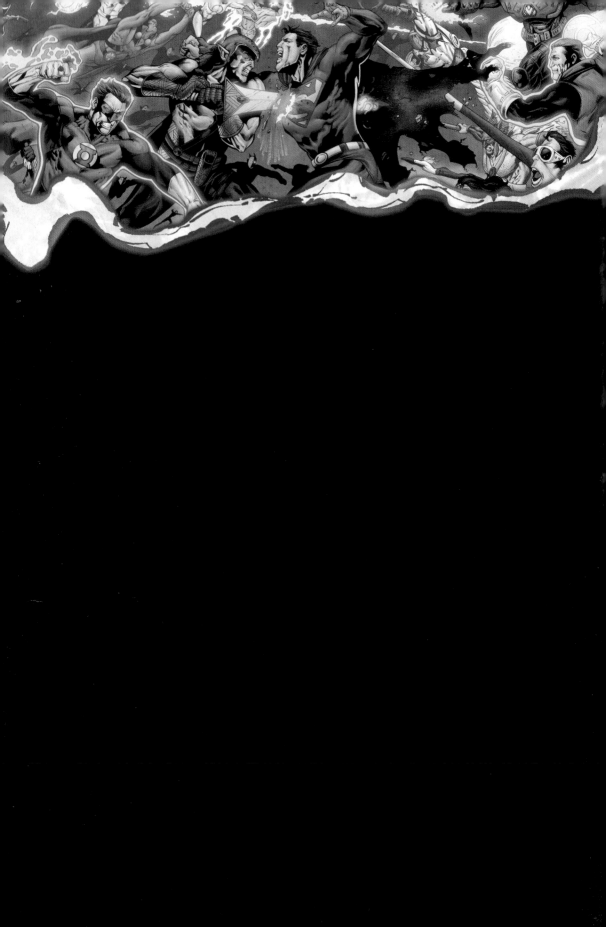

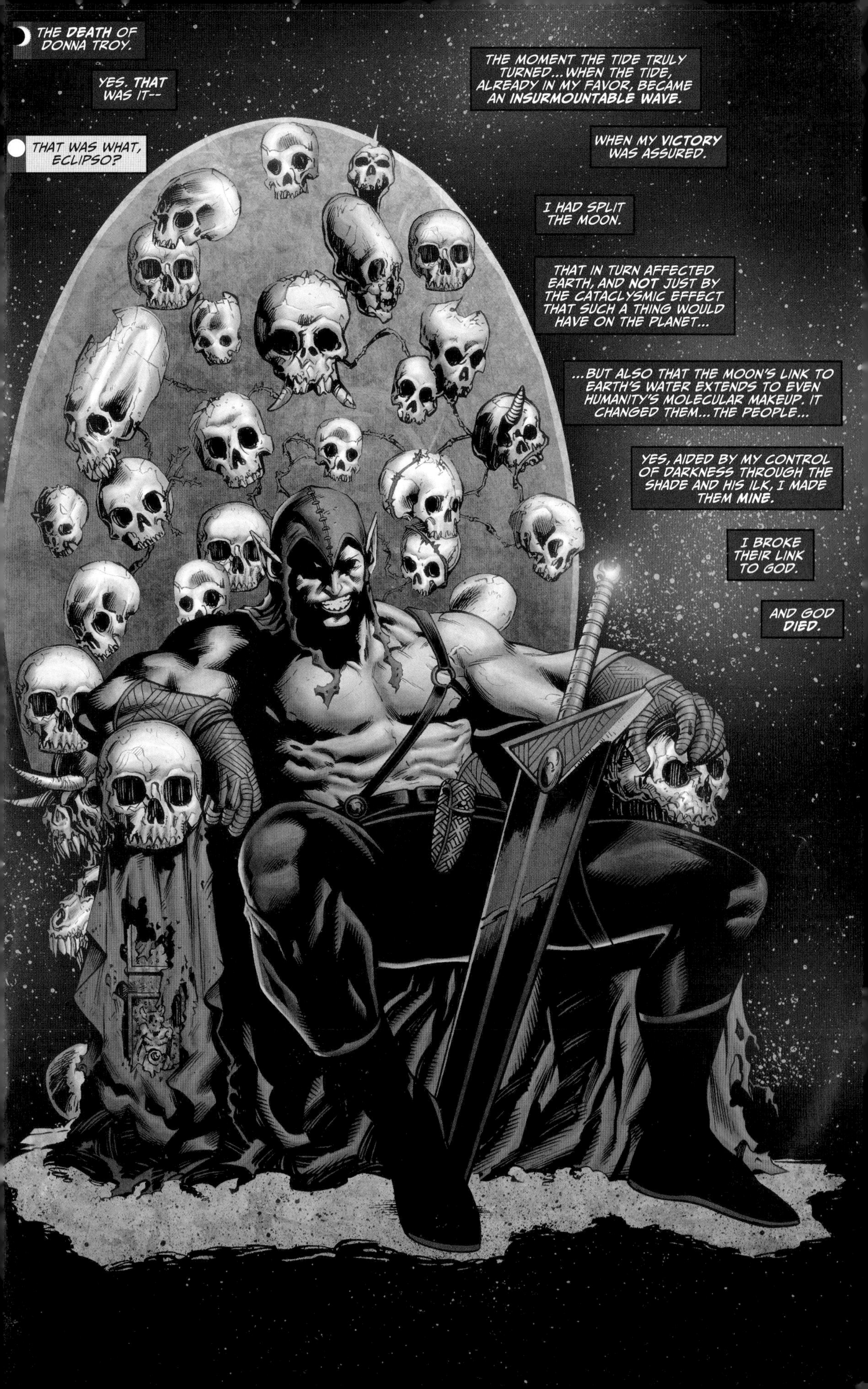
THE DEATH OF DONNA TROY.
YES. THAT WAS IT--
THAT WAS WHAT, ECLIPSO?
THE MOMENT THE TIDE TRULY TURNED...WHEN THE TIDE, ALREADY IN MY FAVOR, BECAME AN INSURMOUNTABLE WAVE.
WHEN MY VICTORY WAS ASSURED.
I HAD SPLIT THE MOON.
THAT IN TURN AFFECTED EARTH, AND NOT JUST BY THE CATACLYSMIC EFFECT THAT SUCH A THING WOULD HAVE ON THE PLANET...
...BUT ALSO THAT THE MOON'S LINK TO EARTH'S WATER EXTENDS TO EVEN HUMANITY'S MOLECULAR MAKEUP. IT CHANGED THEM...THE PEOPLE...
YES, AIDED BY MY CONTROL OF DARKNESS THROUGH THE SHADE AND HIS ILK, I MADE THEM MINE.
I BROKE THEIR LINK TO GOD.
AND GOD DIED.

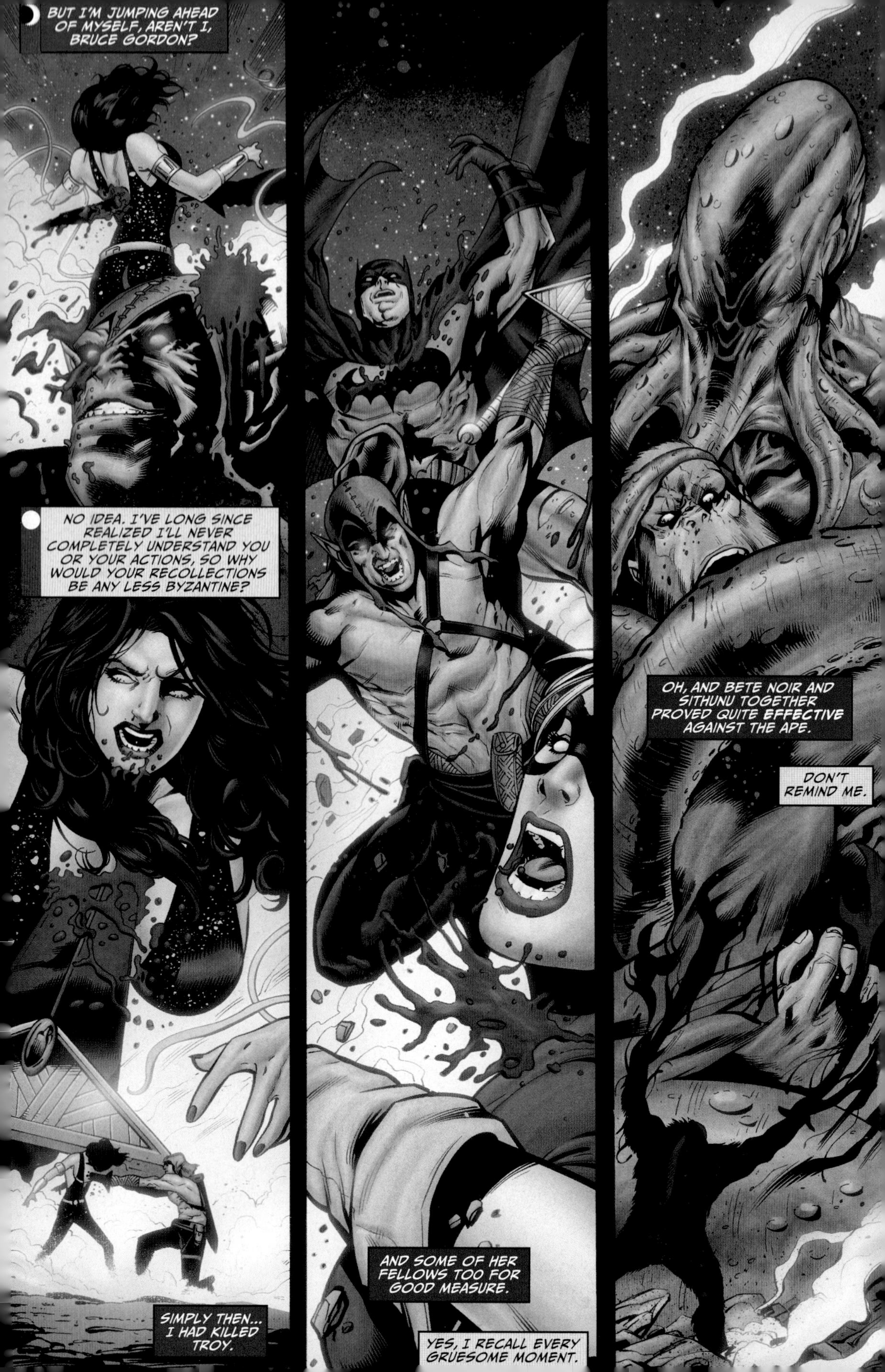
BUT I'M JUMPING AHEAD OF MYSELF, AREN'T I, BRUCE GORDON?
NO IDEA. I'VE LONG SINCE REALIZED I'LL NEVER COMPLETELY UNDERSTAND YOU OR YOUR ACTIONS, SO WHY WOULD YOUR RECOLLECTIONS BE ANY LESS BYZANTINE?
SIMPLY THEN... I HAD KILLED TROY.
AND SOME OF HER FELLOWS TOO FOR GOOD MEASURE.
YES, I RECALL EVERY GRUESOME MOMENT.
OH, AND BETE NOIR AND SITHUNU TOGETHER PROVED QUITE EFFECTIVE AGAINST THE APE.
DON'T REMIND ME.

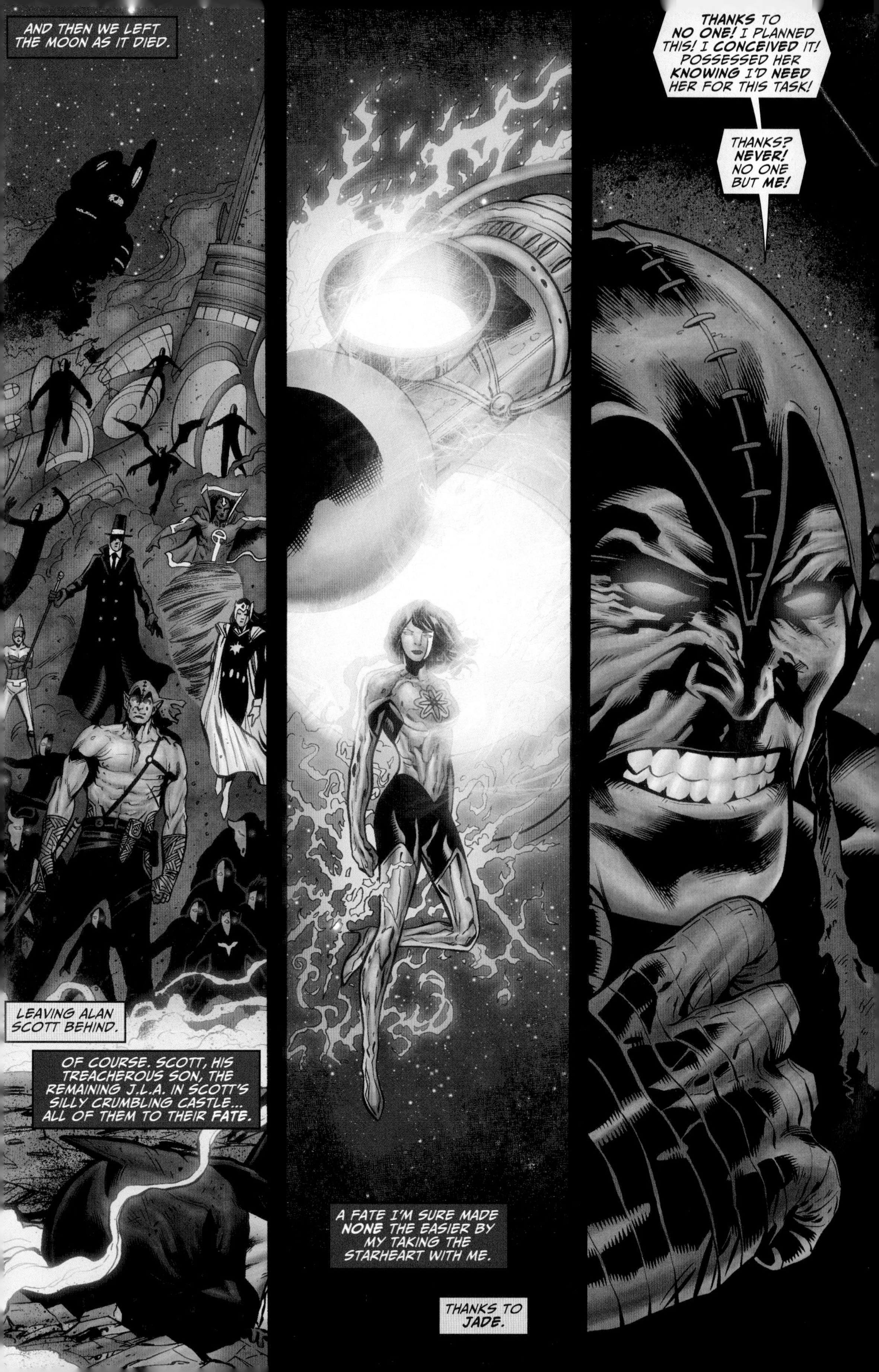
AND THEN WE LEFT THE MOON AS IT DIED.
LEAVING ALAN SCOTT BEHIND.
OF COURSE. SCOTT, HIS TREACHEROUS SON, THE REMAINING J.L.A. IN SCOTT'S SILLY CRUMBLING CASTLE... ALL OF THEM TO THEIR FATE.
A FATE I'M SURE MADE NONE THE EASIER BY MY TAKING THE STARHEART WITH ME.
THANKS TO JADE.
THANKS TO NO ONE! I PLANNED THIS! I CONCEIVED IT! POSSESSED HER KNOWING I'D NEED HER FOR THIS TASK!
THANKS? NEVER! NO ONE BUT ME!

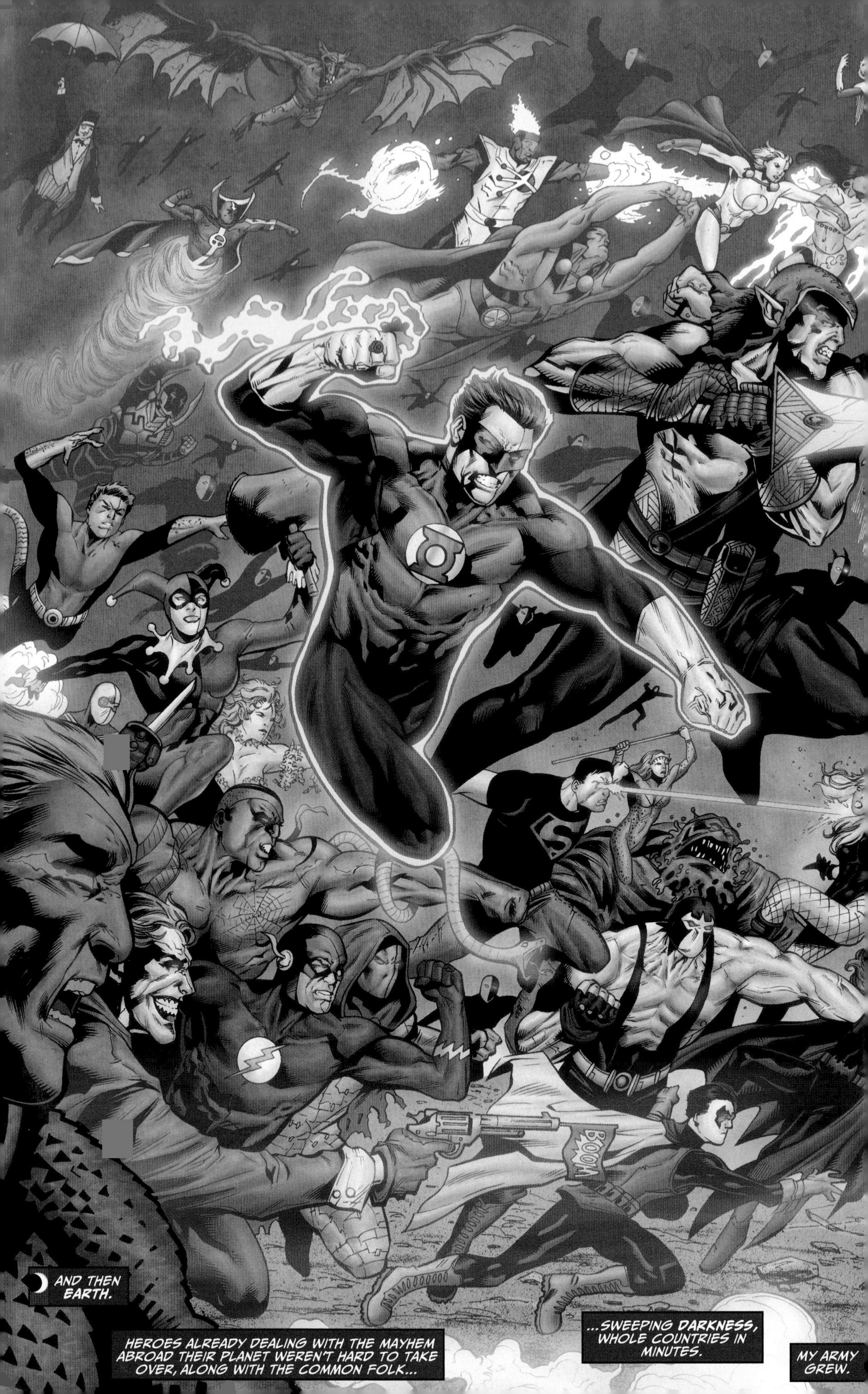
BOOM
AND THEN EARTH.
HEROES ALREADY DEALING WITH THE MAYHEM ABROAD THEIR PLANET WEREN'T HARD TO TAKE OVER, ALONG WITH THE COMMON FOLK...
...SWEEPING DARKNESS, WHOLE COUNTRIES IN MINUTES.
MY ARMY GREW.

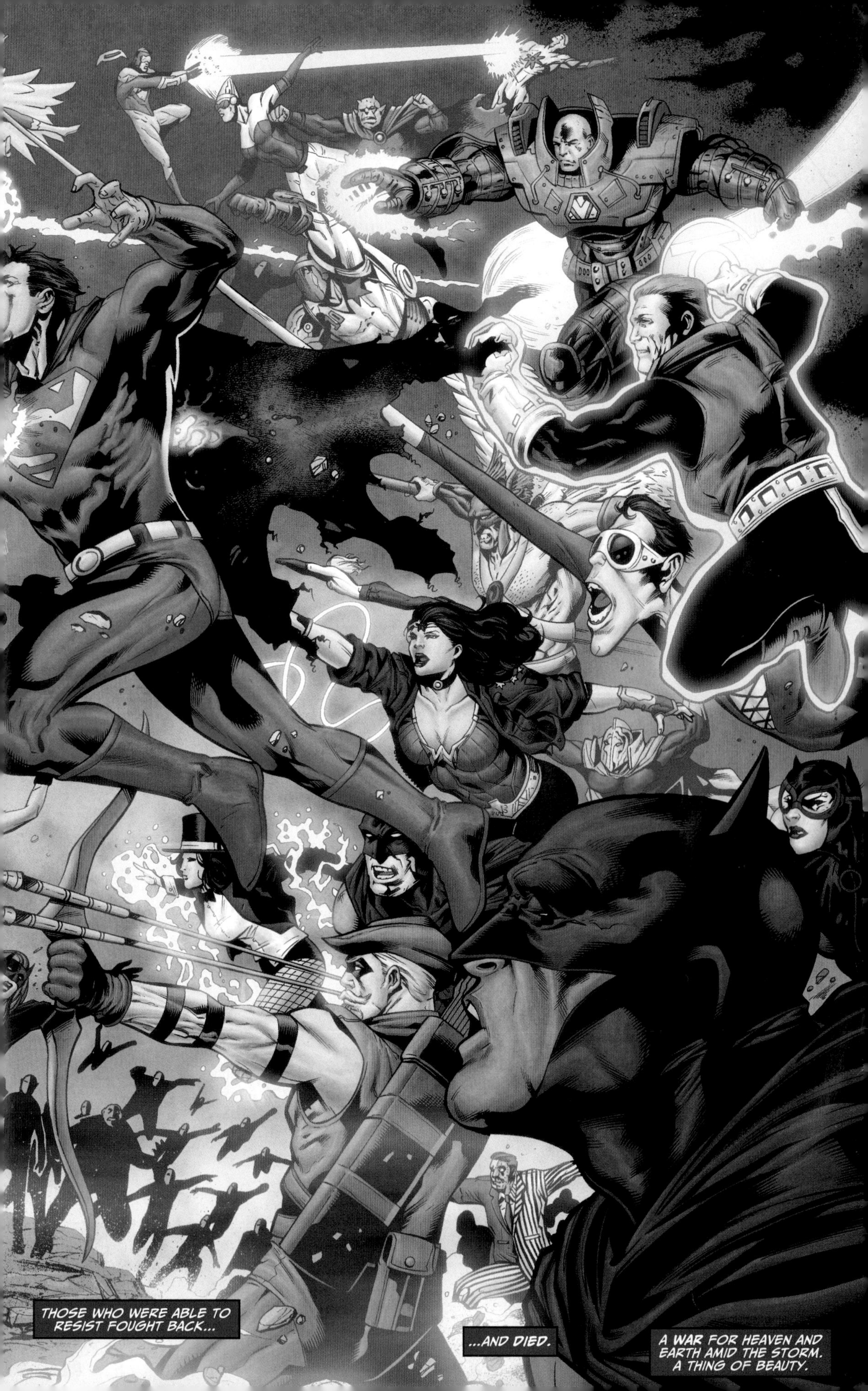
THOSE WHO WERE ABLE TO RESIST FOUGHT BACK...
...AND DIED.
A WAR FOR HEAVEN AND EARTH AMID THE STORM. A THING OF BEAUTY.

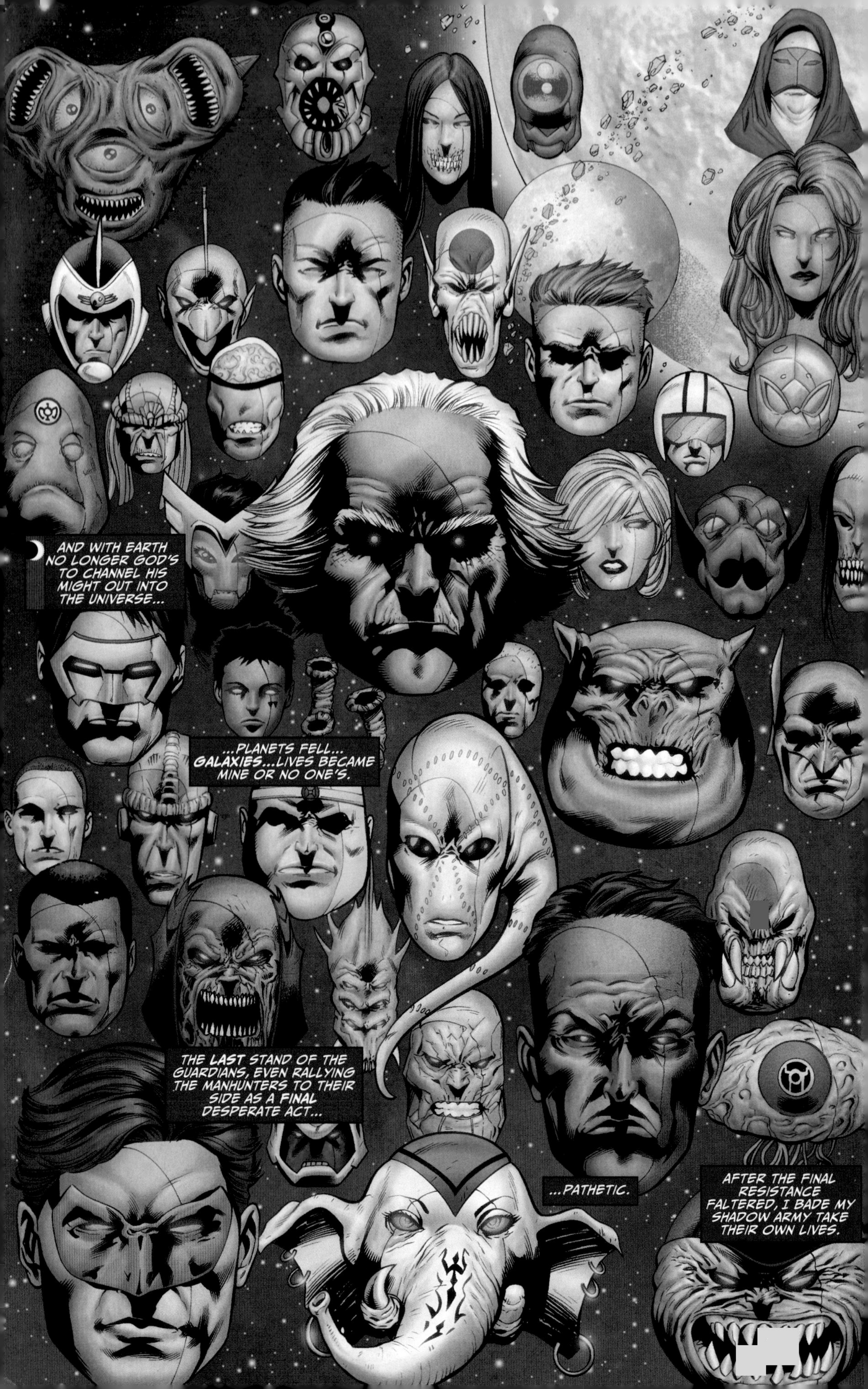
AND WITH EARTH NO LONGER GOD'S TO CHANNEL HIS MIGHT OUT INTO THE UNIVERSE...
...PLANETS FELL... GALAXIES...LIVES BECAME MINE OR NO ONE'S.
THE LAST STAND OF THE GUARDIANS, EVEN RALLYING THE MANHUNTERS TO THEIR SIDE AS A FINAL DESPERATE ACT...
...PATHETIC.
AFTER THE FINAL RESISTANCE FALTERED, I BADE MY SHADOW ARMY TAKE THEIR OWN LIVES.

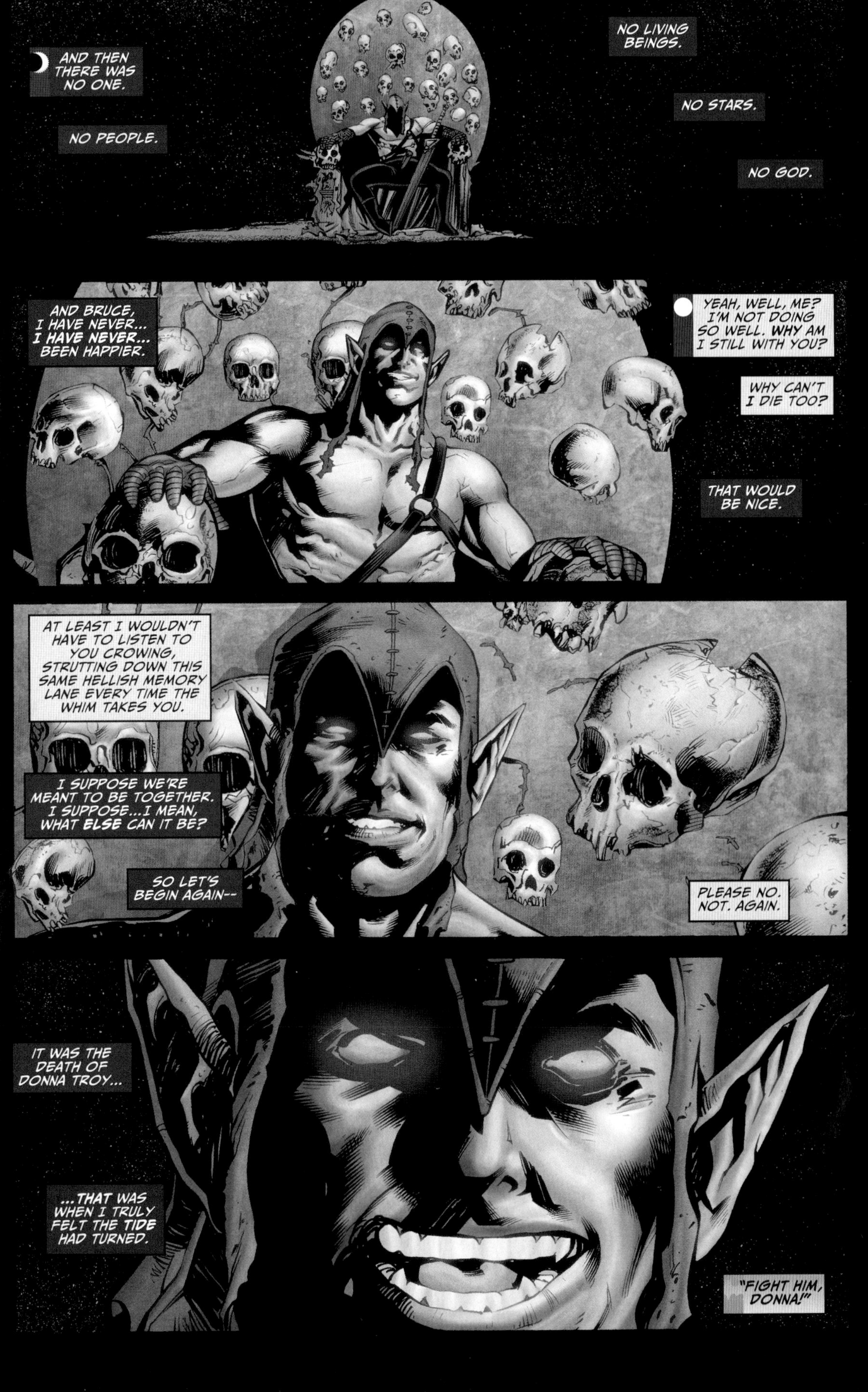
AND THEN THERE WAS NO ONE.
NO PEOPLE.
NO LIVING BEINGS.
NO STARS.
NO GOD.
AND BRUCE, I HAVE NEVER... I HAVE NEVER... BEEN HAPPIER.
YEAH, WELL, ME? I'M NOT DOING SO WELL. WHY AM I STILL WITH YOU?
WHY CAN'T I DIE TOO?
THAT WOULD BE NICE.
AT LEAST I WOULDN'T HAVE TO LISTEN TO YOU CROWING, STRUTTING DOWN THIS SAME HELLISH MEMORY LANE EVERY TIME THE WHIM TAKES YOU.
I SUPPOSE WE'RE MEANT TO BE TOGETHER. I SUPPOSE...I MEAN, WHAT ELSE CAN IT BE?
SO LET'S BEGIN AGAIN--
PLEASE NO. NOT. AGAIN.
IT WAS THE DEATH OF DONNA TROY...
...THAT WAS WHEN I TRULY FELT THE TIDE HAD TURNED.
"FIGHT HIM, DONNA!"

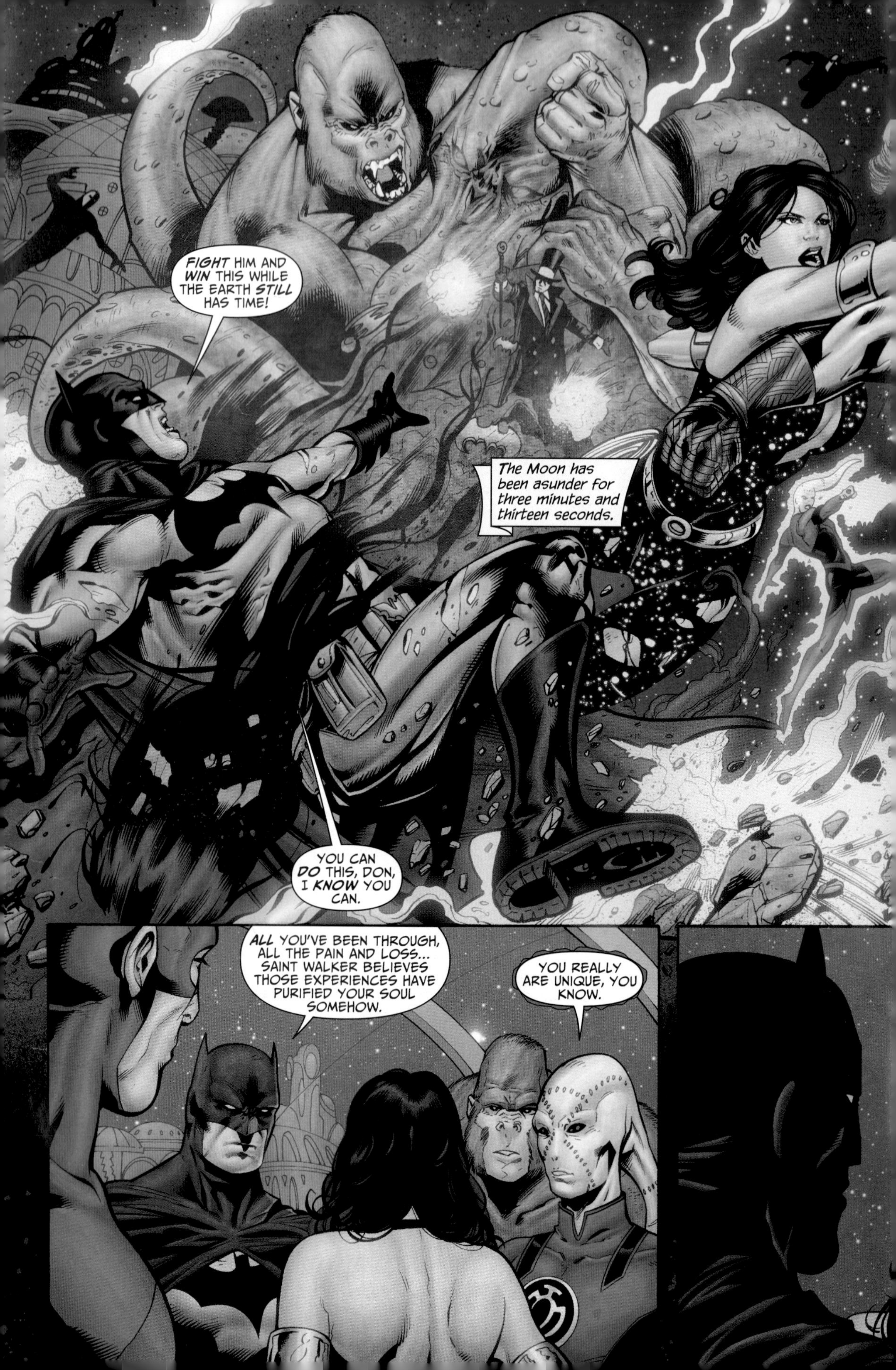

FIGHT HIM AND WIN THIS WHILE THE EARTH STILL HAS TIME!
The Moon has been asunder for three minutes and thirteen seconds.
YOU CAN DO THIS, DON, I KNOW YOU CAN.
ALL YOU'VE BEEN THROUGH, ALL THE PAIN AND LOSS... SAINT WALKER BELIEVES THOSE EXPERIENCES HAVE PURIFIED YOUR SOUL SOMEHOW.
YOU REALLY ARE UNIQUE, YOU KNOW.

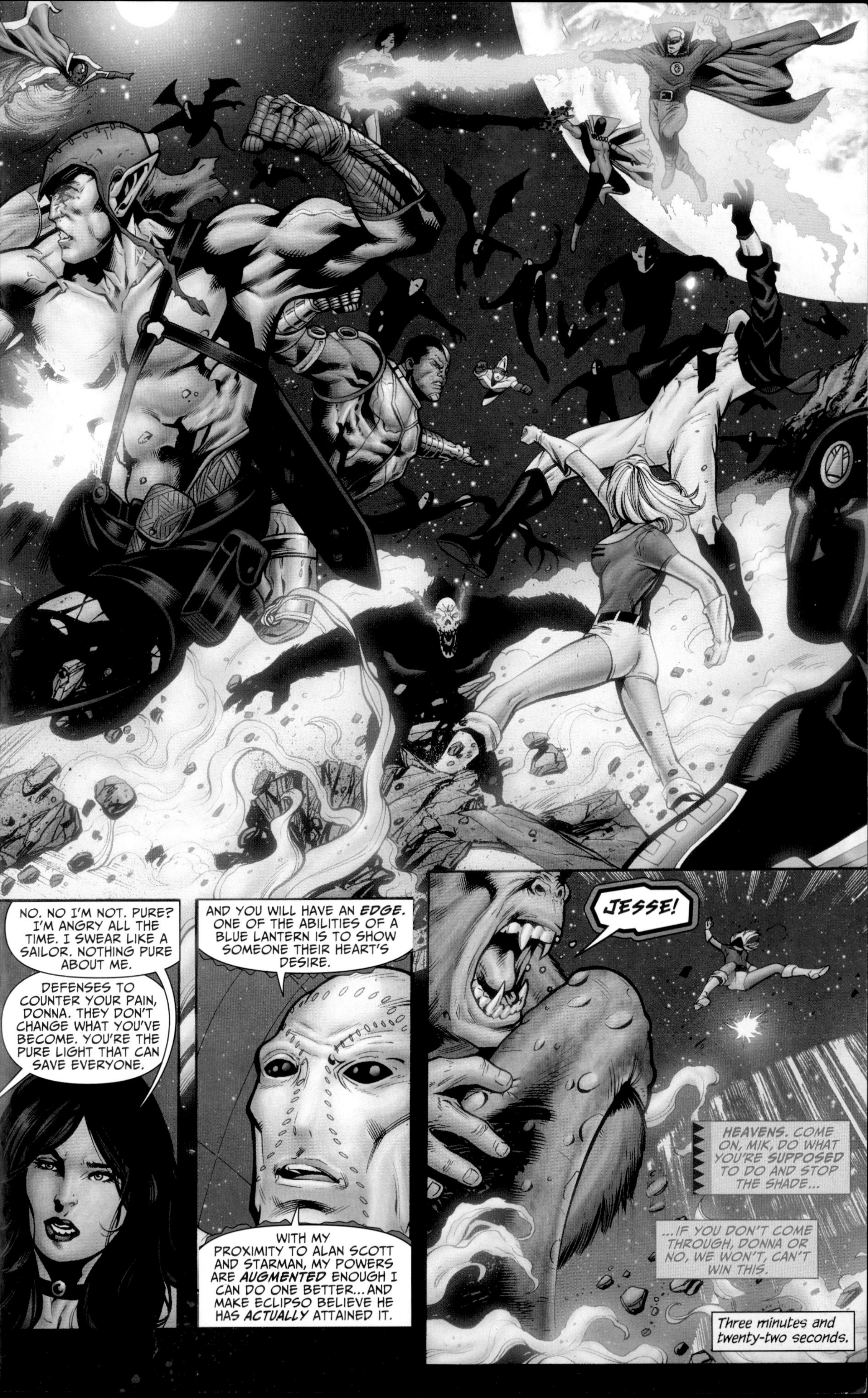

NO. NO I'M NOT. PURE? I'M ANGRY ALL THE TIME. I SWEAR LIKE A SAILOR. NOTHING PURE ABOUT ME.
DEFENSES TO COUNTER YOUR PAIN, DONNA. THEY DON'T CHANGE WHAT YOU'VE BECOME. YOU'RE THE PURE LIGHT THAT CAN SAVE EVERYONE.
AND YOU WILL HAVE AN EDGE. ONE OF THE ABILITIES OF A BLUE LANTERN IS TO SHOW SOMEONE THEIR HEART'S DESIRE.
WITH MY PROXIMITY TO ALAN SCOTT AND STARMAN, MY POWERS ARE AUGMENTED ENOUGH I CAN DO ONE BETTER... AND MAKE ECLIPSO BELIEVE HE HAS ACTUALLY ATTAINED IT.
JESSE!
HEAVENS. COME ON, MIK, DO WHAT YOU'RE SUPPOSED TO DO AND STOP THE SHADE...
...IF YOU DON'T COME THROUGH, DONNA OR NO, WE WON'T, CAN'T WIN THIS.
Three minutes and twenty-two seconds.

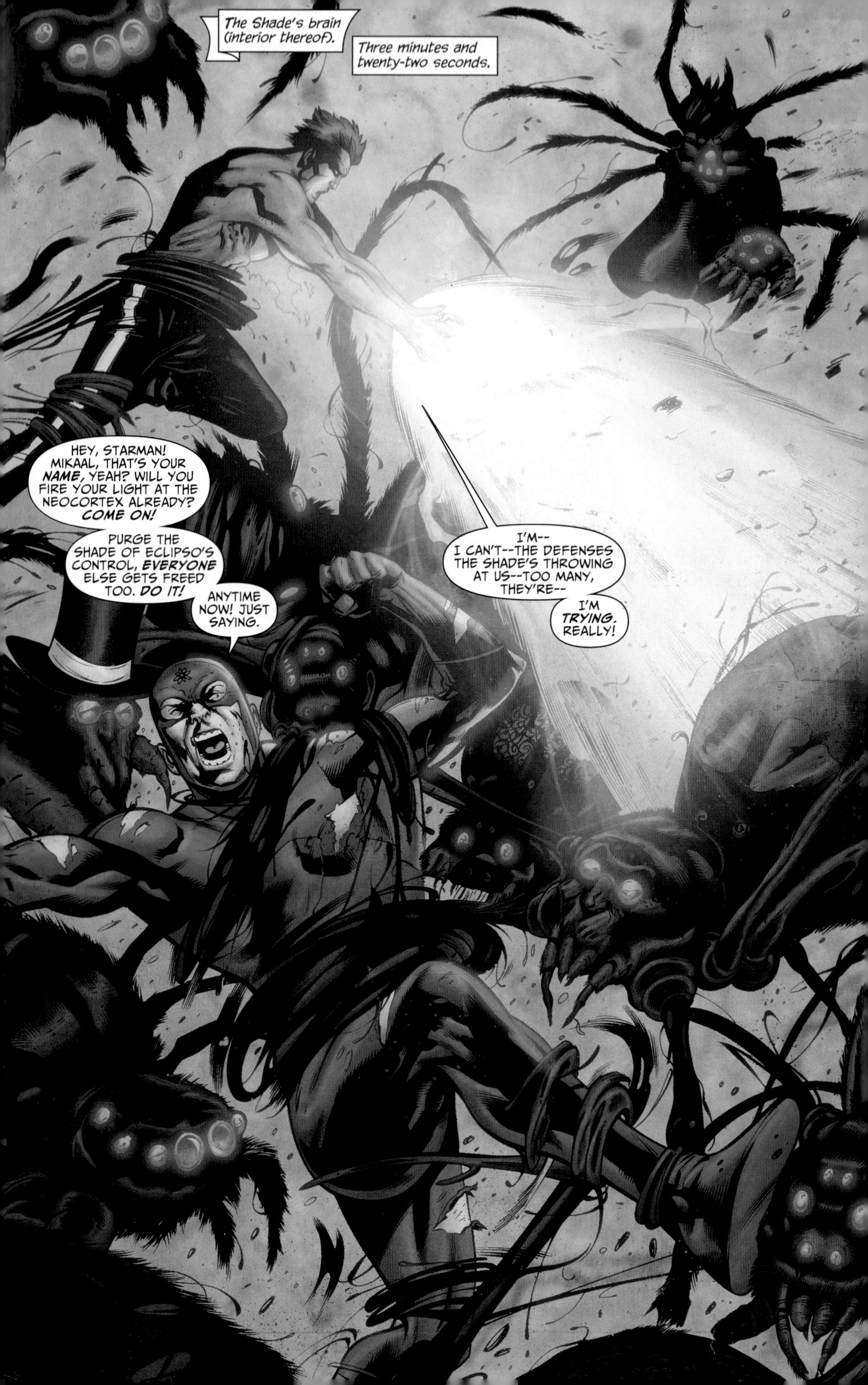
The Shade's brain (interior thereof).
Three minutes and twenty-two seconds.
HEY, STARMAN! MIKAAL, THAT'S YOUR NAME, YEAH? WILL YOU FIRE YOUR LIGHT AT THE NEOCORTEX ALREADY? COME ON!
PURGE THE SHADE OF ECLIPSO'S CONTROL, EVERYONE ELSE GETS FREED TOO. DO IT!
ANYTIME NOW! JUST SAYING.
I'M-- I CAN'T--THE DEFENSES THE SHADE'S THROWING AT US--TOO MANY, THEY'RE--
I'M TRYING. REALLY!

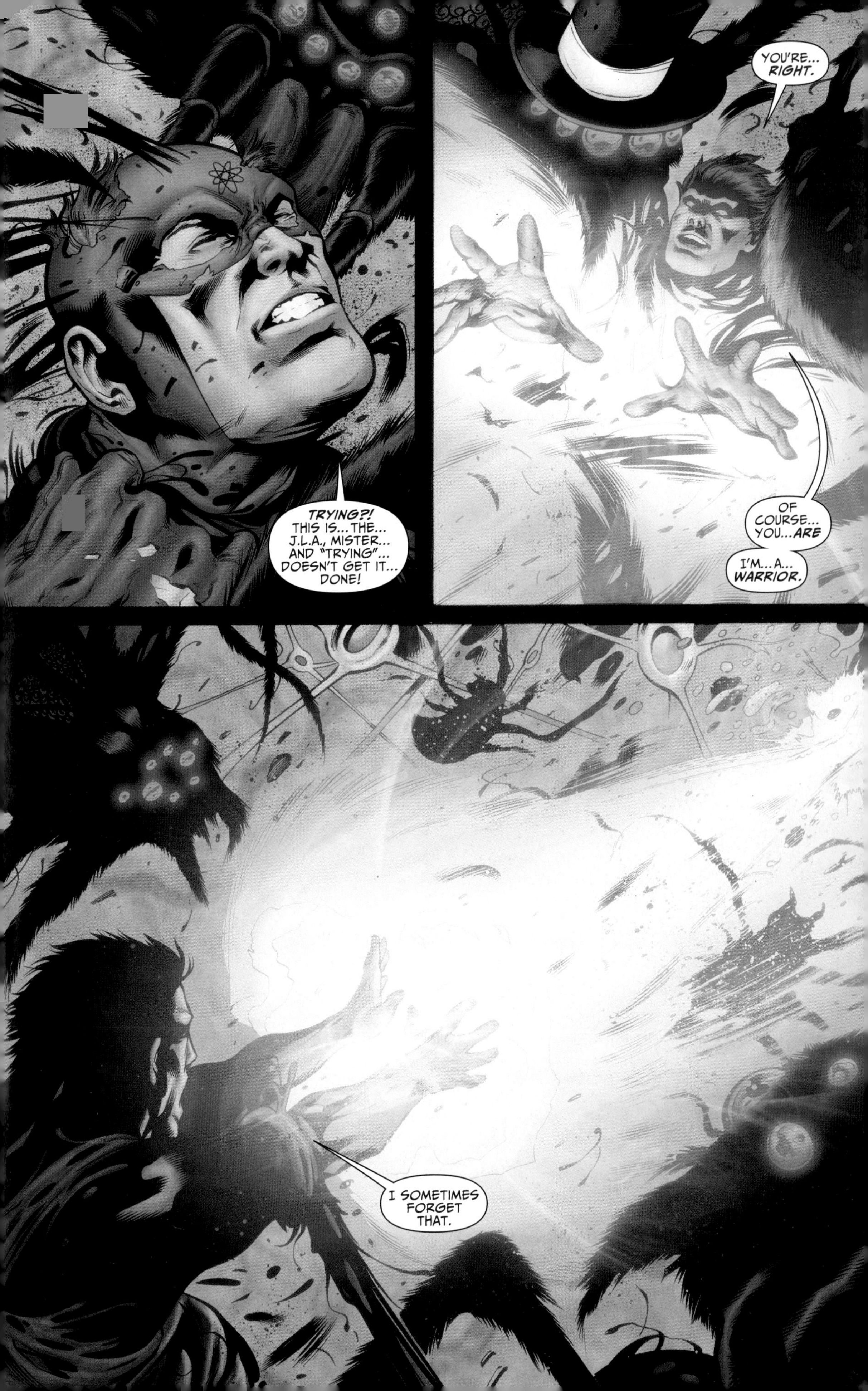
TRYING?! THIS IS... THE... J.L.A., MISTER... AND "TRYING"... DOESN'T GET IT... DONE!
YOU'RE... RIGHT.
OF COURSE... YOU... ARE
I'M... A... WARRIOR.
I SOMETIMES FORGET THAT.

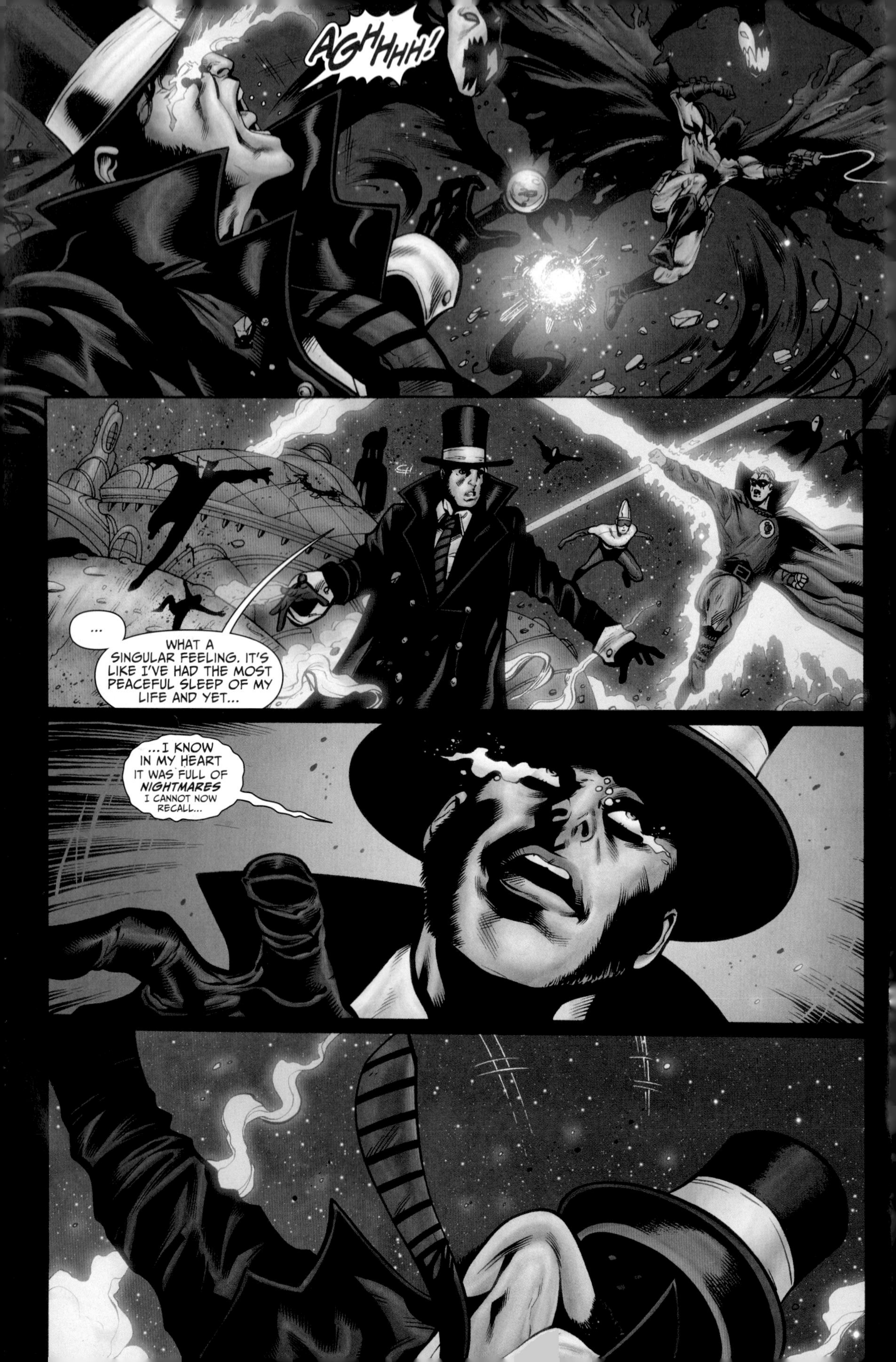
AGHHHH!
...
WHAT A SINGULAR FEELING. IT'S LIKE I'VE HAD THE MOST PEACEFUL SLEEP OF MY LIFE AND YET...
...I KNOW IN MY HEART IT WAS FULL OF NIGHTMARES I CANNOT NOW RECALL...

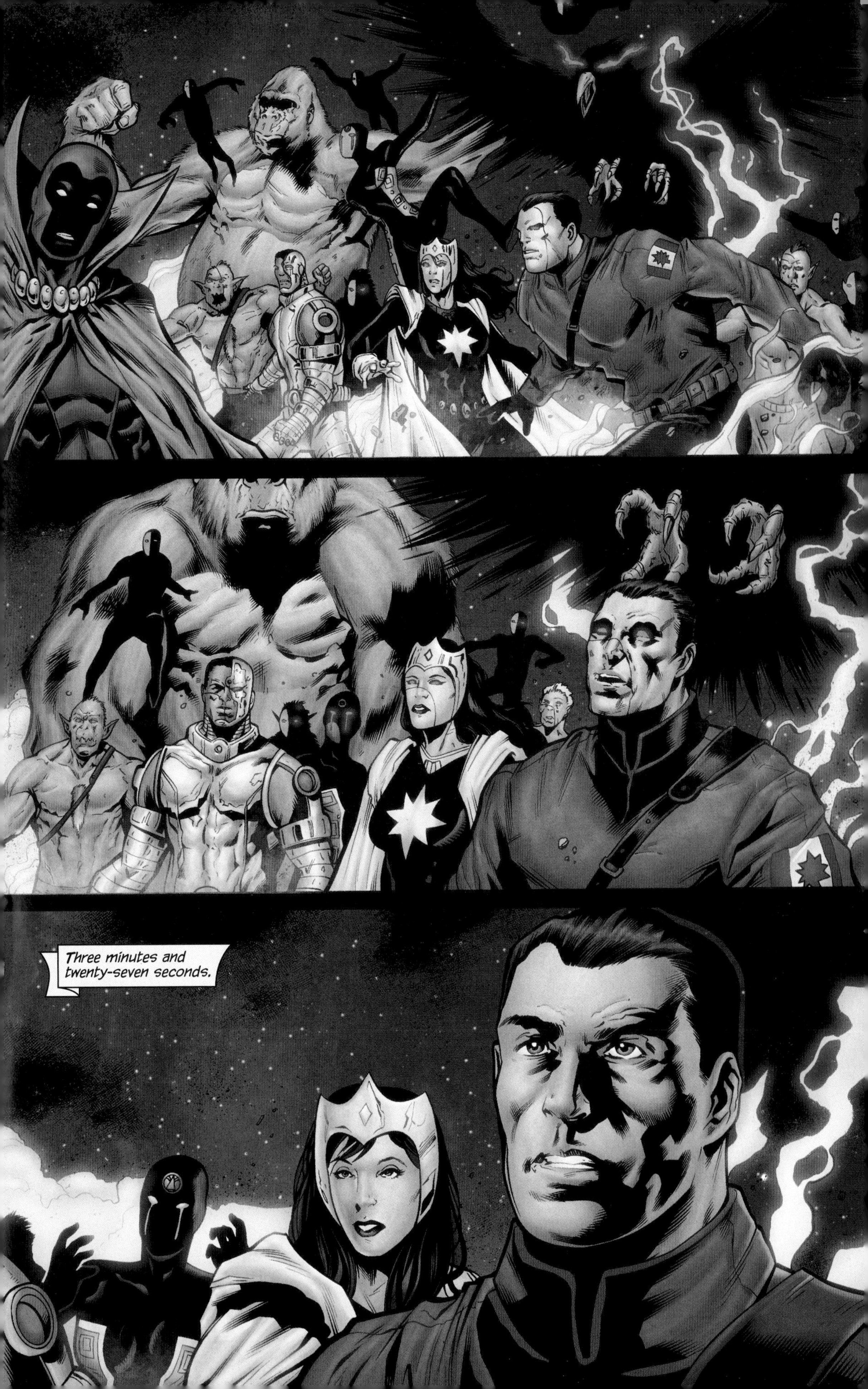
Three minutes and
twenty-seven seconds.

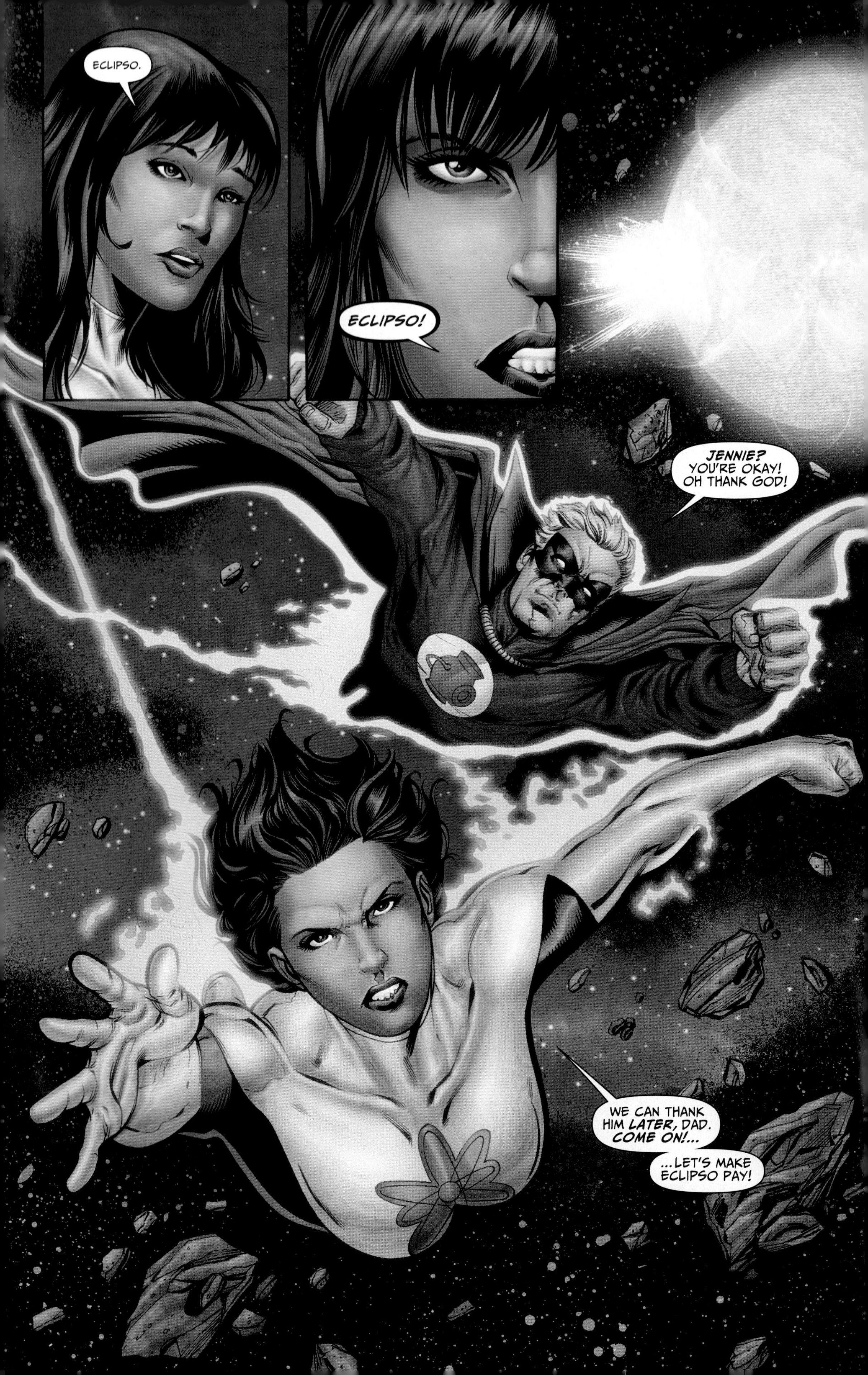
ECLIPSO.
ECLIPSO!
JENNIE? YOU'RE OKAY! OH THANK GOD!
WE CAN THANK HIM LATER, DAD. COME ON!...
...LET'S MAKE ECLIPSO PAY!

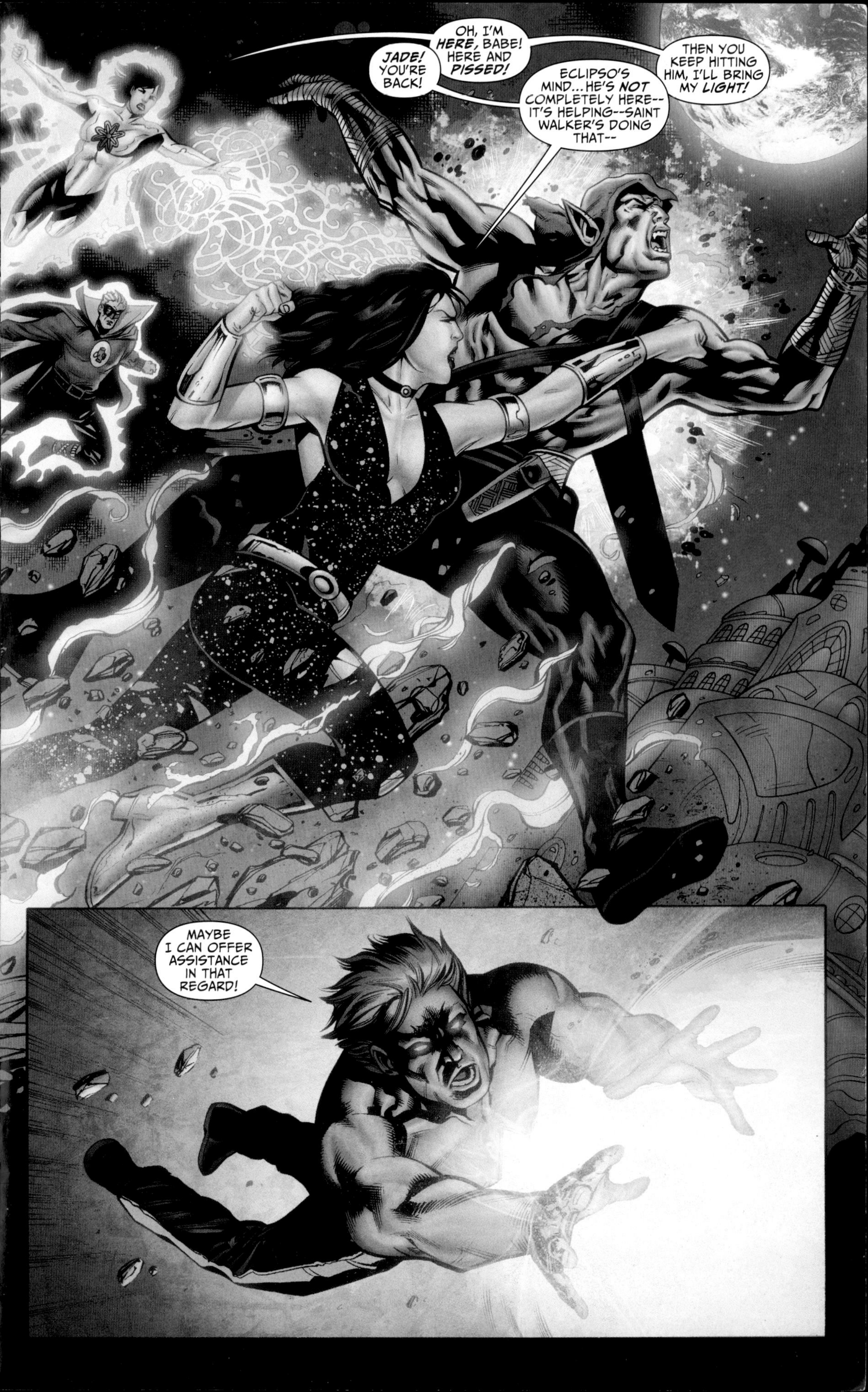
JADE! YOU'RE BACK!
OH, I'M HERE, BABE! HERE AND PISSED!
THEN YOU KEEP HITTING HIM, I'LL BRING MY LIGHT!
ECLIPSO'S MIND... HE'S NOT COMPLETELY HERE-- IT'S HELPING--SAINT WALKER'S DOING THAT--
MAYBE I CAN OFFER ASSISTANCE IN THAT REGARD!

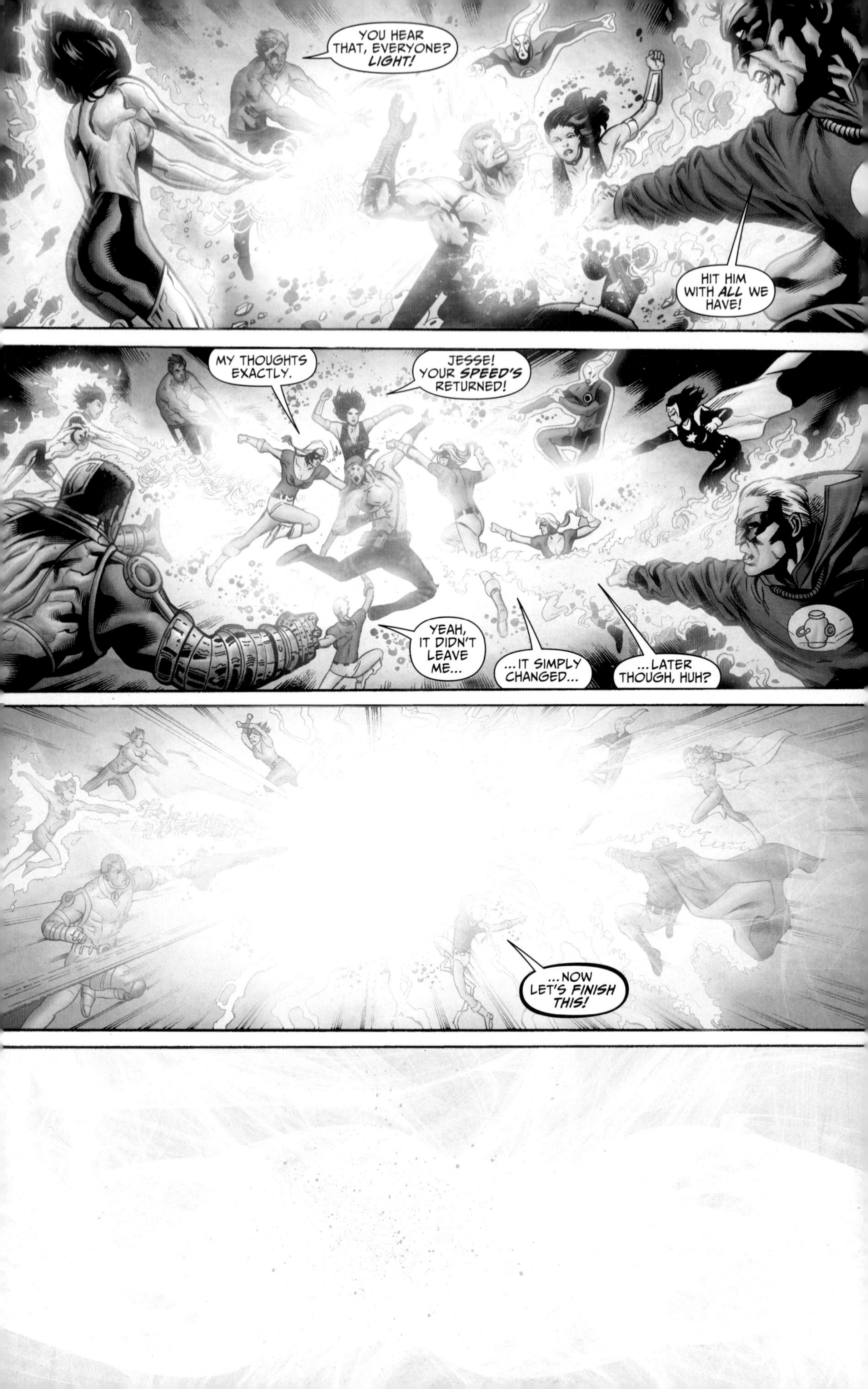

YOU HEAR THAT, EVERYONE? LIGHT!
HIT HIM WITH ALL WE HAVE!
MY THOUGHTS EXACTLY.
JESSE! YOUR SPEED'S RETURNED!
YEAH, IT DIDN'T LEAVE ME...
...IT SIMPLY CHANGED...
...LATER THOUGH, HUH?
...NOW LET'S FINISH THIS!

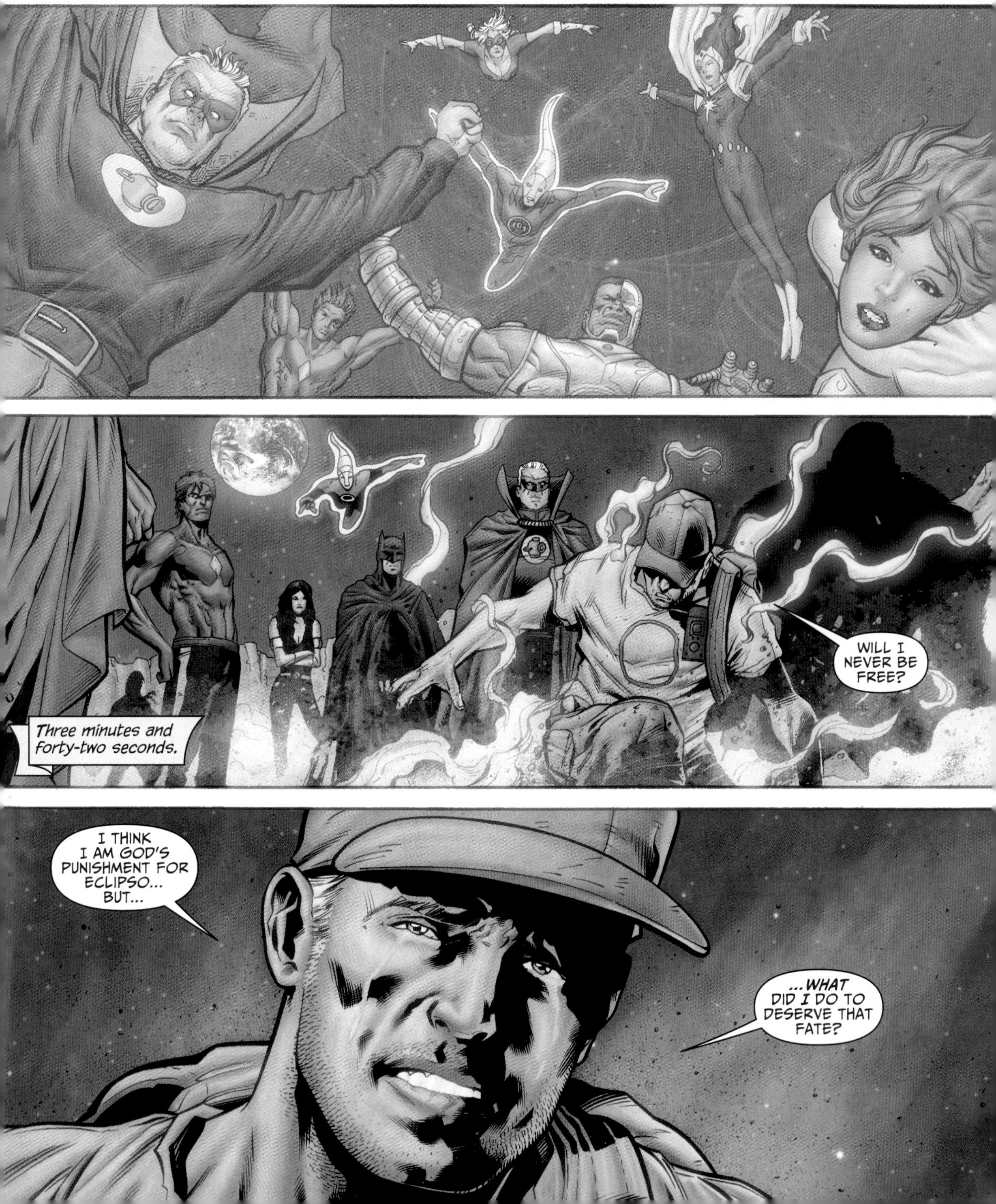
WILL I NEVER BE FREE?
Three minutes and forty-two seconds.
I THINK I AM GOD'S PUNISHMENT FOR ECLIPSO... BUT...
...WHAT DID I DO TO DESERVE THAT FATE?

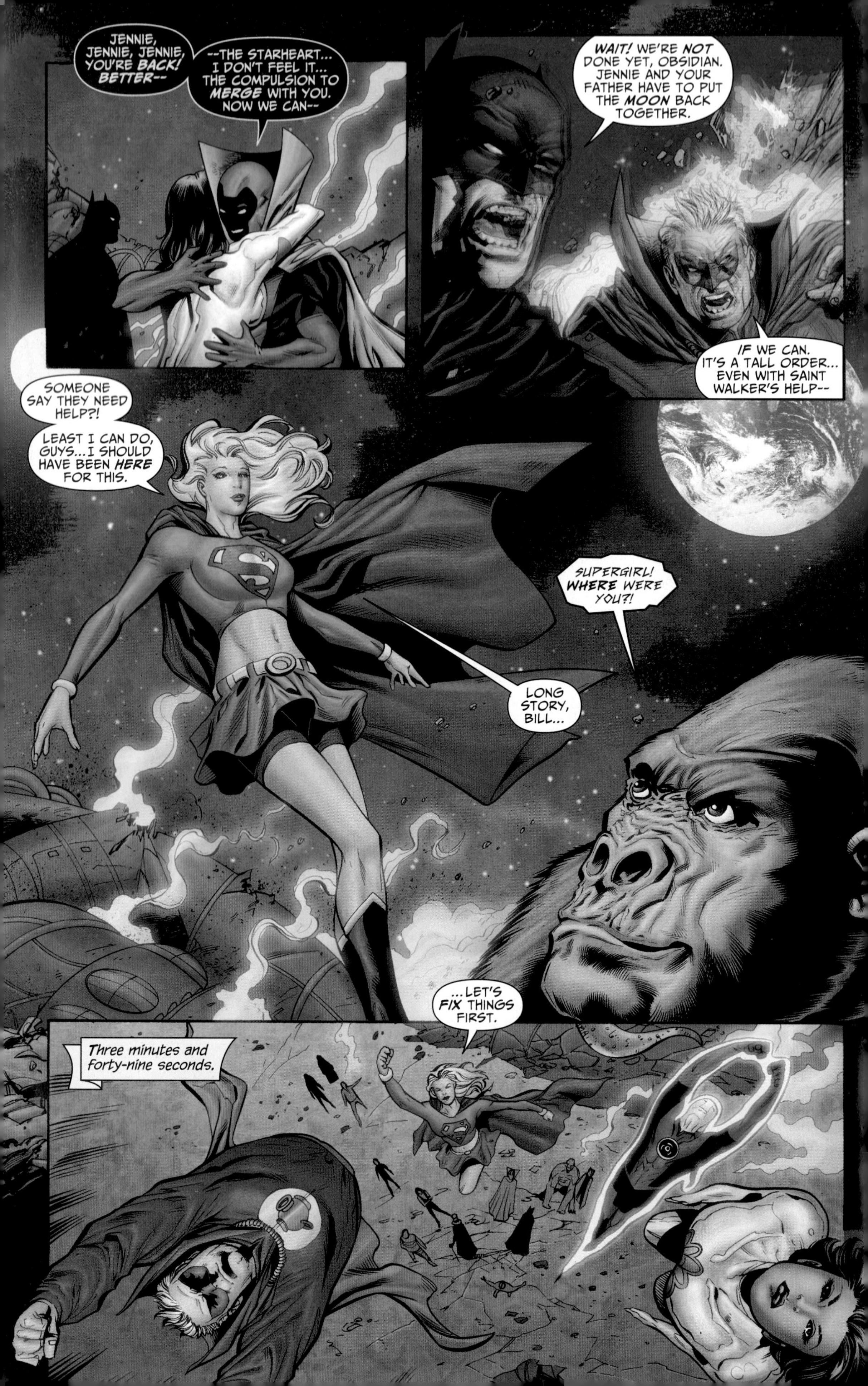
JENNIE, JENNIE, JENNIE, YOU'RE *BACK!* *BETTER--*
--THE STARHEART... I DON'T FEEL IT... THE COMPULSION TO *MERGE* WITH YOU. NOW WE CAN--
WAIT! WE'RE *NOT* DONE YET, OBSIDIAN. JENNIE AND YOUR FATHER HAVE TO PUT THE *MOON* BACK TOGETHER.
IF WE CAN. IT'S A TALL ORDER... EVEN WITH SAINT WALKER'S HELP--
SOMEONE SAY THEY NEED HELP?!
LEAST I CAN DO, GUYS...I SHOULD HAVE BEEN *HERE* FOR THIS.
SUPERGIRL! WHERE WERE YOU?!
LONG STORY, BILL...
...LET'S *FIX* THINGS FIRST.
Three minutes and forty-nine seconds.

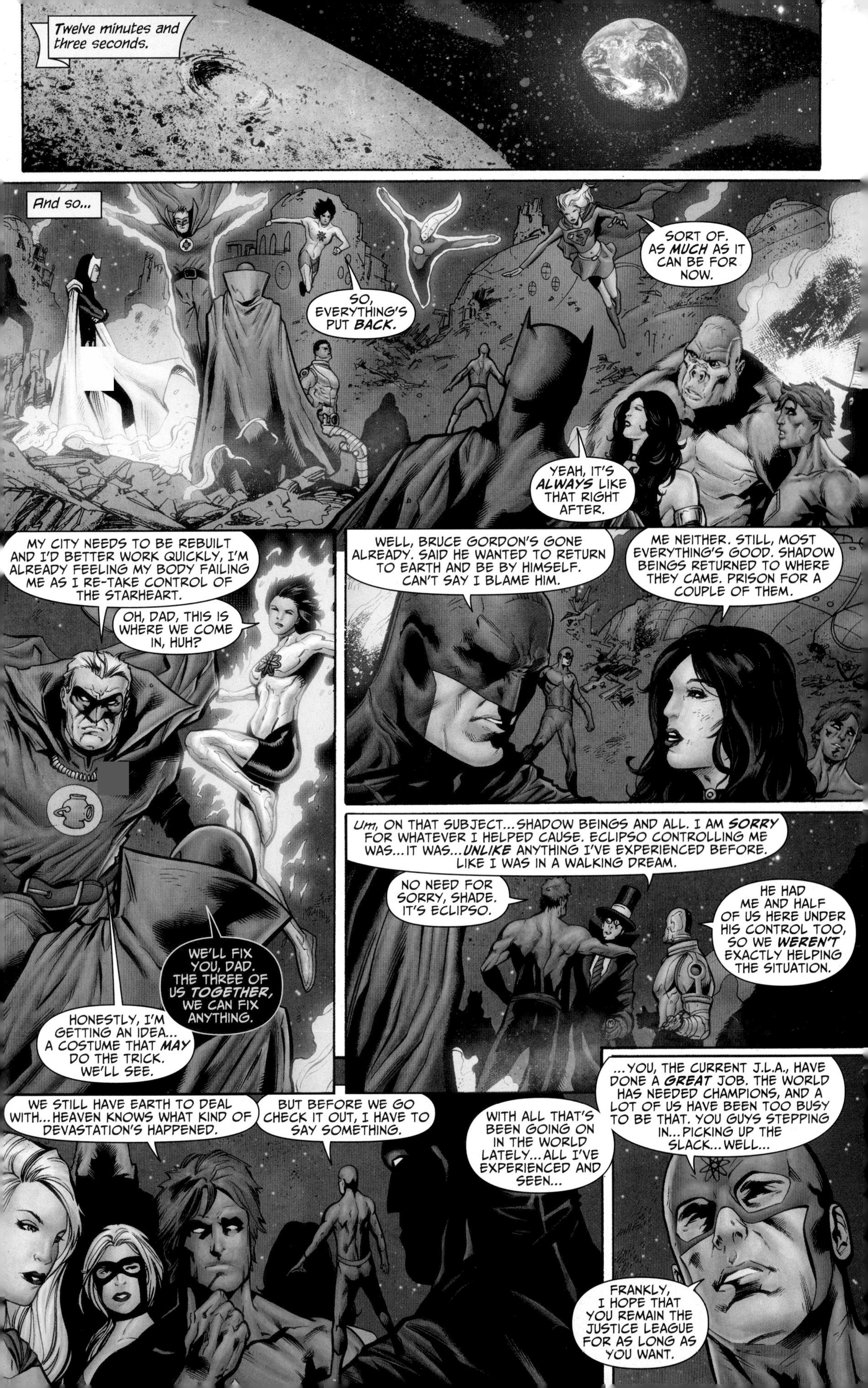
Twelve minutes and three seconds.
And so...
SO, EVERYTHING'S PUT BACK.
SORT OF. AS MUCH AS IT CAN BE FOR NOW.
YEAH, IT'S ALWAYS LIKE THAT RIGHT AFTER.
MY CITY NEEDS TO BE REBUILT AND I'D BETTER WORK QUICKLY, I'M ALREADY FEELING MY BODY FAILING ME AS I RE-TAKE CONTROL OF THE STARHEART.
OH, DAD, THIS IS WHERE WE COME IN, HUH?
WE'LL FIX YOU, DAD. THE THREE OF US TOGETHER, WE CAN FIX ANYTHING.
HONESTLY, I'M GETTING AN IDEA... A COSTUME THAT MAY DO THE TRICK. WE'LL SEE.
WELL, BRUCE GORDON'S GONE ALREADY. SAID HE WANTED TO RETURN TO EARTH AND BE BY HIMSELF. CAN'T SAY I BLAME HIM.
ME NEITHER. STILL, MOST EVERYTHING'S GOOD. SHADOW BEINGS RETURNED TO WHERE THEY CAME. PRISON FOR A COUPLE OF THEM.
Um, ON THAT SUBJECT... SHADOW BEINGS AND ALL. I AM SORRY FOR WHATEVER I HELPED CAUSE. ECLIPSO CONTROLLING ME WAS... IT WAS... UNLIKE ANYTHING I'VE EXPERIENCED BEFORE. LIKE I WAS IN A WALKING DREAM.
NO NEED FOR SORRY, SHADE. IT'S ECLIPSO.
HE HAD ME AND HALF OF US HERE UNDER HIS CONTROL TOO, SO WE WEREN'T EXACTLY HELPING THE SITUATION.
WE STILL HAVE EARTH TO DEAL WITH... HEAVEN KNOWS WHAT KIND OF DEVASTATION'S HAPPENED.
BUT BEFORE WE GO CHECK IT OUT, I HAVE TO SAY SOMETHING.
WITH ALL THAT'S BEEN GOING ON IN THE WORLD LATELY... ALL I'VE EXPERIENCED AND SEEN...
...YOU, THE CURRENT J.L.A., HAVE DONE A GREAT JOB. THE WORLD HAS NEEDED CHAMPIONS, AND A LOT OF US HAVE BEEN TOO BUSY TO BE THAT. YOU GUYS STEPPING IN... PICKING UP THE SLACK... WELL...
FRANKLY, I HOPE THAT YOU REMAIN THE JUSTICE LEAGUE FOR AS LONG AS YOU WANT.

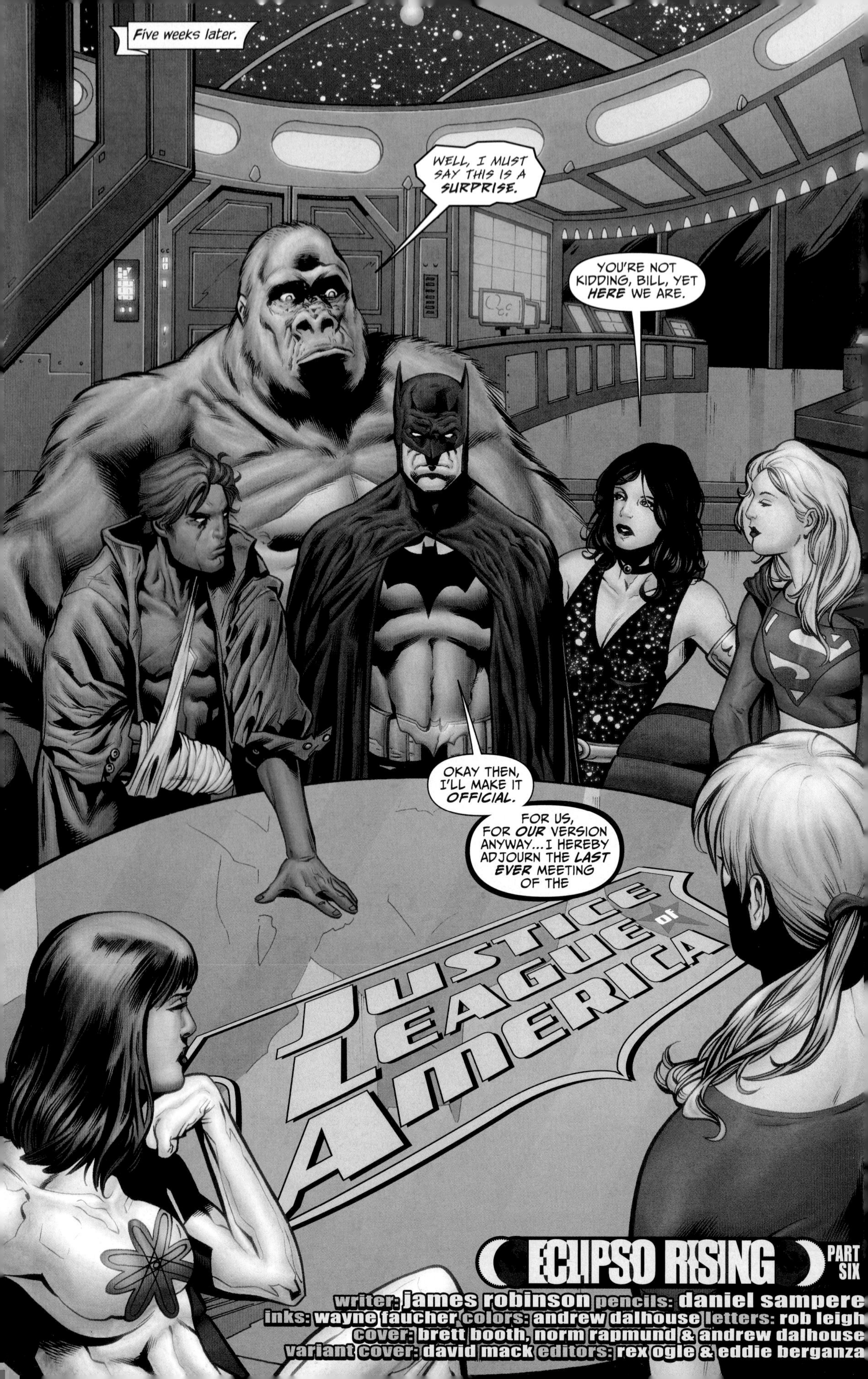

Five weeks later.
WELL, I MUST SAY THIS IS A SURPRISE.
YOU'RE NOT KIDDING, BILL, YET HERE WE ARE.
OKAY THEN, I'LL MAKE IT OFFICIAL.
FOR US, FOR OUR VERSION ANYWAY...I HEREBY ADJOURN THE LAST EVER MEETING OF THE
JUSTICE LEAGUE of AMERICA
ECLIPSO RISING PART SIX
writer: james robinson pencils: daniel sampere
inks: wayne faucher colors: andrew dalhouse letters: rob leigh
cover: brett booth, norm rapmund & andrew dalhouse
variant cover: david mack editors: rex ogle & eddie berganza

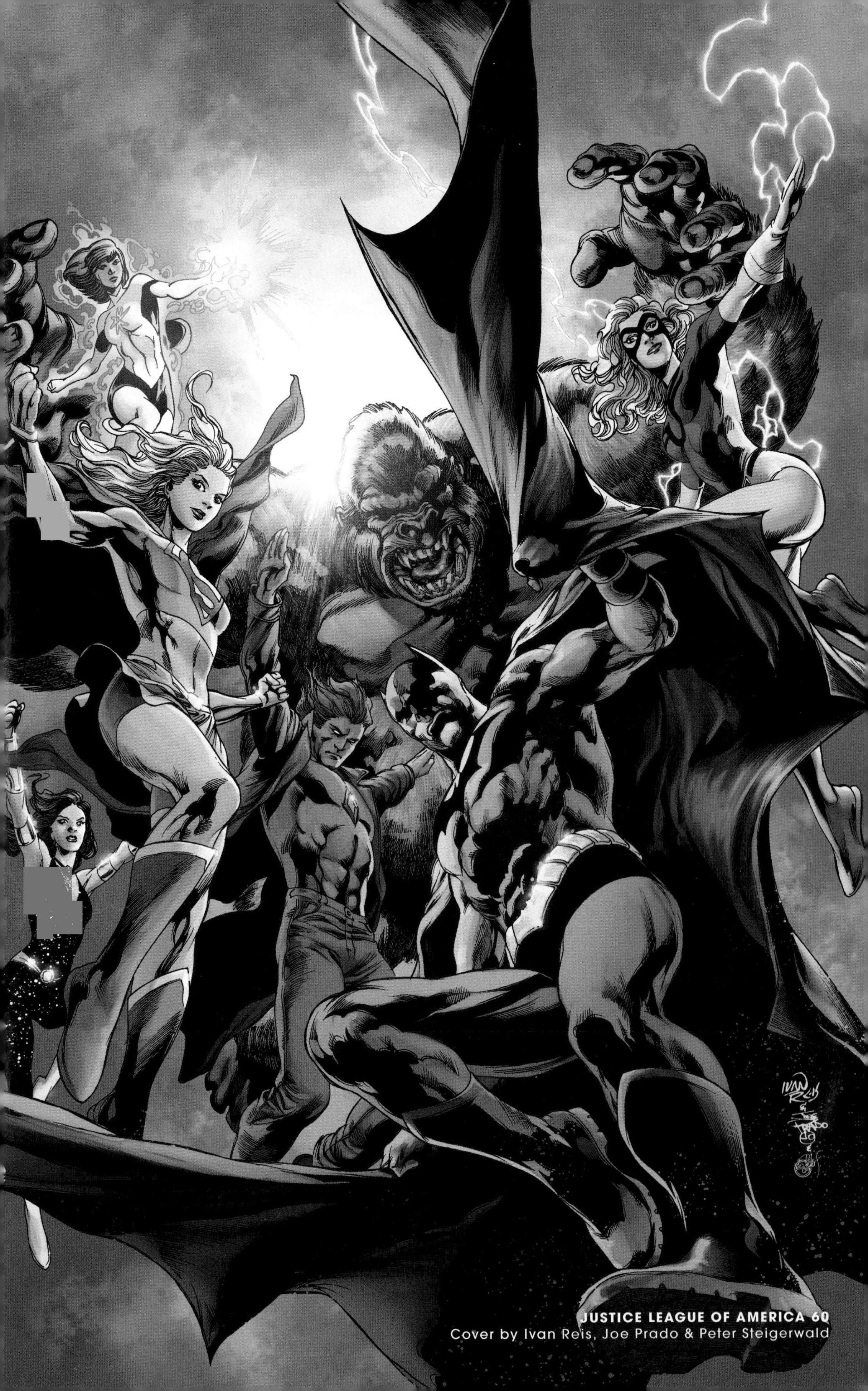

JUSTICE LEAGUE OF AMERICA 60
Cover by Ivan Reis, Joe Prado & Peter Steigerwald

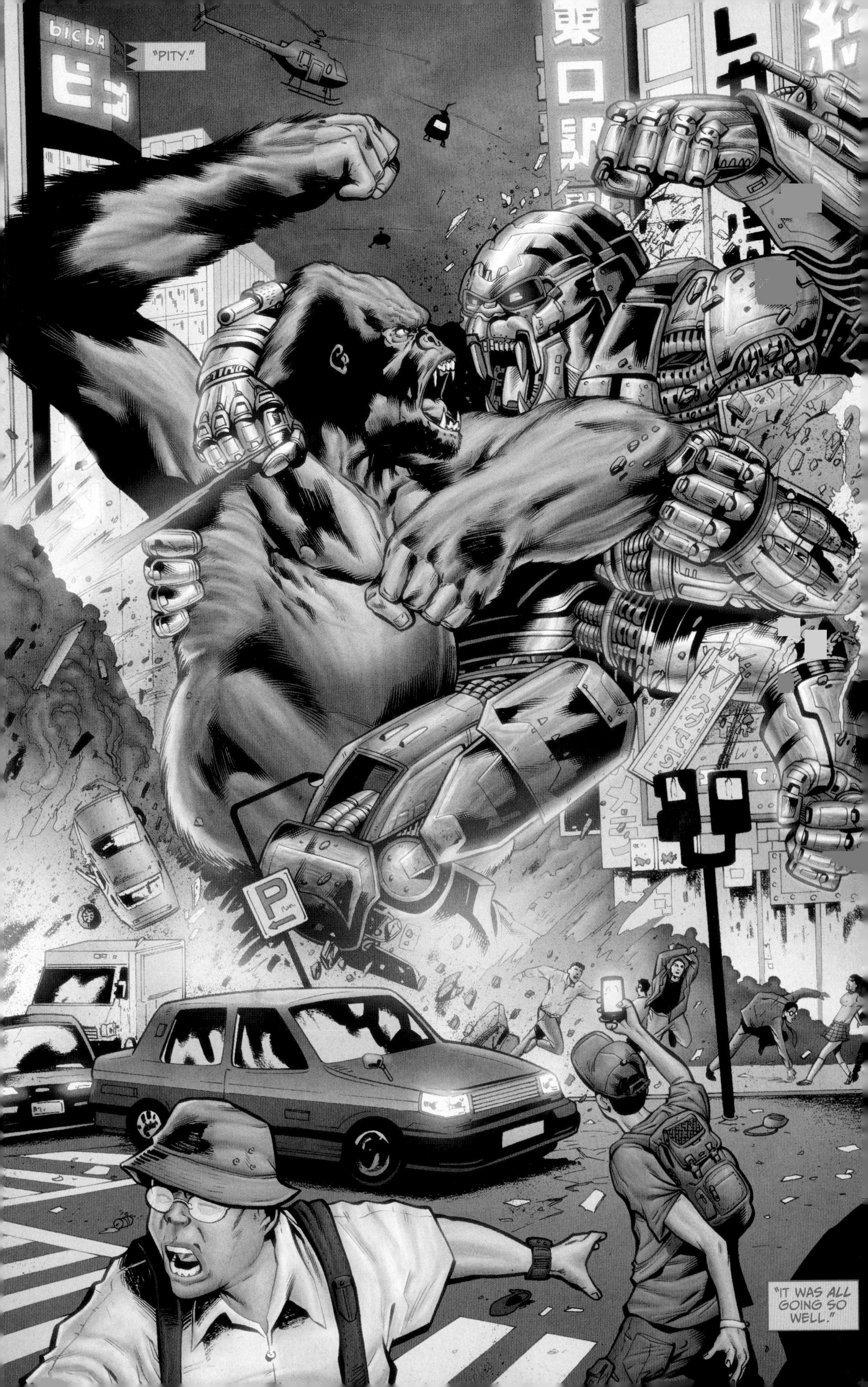
"PITY."
"IT WAS ALL GOING SO WELL."

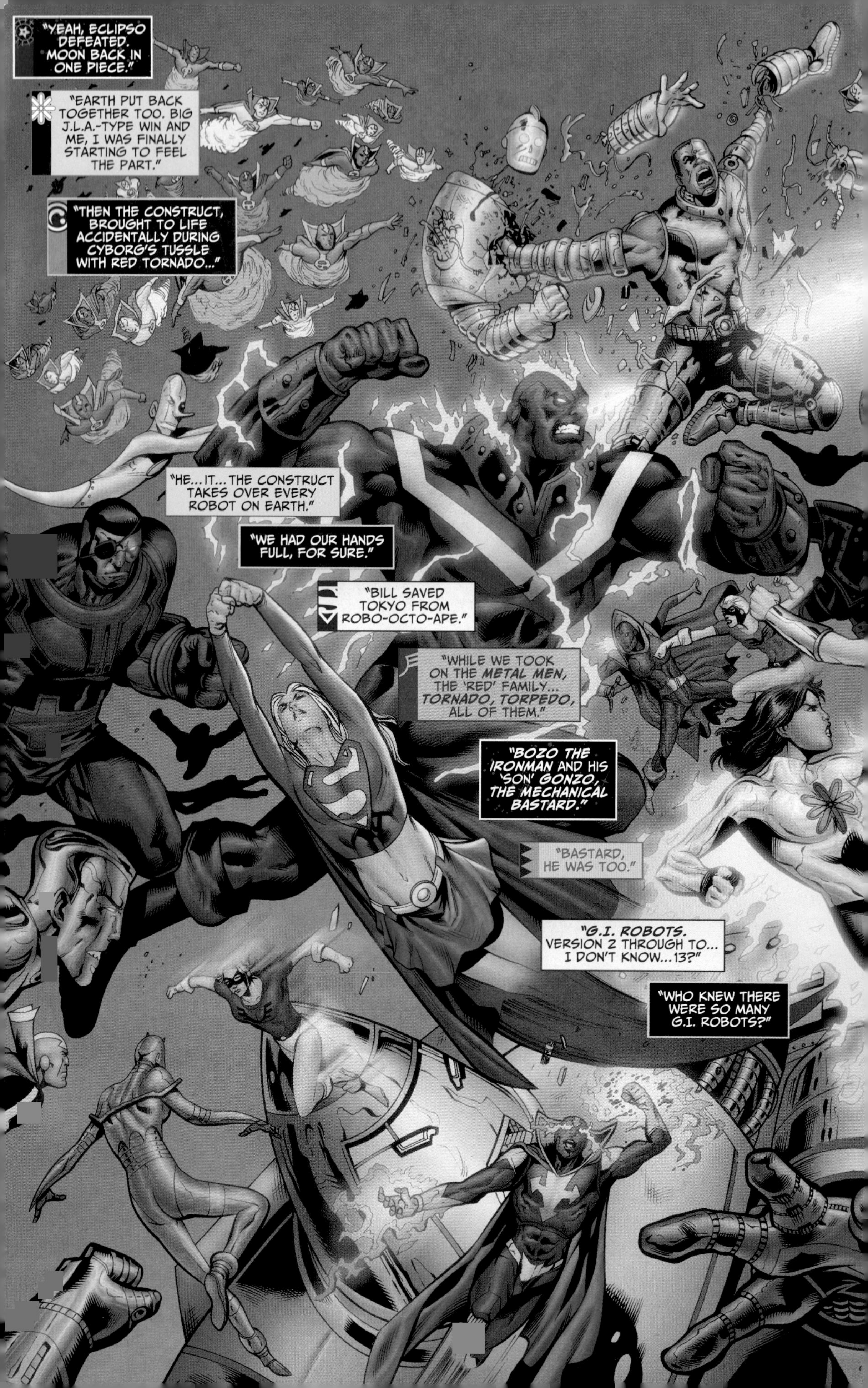
"YEAH, ECLIPSO DEFEATED. MOON BACK IN ONE PIECE."
"EARTH PUT BACK TOGETHER TOO. BIG J.L.A.-TYPE WIN AND ME, I WAS FINALLY STARTING TO FEEL THE PART."
"THEN THE CONSTRUCT, BROUGHT TO LIFE ACCIDENTALLY DURING CYBORG'S TUSSLE WITH RED TORNADO..."
"HE...IT...THE CONSTRUCT TAKES OVER EVERY ROBOT ON EARTH."
"WE HAD OUR HANDS FULL, FOR SURE."
"BILL SAVED TOKYO FROM ROBO-OCTO-APE."
"WHILE WE TOOK ON THE METAL MEN, THE 'RED' FAMILY... TORNADO, TORPEDO, ALL OF THEM."
"BOZO THE IRONMAN AND HIS 'SON' GONZO, THE MECHANICAL BASTARD."
"BASTARD, HE WAS TOO."
"G.I. ROBOTS. VERSION 2 THROUGH TO... I DON'T KNOW...13?"
"WHO KNEW THERE WERE SO MANY G.I. ROBOTS?"

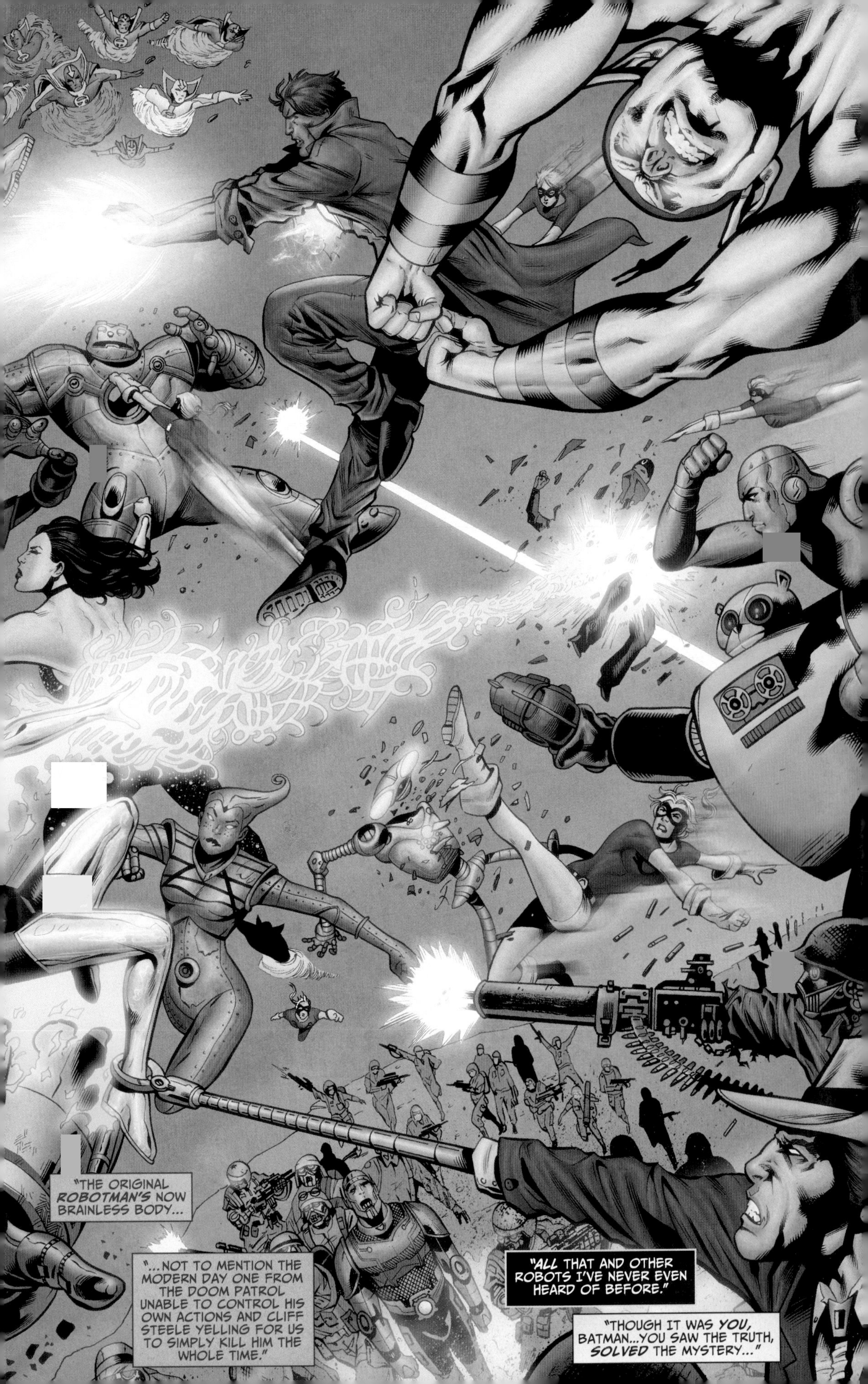
"THE ORIGINAL ROBOTMAN'S NOW BRAINLESS BODY...
"...NOT TO MENTION THE MODERN DAY ONE FROM THE DOOM PATROL UNABLE TO CONTROL HIS OWN ACTIONS AND CLIFF STEELE YELLING FOR US TO SIMPLY KILL HIM THE WHOLE TIME."
"ALL THAT AND OTHER ROBOTS I'VE NEVER EVEN HEARD OF BEFORE."
"THOUGH IT WAS YOU, BATMAN...YOU SAW THE TRUTH, SOLVED THE MYSTERY..."

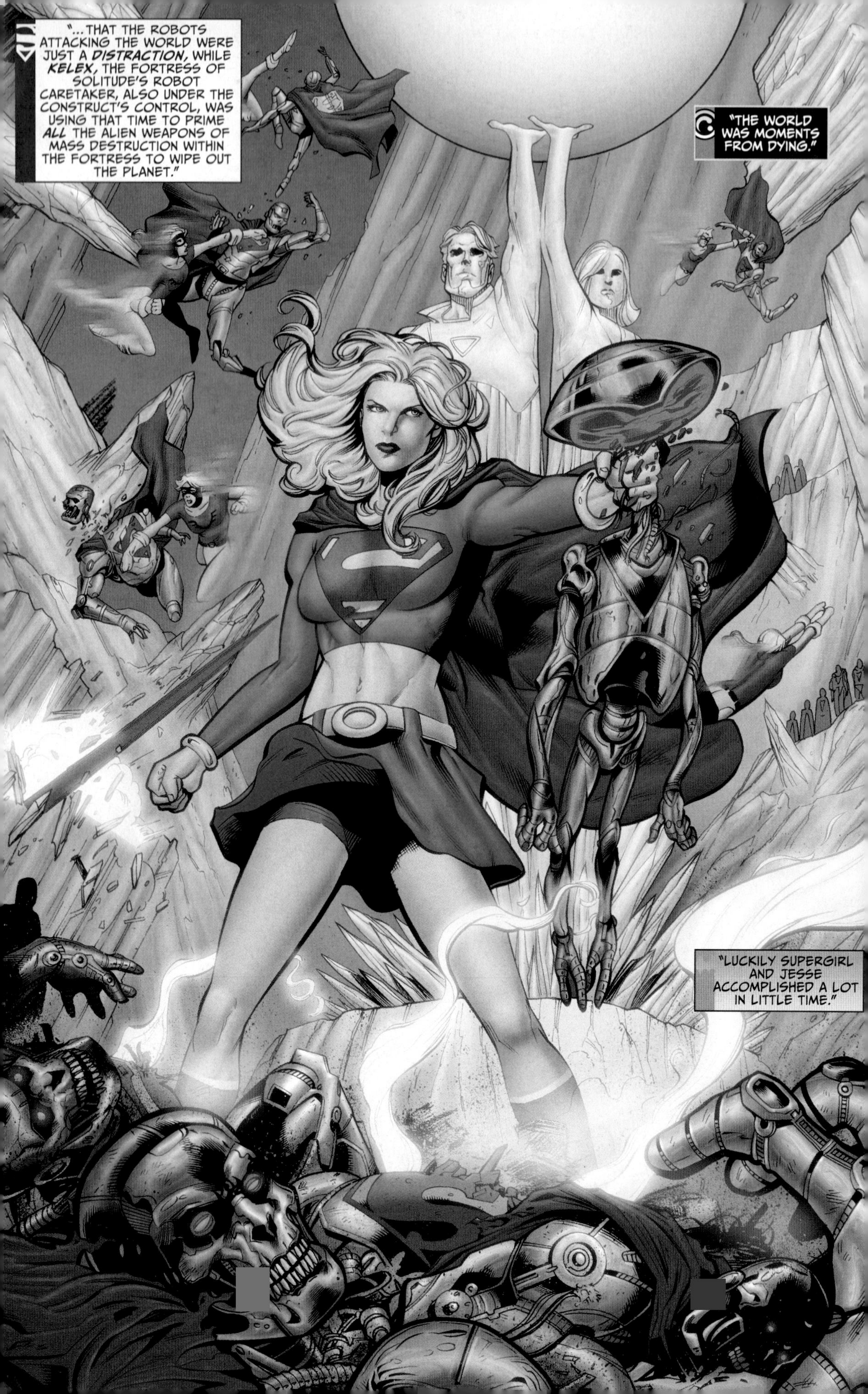
"...THAT THE ROBOTS ATTACKING THE WORLD WERE JUST A *DISTRACTION,* WHILE *KELEX,* THE FORTRESS OF SOLITUDE'S ROBOT CARETAKER, ALSO UNDER THE CONSTRUCT'S CONTROL, WAS USING THAT TIME TO PRIME *ALL* THE ALIEN WEAPONS OF MASS DESTRUCTION WITHIN THE FORTRESS TO WIPE OUT THE PLANET."
"THE WORLD WAS MOMENTS FROM DYING."
"LUCKILY SUPERGIRL AND JESSE ACCOMPLISHED A LOT IN LITTLE TIME."

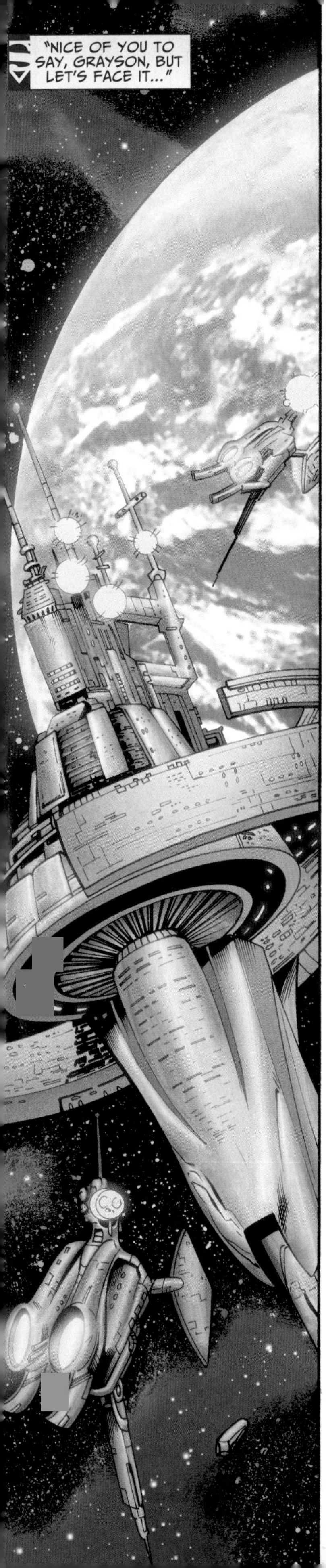
"NICE OF YOU TO SAY, GRAYSON, BUT LET'S FACE IT..."

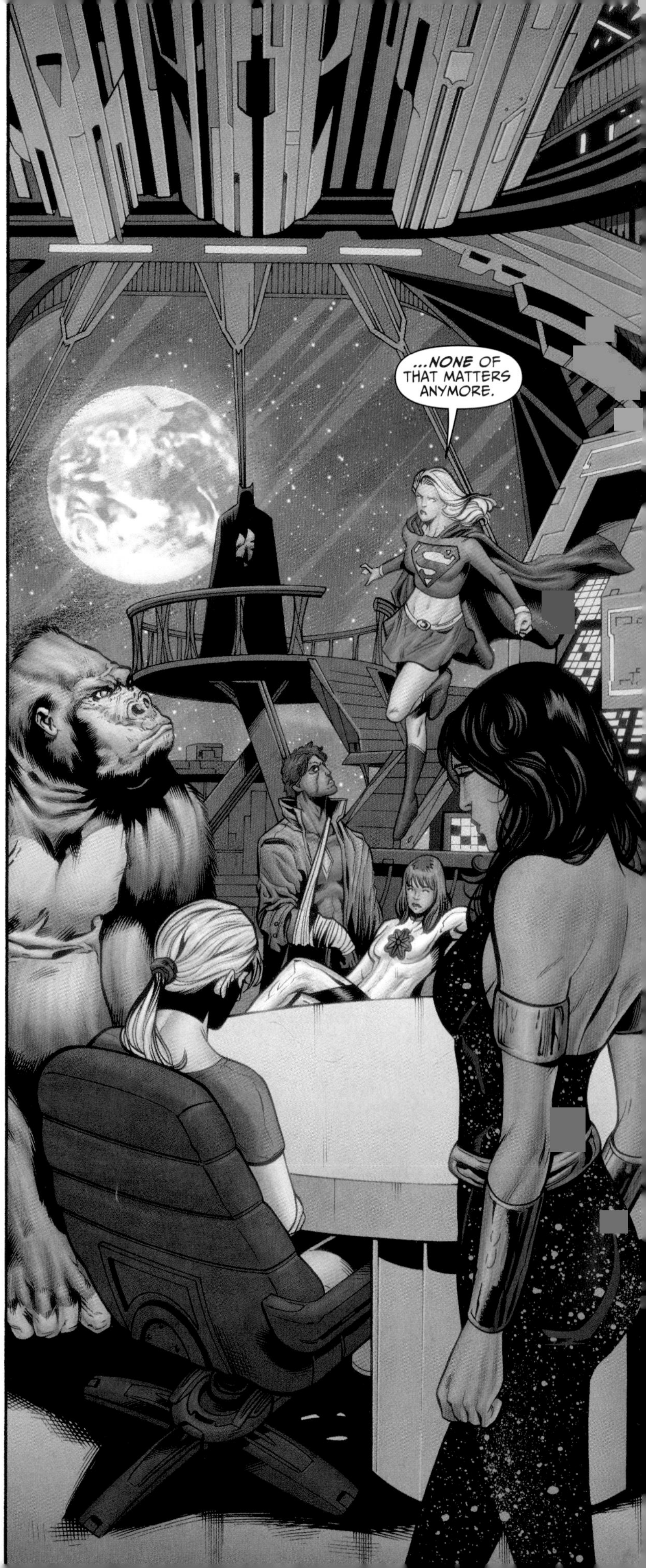
...NONE OF THAT MATTERS ANYMORE.

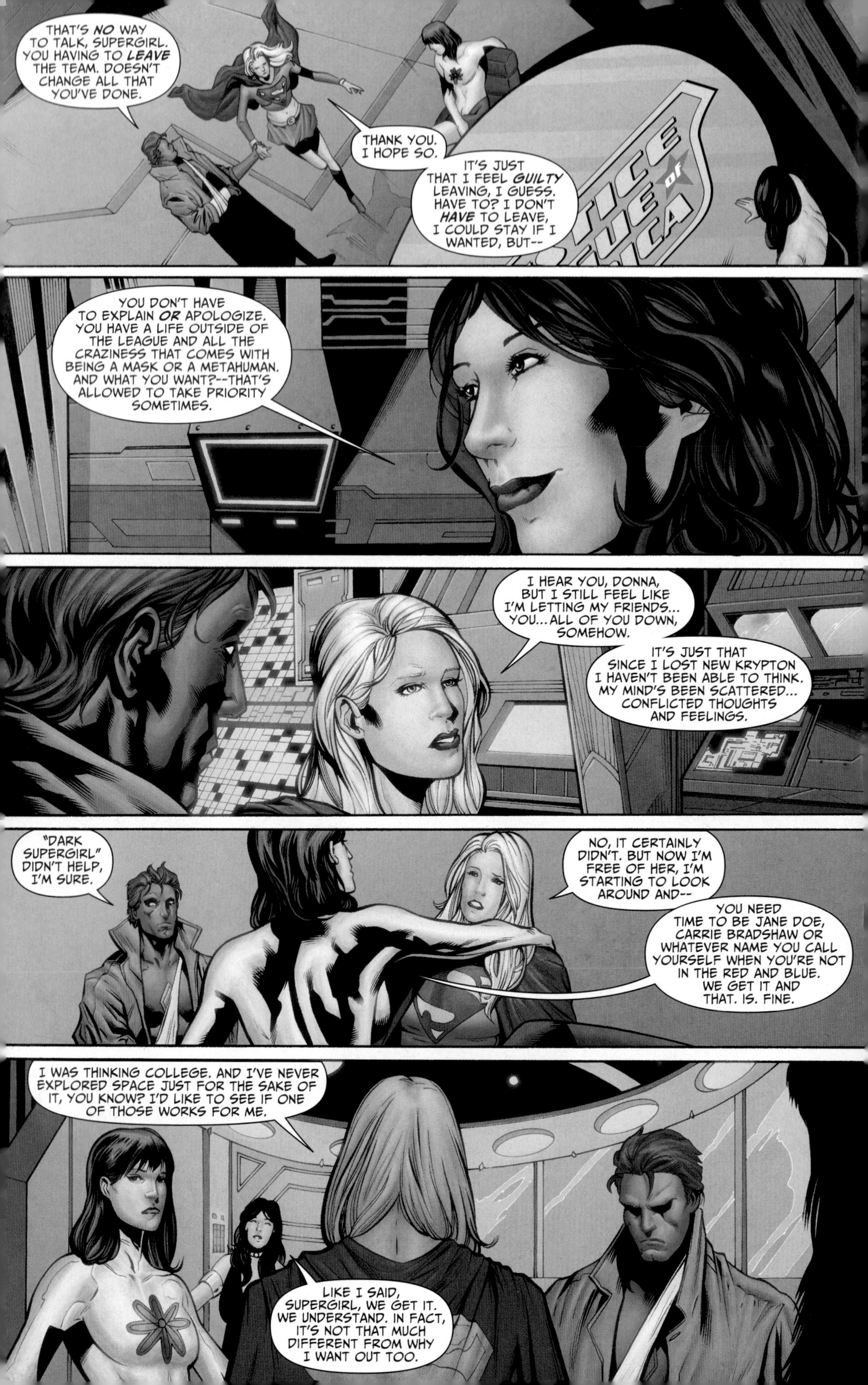
THAT'S NO WAY TO TALK, SUPERGIRL. YOU HAVING TO LEAVE THE TEAM. DOESN'T CHANGE ALL THAT YOU'VE DONE.
THANK YOU. I HOPE SO.
IT'S JUST THAT I FEEL GUILTY LEAVING, I GUESS. HAVE TO? I DON'T HAVE TO LEAVE, I COULD STAY IF I WANTED, BUT--
YOU DON'T HAVE TO EXPLAIN OR APOLOGIZE. YOU HAVE A LIFE OUTSIDE OF THE LEAGUE AND ALL THE CRAZINESS THAT COMES WITH BEING A MASK OR A METAHUMAN. AND WHAT YOU WANT?--THAT'S ALLOWED TO TAKE PRIORITY SOMETIMES.
I HEAR YOU, DONNA, BUT I STILL FEEL LIKE I'M LETTING MY FRIENDS... YOU... ALL OF YOU DOWN, SOMEHOW.
IT'S JUST THAT SINCE I LOST NEW KRYPTON I HAVEN'T BEEN ABLE TO THINK. MY MIND'S BEEN SCATTERED... CONFLICTED THOUGHTS AND FEELINGS.
"DARK SUPERGIRL" DIDN'T HELP, I'M SURE.
NO, IT CERTAINLY DIDN'T. BUT NOW I'M FREE OF HER, I'M STARTING TO LOOK AROUND AND--
YOU NEED TIME TO BE JANE DOE, CARRIE BRADSHAW OR WHATEVER NAME YOU CALL YOURSELF WHEN YOU'RE NOT IN THE RED AND BLUE. WE GET IT AND THAT. IS. FINE.
I WAS THINKING COLLEGE. AND I'VE NEVER EXPLORED SPACE JUST FOR THE SAKE OF IT, YOU KNOW? I'D LIKE TO SEE IF ONE OF THOSE WORKS FOR ME.
LIKE I SAID, SUPERGIRL, WE GET IT. WE UNDERSTAND. IN FACT, IT'S NOT THAT MUCH DIFFERENT FROM WHY I WANT OUT TOO.

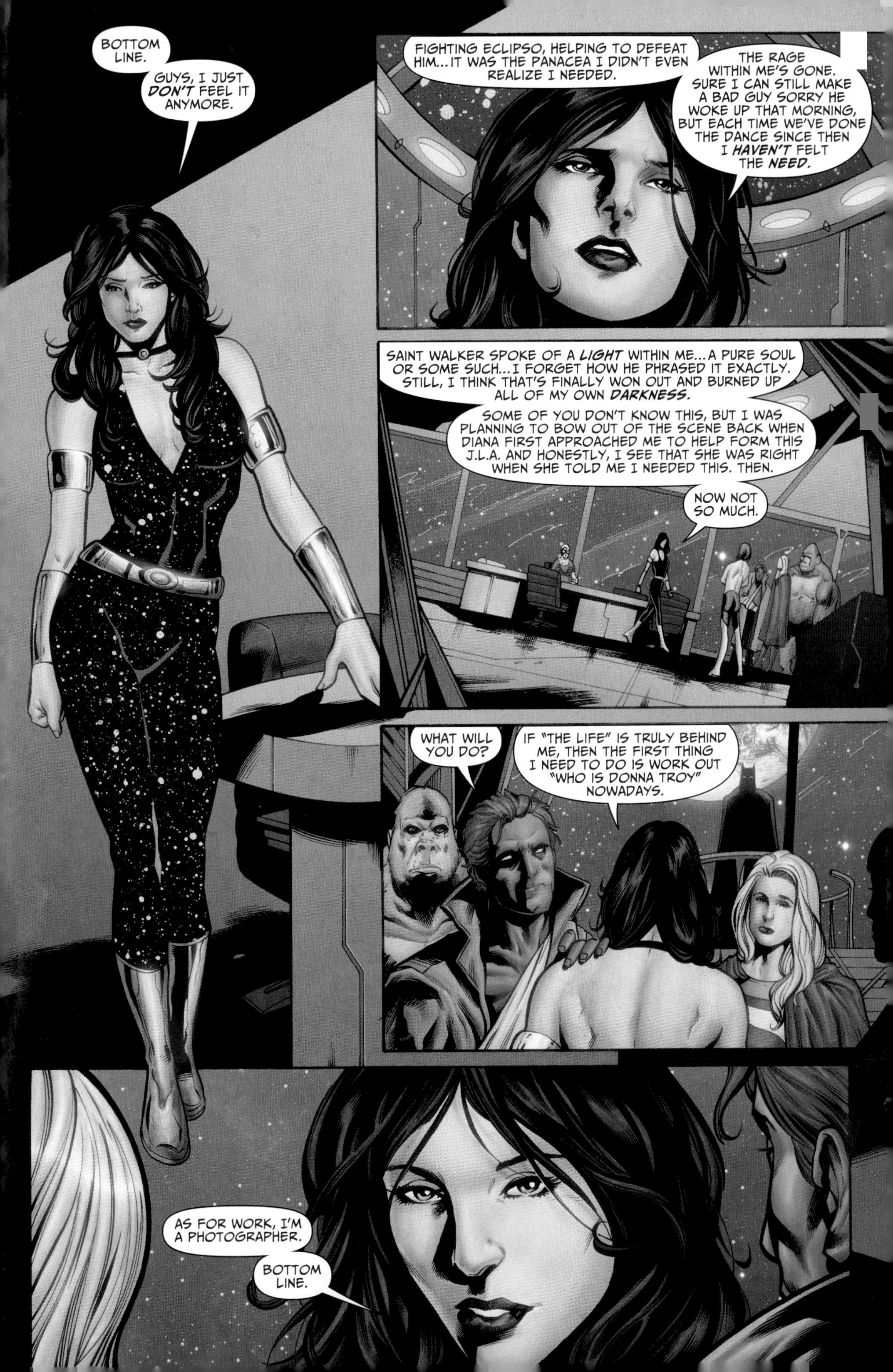
BOTTOM LINE.
GUYS, I JUST DON'T FEEL IT ANYMORE.
FIGHTING ECLIPSO, HELPING TO DEFEAT HIM...IT WAS THE PANACEA I DIDN'T EVEN REALIZE I NEEDED.
THE RAGE WITHIN ME'S GONE. SURE I CAN STILL MAKE A BAD GUY SORRY HE WOKE UP THAT MORNING, BUT EACH TIME WE'VE DONE THE DANCE SINCE THEN I HAVEN'T FELT THE NEED.
SAINT WALKER SPOKE OF A LIGHT WITHIN ME...A PURE SOUL OR SOME SUCH...I FORGET HOW HE PHRASED IT EXACTLY. STILL, I THINK THAT'S FINALLY WON OUT AND BURNED UP ALL OF MY OWN DARKNESS.
SOME OF YOU DON'T KNOW THIS, BUT I WAS PLANNING TO BOW OUT OF THE SCENE BACK WHEN DIANA FIRST APPROACHED ME TO HELP FORM THIS J.L.A. AND HONESTLY, I SEE THAT SHE WAS RIGHT WHEN SHE TOLD ME I NEEDED THIS. THEN.
NOW NOT SO MUCH.
WHAT WILL YOU DO?
IF "THE LIFE" IS TRULY BEHIND ME, THEN THE FIRST THING I NEED TO DO IS WORK OUT "WHO IS DONNA TROY" NOWADAYS.
AS FOR WORK, I'M A PHOTOGRAPHER.
BOTTOM LINE.

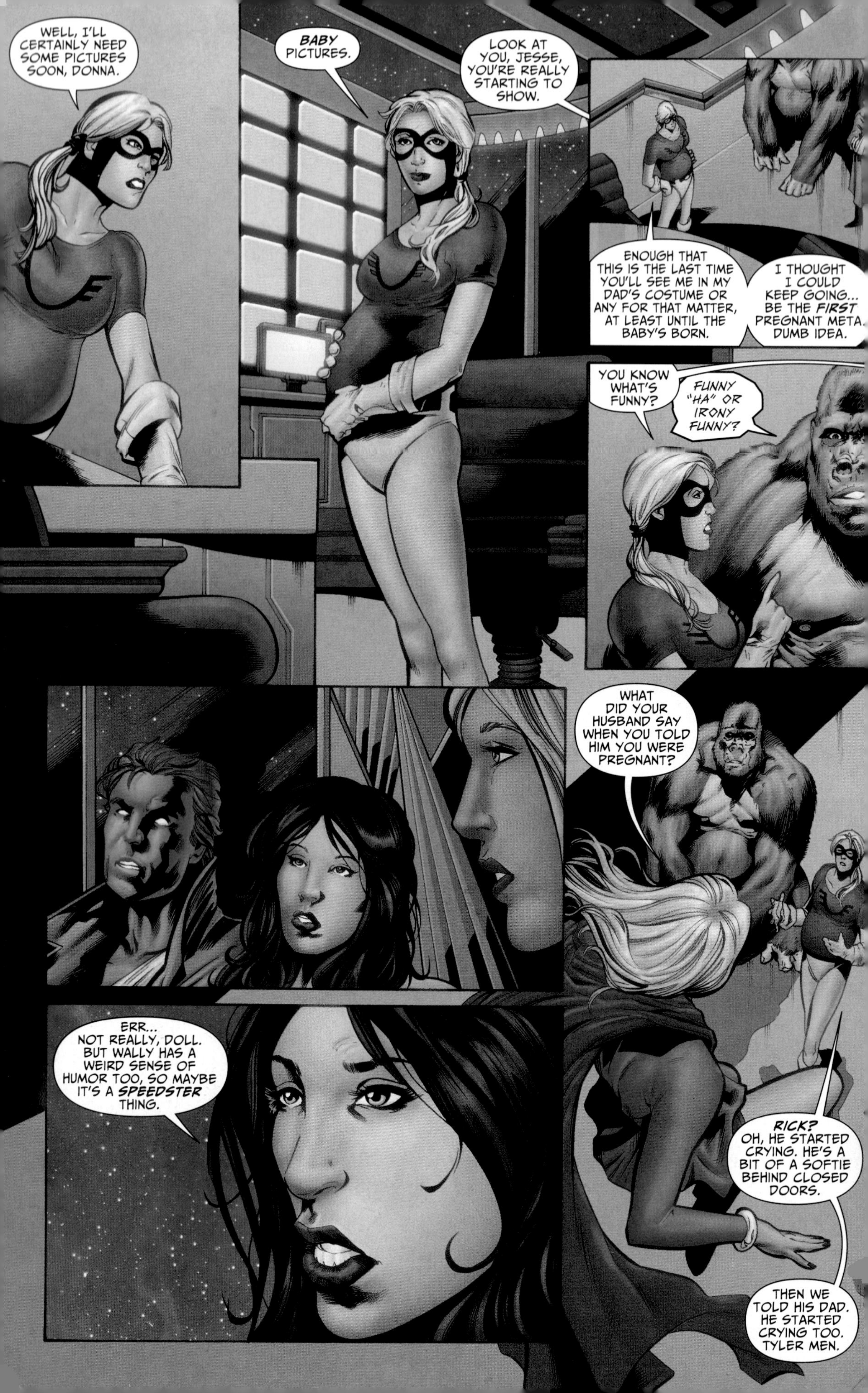
WELL, I'LL CERTAINLY NEED SOME PICTURES SOON, DONNA.
BABY PICTURES.
LOOK AT YOU, JESSE, YOU'RE REALLY STARTING TO SHOW.
ENOUGH THAT THIS IS THE LAST TIME YOU'LL SEE ME IN MY DAD'S COSTUME OR ANY FOR THAT MATTER, AT LEAST UNTIL THE BABY'S BORN.
I THOUGHT I COULD KEEP GOING... BE THE FIRST PREGNANT META. DUMB IDEA.
YOU KNOW WHAT'S FUNNY?
FUNNY "HA" OR IRONY FUNNY?
WHAT DID YOUR HUSBAND SAY WHEN YOU TOLD HIM YOU WERE PREGNANT?
ERR... NOT REALLY, DOLL. BUT WALLY HAS A WEIRD SENSE OF HUMOR TOO, SO MAYBE IT'S A SPEEDSTER THING.
RICK? OH, HE STARTED CRYING. HE'S A BIT OF A SOFTIE BEHIND CLOSED DOORS.
THEN WE TOLD HIS DAD. HE STARTED CRYING TOO. TYLER MEN.

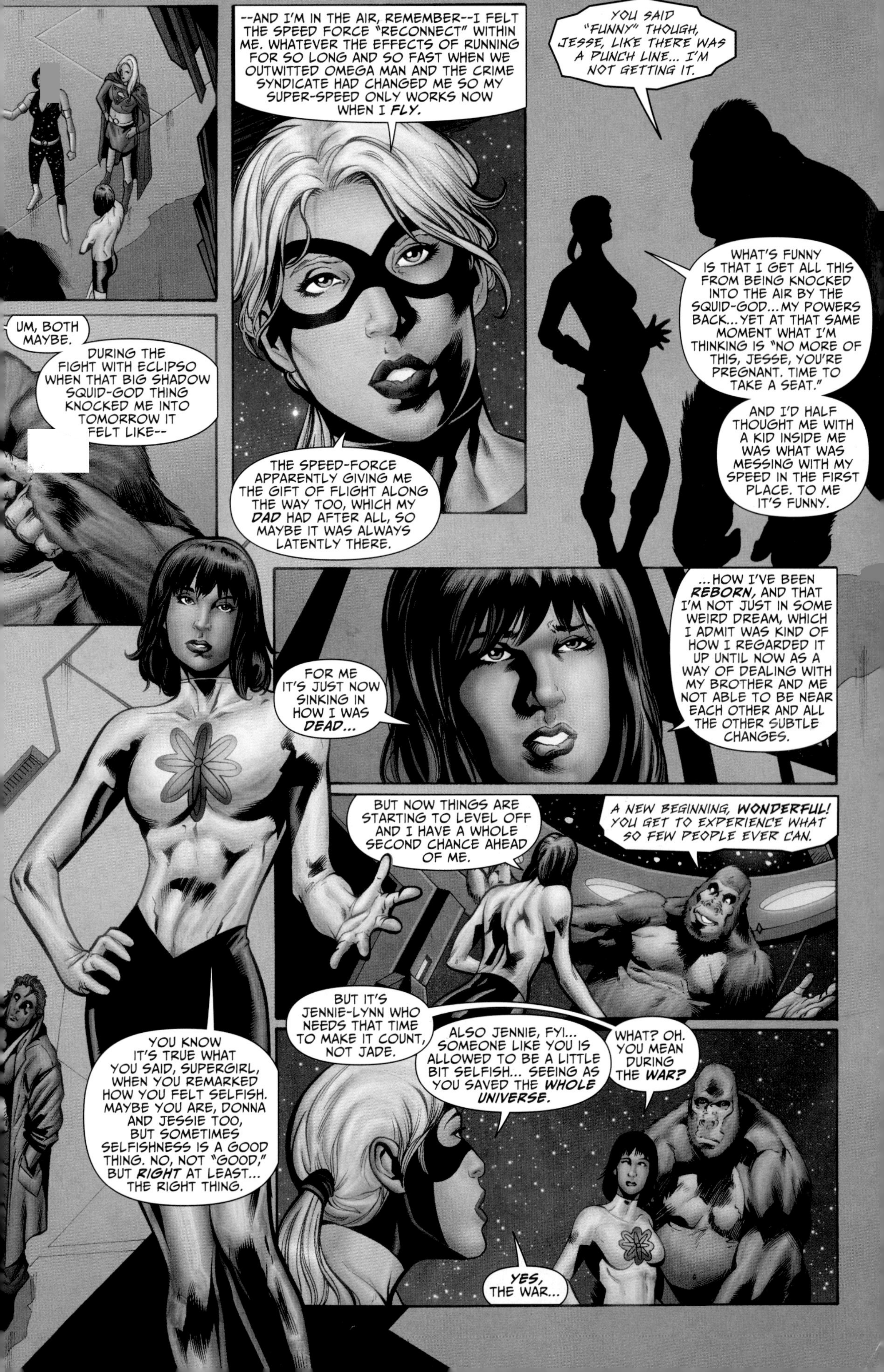
UM, BOTH MAYBE.
DURING THE FIGHT WITH ECLIPSO WHEN THAT BIG SHADOW SQUID-GOD THING KNOCKED ME INTO TOMORROW IT FELT LIKE--
--AND I'M IN THE AIR, REMEMBER--I FELT THE SPEED FORCE "RECONNECT" WITHIN ME. WHATEVER THE EFFECTS OF RUNNING FOR SO LONG AND SO FAST WHEN WE OUTWITTED OMEGA MAN AND THE CRIME SYNDICATE HAD CHANGED ME SO MY SUPER-SPEED ONLY WORKS NOW WHEN I FLY.
THE SPEED-FORCE APPARENTLY GIVING ME THE GIFT OF FLIGHT ALONG THE WAY TOO, WHICH MY DAD HAD AFTER ALL, SO MAYBE IT WAS ALWAYS LATENTLY THERE.
YOU SAID "FUNNY" THOUGH, JESSE, LIKE THERE WAS A PUNCH LINE... I'M NOT GETTING IT.
WHAT'S FUNNY IS THAT I GET ALL THIS FROM BEING KNOCKED INTO THE AIR BY THE SQUID-GOD... MY POWERS BACK... YET AT THAT SAME MOMENT WHAT I'M THINKING IS "NO MORE OF THIS, JESSE, YOU'RE PREGNANT. TIME TO TAKE A SEAT."
AND I'D HALF THOUGHT ME WITH A KID INSIDE ME WAS WHAT WAS MESSING WITH MY SPEED IN THE FIRST PLACE. TO ME IT'S FUNNY.
FOR ME IT'S JUST NOW SINKING IN HOW I WAS DEAD...
...HOW I'VE BEEN REBORN, AND THAT I'M NOT JUST IN SOME WEIRD DREAM, WHICH I ADMIT WAS KIND OF HOW I REGARDED IT UP UNTIL NOW AS A WAY OF DEALING WITH MY BROTHER AND ME NOT ABLE TO BE NEAR EACH OTHER AND ALL THE OTHER SUBTLE CHANGES.
BUT NOW THINGS ARE STARTING TO LEVEL OFF AND I HAVE A WHOLE SECOND CHANCE AHEAD OF ME.
A NEW BEGINNING, WONDERFUL! YOU GET TO EXPERIENCE WHAT SO FEW PEOPLE EVER CAN.
YOU KNOW IT'S TRUE WHAT YOU SAID, SUPERGIRL, WHEN YOU REMARKED HOW YOU FELT SELFISH. MAYBE YOU ARE, DONNA AND JESSIE TOO, BUT SOMETIMES SELFISHNESS IS A GOOD THING. NO, NOT "GOOD," BUT RIGHT AT LEAST... THE RIGHT THING.
BUT IT'S JENNIE-LYNN WHO NEEDS THAT TIME TO MAKE IT COUNT, NOT JADE.
WHAT? OH. YOU MEAN DURING THE WAR?
ALSO JENNIE, FYI... SOMEONE LIKE YOU IS ALLOWED TO BE A LITTLE BIT SELFISH... SEEING AS YOU SAVED THE WHOLE UNIVERSE.
YES, THE WAR...

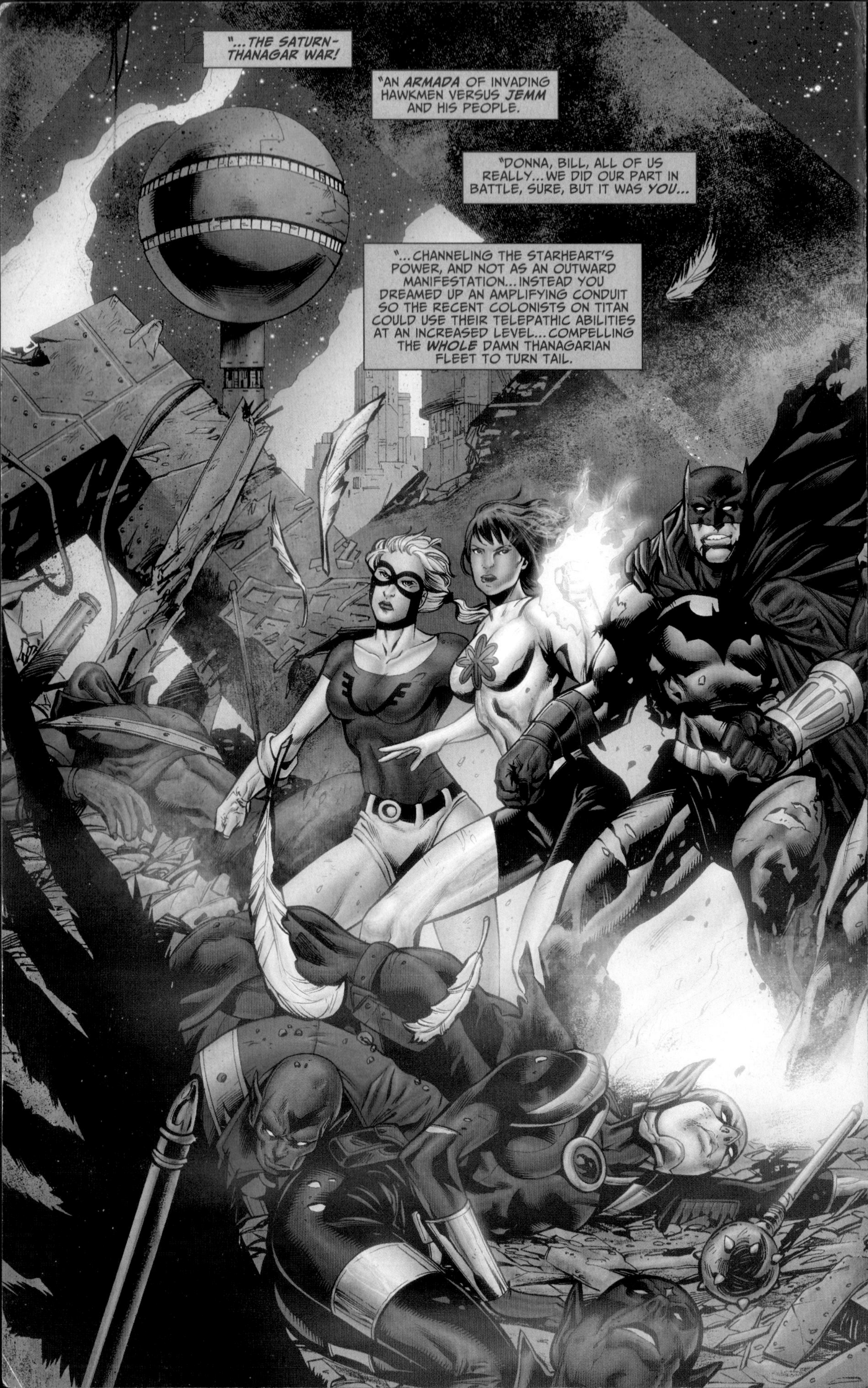
"...THE SATURN-THANAGAR WAR!
"AN ARMADA OF INVADING HAWKMEN VERSUS JEMM AND HIS PEOPLE.
"DONNA, BILL, ALL OF US REALLY...WE DID OUR PART IN BATTLE, SURE, BUT IT WAS YOU...
"...CHANNELING THE STARHEART'S POWER, AND NOT AS AN OUTWARD MANIFESTATION...INSTEAD YOU DREAMED UP AN AMPLIFYING CONDUIT SO THE RECENT COLONISTS ON TITAN COULD USE THEIR TELEPATHIC ABILITIES AT AN INCREASED LEVEL...COMPELLING THE WHOLE DAMN THANAGARIAN FLEET TO TURN TAIL.

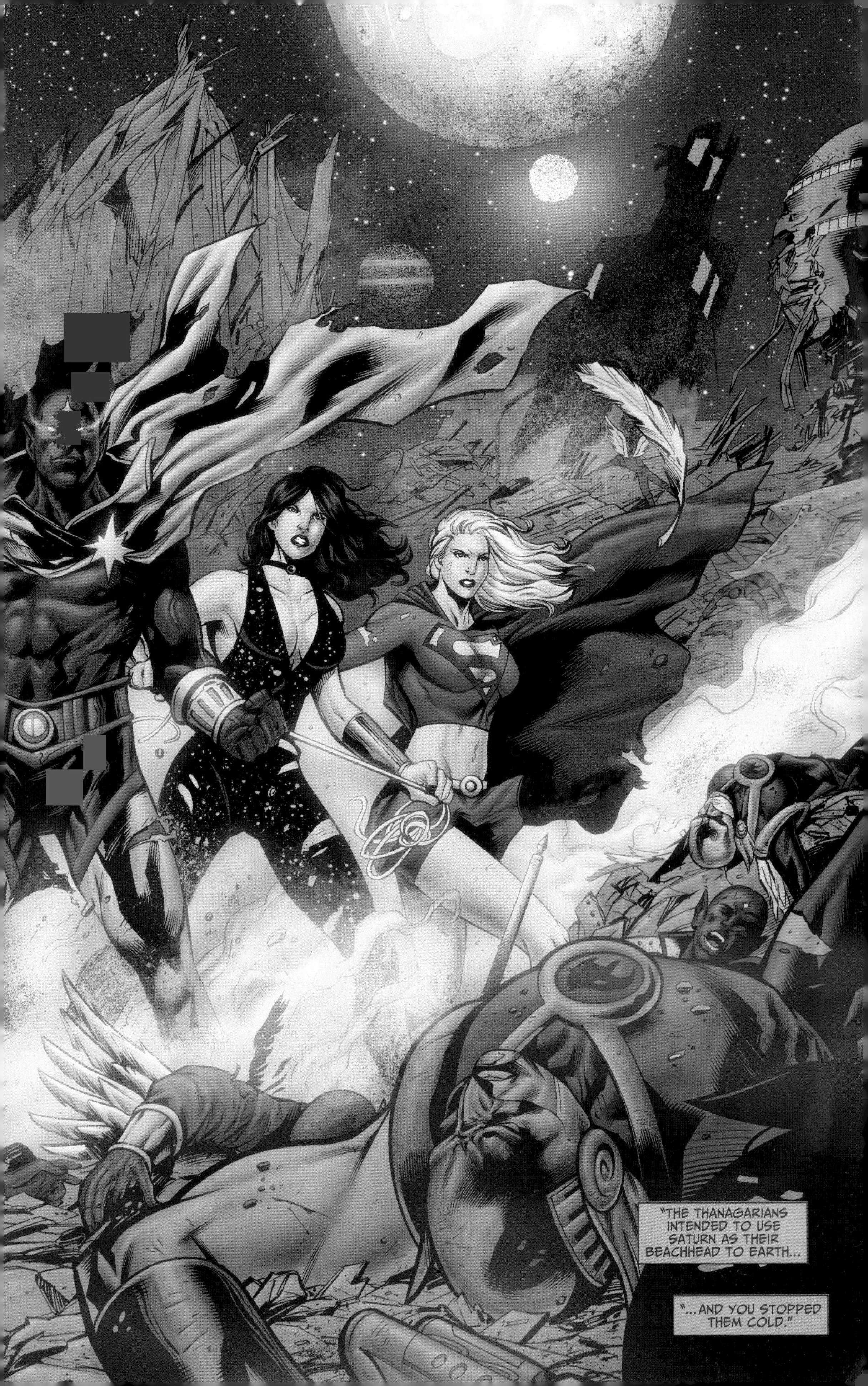
"THE THANAGARIANS INTENDED TO USE SATURN AS THEIR BEACHHEAD TO EARTH...
"...AND YOU STOPPED THEM COLD."

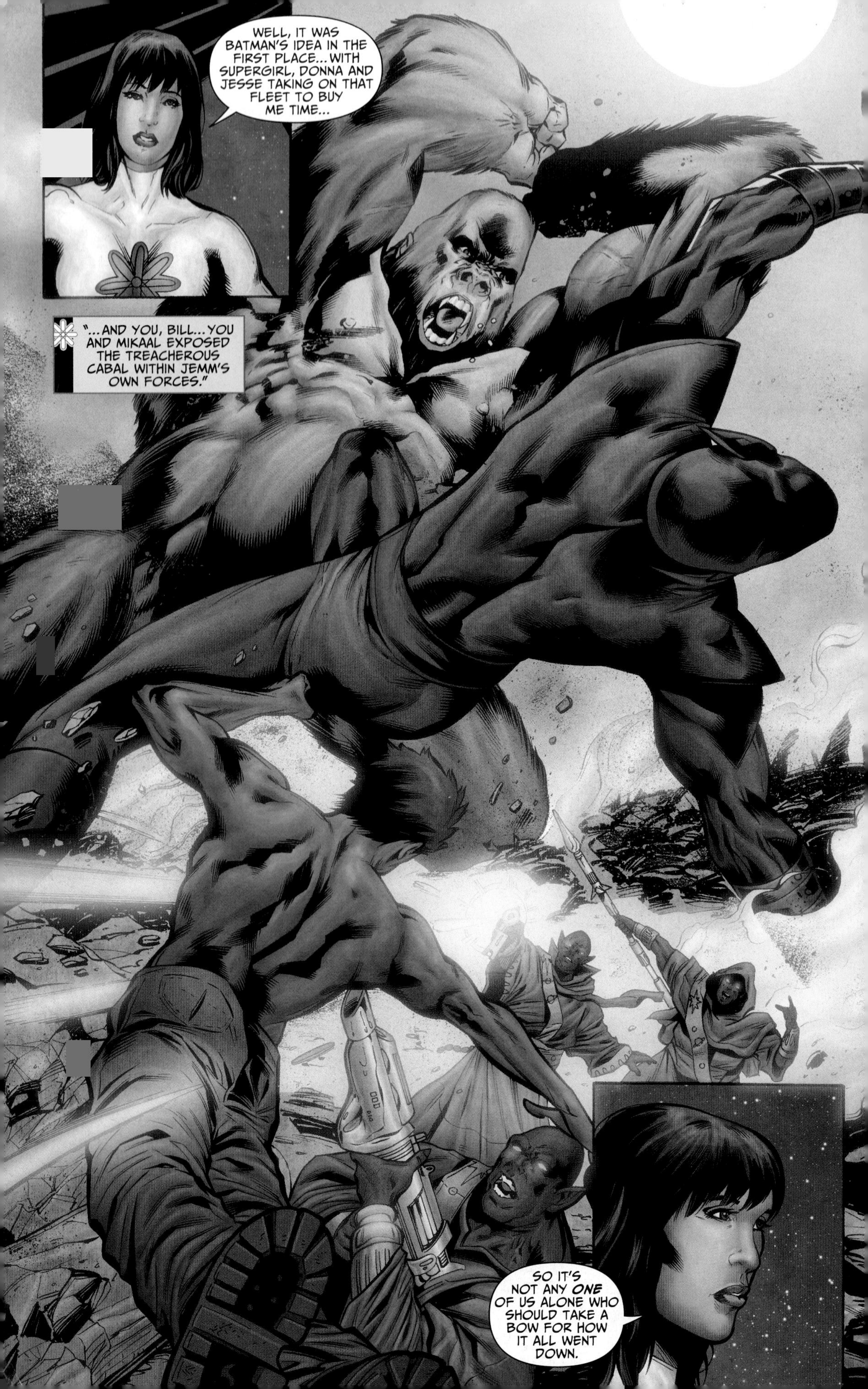
WELL, IT WAS BATMAN'S IDEA IN THE FIRST PLACE... WITH SUPERGIRL, DONNA AND JESSE TAKING ON THAT FLEET TO BUY ME TIME...
"...AND YOU, BILL... YOU AND MIKAAL EXPOSED THE TREACHEROUS CABAL WITHIN JEMM'S OWN FORCES."
SO IT'S NOT ANY *ONE* OF US ALONE WHO SHOULD TAKE A BOW FOR HOW IT ALL WENT DOWN.

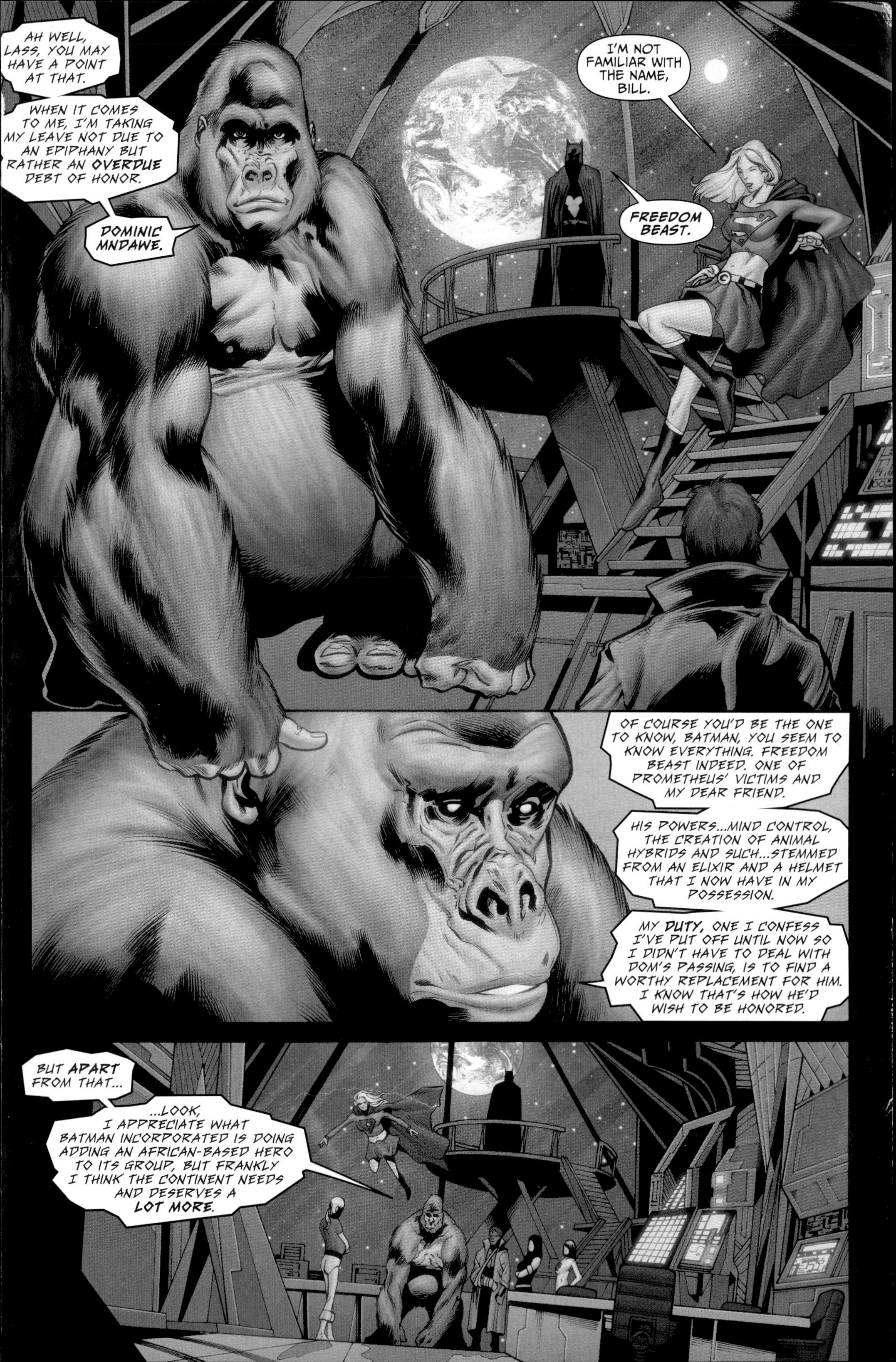
AH WELL, LASS, YOU MAY HAVE A POINT AT THAT.
WHEN IT COMES TO ME, I'M TAKING MY LEAVE NOT DUE TO AN EPIPHANY BUT RATHER AN **OVERDUE** DEBT OF HONOR.
I'M NOT FAMILIAR WITH THE NAME, BILL.
FREEDOM BEAST.
DOMINIC MNDAWE.
OF COURSE YOU'D BE THE ONE TO KNOW, BATMAN, YOU SEEM TO KNOW EVERYTHING. FREEDOM BEAST INDEED. ONE OF PROMETHEUS' VICTIMS AND MY DEAR FRIEND.
HIS POWERS...MIND CONTROL, THE CREATION OF ANIMAL HYBRIDS AND SUCH...STEMMED FROM AN ELIXIR AND A HELMET THAT I NOW HAVE IN MY POSSESSION.
MY **DUTY,** ONE I CONFESS I'VE PUT OFF UNTIL NOW SO I DIDN'T HAVE TO DEAL WITH DOM'S PASSING, IS TO FIND A WORTHY REPLACEMENT FOR HIM. I KNOW THAT'S HOW HE'D WISH TO BE HONORED.
BUT **APART** FROM THAT...
...LOOK, I APPRECIATE WHAT BATMAN INCORPORATED IS DOING ADDING AN AFRICAN-BASED HERO TO ITS GROUP, BUT FRANKLY I THINK THE CONTINENT NEEDS AND DESERVES A **LOT MORE**.

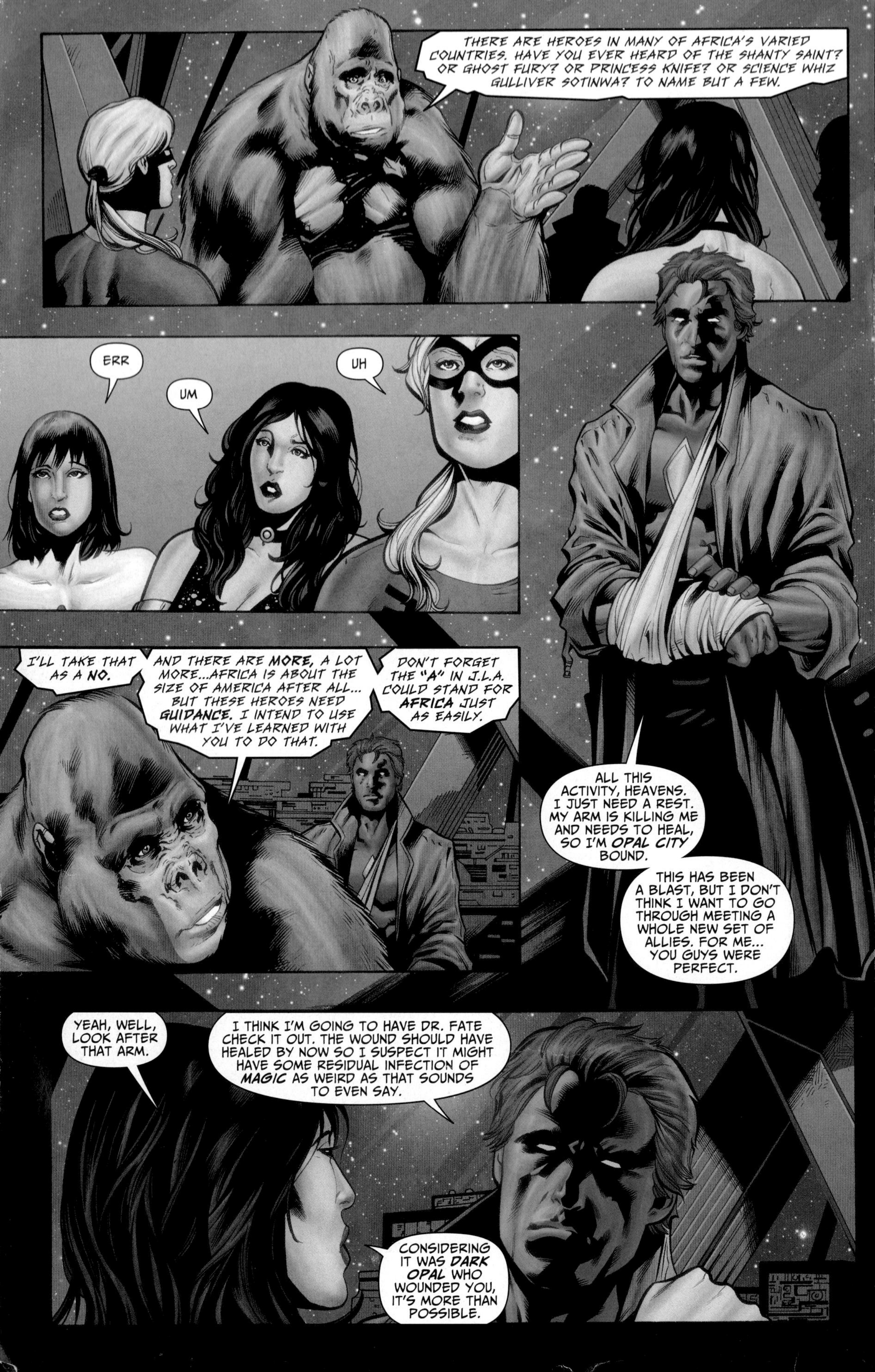
THERE ARE HEROES IN MANY OF AFRICA'S VARIED COUNTRIES. HAVE YOU EVER HEARD OF THE SHANTY SAINT? OR GHOST FURY? OR PRINCESS KNIFE? OR SCIENCE WHIZ GULLIVER SOTINWA? TO NAME BUT A FEW.
ERR
UM
UH
I'LL TAKE THAT AS A NO.
AND THERE ARE MORE, A LOT MORE...AFRICA IS ABOUT THE SIZE OF AMERICA AFTER ALL... BUT THESE HEROES NEED GUIDANCE. I INTEND TO USE WHAT I'VE LEARNED WITH YOU TO DO THAT.
DON'T FORGET THE "A" IN J.L.A. COULD STAND FOR AFRICA JUST AS EASILY.
ALL THIS ACTIVITY, HEAVENS. I JUST NEED A REST. MY ARM IS KILLING ME AND NEEDS TO HEAL, SO I'M OPAL CITY BOUND.
THIS HAS BEEN A BLAST, BUT I DON'T THINK I WANT TO GO THROUGH MEETING A WHOLE NEW SET OF ALLIES. FOR ME... YOU GUYS WERE PERFECT.
YEAH, WELL, LOOK AFTER THAT ARM.
I THINK I'M GOING TO HAVE DR. FATE CHECK IT OUT. THE WOUND SHOULD HAVE HEALED BY NOW SO I SUSPECT IT MIGHT HAVE SOME RESIDUAL INFECTION OF MAGIC AS WEIRD AS THAT SOUNDS TO EVEN SAY.
CONSIDERING IT WAS DARK OPAL WHO WOUNDED YOU, IT'S MORE THAN POSSIBLE.

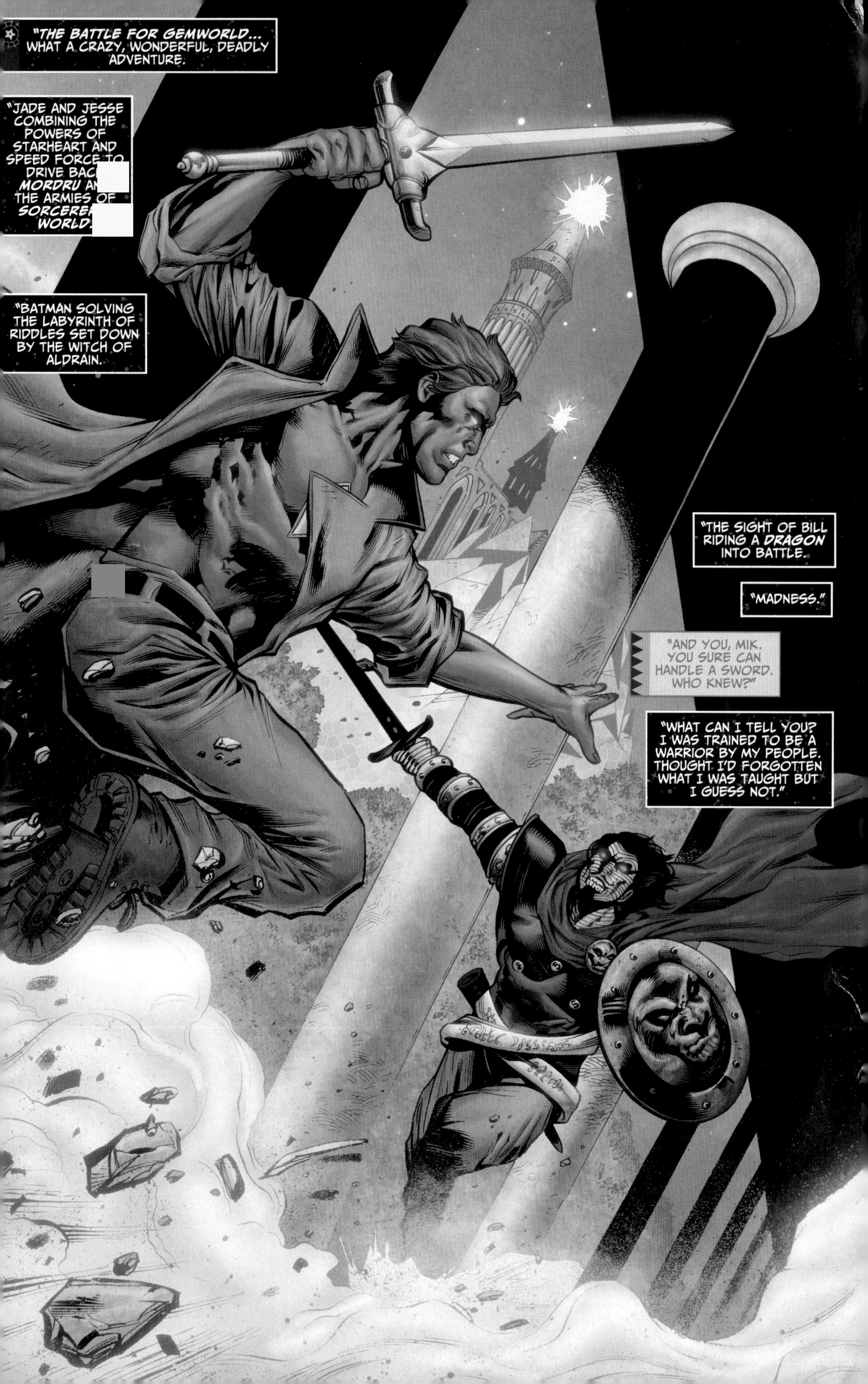
"THE BATTLE FOR GEMWORLD... WHAT A CRAZY, WONDERFUL, DEADLY ADVENTURE.
"JADE AND JESSE COMBINING THE POWERS OF STARHEART AND SPEED FORCE TO DRIVE BAC MORDRU AN THE ARMIES OF SORCERER WORLD.
"BATMAN SOLVING THE LABYRINTH OF RIDDLES SET DOWN BY THE WITCH OF ALDRAIN.
"THE SIGHT OF BILL RIDING A DRAGON INTO BATTLE.
"MADNESS."
"AND YOU, MIK. YOU SURE CAN HANDLE A SWORD. WHO KNEW?"
"WHAT CAN I TELL YOU? I WAS TRAINED TO BE A WARRIOR BY MY PEOPLE. THOUGHT I'D FORGOTTEN WHAT I WAS TAUGHT BUT I GUESS NOT."

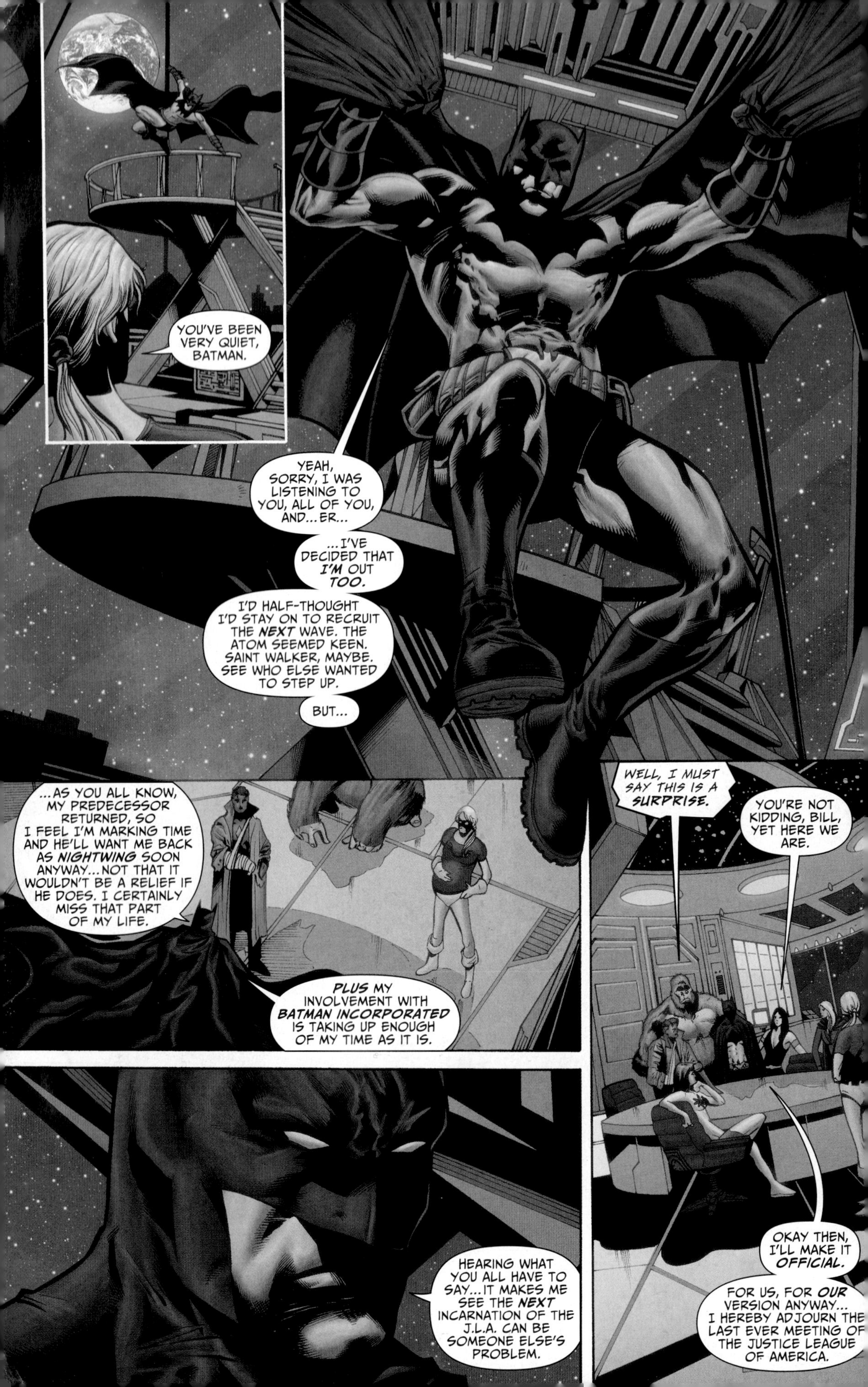
YOU'VE BEEN VERY QUIET, BATMAN.
YEAH, SORRY, I WAS LISTENING TO YOU, ALL OF YOU, AND... ER...
...I'VE DECIDED THAT I'M OUT TOO.
I'D HALF-THOUGHT I'D STAY ON TO RECRUIT THE NEXT WAVE. THE ATOM SEEMED KEEN. SAINT WALKER, MAYBE. SEE WHO ELSE WANTED TO STEP UP.
BUT...
...AS YOU ALL KNOW, MY PREDECESSOR RETURNED, SO I FEEL I'M MARKING TIME AND HE'LL WANT ME BACK AS NIGHTWING SOON ANYWAY... NOT THAT IT WOULDN'T BE A RELIEF IF HE DOES. I CERTAINLY MISS THAT PART OF MY LIFE.
PLUS MY INVOLVEMENT WITH BATMAN INCORPORATED IS TAKING UP ENOUGH OF MY TIME AS IT IS.
WELL, I MUST SAY THIS IS A SURPRISE.
YOU'RE NOT KIDDING, BILL, YET HERE WE ARE.
HEARING WHAT YOU ALL HAVE TO SAY... IT MAKES ME SEE THE NEXT INCARNATION OF THE J.L.A. CAN BE SOMEONE ELSE'S PROBLEM.
OKAY THEN, I'LL MAKE IT OFFICIAL.
FOR US, FOR OUR VERSION ANYWAY... I HEREBY ADJOURN THE LAST EVER MEETING OF THE JUSTICE LEAGUE OF AMERICA.

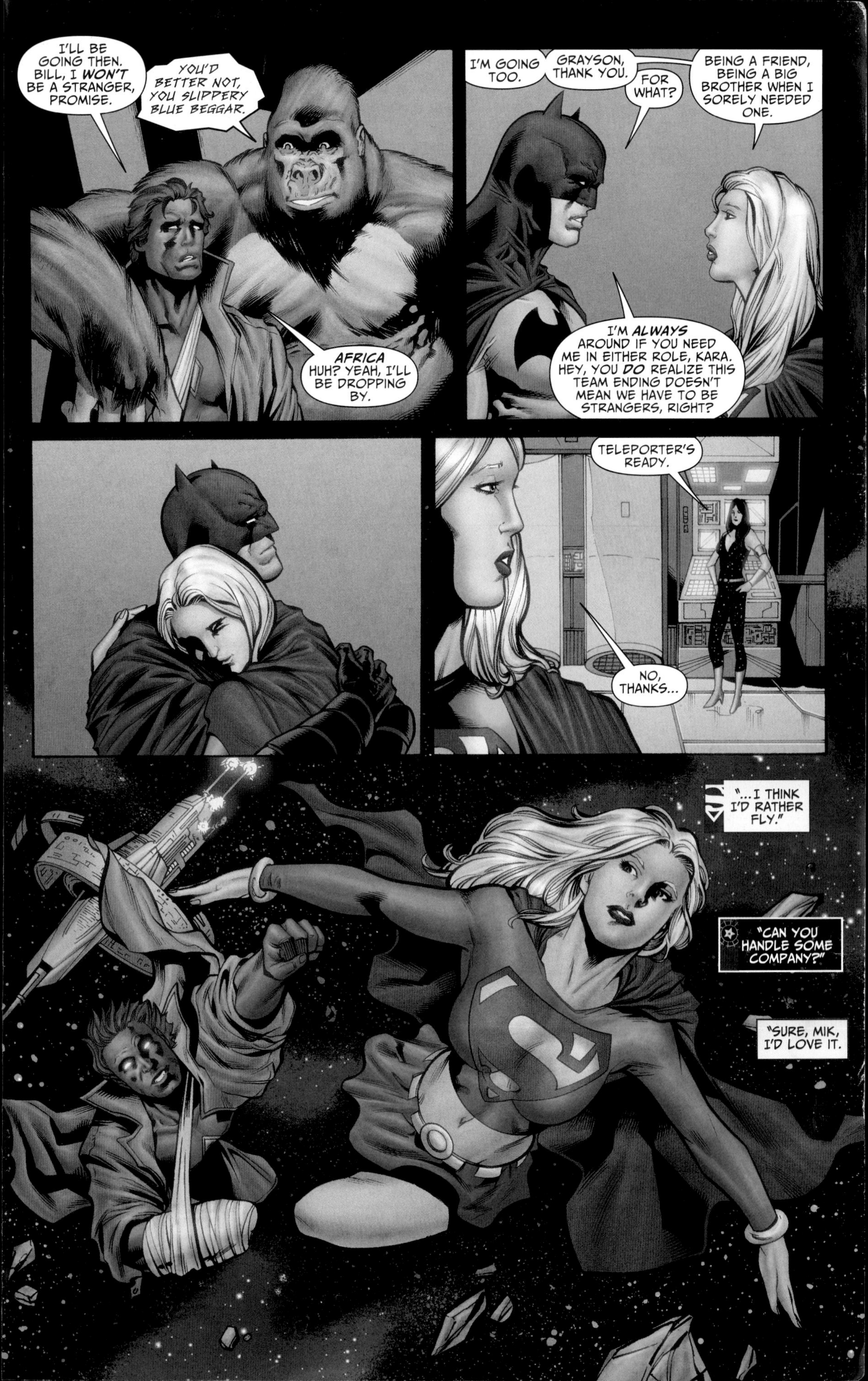
I'LL BE GOING THEN. BILL, I WON'T BE A STRANGER, PROMISE.
YOU'D BETTER NOT, YOU SLIPPERY BLUE BEGGAR.
AFRICA HUH? YEAH, I'LL BE DROPPING BY.
I'M GOING TOO.
GRAYSON, THANK YOU.
FOR WHAT?
BEING A FRIEND, BEING A BIG BROTHER WHEN I SORELY NEEDED ONE.
I'M ALWAYS AROUND IF YOU NEED ME IN EITHER ROLE, KARA. HEY, YOU DO REALIZE THIS TEAM ENDING DOESN'T MEAN WE HAVE TO BE STRANGERS, RIGHT?
TELEPORTER'S READY.
NO, THANKS...
"...I THINK I'D RATHER FLY."
"CAN YOU HANDLE SOME COMPANY?"
"SURE, MIK, I'D LOVE IT.

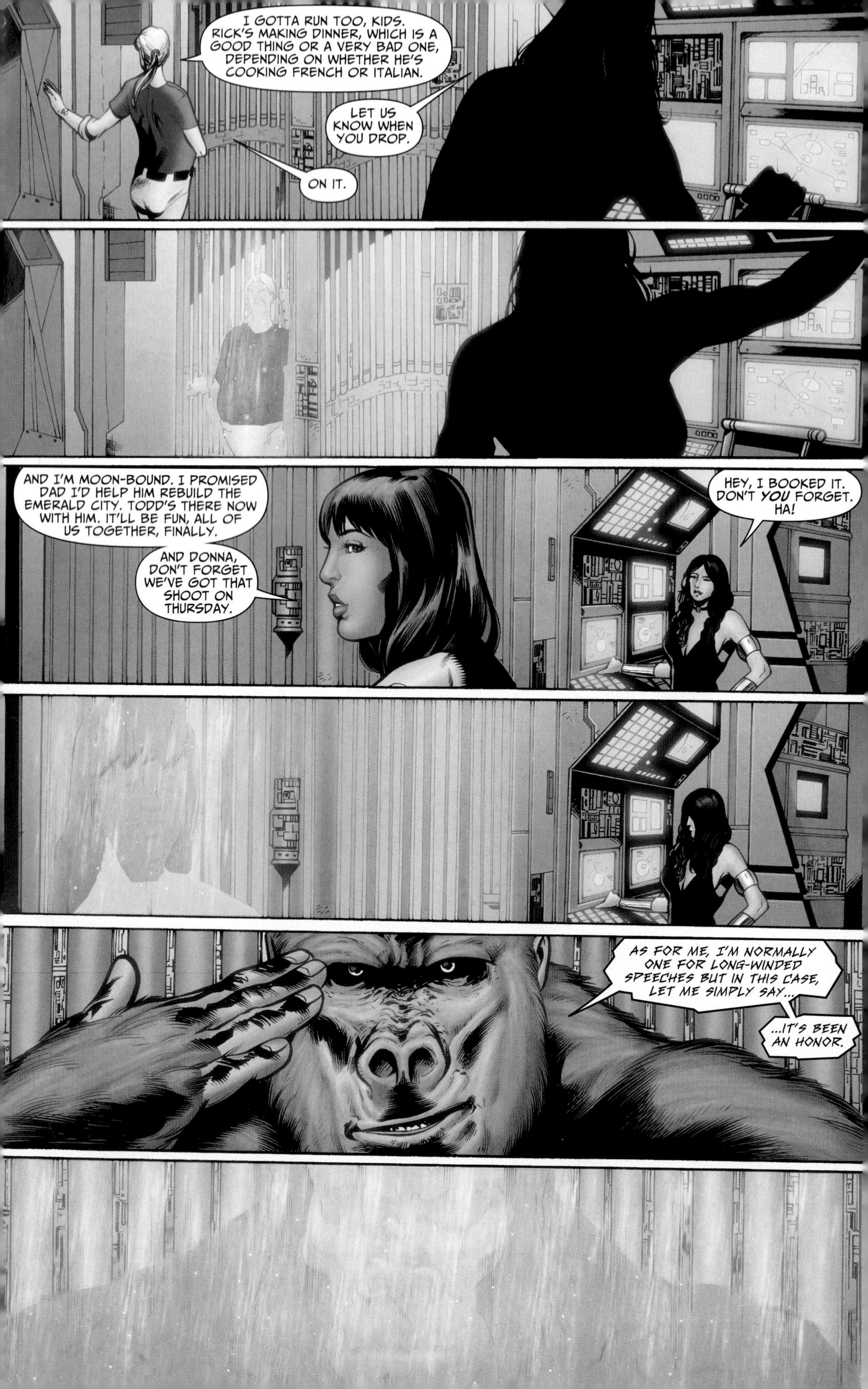
I GOTTA RUN TOO, KIDS. RICK'S MAKING DINNER, WHICH IS A GOOD THING OR A VERY BAD ONE, DEPENDING ON WHETHER HE'S COOKING FRENCH OR ITALIAN.
LET US KNOW WHEN YOU DROP.
ON IT.
AND I'M MOON-BOUND. I PROMISED DAD I'D HELP HIM REBUILD THE EMERALD CITY. TODD'S THERE NOW WITH HIM. IT'LL BE FUN, ALL OF US TOGETHER, FINALLY.
AND DONNA, DON'T FORGET WE'VE GOT THAT SHOOT ON THURSDAY.
HEY, I BOOKED IT. DON'T YOU FORGET. HA!
AS FOR ME, I'M NORMALLY ONE FOR LONG-WINDED SPEECHES BUT IN THIS CASE, LET ME SIMPLY SAY...
...IT'S BEEN AN HONOR.

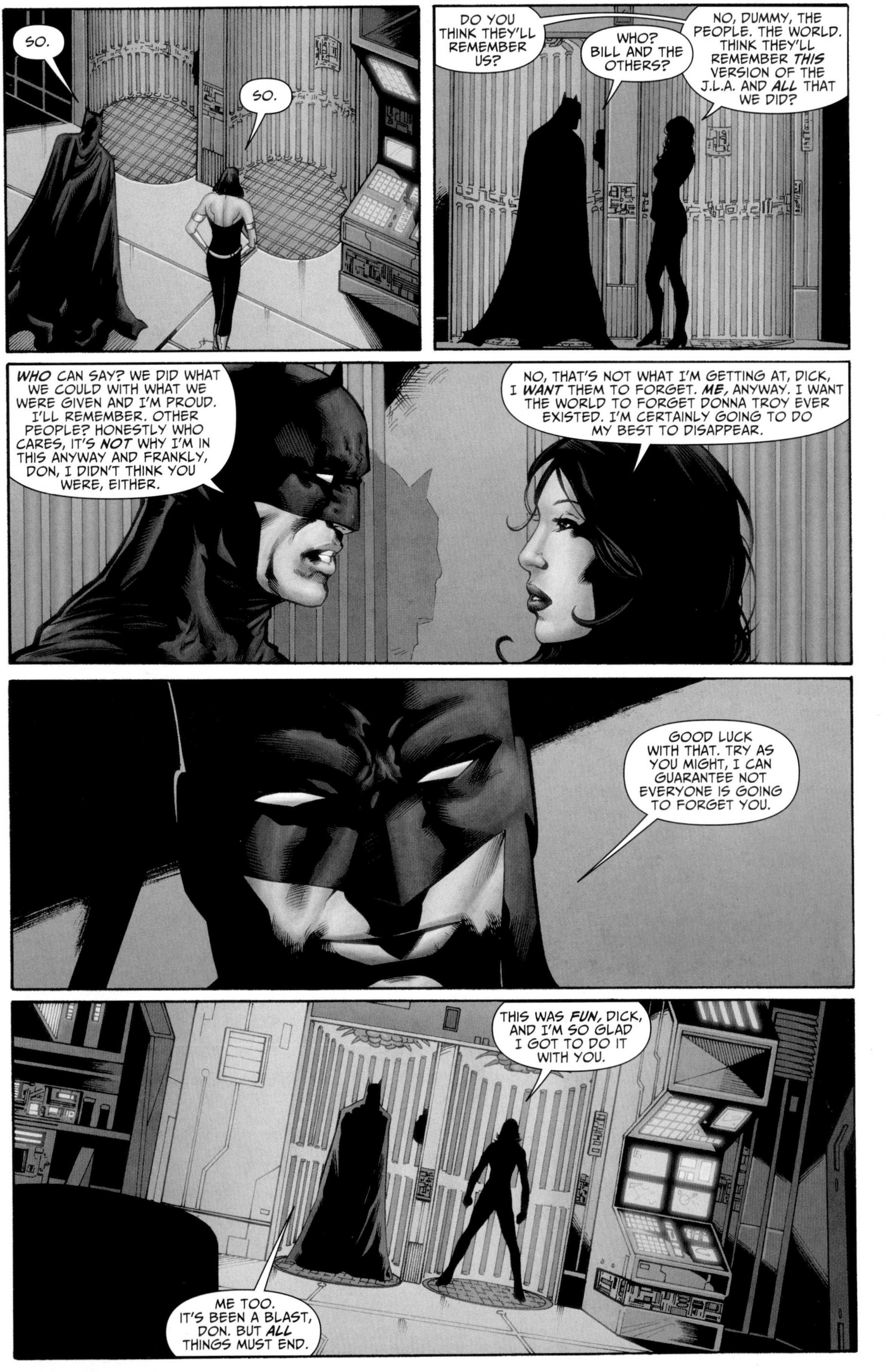
SO.
SO.
DO YOU THINK THEY'LL REMEMBER US?
WHO? BILL AND THE OTHERS?
NO, DUMMY, THE PEOPLE. THE WORLD. THINK THEY'LL REMEMBER THIS VERSION OF THE J.L.A. AND ALL THAT WE DID?
WHO CAN SAY? WE DID WHAT WE COULD WITH WHAT WE WERE GIVEN AND I'M PROUD. I'LL REMEMBER. OTHER PEOPLE? HONESTLY WHO CARES, IT'S NOT WHY I'M IN THIS ANYWAY AND FRANKLY, DON, I DIDN'T THINK YOU WERE, EITHER.
NO, THAT'S NOT WHAT I'M GETTING AT, DICK, I WANT THEM TO FORGET. ME, ANYWAY. I WANT THE WORLD TO FORGET DONNA TROY EVER EXISTED. I'M CERTAINLY GOING TO DO MY BEST TO DISAPPEAR.
GOOD LUCK WITH THAT. TRY AS YOU MIGHT, I CAN GUARANTEE NOT EVERYONE IS GOING TO FORGET YOU.
THIS WAS FUN, DICK, AND I'M SO GLAD I GOT TO DO IT WITH YOU.
ME TOO. IT'S BEEN A BLAST, DON. BUT ALL THINGS MUST END.

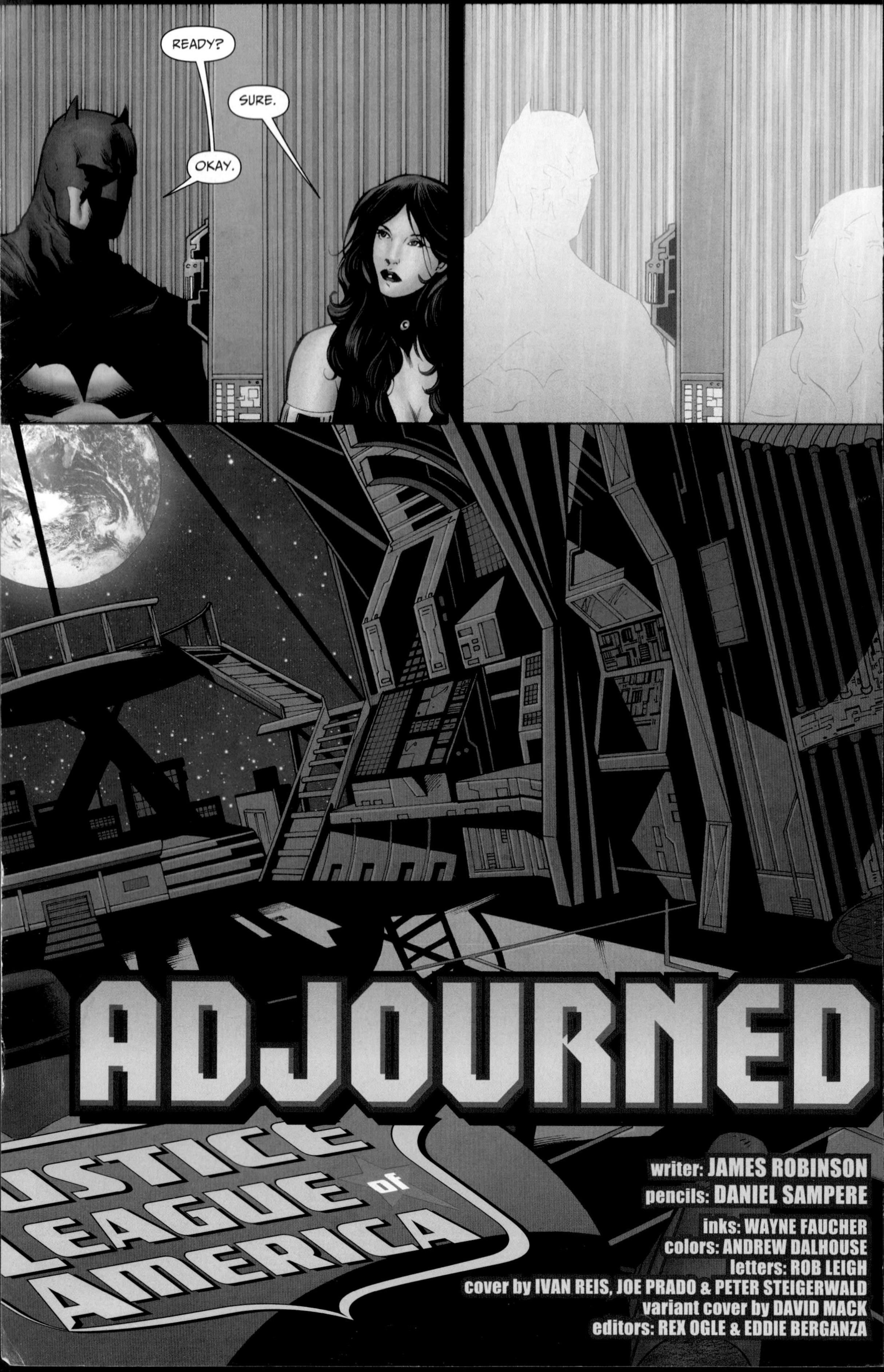
READY?
SURE.
OKAY.
ADJOURNED
JUSTICE LEAGUE of AMERICA
writer: JAMES ROBINSON
pencils: DANIEL SAMPERE
inks: WAYNE FAUCHER
colors: ANDREW DALHOUSE
letters: ROB LEIGH
cover by IVAN REIS, JOE PRADO & PETER STEIGERWALD
variant cover by DAVID MACK
editors: REX OGLE & EDDIE BERGANZA

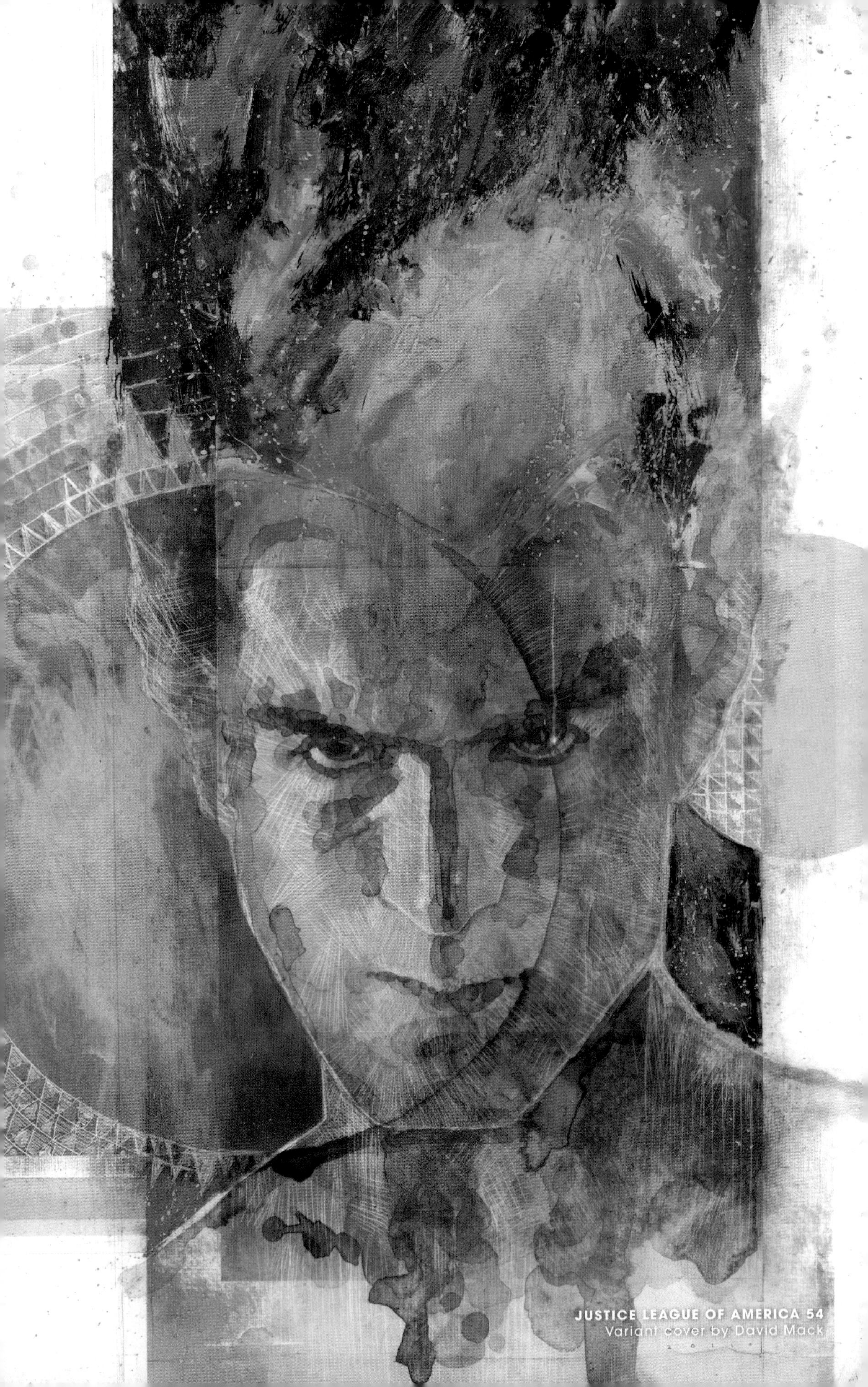

JUSTICE LEAGUE OF AMERICA 54
Variant cover by David Mack

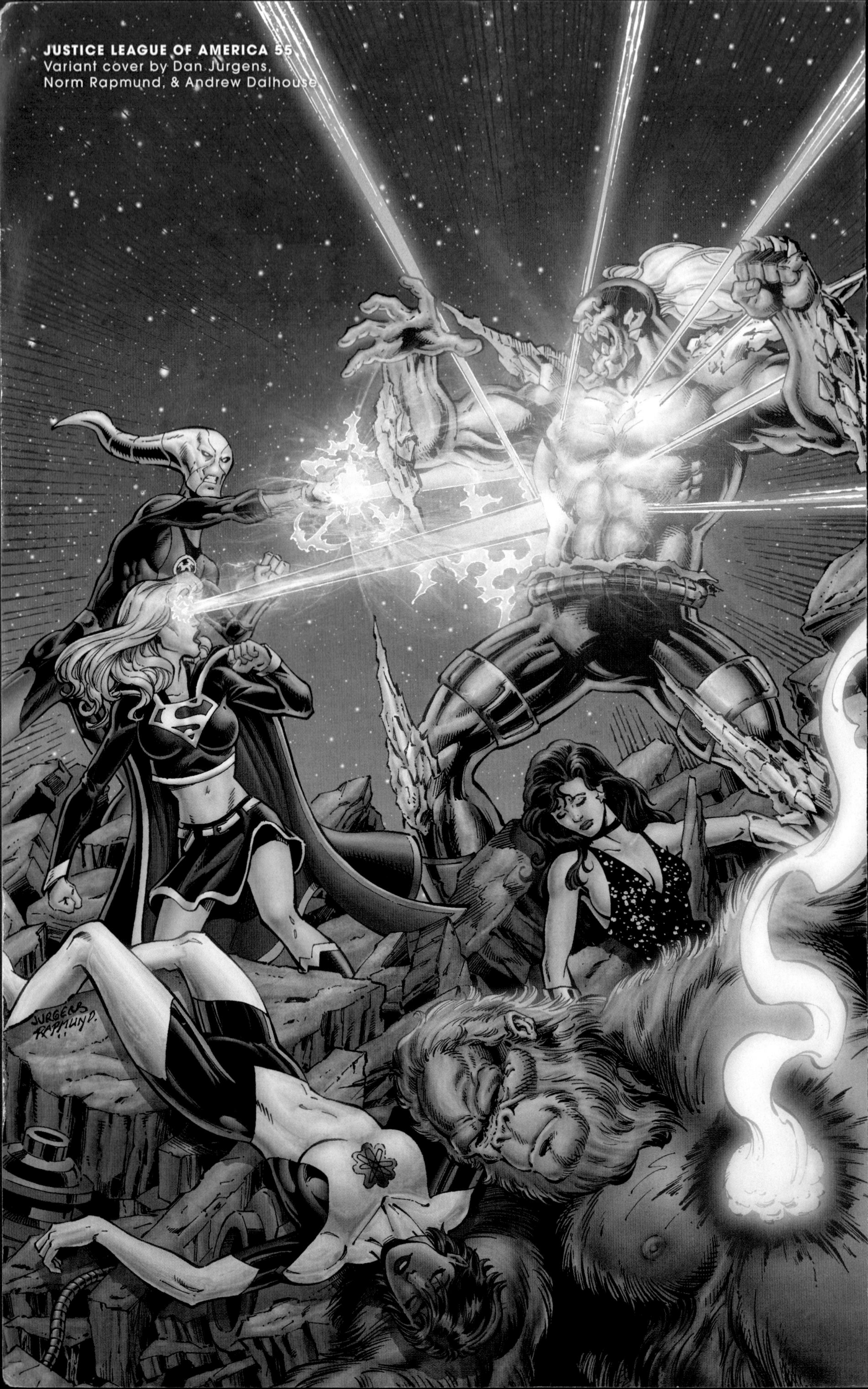
JURGENS RAPMUND.

JUSTICE LEAGUE OF AMERICA 55
Variant cover by Dan Jurgens,
Norm Rapmund, & Andrew Dalhouse

JUSTICE LEAGUE OF AMERICA 56
Variant cover by David Mack

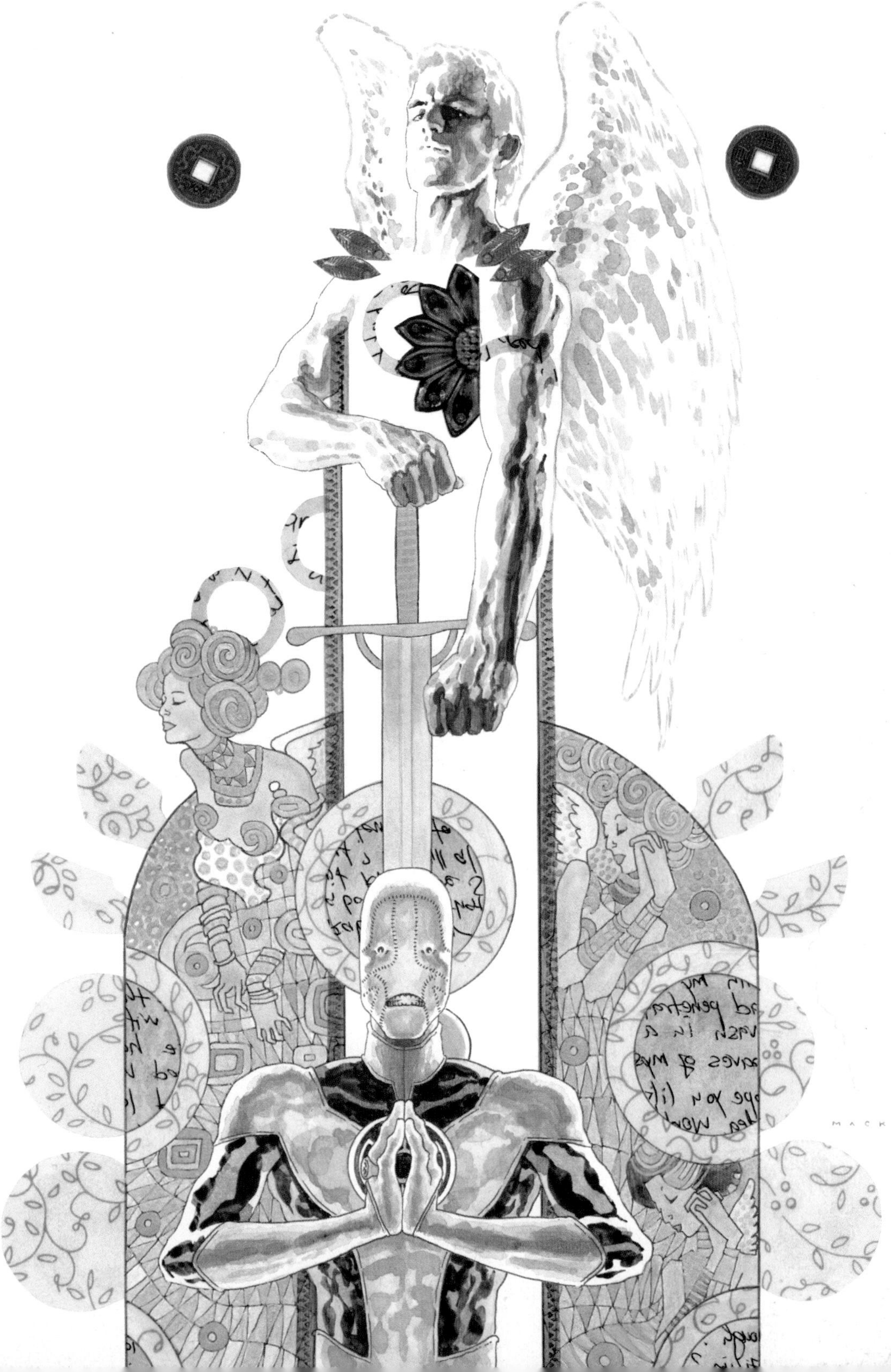
MACK

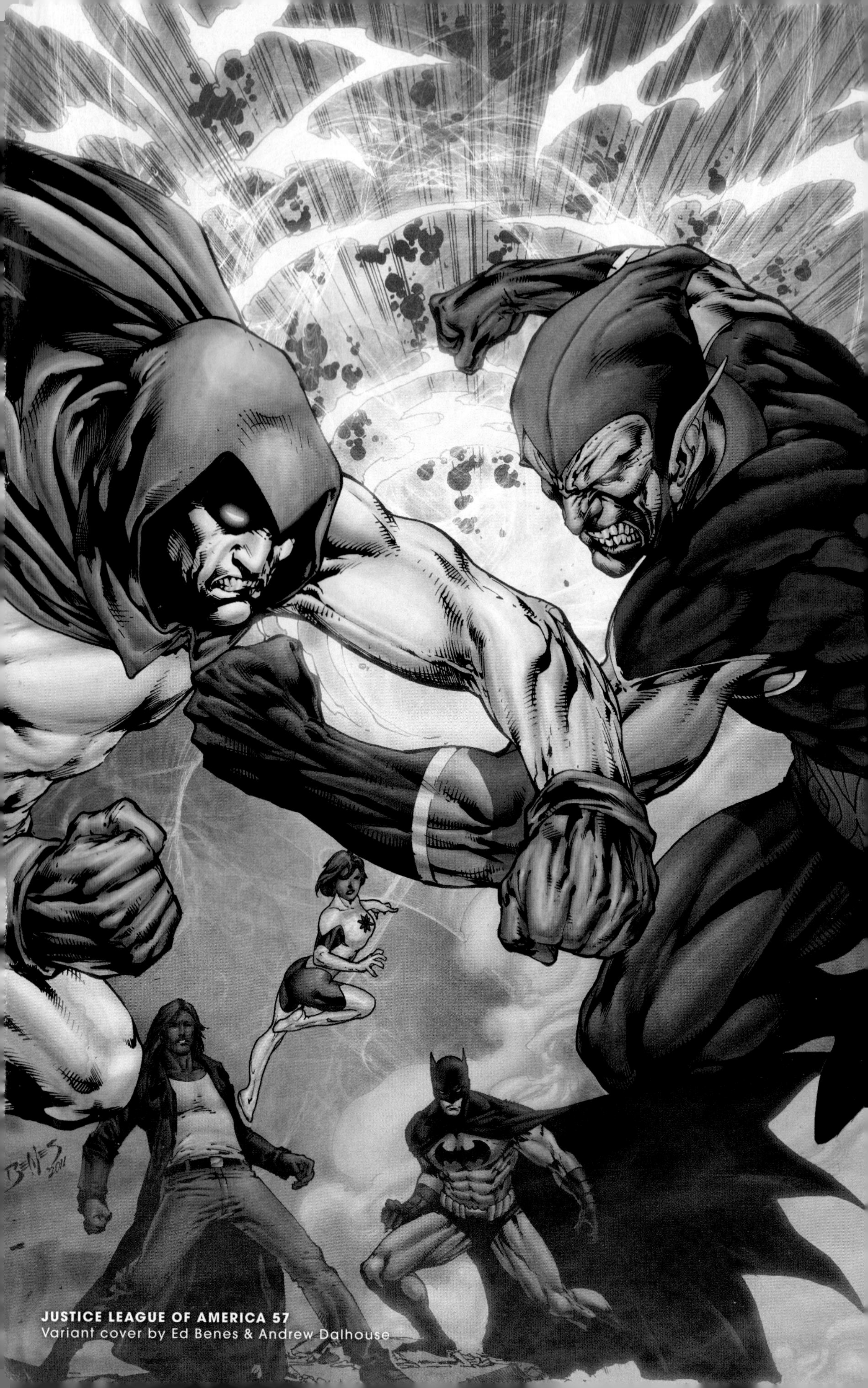
BENES 2011

JUSTICE LEAGUE OF AMERICA 57
Variant cover by Ed Benes & Andrew Dalhouse

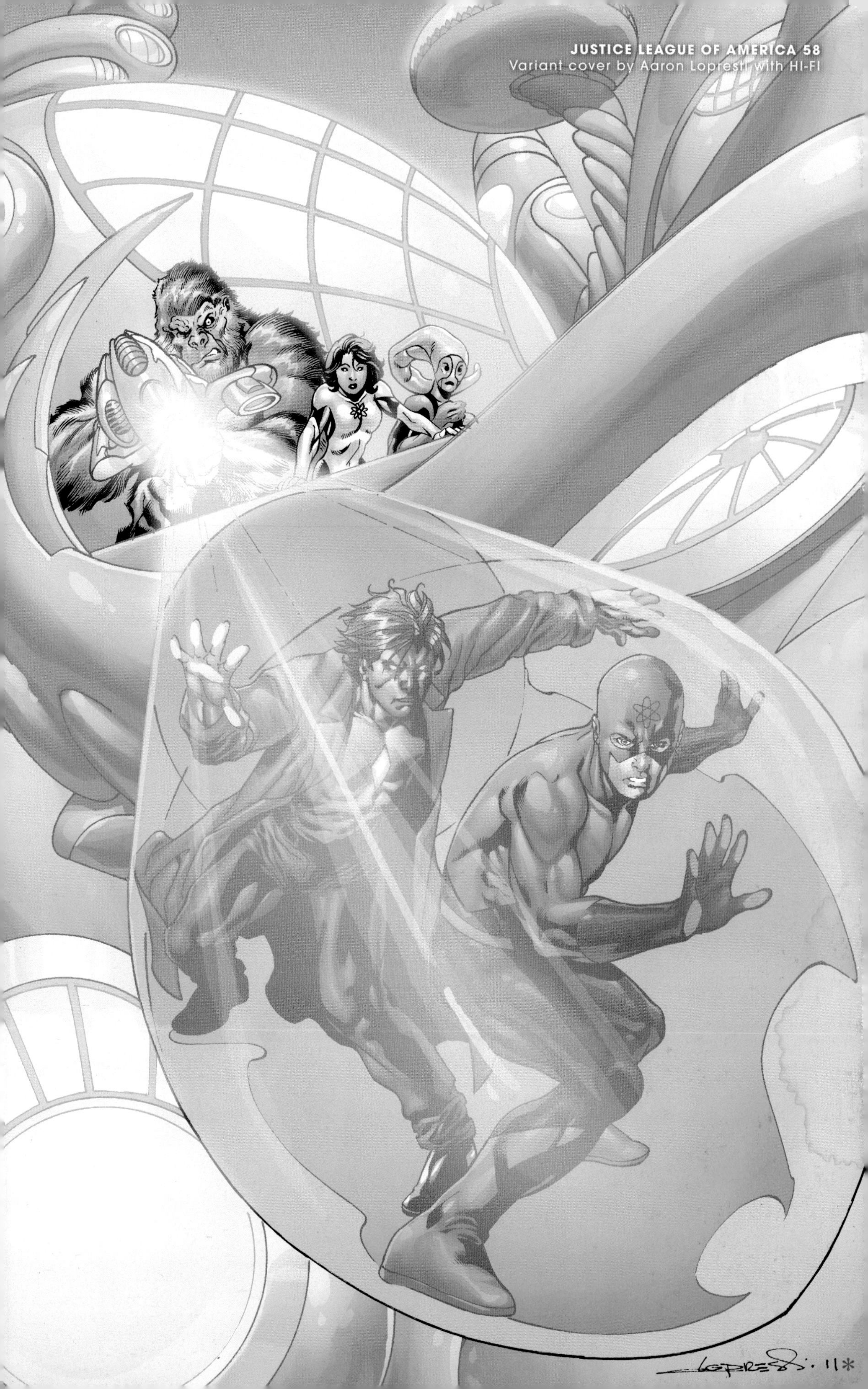

JUSTICE LEAGUE OF AMERICA 58
Variant cover by Aaron Lopresti with HI-FI

JUSTICE LEAGUE OF AMERICA 59
Variant cover by David Mack

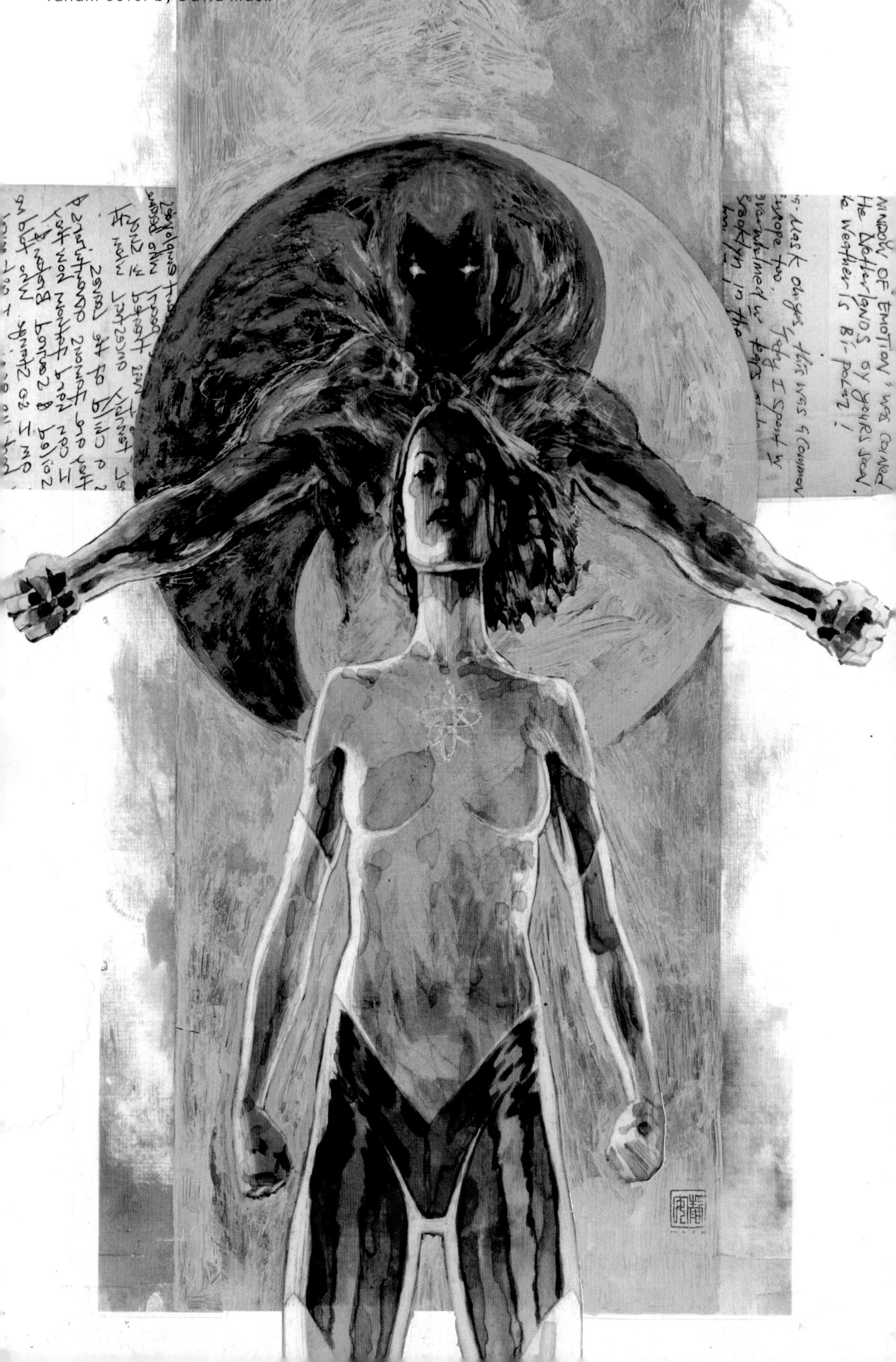

JUSTICE LEAGUE OF AMERICA 60
Variant cover by David Mack

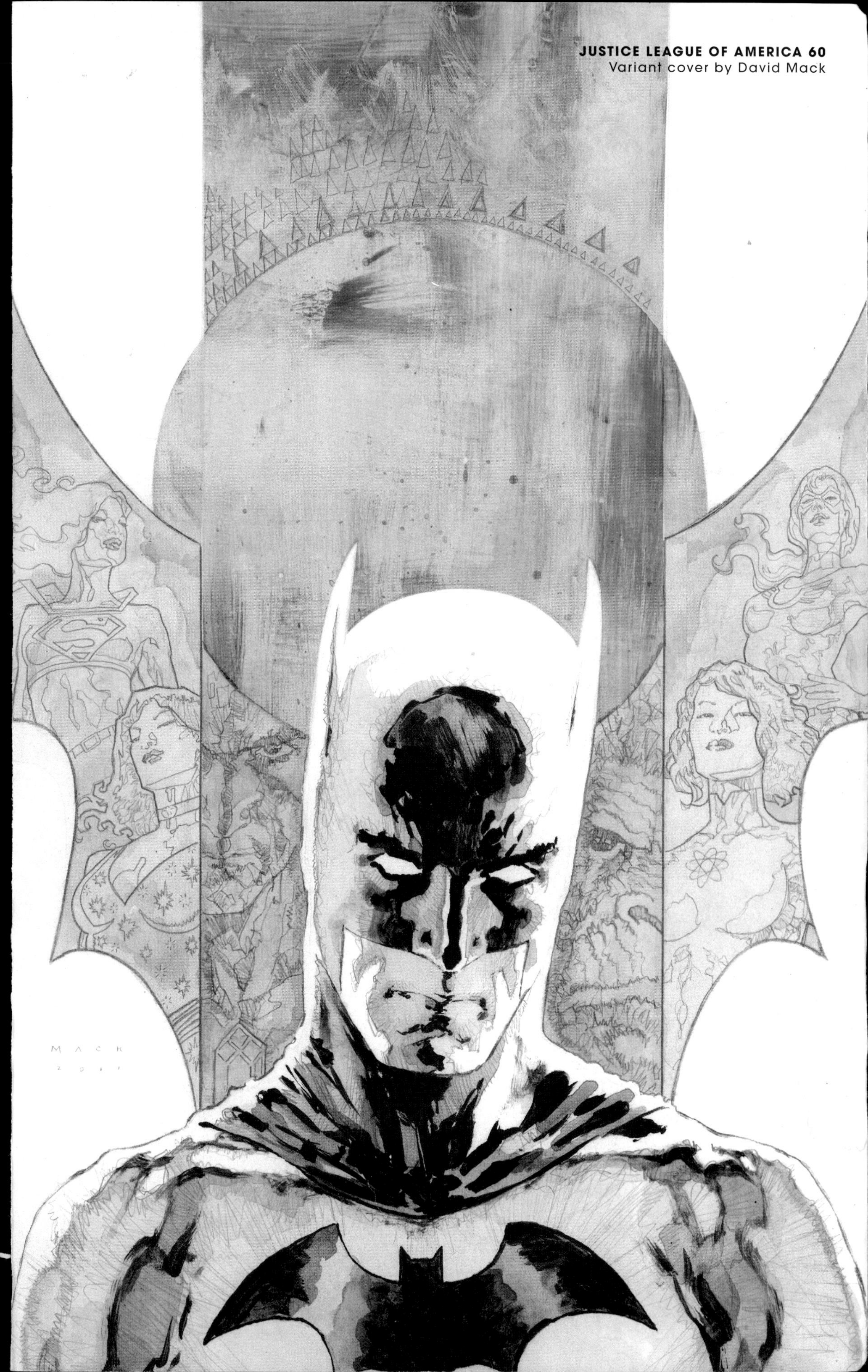
MACK

DC COMICS™

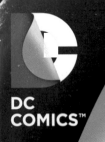

"[A] comic legend." —ROLLING STONE

"[Grant Morrison is] comics' high shaman." —WASHINGTON POST

"[Grant Morrison] is probably my favorite writer. That guy has more ideas in his pinky than most people do in a lifetime." — Gerard Way from MY CHEMICAL ROMANCE

FROM THE WRITER OF *ALL-STAR SUPERMAN* AND *BATMAN & ROBIN*

GRANT MORRISON

with HOWARD PORTER

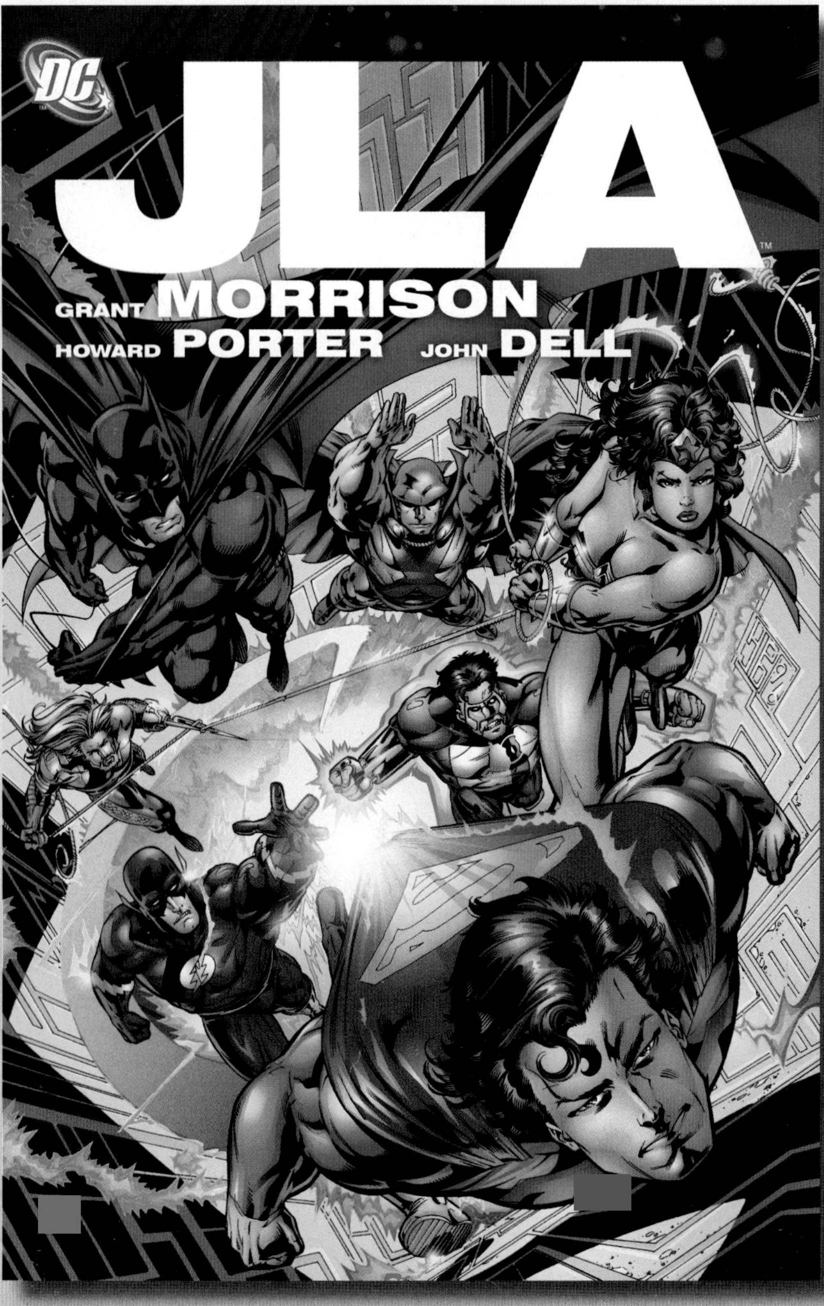

JLA
GRANT MORRISON
HOWARD PORTER JOHN DELL

JLA VOL. 2

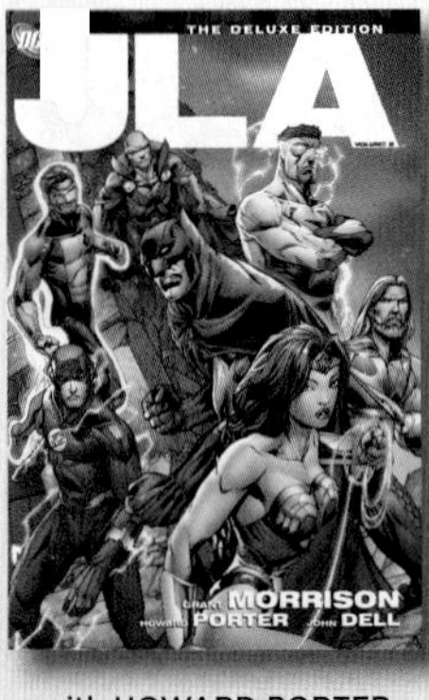

THE DELUXE EDITION
JLA
GRANT MORRISON
HOWARD PORTER JOHN DELL

with HOWARD PORTER

JLA VOL. 3

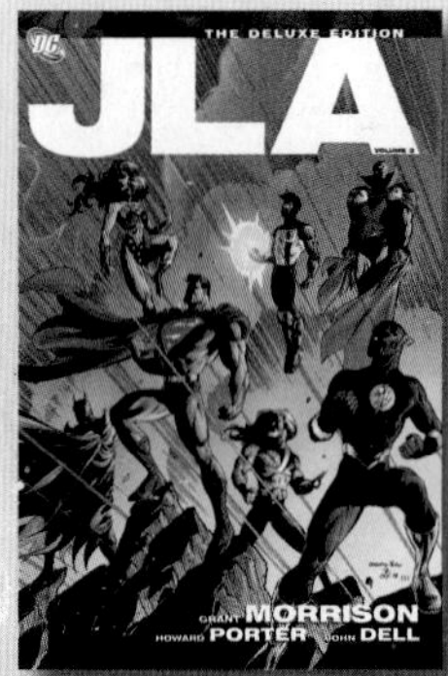

THE DELUXE EDITION
JLA
GRANT MORRISON
HOWARD PORTER JOHN DELL

with HOWARD PORTER

JLA VOL. 4

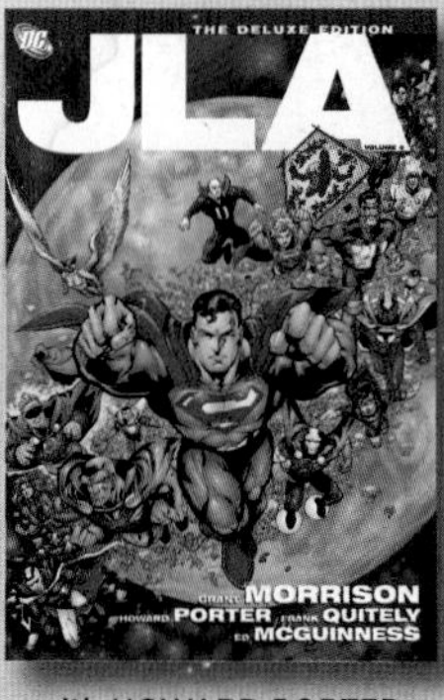

THE DELUXE EDITION
JLA
GRANT MORRISON
HOWARD PORTER FRANK QUITELY
ED McGUINNESS

with HOWARD PORTER, FRANK QUITELY and ED McGUINNESS